THE WHITE LADDER

THE WHITE LADDER

Triumph and Tragedy at the Dawn of Mountaineering

DANIEL LIGHT

W. W. NORTON & COMPANY

Independent Publishers Since 1923

For information about permission to reproduce selections from this book, write to
Permissions, W. W. Norton & Company, Inc., 500 Fifth Avenue, New York, NY 10110

For information about special discounts for bulk purchases, please contact
W. W. Norton Special Sales at specialsales@wwnorton.com or 800-233-4830

Manufacturing by Lake Book Manufacturing
Production manager: Delaney Adams

ISBN 978-1-324-06621-7

W. W. Norton & Company, Inc., 500 Fifth Avenue, New York, NY 10110
www.wwnorton.com

W. W. Norton & Company Ltd., 15 Carlisle Street, London W1D 3BS

1 2 3 4 5 6 7 8 9 0

For my mother

Contents

THE WHITE LADDER

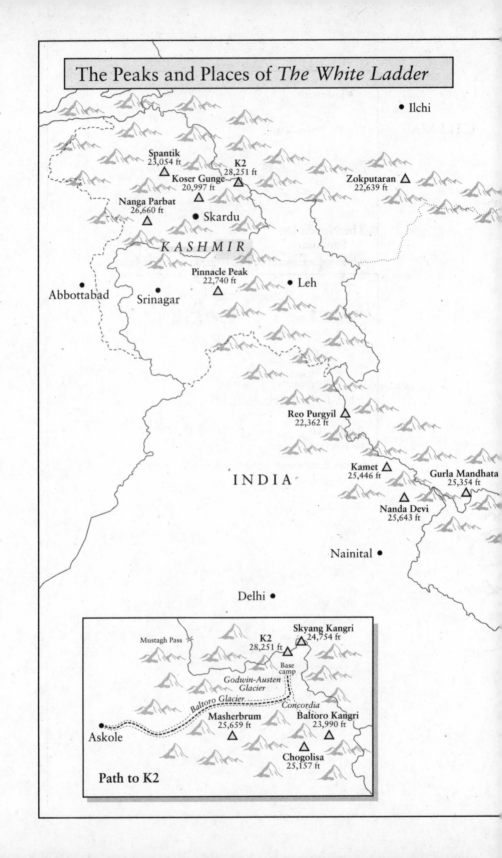

The Peaks and Places of *The White Ladder*

- Ilchi

Spantik
23,054 ft
K2
28,251 ft
Koser Gunge
20,997 ft
Zokputaran
22,639 ft

Nanga Parbat
26,660 ft
- Skardu

KASHMIR

Pinnacle Peak
22,740 ft
- Leh

- Abbottabad
- Srinagar

Reo Purgyil
22,362 ft

Kamet
25,446 ft
Gurla Mandhata
25,354 ft

INDIA

Nanda Devi
25,643 ft

Nainital •

Delhi •

Mustagh Pass
Skyang Kangri
24,754 ft
K2
28,251 ft
Base
camp
Godwin-Austen
Glacier
Baltoro Glacier
Concordia
Masherbrum
25,659 ft
Baltoro Kangri
23,990 ft
Askole
Chogolisa
25,157 ft

Path to K2

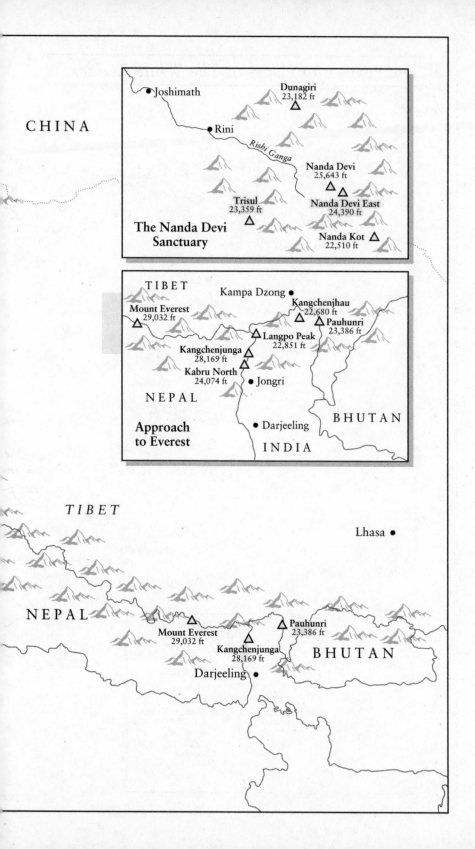

CHINA

The Nanda Devi Sanctuary

Joshimath

Dunagiri
23,182 ft

Rini

Rishi Ganga

Nanda Devi
25,643 ft

Nanda Devi East
24,390 ft

Trisul
23,359 ft

Nanda Kot
22,510 ft

The Nanda Devi Sanctuary

Approach to Everest

TIBET

Kampa Dzong

Kangchenjhau
22,680 ft

Pauhunri
23,386 ft

Mount Everest
29,032 ft

Langpo Peak
22,851 ft

Kangchenjunga
28,169 ft

Kabru North
24,074 ft

Jongri

NEPAL

BHUTAN

Darjeeling

INDIA

Approach to Everest

TIBET

Lhasa

NEPAL

Mount Everest
29,032 ft

Pauhunri
23,386 ft

Kangchenjunga
28,169 ft

BHUTAN

Darjeeling

We attacked the wall immediately after starting, making short and frequent halts for rest and breath, as we trod silently the white ladder of approach to the mysterious unknown.

FANNY BULLOCK WORKMAN, 1909

Author's Note

The notion that early European mountain-explorers were lone, pioneering figures endures even today. In truth, every expedition included those whose names and identities were not a matter of record. Who kept no account of their experiences, or whose stories have been lost. Theirs were the shoulders the Europeans stood on. Theirs were the backs they broke.

I have tried to do justice to the part played by these local intermediaries. I give their names where I have been able to discover them. I make as full an account of their involvement as sources allow. At the same time, I sometimes employ the same shorthand as the sources themselves. I use 'Baltis', 'Bhotias' and 'Lepchas' to refer to what may have been more intermixed ethnic groups. I use 'porter' and 'guide' to describe roles that were more complex and multifarious. I refer to groups of 'men' that may have included small minorities of women. The word 'coolie' – a pejorative term for porters – appears only in direct quotations.

For the names of the places we travel to and the people we meet, I favour whatever spellings appear most frequently in the sources I use. Some places – 'Bombay', for example, 'Calcutta' and 'Rangoon' – are referred to by their English-language names at the time of the events described. Some names are spelled differently when they appear in extracts or quotations.

It is impossible to cover such a broad sweep of history without making some mistakes. Mountaineers climb with force of personality and find plenty to disagree about, even from two ends of the same rope. Some dangers might be exaggerated, others underplayed. Some heights have been mismeasured, disputed and revised. Some people tell bare-faced lies. I have recounted the climbs as the climbers told them, leaving the reader to decide what to believe.

There will be moments when this book betrays the fact that I am not a serious mountaineer. A keen climber, yes, who knows what it is to move, un-roped, at the edge of my comfort zone. But made from nothing like the same stuff as most of the people you are about to meet.

I am, I suppose, like the military historian who writes about battle without ever having gone to war. An enthusiast, who loves mountains, and who found, in the writing of this book, a way to always be among them.

PROLOGUE

Because It Is There

Mallory was bored.

Bored of giving the same old talk, with the same old photographs, on the same old lecture tour. Disheartened by the mixed reception on the other side of the Atlantic, by half-full venues and lacklustre reviews. And, when the lights came up, always the same question.

Why?

Might as well ask a dog why it howls at the moon. Mallory was a *climber*. At seven, he'd been scampering up drainpipes on his father's church; at twelve, it was the chapel of Winchester College. Mount Everest was a higher calling, of course, but at heart he was still that boy from Birkenhead, climbing 'like he did not expect to fall'.

Why?

Some question for a soldier, a veteran of the Great War. Mallory had served in the Royal Artillery, had made a target of himself scaling trees and church towers, spotting for his battery. He had gone to the trenches on reconnaissance missions, had seen bodies sinking into Picardy clay. Those who had seen so much death knew life was for living. Those who had been to such depths knew mountains were for climbing.

Why?

He had a family to think about. He and Ruth had married six days before Britain entered the war; the children barely knew him. Why disappear into the mountains when everything that mattered most was

1

back home? Except Mallory didn't know how to be a husband or a father, any more than he knew how to be a soldier or a teacher. The only thing that came naturally to him was to climb.

But why? Why put yourself in such danger?

Because it *was* dangerous. Seven men had died on the last Everest expedition, Sherpas killed in an avalanche. For many, they were just porters, indigenous intermediaries pressed into the service of the British. Mallory knew them as skilled guides and mountaineers, men with their own understanding of what it meant to walk in Everest's shadow. They had names – Dorje, Lhakpa, Norbu, Pasang, Pema, Sange and Temba. They had families.

Mallory blamed himself. He had led them into trouble. They shouldn't have been on the mountain so late in the summer. Then a weather window opened, tempting good mountaineers into bad decisions. So much experience among the British. Everest made novices of them all.

Now there was talk of having another go. Why? *Because they almost had it.* George Finch and Geoffrey Bruce had gone to within two thousand feet of the summit, until Everest was the only mountain they could see 'without turning our gaze downwards'. Exhausted, with time against them, a malfunction with their oxygen equipment turned them back. But for one stroke of bad luck, they might have climbed the world's highest mountain. How could they give up now?

'So,' said the reporter, a young lady from the *New York Times*. 'Why *exactly* is it that you want to climb?'

Mallory sighed.

Go ask the past.

Go ask the pioneers.

Go ask the mercenaries and spies, risking their lives, wearing disguises so good they fooled themselves. Ask soldiers and surveyors, labouring through the lowlands, forcing frozen passes, in the stamping ground of somebody else's gods. Ask the alpinists and cragsmen, showmen and charlatans, peasants and princes, writing their names into record books and sometimes into stone. Ask the amateurs and professionals... ask them all, who first clapped eyes, set hearts, fixed hands on the highest mountains in the world. Go ask the past, demand your truth from visionaries and seers.

Then listen, as their answers echo back across the years.

A traveller following a trail up the Sutlej valley in Himachel Pradesh, India, c. 1865.
Photograph by Samuel Bourne.

PART 1

ALL THEY
SURVEYED

And, all the time, there it was ahead of them.

Diego de Ordás Reconocé el bolcan de Tlascala

Then, just as they were beginning to despair,
a vision appeared to stir their cavalier spirits…

Two illustrations of the first attempt on Popocatépetl (top) from the title page to
Herrera's *Historia*, 1601 and (bottom) from an engraving in Ogilvy's *America*, 1671.

CHAPTER 1

Under a Foreign Sky

'I hold out to you a glorious prize,' Don Hernán Cortés told his assembled forces, 'but it is to be won by incessant toil. Great things are achieved only by great exertions.' That was the conquistador's promise, as he and his followers prepared to sail for the place they called 'Yucatán'. The year was 1519, the 'glorious prize' in question – Aztec Mexico.

Cortés had mustered his army on the shore at Cuba's Cape Corrientes, a force of around five hundred Spanish soldiers accompanied by several hundred native Cubans. A fleet of eleven ships lay just offshore, loaded with horses, assorted weapons and artillery, and as much cassava bread and salt pork as he had been able to lay in stock. Cortés was not a tall man – by some accounts he stood at just five foot four – but since being appointed captain-general of the armada he had taken to wearing a hat with a large plume of feathers. This was complemented by a black velvet coat with golden knots and a gold medallion, heralding the glittering promise of great riches waiting just across the opal sea.

Cortés was true to his word. Battered by a violent storm, they made land at Yucatán to be faced by hostile Mayan warriors vastly outnumbering them. Arrows and spears were no match for the 'fiery lightning' of Spanish cannon and musket but, for Cortés and his exhausted army, victory brought no respite. Making camp on the burning sands of the *tierra caliente*, they were tormented by swarms of parasitic insects. The heat was unbearable, but Cortés insisted his soldiers keep their armour on at all times. Even when they slept, it was with weapons at hand.

Marching east into the snow-clad mountains of the Cordillera, the Spanish were ambushed by their enemies and besieged by cold. This, though, was life in the army of Cortés, a general whose mantra was 'succeed or perish'. Upon hearing that some of his soldiers were considering retreat, 'their patience exhausted by a life of fatigue and peril', the conquistador acted decisively – he sent back orders to sink their own ships.

Then, just as they were beginning to despair, a vision appeared to stir their cavalier spirits – a thin column of smoke, rising from a mountain's summit. Drawing closer, they saw the smoke coming from *within* the mountain. High on Mexico's Sierra Nevada, it was the 17,694-foot stratovolcano Popocatépetl.

Many of the Spanish had never seen an active volcano before. Transfixed by 'the wild terrors which hung over the spot' and possessed by 'the wild love of adventure', a decorated captain named Diego de Ordaz saw an opportunity to further enhance his reputation. He went to Cortés and 'begged leave… to ascend the mountain' to 'inspect this wonder more minutely'.

Cortés sensed an opportunity of his own. He had been manipulating local factions from the moment they made land at Yucatán, gaining their allegiance then turning them against one another. Now he would show 'that no achievement was above the dauntless daring of his followers', for whom 'the most appalling and mysterious perils were as pastimes'.

With some of the Tlaxcalans as their guides, Ordaz and a small party of Spaniards started towards the volcano. They passed through dense forest, the pine trees mutilated and misshapen, scarred by debris from past eruptions. Then there were no trees at all, only shrubs and stunted vegetation, as they moved onto the slopes of Popocatépetl, 'a black surface of glazed volcanic sand and lava… arrested in a thousand fantastic forms'.

As if awoken by the footsteps troubling its lower reaches, the volcano began to stir. According to the Spanish, the Tlaxcalans believed

Popocatépetl to be 'the abode of the departed spirits of wicked rulers, whose fiery agonies in their prison-house caused the fearful bellowings and convulsions in times of eruption'. Now, hearing these 'strange subterranean sounds', the local guides decided they would go no further.

There is no way of knowing whether, to the minds of the Tlaxcalans, the noise they heard was indeed the anguish of vengeful souls, trapped in a prison of fire. Just as it befitted the Catholic conquistadors to see their indigenous counterparts as fearful and superstitious, with a homeland waiting to be claimed for the Holy Roman Emperor and his one true god, it well suited the Tlaxcalans *not* to climb an active volcano. Putting such questions – and their guides – behind them, the Spanish went on alone.

Mist closed in and smoke drifted down to join it. Gone was the sky, the bright sunlight, the sprawling tableland beneath. It grew colder as they passed the snowline, and the rocky mountainside disappeared beneath a thick coating of ice and snow. Wrapped in cloud, they had entered a white world, where 'a false step might precipitate them into the frozen chasms that yawned around'. Their quilted cotton armour insulated them against the gathering cold; their steel helmets and cuirasses afforded some protection against volcanic debris, or a serious fall. But armour weighed heavily at 17,000 feet and more, where breathing grew difficult, 'every effort... attended with sharp pains in the head and limbs'.

Ordaz urged them on. Then, with the lip of the crater visible above, the volcano burst into life. It 'began to throw out great tongues of flame', 'such volumes of smoke, sparks, and cinders belched forth from its burning entrails, and driven down the sides of the mountain, as nearly suffocated and blinded them'. They had reached the last circle of hell, except here the circles rose upwards. 'Two lances' distant' from the summit, they could go no further. At the last, they turned back.

'They went, and strove, and did all that was possible to scale it,' wrote Cortés in a letter to the Holy Roman Emperor, 'but never were able to do so.' He might have given them a little more credit. Ordaz had brought back more than just a tale of high adventure from the near-summit of Popocatépetl. He had looked deep into the homeland of the Aztec ruler, Montezuma. Cortés could now lead his army over the high mountain pass to the north, approaching the city of Tenochtitlan with the element of surprise. 'They came back very glad at having discovered such a road,' wrote Cortés, 'and God knows how happy I was about it.'

Ordaz had observed something else, high on the slopes of Popocatépetl: the foul smell of sulphur dioxide, emanating from the crater. Sulphur, Ordaz knew, was necessary for the production of gunpowder. And gunpowder was necessary for the waging of war. When their supplies ran short, Cortés would send another of his captains, Francisco de Montaño, to the summit of Popocatépetl. To the conquistador's delight, Montaño returned with all the sulphur they could possibly need, describing how he had been lowered into the crater to collect it. In a letter to the emperor, Cortés struck a more circumspect note. 'It would be less inconvenient, on the whole,' he observed, 'to import our powder from Spain.'

The ascent of Popocatépetl is *not* the first historically documented account of a mountain being climbed. For that, we turn to the *Shujing*, one of the oldest books in the world, to find the ruler of China, Emperor Shun, atop the highest peak of the eastern Shandong province, the 5,029-foot Mount Tai, in around 2284 BCE. Standing on the first part of the Chinese landmass to feel the light of a new day, Shun made burnt offerings to the Jade Emperor of Heaven, and gave thanks for the gifts of light and life, symbolised by the break of dawn.

Other high ascents predate the Spanish on Popocatépetl. A Buddhist monk named Matsudai Shonin is known to have ascended Japan's 12,395-foot Mount Fuji in 1149 CE. Shonin was a follower of Shugendo, a Buddhist sect whose disciples, the Yamabushi, climbed as an act of ritual religious observance, an opportunity to test their faith. At the same time, thousands of miles away, Native Americans are said to have ascended mountains of 12,000 feet and more to commune with their ancestral spirits. For some, the height of the peak climbed was a measure of a young warrior's spiritual ambition.

The ascent of Popocatépetl was different. From medieval times, Europeans had contemplated mountains with fear and superstition, their frozen heights the haunts of witches and the lairs of dragons, with the souls of the damned lying incarcerated in the glaciers below. A few out-riders of the Enlightenment had ventured into the Alps – most famously, Leonardo da Vinci. Towards the end of the fifteenth century, Da Vinci climbed a mountain called Monboso, a spur of the Monte Rosa, where he drew sketches of the range appearing in the background of the *Mona Lisa*. Da Vinci, though, was ahead of the curve. In the early sixteenth century most Europeans agreed that Alpine passes were to be hurried over, and the mountains themselves avoided altogether.

Now, on the other side of the world, Ordaz and Montaño had led attempts on a summit higher than any in Europe, not as an act of reli-gious homage or contrition, but in the name of conquest. Driven by 'the chimerical spirit of enterprise... which glowed in the breast of the Spanish cavalier', they evoked something of the spirit of the modern-day mountaineer. Which is why, five hundred years later, in a chronicle of the highest ascents on record, that is where our story begins.

Baron Alexander von Humboldt was asleep in his hammock when the world began to shake. The day was hot and humid, and thunderclouds had cast the Venezuelan city of Cumaná into darkness, foreshadowing the violent earthquake now rocking the city to its very foundations. Humboldt watched as his friend Aimé Bonpland was thrown to the ground. In the streets nearby he could hear people crying out in terror. Panic was spreading fast.

Humboldt rose to his feet and began to set up his instruments. He had come to South America to gain a better understanding of the inner workings of the earth. This was too good an opportunity to miss.

Earthquakes were just one of the dangers Humboldt would encounter during his five-year expedition to South America. Arriving in 1799, he and Bonpland travelled thousands of miles, taking heavily laden mules across the highest and most precipitous passes of the Andes, then ven-turing deep into the 'howling wilderness' of the Amazonian rainforest. There, they conducted dangerous experiments with deadly poisons, and bathed in waters infested with alligators and crocodiles, giant anacondas and electric eels.

In June 1802 they came within sight of the 20,549-foot Ecuadorean stratovolcano Chimborazo. Humboldt and Bonpland intended to climb it.

Humboldt was fascinated with volcanoes. He envisaged nature as a single interconnected system, a web of life 'animated and moved by inward forces'. To Humboldt, volcanoes were openings to the heart of nature, manifesting all its creative – and destructive – force. Now he would take his work onto the slopes of one unmatched in reputation and stature, in search of the ultimate prize – vital evidence for how the earth itself had formed.

Humboldt knew the stories of the Spanish on Popocatépetl. He doubted whether they had gone into the crater, or to the summit, thinking it more likely they had collected the sulphur, 'as several persons in Mexico suppose, from a lateral crevice of the volcano'. His ascent of Chimborazo would be different. He would bring a scientific rigour to proceedings, and a scientist's reputation. He would open the book on the world altitude record – and close it – by climbing what most Europeans then believed to be the highest mountain on earth.

A painting by Friedrich Weitsch shows Humboldt and Bonpland en route to Chimborazo, camped on the grassland plains leading to its foot. Humboldt stands, inspecting an intricate brass theodolite – a telescope that reports the angle of an object from the horizontal – cradled by one of the local guides. Bonpland sits taking notes in the shade of a tree. Both men wear frock coats, loose-fitting trousers and thin-soled shoes. Nearby, on a wooden box, is a top hat.

Humboldt was nothing if not ambitious – he meant to climb Chimborazo in a single day. That night, heavy snow fell, but it did nothing to deter him. He and Bonpland were away early the next morning, accompanied by their friend Carlos Montúfar, their Mestizo manservant José de la Cruz, and a party of local porters and guides. They crossed the tableland then started up a series of giant step-like plains, Humboldt and Bonpland riding on mules. Coming to the snowline, Humboldt understood that their guides had little sense of what lay ahead. They had chosen this route up the mountain, but 'few had ever reached the limit of perpetual snow'.

Leaving their mules, they climbed through an 'enchanted forest of stone', leading to the foot of 'a narrow ridge of rock… by which alone it was possible for us to advance'. The ridge looked badly weathered, narrowing to just a few inches. The locals knew it as the *cuchilla*. A word which means 'knife-edge'.

Humboldt saw the guides and porters preparing to abandon them. The locals might visit the lower reaches of Chimborazo to hunt game or gather firewood, but they had no reason to climb the cuchilla. When 'all entreaties and threats were unavailing', Humboldt understood that he and his three companions were on their own.

They began to climb. Soon the ridge was all there was, rising out of a sea of mist, disappearing into a canopy of cloud. 'On the left the precipice was concealed by snow,' wrote Humboldt, 'on the right our view sank shuddering 800 or 1,000 feet into an abyss.' 'As the rock was very keenly angular, we were painfully hurt, especially in the hands.' And still they went up.

Occasionally, where the ridge was wide enough, they stopped to rest. Here Humboldt measured altitude, gravity, temperature and humidity, balancing his instruments on the rocks around him and scribbling notes with frozen and bloody fingers. Little trace of life remained, only stone-lichen and moss. 'A butterfly (sphinx) was caught by M. Bonpland at the height of 15,000 feet,' noted Humboldt. 'We saw a fly 1,600 feet higher.' From the slopes of other volcanoes, they had looked down onto the backs of soaring condor. On Chimborazo those were nowhere to be seen.

The longer they climbed, the more they felt the effects of altitude. 'We began gradually to suffer from great nausea,' wrote Humboldt. 'We had haemorrhage from the gums and lips. The conjunctiva of the eyes likewise, was, in all, gorged with blood.' The men grew giddy as the world swam around them, with no horizon to orient them, no summit to hold their gaze. All they could do was climb, up the crumbling crest of the cuchilla, hoping up was still up, down still down.

Then, like that, the mist was gone, revealing the dome-shaped summit of Chimborazo. All that stood between the four men and, to the best of their knowledge, the highest position on the surface of the earth, was a distance 'thrice the height of St Peter's church in Rome'. 'It was an earnest, momentous gaze,' wrote Humboldt, one that 'animated our powers anew'.

The men 'hastened onwards, with certain steps', believing the summit now within their grasp, only for fate to snatch it from them. 'All at once a ravine of some 400 feet in depth, and fifty broad, set an insurmountable barrier to our undertaking.' With no way round the giant crevasse, there was no alternative but to turn back.

According to Humboldt's measurements, they had reached a height of 19,286 feet above sea level. Higher than the top of Popocatépetl, higher than the highest summits of the Alps. Higher than any European was known to have gone before. Looking out across the neighbouring mountains, Humboldt might have felt a supreme satisfaction. He did not. Gazing upwards with a sense of 'mournful solitude', he could only watch as the mist closed in once again. It was one o'clock in the afternoon. He and his companions turned and began to climb down.

Arriving back in Europe two years later, Humboldt doubted whether his near ascent of Chimborazo was of 'serious scientific interest'. In a place where flora and fauna were largely absent, and the finest instruments prone to error, 'the efforts of travelling natural philosophers' were, in his view, 'scarcely rewarded'. 'There is, on the other hand, an active popular participation in such endeavours,' offered Humboldt. 'That which seems unobtainable has a mysterious attractive power.'

Humboldt embarked on a European lecture tour, recounting all he had learned on his 'great voyage', to find that his tale of Chimborazo was the real draw. Crowds of people turned out to see the man who had climbed, in his own words, to 'a place higher than all others that men had reached on the backs of mountains'. The story of the world altitude record was just beginning, and already it was a box office hit.

*

For years, rumours had been circulating among the British, swirling around the East India Company offices in Calcutta, fogging the corridors of the Royal Geographical Society. Talk of mountains so big it made you breathless just to look at them. This had been met for the most part with scepticism and disbelief, but in the early nineteenth century men like James and Alexander Gerard saw for themselves that the rumours were true.

The Gerards were soldiers in the Bengal Infantry, the private army of the East India Company. Formed to trade on behalf of the British in the Indian Ocean, the Company controlled a force of more than 200,000 men, their mission to defend British interests against colonial rivals like the French, and regional powers like the Gurkhas and Murathas. The Company's armies had fought a series of wars around the turn of the century and, by 1818, large swathes of the subcontinent were under British control.

With the advent of peacetime, the British found good use for officers like the Gerards, men who enjoyed the benefit of a 'liberal education'. They were sent to conduct 'route surveys', following the course of a road or a river through newly acquired territory. They collected information about the character and constituents of an area, about infrastructure and agriculture, about trade and commerce. They might make a few notes on how best to defend a position against musketry, but for the most part their soldiering days were over. If either was to kill anybody now it would be the result of bad luck rather than good judgement.

In September 1818, the brothers embarked on their most ambitious expedition yet, along the mountainous northern frontier of British-administered India. They marched up the valley of the Sutlej river into the mountains of Himachal Pradesh, at the head of almost one hundred indigenous porters and guides. There they found a world 'more of magnificence than of beauty', where pine trees clung to the mountainside, roots grasping at the slenderest of cracks. Alexander thought the landscape 'on the grandest scale, fragments of fallen rocks of immense bulk, hurled from the peaks above, and vast impending

cliffs fringed with dark forests, and topped with mountains of inde-
structible snow'.

And, all the time, there *it* was ahead of them. A 22,362-foot pyramidal peak rising out of the surrounding massif, a giant triangular notch
in the skyline.

Reo Purgyil. *Abode of the Demon.*

The Gerards marched for two weeks, bringing them to the village
of Shipki, at the limit of British-administered India. To the east was a
high mountain pass, the Shipki La; for the British, it was a gateway to
all the secrets of Chinese Tartary. To the north stood Reo Purgyil, now
just a few miles away. To climb it would be to gain the ultimate vantage
point, a chance to look deep into territory they were forbidden from
entering. But the brothers had ambitions of their own. They were well
aware of Humboldt's record, and they meant to break it.

After a long march through a tangled mass of vicious thorns, the
brothers and their guides moved onto 'enormous blocks of stone' that
teetered beneath them as they hopped from one to the next. Then, as
the ground grew steeper, they 'were obliged to use both hands and feet,
now climbing up almost perpendicular rocks and now leaping from
one to the other'. Knowing 'a single false step might have been attended
with fatal consequences', they crossed 'deep chasms, which we could
scarcely view without shuddering'. 'I never saw such a horrid-looking
place,' wrote Alexander. 'It seemed the wreck of some towering peak,
burst asunder by severe frost.'

The Gerards had set their minds on reaching a 'near' pinnacle, 'but
were never so much deceived in distance. It took us full three hours
to reach its top, and the ascent was very tiresome.' Meanwhile, as they
gained height, they met the enemy within. Pain rose behind their eyes
and in their ears, and their chests tightened like drums. As a doctor,
James was well equipped to ward off many hazards of Himalayan travel,
but where his knowledge fell short – where all knowledge fell short –
was the operation of altitude on the human frame. Constant headaches,
breathing difficulties, loss of appetite, exhaustion and insomnia, these
were just some of the symptoms of *hypoxia*, a shortage of oxygen in the

blood. The Gerards knew it as 'mountain sickness' and it left them, in Alexander's words, 'completely debilitated'.

And yet they soldiered on, as soldiers do. When they finally called a halt, it was deep into the afternoon, with the temperature falling fast and darkness close behind. Stopping on a saddle slung between two peaks, they fumbled with their equipment, anxious to know how high they had climbed. Their three homemade barometers all agreed: they were 18,683 feet above sea level. Just a few hundred feet short of the height Humboldt claimed to have reached on Chimborazo. It was too late, though, to go on.

Retreating only some of the way down the mountain, the Gerards took shelter in a hollow among the rocks, hopeful that the warmth of a blanket and a campfire would stave off hypothermia. Their spirits were warmed, too, by 'a large quantity of punch, which we continued drinking till near two in the morning. I do not recollect anything,' wrote Alexander, 'that ever refreshed me so much.'

Conditions deteriorated overnight. Starting out at sunrise, they met a bitter wind that strengthened as they climbed. The porters stopped more often to rest, the Gerards 'at one time threatening, and at another coaxing them'. 'To tell the truth, however', wrote Alexander, 'we could not have walked much faster ourselves.' Finally, 'the man who carried the bundle of sticks sat down and said he must die, as he could not proceed a step farther.' He was 'like the man in the fable', wrote James, 'who called on death to relieve him of his load'.

The Gerards took stock. There above them was a pinnacle of rock, overlooking the place they had turned back. Sensing the record within their grasp, they left the stricken man to rest. This would be their peak within a peak, their summit beneath the summit, at what they hoped would be a record-breaking height.

The wind had been 'irresistibly violent' all day, but finally, mercifully, it died down. Then, before they knew it, they were there. Thousands of feet of mountain towered above, but this was the apex of their ambition. High enough, they believed, to earn them a new world altitude record.

The wind had calmed, but their hands were numb with cold and the ink in their pot had frozen solid. Turning again to their homemade barometers, they made hurried notes in pencil.

They watched each instrument settle in turn at the same mark.

They were 19,411 feet above sea level.

The record was theirs.

Below lay Chinese Tartary, stretching away to the east. But the Gerards recorded no further observations. They wrote nothing of what they saw. They had what they came for.

So, under the failing light, they started back down the mountain. Night was falling, a vale of shadow pulled down over this jagged frontier, a range of mountains like no other. A range 'so elevated', wrote James, 'that Chimborazo would look like a mole-hill'.

Diego de Ordaz. Baron Alexander von Humboldt. James and Alexander Gerard. Theirs are the names associated with the earliest ascents of what were then believed to be some of the world's highest mountains.

The story of mountaineering's world altitude record is, in that respect, a history told by the victors: men – predominantly men – who climbed, they thought, beyond the reach of contradiction.

Whether for the advancement of science or the prosecution of empire, each of these first 'mountaineers' had his own reasons to climb.

And, whatever their motives, however imprecise their measurements, Ordaz, Humboldt and the Gerards had one thing in common – all believed they had gone higher than any man, woman or child before them.

All were wrong.

What none of them could know was that evidence existed of an ascent to eclipse all their best efforts. Unearthed by Johan Reinhard and his archaeological team in 1999, it is a reminder that initiative and ambition did not begin with European colonial endeavour. That men and women have forever looked to the heavens and tried to draw them closer.

Everything we know about their 'expedition' has been pieced together from Reinhard's discovery. It speaks to a journey that began in the twilight of the fifteenth century, as a party of Incas started south from their capital of Cusco, high in the Andes Mountains of South America. Skirting the crystal waters of Lake Titicaca, crossing the sprawling salt flats of the Salar de Uyuni, then braving the shifting sands of the Atacama Desert, they travelled over a thousand miles through some of the most beautiful and forbidding terrain on earth, until they arrived at the foot of the 22,110-foot stratovolcano Lluillaillaco.

These were not the first Incas to climb Lluillaillaco. Others had gone before, following a trail all the way to the summit. Nor were there any great obstacles to overcome; the volcano's slopes were formed of layer upon layer of lava and ash, the legacy of countless eruptions. But it was bitterly cold even at the height of summer and, as the day wore on, with more of their path lying within the shade, it would have grown colder still.

At around 17,000 feet, with darkness almost upon them, they pre-pared to spend the night on the mountain. They left the main trail to reach a *tambo*, an Incan waystation, a dozen buildings with walls of stone and roofs of matted straw. The Inca priests could now check on the condition of the three children they had with them. The oldest was a thirteen-year-old girl, who had lived for six months as one of the *aclla*, or chosen women, under the guidance of high priestesses. With her was a boy and another girl, each barely five years old. All had been given coca leaves to chew and *chicha*, a fermented alcoholic drink, enough that they were barely conscious. They, at least, would have no difficulty sleeping that night.

The next day they started out again. Many of the Incas lived at alti-tudes of 10,000 feet or more, but even they would have felt the leaden weight on their feet, the clouds gathering in their minds, at 20,000 feet and climbing. Finally, with the wind howling around them, they saw the summit above.

There, a short distance beneath it, was another building. The priests laid the still-unconscious children on the matted floor. They dressed them in elaborate headdresses made of white feathers, wrapped them in richly coloured tunics and adorned their bodies with intricate silver jewellery.

Then, once all the preparations were complete, they carried their little bodies to a place just beneath the summit, where three chambers awaited. Placing them inside, they arranged precious artefacts around them, intricate figurines made of spondylus shells, ceramic vessels, wooden cups, spoons and combs. Gifts for the gods from across the Inca empire, the children would take them to the afterlife.

There is no way of knowing exactly how the children died. Hypothermia might have taken them long before they reached the summit; the boy's legs were bound, perhaps to make his lifeless body easier to carry. There is other evidence to suggest they were suffocated, that the priests forced handfuls of coca leaves into their mouths, then kept their hands clasped over the children's faces until the light died in their eyes. More chilling is the possibility they were still breathing as the priests prepared to leave them, drugged and slowly dying, buried alive beneath a thin layer of gravel.

What is certain is that the 'Children of Lluillaillaco' knew nothing of scientists or surveyors, of alpinists or altitude records. Nor could they know that their bodies would be discovered by a team of archaeologists five hundred years after their deaths and that they would one day be commemorated in the same breath as pioneering adventurers from Spain, Prussia and Scotland. All they knew, in the final reckoning, was an end to the cold, the confusion, the suffering. Alone together, just shy of the 22,110-foot summit of a volcano, that much closer to the gods they were being sent to join.

*...the Schlagintweits began conducting experiments of their own,
styling themselves a new generation of Humboldtian adventurer.*

German naturalist and explorer Adolph Schlagintweit. Portrait by A. Graefle.

CHAPTER 2

Ahead of the Game

Adolph Schlagintweit had seen better days.

Three years on the road would do that to a man, especially the kind of 'roads' he had been taking. Since making port at Bombay in 1854, Adolph and his two brothers had travelled all over India, covering more than 16,000 miles. Now, three years later, their expedition was almost at an end. Hermann and Robert had already sailed for Europe, where they would start work sorting through the many journals they had kept, the hundreds of sketches they had produced. They had left Adolph to find his way back over land, braving a journey through Chinese Turkestan.

A column of smoke rose over the pinch of higher ground where Adolph and a handful of men were camped. They were all that remained of an expedition once numbering in the hundreds. Kneeling over the pot was Abdullah, a Kashmiri Muslim who had been with the Schlagintweits since they first arrived in India. He was an accomplished draughtsman with a talent for reading the landscape and filling in the blanks; nobody had contributed more to the maps and charts they produced. Often Abdullah was forced to work with more blank than landscape, so it helped that he was expert at teasing out local knowledge. A flash of those kind eyes quickly gained him the confidence of a total stranger.

Muraj the merchant sat cross-legged; hands clasped. All the men were masquerading as caravan traders, but Muraj was the real deal. With his stock of furs and silks he added a note of authenticity to proceedings and was always ready to do a little business on the side. He knew the roads they travelled on, and the roads knew him.

Mohammed Amin was a less wholesome character, 'a person of questionable antecedents' said to have once worked as a gang-robber. That should not have come as a complete surprise, given the task for which he had been recruited – guiding Europeans through Chinese-controlled territory – was itself a criminal one. He lay in the warmth of the fire, puffing clouds of thick smoke from his water pipe.

Adolph would be relying on these men, now more than ever. They had made it over the mountains to find that war had broken out in Kashgar. Kokandi Turks had invaded, driving out the ruling Chinese and laying claim to the region. Their leader, a warlord named Wali Khan, had a reputation as an impetuously violent man; he was rumoured to have killed so many Muslims that six minarets had been erected from the skulls. Legend had it that, on the occasion of receiving a newly forged sabre, he put it to the test by decapitating the son of the man who had just presented it to him.

Adolph's path back to Europe took him through the heart of the conflict. His one alternative was retreat, but that carried risks of its own. The crossing of the Khunjerab pass had pushed them to their limits, their bodies wracked by cold and driven to exhaustion. Some of the porters had lain down in the snow, asking to be left to die. Retreading those frozen heights, Adolph might simply lie down and join them.

The last light of a long day caught the snow-capped peaks to the south. The wisest course was to recross the mountains. They would find fresh porters, would find their way back to India. There, boats would be waiting, steamers bound for Europe.

And yet. The spirit of adventure drew Adolph forward. Into the heart of Kashgar. Into the arms of Wali Khan.

In August 1818, almost forty years before Adolph Schlagintweit arrived in the borderlands of Chinese Turkestan, the carriage of Baron Alexander von Humboldt pulled up outside East India House in London's Leadenhall Street.

Humboldt had returned from South America believing he had climbed to within a thousand feet of the highest point on earth. Now he understood that there were mountains in Asia to dwarf Chimborazo. Seeing the British sending soldiers rather than scientists to investigate, Humboldt hoped to mount an expedition of his own. He would discover all that connected the two greatest mountain ranges on earth – the Andes and the Himalaya – and learn everything he could about the planet in between.

Humboldt enjoyed considerable influence in London. The Prince Regent and the foreign secretary both knew him as a trusted advisor of King Friedrich of Prussia and looked approvingly on his plans. All that remained was to secure permission to pass through British-administered territory. For that, Humboldt needed the blessing of the East India Company.

Humboldt left London a few days later believing his meeting with the Company's Court of Directors had gone well. But, as the months went by, he came to understand that they opposed his plans. Humboldt had returned from Latin America railing against the excesses of Spanish colonialism in the 'New World', giving inspiration to a revolution led by his young friend, Simón Bolívar. Worse still, he had been openly critical of the 'civil and military despotism' of the British in India, drawing parallels with the violence and brutality he had witnessed on his travels. For all his courtly influence, Humboldt's reputation preceded him – the Court of Directors saw him stirring up precisely the kind of trouble they didn't need.

Months turned to years, years to decades. Humboldt became an old man, for whom the only journeys that remained were great flights of the imagination. He poured himself into literary projects, each more ambitious than the last, culminating with *Cosmos*, an opus promising to encompass the entire universe and all of existence. By now Humboldt had accepted that he would never see 'High Asia'; it was his most intense regret. Then, in 1849, he met the Schlagintweits.

The sons of a distinguished Bavarian eye surgeon, Hermann, Adolph and Robert Schlagintweit had received a prestigious education, proving themselves exceptional students in the field of geographical science. In 1845, when the first volume of *Cosmos* was published, they were among the crowds jostling for copies. Inspired by what the tome contained, the Schlagintweits began conducting experiments of their own, styling themselves a new generation of Humboldtian adventurer.

In May 1849 Hermann and Adolph left Munich and moved to Berlin. There they secured an audience with Humboldt, who saw that they were just what he needed – able-bodied young acolytes, ready to undertake a pilgrimage on his behalf. He was already planning future volumes of *Cosmos*, expanding its celestial scope to include 'both heaven and earth'. There could be no getting closer to the heavens, reasoned Humboldt, than to stand on the shoulders of the world's highest peaks.

Then, in 1852, he saw his chance. For thirteen years the Company had been conducting its Magnetic Crusade, an investigation into the forces of geomagnetism in the 'Eastern Archipelago'. When its leader, Captain Charles M. Elliot, suddenly succumbed to fever and died, Humboldt put the Schlagintweits forward as candidates to complete the work. Some in Britain questioned the need to recruit fresh-faced foreigners 'to a duty which some of our Indian officers were both anxious and competent to perform', but the Court of Directors was not listening; they were more interested in the generous sums offered by the kings of Prussia and Bavaria, who had agreed to part-fund a Schlagintweit-led expedition. The Company promptly agreed terms with the brothers, and preparations for their Scientific Mission to India and High Asia began.

The steamer *Indus* made port at Alexandria in September 1854 and the Schlagintweits came ashore. With all their equipment packed onto camels, Hermann, Adolph and Robert raced through the desert to the port of Suez, where they traded the stifling heat of covered wagons for the top deck of a paddle steamer, sipping champagne as they chuntered along the length of the Red Sea. Tragically, with no ice available, they drank it warm.

The brothers boarded a steamship at Aden and, one week later, disembarked at Bombay. From there they travelled cross-country to Madras, then north by boat to Calcutta, where their first engagement was a meeting with George Everest. Everest was credited with masterminding the Great Trigonometrical Survey, a project to measure the length and breadth of India. It was 'one of the most stupendous works in the whole history of science', gushed one of his contemporaries. 'Everest's was a creative genius. The whole conception of the survey, as it now exists, was the creation of his brain.'

Not everybody was quite so enthusiastic. 'We believe', reported the *Calcutta Review* in 1851, 'that there are very few persons, even in India, who have any notion whatever of what the Trigonometrical Survey really is, or what it does for geography or science: or who can comprehend what has been already done, and why it has not long since been brought to a conclusion.' Established in 1802, the work had been expected to take five years. Five *decades* later it was still far from complete, testament to the hallowed British tradition of underestimating the task at hand.

The Schlagintweits did not have the luxury of half a century at their disposal – they had funding for three years. Three years to complete a wildly ambitious programme of scientific enquiry, encompassing geography, geology, zoology, botany, palaeontology, mineralogy and meteorology. It is easy to see the hand of Humboldt in this. His holistic view of nature demanded that, to investigate any one of the natural sciences, you had to investigate them all.

At Calcutta the brothers divided into two separate expeditions. Hermann travelled north to Darjeeling, and Adolph and Robert boarded a train northeast to Patna. There they transferred to *palkis*, a type of sedan chair carried by bearers, and joined the course of the Ganges. They followed the river upstream towards its source; heaven itself, if Hindu fables were to be believed. Summer was coming, bringing a heat to the plains most Europeans would find unbearable. The Schlagintweits let it chase them up into the coolness of the mountains.

*

Arriving at the British hill station of Nainital in May 1855, Adolph and Robert got their first good look at a true Himalayan giant. To the north was Nanda Devi, the highest mountain in the Kumaon region of the Himalaya, towering above the band of cloud masking its hazy lower reaches. Within weeks they crossed a high pass to the east of the mountain, coming to the village of Milam by the start of June.

Out of Milam they led a series of expeditions into the surrounding mountains, going to heights of 17,000 feet and more. On the Milam glacier they forced their way up a broken icefall to around 19,000 feet, four hundred feet short of the mark reached by the Gerards on Reo Purgyil. The Schlagintweits had arrived in High Asia intent on emulating the greatest accomplishments of Baron von Humboldt – including a world altitude record of their own.

Their chance came late in the summer as they approached a 25,446-foot peak named Kamet. Attended by three smaller peaks, Kamet is a pyramidal mass of red granite schist, burnished gold at dawn and dusk by the sun's slanting rays, setting its hanging glaciers aglow. Deep into the summer it is caught between the worst excesses of the Himalayan monsoon coming up from the south and the attenuating influence of dry westerly winds swooping in from Tibet. Amid the cut and thrust of this elemental struggle, peace occasionally breaks out, producing favourable conditions for climbing.

On the evening of 18 August, the two brothers arrived high on the slopes of Ibi Gamin, a 24,131-foot peak a mile northeast of Kamet. With them were eight other men: 'Bhútias from Mílum,' wrote Robert, 'and Tibetans'. Together they had been exploring the surrounding glaciers for five days already, 'encamped… at very unusual heights'. Consulting their barometers, Adolph and Robert saw that this was 'the greatest height at which we ever passed the night'. They were 19,326 feet above sea level – less than one hundred feet shy of the Gerards.

It was a stormy night, but the next day dawned clear. The ten men started out early, determined to see how high they could go, but as they climbed the snow-covered slopes of Kamet's eastern peak, they found their path blocked by crevasses and were forced to take lengthy detours in search of 'snow-bridges' to see them safely over. Adolph and Robert had taken their experiments high on the slopes of the European Alps, but here they were contending with obstacles of a whole new order of magnitude. 'Apart from the extreme elevation and consequent cold,' wrote Robert, 'the bodily exertions… proved a great tax on our powers.'

The men kept climbing, through the morning and into the afternoon. Then, cresting the mountain's east ridge, they were brought to a halt by a vicious north wind. One of their party suffered a haemorrhage of some kind – he began 'to bleed uncontrollably' and 'lost all his strength'. For all the brothers knew, this was what happened at such heights. They might be moments away from suffering the same fate themselves.

Exhausted, they stopped to rest. Adolph and Robert already knew they had surpassed the height reached by the Gerards – the question was by how much. They checked their barometers, noting down the readings then, with one of their party seriously unwell, started down.

It was only later, when they completed their computations, that the brothers saw how high they had gone. 'We had ascended the flanks of Íbi Gámin,' wrote Robert, 'to a height of 22,259 feet. This, as far as we know, is the greatest height yet reached on any mountain.'

The Schlagintweits had not just broken the Gerards' record – they had left it in smithereens three thousand feet below. 'Theirs was an amazing performance,' wrote the English mountaineer Frank Smythe, who would climb Kamet for himself in 1931, 'especially if it be remembered that at that date many of the great Alpine peaks had not yet been climbed.' Years later, Smythe would sense their hands on his shoulder, approaching the summit of his own desires. 'In the shadow of Kamet', he wrote, 'in the silence and the loneliness about us, we felt that the pioneers who had crossed their "last pass" were watching our progress, even perhaps instilling into us their own determination, and passing on to us the bright torch of their own pioneering. If success was to be ours, we should be completing work well begun, and in realising our own ambitions realise theirs.'

*

Over the next two years the Schlagintweits conducted a sprawling survey of the Indian subcontinent. They went as far east as Assam, as far west as Karachi, all the way south to Ceylon and always north in the summer, into the mountains, to the northernmost extremities of British-administered territory. The resulting map is a cat's cradle of red lines, dotted and dashed to signify each brother's progress, draped between major cities and along the sprawling coastlines of the south, and looped in bunches around the great regional centres of the north.

Each brother travelled with as many as fifty indigenous intermediaries, from watchmen to watercarriers, taxidermists to torch-bearers, woodcutters to bone-boilers. Together they amassed a huge collection of scientific and cultural objects, including a macabre inventory of anthropological artefacts. They collected human remains from colonial hospitals, the bodies of convicts plundered from Indian prisons, skeletons robbed from graveyards; in all, more than forty thousand items. Their hope was to establish an 'India Museum' in Berlin, adorning its walls with the pick of 750 sketches and watercolours produced along the way.

Meanwhile, the cost of the enterprise ballooned. There were wages to be paid, collectables to be transported and the Schlagintweits themselves, making use of every available mode of conveyance. They travelled by steamer and railway, by elephant and *palanquin* – a covered litter carried on poles on the shoulders of four to six men – and made use of the Nepalese *dari*, 'a type of portable hammock, which allows all kinds of observations of the traversed region'. They only pitched their tents where no alternative presented itself, preferring to stay in bungalows and hotels, or at British hill stations. At times they behaved more like tourists than scientific travellers, spending their money accordingly.

Except it wasn't *their* money. The Company had given them a budget, but when that ran out the brothers continued to draw on a line of credit they had negotiated with the Indian government. There were rumours they had run up debts of £18,000 – approximately £1.5 million in today's money – prompting some to ponder what returns could be expected on such a sizeable investment. For all the ground they had covered, all the measurements they had taken, all the specimens they had collected, the brothers seemed to have 'discovered' nothing not already perfectly well-known to the British.

Intent on silencing their critics, Hermann and Robert left Adolph and made their way back to Europe, where they started work on *Results Of A Scientific Mission To India And High Asia*. The brothers hoped this exhaustive compendium of facts and figures would more than offset the expense of the enterprise, planning to produce a work of nine volumes. Only four were ever completed and they were not well-received. *The Athenaeum*, the pre-eminent British literary periodical of its day, pronounced the published volumes 'unreadable' and the Schlagintweits themselves 'remarkably ill-chosen for undertaking the lead of a great scientific mission'.

Robert Schlagintweit did eventually find an audience for their work. Taking a leaf out of Humboldt's book, he embarked on a lecture tour. Robert travelled the world with his presentation of paintings, letters and postcards, conjuring an image of himself exploring India in the manner of 'a thoroughly independent sovereign, who governs absolutely over an immense kingdom adorned with the rarest charms of nature… Every European, whom he may meet is a friend, every other person an obedient subject.' It was a fanciful depiction, and, well, where 'obedient servants' were concerned, Robert – unlike his brother Adolph – had never met Wali Khan.

As he prepared to continue north towards the city of Yarkand, Adolph instructed two men to recross the mountains to the south, taking many of his journals and papers with them. He was anxious to preserve his legacy, knowing danger lay ahead.

Danger yes, but also opportunity. Chinese Turkestan was more fertile than India, its weather more temperate, where fine dust blowing in from the Gobi Desert breathed new life into the soil. Crops grew prodigiously, the grain was superior, the fruit more flavoursome and abundant. There was gold, washing down from the mountains, so plentiful it changed hands for half its value in the markets to the south. There were precious stones, and metals and minerals – iron, lead, copper, antimony, salt, saltpetre, sulphur, soda and coal – and there was talk of other treasures lying hidden beneath the ground. Whole cities were said to have been swallowed up by the shifting sands, in the ruins of which lay great hoards of gold coins.

Adolph was well aware of the Schlagintweits' spiralling debts – it was one of the main reasons he had decided to return to Europe overland. The journey should enable him to open up new trade routes, not to mention the regional intelligence he could gather and the soft power he could wield from socialising with potential allies and trading partners. Hermann and Robert were already back in Berlin trying to assuage the Company's concerns; here was Adolph's shot at finding a solution of his own.

Things went well at first. Masquerading as a caravan of merchants, they passed undetected through the city of Ilchi and carried on towards Yarkand, relying on Muraj to scout ahead. Then, three weeks into their journey, he returned with news of a dramatic development. Wali Khan had sent his armies east with orders to seize Yarkand, long held by the Chinese. The Turks had laid siege to the city, pinning their beleaguered enemy inside their fort.

Adolph and his companions reached Yarkand to witness a spectacular counterattack. With the Turks camped outside the city, the Chinese poured out of their garrison and caught their besiegers off-guard, routing them in the open field. In the chaos that ensued, Adolph and his men found themselves caught up in Wali Khan's retreating army.

Things were amicable at first, but the Turks grew suspicious of this fair-skinned 'feringhi' with detailed drawings of rivers, mountains and settlements about his person. Adolph and his companions had their arms taken; they were going to Kashgar, whether they cared to or not.

When they reached the city Adolph was taken directly before Wali Khan. Putting his faith in the maxim that fortune favours the bold, he introduced himself as an envoy of the Honourable East India Company, a man of great importance to the British. He intimated that, should any harm come to him or his men, no stone would be left unturned in the quest for justice and retribution. As he spoke, Adolph described the man he had always hoped to become – a great Humboldtian adventurer, an emissary of enterprise and enlightenment, shining the lamp of science into the darkest corners of the world.

Wali Khan said nothing. His siege on Yarkand had failed and now the armies of the Khatais were coming. Strength rather than diplomacy would dictate the fate of Kashgar, and of Wali Khan. What better time to remind his followers that he answered to nobody, least of all an agent of the British, sent deep, too deep, into territory he and his followers called home?

Turning to his men, Khan spoke. His instructions were simple and clear. The other members of the party were to be taken to his prisons, where they could hope to die or, worse, be sold into slavery. Meanwhile, Adolph was to be taken to the gates of the city.

There, at four in the afternoon, he had his head chopped off.

Gone was the accident-prone ensign of the past,
replaced by a determined young officer.

English naturalist, soldier and surveyor Henry 'Haversham' Godwin-Austen
at Cherraponjee, India. Photographer unknown (1869).

CHAPTER 3

Fresh Blood

In January 1848 Henry 'Haversham' Godwin-Austen arrived at Sandhurst, England's leading military academy, as green as its playing fields. Thirteen years old, he showed promise as an artist, but lapsed into complacency, becoming so idle it earned him a night in the cells.

Word of his behaviour reached his grandfather, General Godwin. The general had pulled strings to ensure Haversham a place at Sandhurst and was dismayed to learn that the young cadet was squandering the opportunity. General Godwin was promptly aboard a train out of London, intent on taking the matter up with his grandson in person.

The first Haversham knew of the general's visit was the appearance of one of the sergeants in his Hall of Study, bearing a summons to the lieutenant governor's office. Ordinarily this meant one of two things: a hamper from home ready for collection, or a disciplinary matter, with whatever punishment that might bring. It was with 'mixed feelings' then that Haversham passed through the green baize door of the office in question. The last thing he expected to see was the stern face of his grandfather awaiting him on the other side.

General Godwin marched Haversham out onto the parade ground. There he disabused his grandson of the notion that his family would buy him a military commission if he did not earn one on merit. By the time the general had finished, Haversham understood that, if he did not pull his socks up, he would be entering the army at the rank of private.

'That was the best and kindest thing he ever did for me,' wrote Haversham, who went on to graduate with distinction. Now a young ensign, his reward was to be posted to Burma, where he would serve as the aide-de-camp to a distinguished British general – his grandfather, General Godwin.

Godwin-Austen had barely made port in Calcutta when he was thrown from a horse and hospitalised with a broken thighbone; his biographer Catherine Moorehead compared the accident with 'the modern phenomenon of an over-enthusiastic young driver trashing his car not long after passing his driving test'.

The Indian subcontinent was just getting started with him. On the boat from Calcutta to Rangoon he contracted smallpox, at a time when it was widespread and commonly fatal. He would eventually recover, but over the next eighteen months he experienced prolonged bouts of illness, including serious eye and ear infections, treated by the generous application of leeches: thirty on his side for a suspected liver infection; six around each eye; twenty on the ear – a triumph of logistics, regardless of its medical efficacy.

Though Godwin-Austen himself was in the wars, he arrived in Rangoon to find peace had broken out. The Second Anglo-Burmese War was at an end, leaving him with few military duties and time to spare. Seeing an opportunity to hone his skills as a surveyor, he started work on a map of the Irrawaddy Delta, a maze of river channels covering an area of eight thousand square miles. The work was an ideal distraction, bringing together his artistic talents, his fascination with natural history and all the knowledge he had picked up from his father, Robert Godwin-Austen, a distinguished geologist, and a member of the Royal Geographical Society.

The resulting map was so impressive – so the story went – it caught the eye of Sir Andrew Waugh, the surveyor-general of India. Without further ado, Godwin-Austen was on his way back to Calcutta, recruited to the ranks of the Survey of India. He did not know it yet, but his appointment owed much to the influence of his father, who had, in his own words, 'set the machinery to work'. For Haversham, the explanation was much simpler: the Survey needed fresh blood, and he was just the man to spill some.

Founded in 1767 to help consolidate territory under the control of the East India Company, the Survey of India had a long tradition of putting men in harm's way. Under the leadership of a young officer named Captain James Rennell – the first surveyor-general of India – its surveyors were charged with exploring the extent of British-administered India. The work took them into a wilderness of the unfamiliar, home to animals they had never encountered and deadly diseases new to their freshly imported immune systems. In those early years an assignment to the Survey was, according to John Wilford in *The Mapmakers*, 'tantamount to a death sentence'.

Rennell led from the front. On one occasion he could only watch as a tiger carried off one of his men, but on another, when a leopard attacked a group of *sepoys* – professional Indian soldiers – Rennell seized a bayonet and thrust it into the creature's mouth. He was ready, too, to draw arms against human attackers – and did not always come off best. During one ambush Rennell received a series of savage blows from a sword, sustaining injuries from which he never fully recovered. He retired from active service in 1777, returning to England with 'a shattered constitution'. He was thirty-five years old.

Rennell had given his all for the Survey, but for some he had not gone far enough. William Lambton, a young British officer bursting with ambition, believed the mapping of India demanded a rigour and exactness beyond even Rennell's best efforts. Rennell and his men had relied on 'route surveys', following roads or rivers and noting down local geography. Lambton argued for a more scientific approach, ascertaining 'the correct positions of the principal geographical points upon correct mathematical principles'. Using a system of triangulation and trigonometry to calculate exact heights and distances, Lambton hoped to create a vast mesh of triangulated positions extending the length and breadth of subcontinental India. His project became known as the Great Trigonometrical Survey.

Work began in 1802 and, from the outset, it was an uphill struggle. Lambton required a theodolite, a telescope that reports the angle of an object from the horizontal; there were only three in the world powerful enough to measure such large distances. When he succeeded in obtaining one, he found it weighed half a tonne. Moreover, to be of any use, the instrument – which needed twelve men just to lift it – had to be raised to a position of significant elevation. With few natural vantage points on the vast southern plains of India, Lambton and his men commandeered temples or conscripted locals to build towers of their own. Forcing men to work long days in suffocating heat, doing damage to hallowed religious buildings in the process, they made enemies everywhere they went.

For Lambton and his surveyors, all nature seemed to be against them: they were plagued by illness, tormented by insects, and attacked by everything from king cobras to rogue elephants. It got worse as they moved north, taking their work into a lowland belt of marshy grassland known as the Terai, where clay-rich swamps teemed with parasites and water-borne disease. Further north still, they entered the jungle, where the atmosphere was so oppressive it was deserted, for the worst heat of the year, by even the birds. Then, moving up into the mountains of the Himalaya, they made enemies of ice and stone.

Decades passed. The Great Trigonometrical Survey swallowed up whole lives and careers. Lambton was succeeded as surveyor-general by George Everest, then Everest by Andrew Waugh, who oversaw the 'discovery' of what he and his fellow Survey men knew as Peak XV. Waugh wrote to his deputy in Calcutta in 1856 confirming it was the highest mountain yet discovered; he suggested naming it after his predecessor, a name that came into common parlance almost a decade before it was officially adopted. But Mount Everest, as far as the British were concerned, could be admired only from afar. It lay fifty miles beyond

India's border with Nepal, and the Nepalese steadfastly refused British applications to inspect it more closely.

Instead, in 1856, the Survey's most experienced men were focusing their attention elsewhere, on a region that had come under British rule following the First Anglo-Sikh War – Kashmir. The British had ceded control to a territorial ally but retained suzerainty over the region, meaning they would help defend its borders. Of course, to do that, they first needed to ascertain where its borders lay.

With Tibet to the east and Chinese Turkestan to the north, Kashmir encompassed a large tract of the Western Himalaya. Much of what the British knew about the region owed itself to the exploits of Godfrey Vigne, a private traveller who, in the 1830s, returned to England describing mountains 'such as would make Mont Blanc look small beside them'. Vigne was not exaggerating – he had passed through the shadow of some of the highest peaks on earth, in a range known as the Karakoram.

Twenty years later, in 1855, these same mountains caught the attention of the British surveyor Colonel Thomas G. Montgomerie. Montgomerie was taking observations from the summit of Mount Harmukh, a minor peak in the lower-lying mountains of the Lesser Himalaya, when he noted in particular 'two fine peaks standing very high above the general range'. Montgomerie recorded them as 'Peak K1' and 'Peak K2', the K standing for Karakoram.

Montgomerie knew he was looking at mountains that formed part of a great natural frontier between Kashmir and Chinese Turkestan, a notional border the British had yet to define. But where – exactly – were they? And to whom did they *belong*? One thing was certain: he would not get answers to his questions from 137 miles away. Sooner or later, somebody would need to take a closer look. That somebody, as it turned out, was Henry Haversham Godwin-Austen.

Appointed to the Survey in 1857, Godwin-Austen joined a subdivision of the Great Trigonometrical Survey known as the Kashmir Series. He was put to work in the Pir Panjal, the largest range of the Lesser Himalaya, where he received a sobering taste of what awaited in the greater ranges to the north. It wasn't enough simply to climb mountains. He and his party would remain at the summits for hours, sometimes days, as they completed observations. Hunkered down at high altitude in sub-zero temperatures, they were freezing cold, brutally exposed and often dangerously short on supplies. 'Minor inconveniences', wrote the surveyor, that 'may serve to give some idea of the amount of labour entailed in the survey of a country such as this'.

For all the difficulties he faced, Godwin-Austen thrived in the mountains. Gone was the accident-prone ensign of the past, replaced by a determined young officer. He carried a length of rope to see him safely over crevasses and a hatchet for cutting steps in the ice; the more precarious his situation, the more sure-footed he became. 'His strength and stamina were amazing,' wrote Moorehead, who considers it 'testimony to his exceptional mental toughness' that he was the often 'the sole Westerner in the party'. For Godwin-Austen, unable to 'discuss the nature of the country and admire its magnificent scenery' with fellow Europeans, his was a particular kind of isolation, a loneliness all of its own.

Most of the men with Godwin-Austen were Balti porters, native to Kashmir and recruited under a system of forced labour known as *begar*. This entitled state and government officials to commandeer porters and provisions at the towns and villages they came to, whether to carry supplies and munitions to outposts along the frontier, as a transport corps for representatives of the Indian government, or to further the objectives of imperial institutions such as the Survey of India. The great virtue of this arrangement, from Godwin-Austen's perspective, was that he could alter the size of his party according to his needs, taking on fresh men in more remote areas where it was necessary to carry more food and fuel. For the villagers themselves, wrested from their families and crops, and forced to carry heavy loads deep into icebound mountains, the system had less to commend it.

Begar was not an invention of the British. The word was Persian in origin; begar had been practised in India since the start of the eighteenth century. In the case of Kashmir, begar had been introduced by the Dogras, a Sikh dynasty that had annexed the region in 1841. Twenty years on, the Dogras still governed Kashmir under the supervision of the British, themselves no strangers to forced labour. In 1861, as Godwin-Austen prepared to lead the expedition that would make him famous, he counted two Dogra Sepoys – Sikh infantrymen – among the ranks. 'In this way,' notes the geographer Kenneth Iain MacDonald, 'the colonialist discourse in India was produced in collusion with the Indian bourgeoisie.'

Godwin-Austen knew better than to rely solely on his Dogra enforcers to keep order. British travellers tended to characterise their Balti porters as lazy, cowardly and dishonest, citing cases of sabotage, theft, deception, feigned illness and desertion. Today these alleged behaviours are better understood as 'acts of resistance', notes MacDonald, 'played out in an effort to exercise a degree of self-determination and retain an element of dignity'. Understanding this, Godwin-Austen had selected a Balti named Mahomed, drawn from among the porters, to be his *sirdar*, or 'man of influence'. The coming expedition would be a constant negotiation, not just of the landscape, but with those who called it home.

On 8 July 1861, Godwin-Austen arrived at the summit of Thyarlung, a 16,844-foot peak at the gateway to the Karakoram mountains – the region he had been sent to explore. 'The view, as usual from these alti-tudes, was grand and magnificent,' he wrote. 'Peak K2, the highest on this side (overtopped only by Mount Everest in the far eastern Himalayas of Nepal), appeared an airy-blue tint, surrounded by the yellower peak K1 (Masherbrum), K3, and others, all over 24,000 ft in height. Other minor peaks, by hundreds, thrust up their heads – some snow-capped, some rounded, some bare and angular, running up as sharp as needles.'

Colonel Montgomerie had first sighted K2 from 137 miles away. Now, at the summit of Thyarlung, Godwin-Austen had halved that distance. That, though, was as the eagle flies; the path of the expedition snaked up the Shigar and Braldu valleys, into the rugged heart of the Karakoram. He and his party would be three weeks reaching Askole, the last village they would come to. Arriving there on 30 July, Godwin-Austen became only the second European ever to pass through; the first, five years earlier, had been Adolph Schlagintweit.

No visit to Askole was complete without a *jhula* crossing. A jhula was a type of bridge made of three strands of rope held apart by forked branches. Jhulas would only be replaced once they had failed – typically at the cost of at least one life – so were often found in states of alarming disrepair. This was certainly true of the jhula spanning the vertiginous gorge of the Braldoh river. 'The passage across', wrote Godwin-Austen, with a tang of Victorian understatement, 'was by no means pleasant'.

This was a taste of what awaited Godwin-Austen and the sixty-six men with him as they marched out of Askole into the Karakoram's deeper interior. Danger was everywhere. It might be darkly beautiful, like the river of stone that rushed past one of their campsites, 'a black mass... of stones and rock, some of great size, all travelling along together like peas shot out of a bag, rumbling and tumbling one over the other, and causing the ground to shake'. Then there were the crevasses, stretched like crooked mouths across the glaciers, 'ugly things to look into, much more so to cross, between walls garnished with magnificent green icicles... looking like rows of great teeth ready to devour one'.

There was no way to explore the Karakoram but by its glaciers, which flowed through the valleys with a directness of their own. Seen from afar they might have appeared sleek and sweeping, but move up close and find a skirmish of the elements, a timeless struggle between ice and stone. 'The devastation and mess created by a glacier surpass the wildest dreams of a construction engineer,' wrote John Keay of the Karakoram. 'Try to ascend them and you find them surrounded by an oozing morass of mud and stone, blocks of ice and shattered rock, as insecure and unpleasant to cross as the worst icefield. This is the world as it must have been at the dawn of creation, cracking and crumbling, oozing and flowing with irresistible elemental forces. No place at all for human beings.'

Nor did the nights bring respite. Camping on the glacier, the men used rocks and stones for a mattress, protection against the cold ghosting up from below. Retreat to the glacier's edge and there was solid rock to sleep on, but within range of blocks of stone falling from the cliffs above. The sound of these thudding down was enough to cheat the tiredest soul of a good night's sleep, so instead they lay awake in the darkness, waiting for the light to break, when dawn summoned them back out onto the remorseless ice.

By the night of 11 August, the expedition was camped midway up the Chiring glacier, a day's march from the top of the Mustagh pass. For centuries, migrants and merchants had used the pass to move between Kashmir and Chinese Turkestan. Godwin-Austen was aware that many local travellers had crossed before him, including some of his own Balti guides, so he might have considered it a formality. What he didn't know was that for the last five years the Chiring glacier had been undergoing a 'surge', moving ten times faster than usual. He found it severely crevassed, with huge blocks of ice obstructing their path.

That evening, his tent pitched in the lee of steep cliffs where the valley narrowed, the surveyor heard 'most disagreeable noises' beneath him. The glacier was making its feelings known, 'crunching, splitting and groaning to an awful extent'. For the Baltis, with only blankets to protect them, 'the cold was very severe… for as our fuel had to be carried with us, no fires could be afforded except for cooking. We all went to rest early,' wrote Godwin-Austen, 'and did not turn out till the sun showed over the immense cliffs above us.'

Starting out the next morning, Godwin-Austen was accompanied by Mahomed and seven other men carrying 'ropes and other appliances'. The pass was less than five miles away but 'progress was provokingly slow'. 'Travelling became so insecure that we had to take to the ropes,' wrote Godwin-Austen, 'and so, like a long chain of criminals, we wound our way along. In this mode we moved much faster,' he went on, 'each man taking his run and clearing even broad crevasses.'

As the day advanced the sun rose and the snow softened. The men's feet broke through the crust of snow on the glacier's surface, sinking down onto the harder ice below. All around they heard avalanches falling down the valley sides. Then, just a mile short of the pass, the weather turned. It began to snow and clouds closed in, leaving Godwin-Austen in the dark as to their exact position. As time ticked by, he stopped to take stock.

Barometers were not the only way to measure altitude. Godwin-Austen was able to calculate their position by observing the boiling point of water, which drops half a degree below 100°C for every five hundred feet above sea level. Using this method, he put them at just a few hundred feet beneath the top of the pass. Even as the water was boiling, however, the men could see the clouds getting thicker, until 'all the peaks around had become quite obscured'. The snow, too, was falling more heavily. 'I thought it best to take the opinions of the men with me,' wrote Godwin-Austen, 'and, guided by their experience, I gave up the idea of proceeding further.'

Here was early Himalayan exploration as few have imagined it. A British officer led to a mountainous frontier that was a mystery only to him, along a surging glacier transformed in ways the local shepherds could describe. A lone European leading by committee, submitting to the instincts and experiences of his guides. Too often the first English-speaking explorers of the Himalaya have been characterised as intrepid pioneers, celebrated for their tenacity and singularity of vision. Here was one who understood that no amount of imperial authority was a substitute for local knowledge.

Accepting defeat, Godwin-Austen cut a rueful figure, part of the dog-tired chain gang trudging back down the Chiring glacier. To have reached the top of the pass would have been to look deep into territory little known to the British – 'but want of time,' wrote the surveyor, 'there still being much work to be done, prevented another attempt.' The Mustagh pass had defeated them, but he had not given up on the search for Peak K2.

Retracing their steps as far as the Braldoh river, the men turned east along one of its tributaries. This brought them to the foot of the Biaho glacier, leading in turn to the Baltoro. Thirty-nine miles long and fed by more than a dozen smaller glaciers, the Baltoro glacier is a vast coronary artery in the frozen heart of the Karakoram. It is not the longest glacier in the range, but it feels the most integral, flowing from some of the largest and most spectacular mountains on earth. Somewhere among them, hoped Godwin-Austen, was Peak K2.

The days to come would be the most exacting yet, as he and his men marched up the corrugated surface of the Baltoro, a sprawling swell of loose stone. On the first day they covered a distance of just four miles. The second was little better. Setting out in the morning, they were met by the full force of a bitter wind, cannonading along the broken surface of the glacier, funnelling through every valley and trench, invading the narrowest fissures and fault lines.

That night on the glacier was colder and harder still. Since all they had for fuel was what they could carry, their fires were parsimonious affairs; flames cowering in the cold, like the men huddled around. Some of the Baltis began to complain, saying if 'Sahib' passed the night with nothing more than a rug to shiver under, retreat would be sounded immediately. Godwin-Austen had already tested their resolve on the Chiring glacier. Now he questioned how much further up the Baltoro they would be willing to go.

And, alongside the weakening resolve of the men, Godwin-Austen harboured misgivings of his own. He felt certain that if they pushed far enough along the Baltoro they would come within sight of Peak K2. 'I knew that it could not be far off,' he wrote, 'but began to have some doubts as to whether it might not be beyond the Karakoram watershed.' At dawn of the third day, he took action, turning the expedition south, as they marched across the glacier to the foot of Masherbrum's great northern spur. Then they began to climb. Rather than see proceedings peter out on the glacier, Godwin-Austen was trying for a glimpse of Peak K2 over the bulwark of mountains to the north.

Climbing upwards on the black granite of the Karakoram, they joined the spur's main ridge, where the going grew steeper still. Feeling the weight on his lungs, the strain on his legs, Godwin-Austen knew they were gaining height fast. Every time they stopped to rest, he turned and gestured to where his mountain should be: 'the peak I had toiled up so far to see'. Then, turning once again, more in hope than expectation, Godwin-Austen saw at his fingertip 'a distant bit of rock and snow... just peering above the nearer snow-line'. The men made one last push, until 'there no longer remained a doubt about it. There, with not a particle of cloud to hide it, stood the great Peak K2, on the watershed of Asia!'

The mountain was fifteen miles away, set back from the Baltoro along one of its larger tributaries. Seeing its southern slopes flowing into the glacier below, Godwin-Austen fixed its position within the territory of Kashmir, and recorded its height as 28,265 feet – a figure that differs by just a few feet from the measurement of 28,251 feet assigned to it today. There, hidden deep in the Karakoram, was the second-highest mountain in the world. And, unlike Everest, it was within British-controlled territory. Where Godwin-Austen had led, others would soon follow. They would go further up the Baltoro, all the way to the foot, and onto the slopes of Peak K2.

With what time he had left, Godwin-Austen produced a charcoal illustration, drawing pictures where others might struggle to draw breath. The resulting watercolour shows Peak K2 high above the surrounding peaks and massifs, as glaciers race downwards through the intervening Biange heights. The Baltoro dominates the midground, dark bands of moraine marking out the lanes on this sweeping super-highway of ice and stone. On the near slopes of Masherbrum's spur, Balti porters can be seen standing beside a freshly constructed cairn. Once he had finished his visual study, Godwin-Austen followed them down the mountainside, but not before adding a stone of his own.

Written in 1955, *Abode of Snow* claims to be a definitive history of the Himalaya. Its author, Kenneth Mason, was a veteran of the Survey of India, a decorated soldier and a respected geographer. Mason offered a glowing appraisal of Haversham Godwin-Austen, hailing him 'probably the greatest mountaineer of his day'.

It was in Mason's nature to revere a fellow Survey man, especially one who had brought such distinction to their profession. It is doubtful, however, whether Godwin-Austen considered himself a 'mountaineer' – he was probably not familiar with the term. He was a naturalist, geologist, surveyor and explorer, doing his most celebrated work in places where mountains happened to be. Famous for taking a first good look at K2, he is just as easily pictured on the shores of some far-off lake, collecting shells, or teaching his men how to use a fishing rod, while the lapping of the water transported him back 'to the beaches of Old England'.

There was much to set Godwin-Austen apart from the crowd: his distinguished family; his artistic talents; his redoubtable resolve. His climbing record, too, was formidable. By the end of his career, he had climbed above twenty thousand feet on at least four occasions and had gone any number of times above the highest summits of the Alps. His ascent, in 1862, of a 20,613-foot mountain called Mata Peak, or Mentok Kangri, is still cited as a world summit record – the highest mountain, up until that time, climbed to the top. But Godwin-Austen was not 'the greatest mountaineer of his day'. He was not even the greatest mountaineer working for the Survey of India.

Their faces told the story of all they had endured...

'Crossing the Burzil Pass', from *Climbing and Exploration in the Karakoram-Himalayas* by William Martin Conway (1894). Illustrator unknown.

CHAPTER 4

The Khan of Khotan

In May 1883 an obituary appeared in *Proceedings of the Royal Geographical Society*, revealing that a man named William Henry Johnson had died 'at Jummoo, on the 3rd of March, under the most melancholy circumstances, being fully persuaded that he had been poisoned'. Johnson had served for two decades as governor and joint-commissioner of Ladakh, in the employment of the Maharajah of Kashmir, a position 'most difficult to fill without creating great jealousy', noted his obituarist, 'and, no doubt, many enemies'.

Johnson had not always worked for the Maharajah. He had spent the formative years of his career with the Survey of India. Indeed, one of his fellow surveyors had written his obituary. 'It has been a sad task looking back on past years,' wrote Haversham Godwin-Austen, 'and recalling thereby many who are now gone. His services have been of no ordinary kind, and I am glad now to be able to bring them to the public notice they deserve.'

Johnson had joined the Survey of India in 1848 at the age of sixteen. Born to Anglo-Indian parents in Dehradun, educated at the hill station of Mussoorie, he had quickly made a name for himself in the civil branch of the Survey. Twice, more experienced men had failed to reach the crest of the Nela pass, high in the Kumaon Himalaya, only to be driven back by freezing temperatures and heavy snow. In May 1854, Johnson succeeded in establishing a triangulation station a quarter of

49

a mile east of the pass, at an altitude of 19,069 feet. At twenty-two, he had set a new Survey altitude record.

Tasked with establishing stations wherever they were needed, Johnson and his men sometimes climbed several different peaks before they found a sufficiently unobstructed view. Then, once a suitable location had been found, the hard work began. The summit was transformed into a building site, as they dug into the snow-capped mountaintop and laid the foundations for masonry pillars to support the big brass theodolite. They raised wooden scaffolds for the heliotrope, a mirrored instrument used to signal from one station to another, and built stone huts for shelter. Until those were ready, they had only tents to protect them from the strong winds and sub-zero temperatures. They might get ill, a storm might roll in, but there was no leaving the summit until their work was done.

Colonel Thomas G. Montgomerie is remembered as the man who 'discovered' the world's second-highest mountain, 'Peak K2'. In truth, Johnson was the first to the summit of Mount Harmukh, leading the work party that built the station used by Montgomerie. In all likelihood, Johnson had already looked north to the Karakoram, had already taken the measure of its highest mountains. He laid the groundwork for those who followed, pioneering the peaks on which higher-ranking men made their reputations.

And he was prolific. Time and again he broke the Survey's altitude record, climbing to 19,600 feet, 19,900 feet and 20,600 feet in successive years. In 1862 he built a station at 21,000 feet and climbed to 22,300 feet. In 1863 he passed a night just shy of 22,000 feet. Haversham Godwin-Austen climbed above twenty thousand feet four times in his career; Johnson established nine stations above that height before he turned thirty, with four of those remaining the highest in the world for the next sixty years. Sometimes the pillars, scaffolds and huts were visible from villages below, evidence that Survey men did not just climb such mountains – they built on them.

Early in 1864 it looked as though Johnson's hard work was about to pay off. Colonel Montgomerie announced he was stepping down as head of the Kashmir Series and Johnson, who had often deputised for Montgomerie, thought himself a shoo-in to replace him. But it was not to be. The position went instead to a young lieutenant named Carter, a man whose only qualification was his military rank.

Johnson's best efforts had been in vain. Passed over for promotion, he would have to seek his own fortune. He began making plans for a different kind of expedition altogether.

The Survey of India existed, first and foremost, to do exactly as its name suggested – to map and measure British-administered India. Though its remit did extend to 'rectifying our imperfect geographical knowledge of the regions beyond British influence', its agents were cautioned not to 'risk the safety of the party nor to entangle Government in political complications'. Johnson left the mountain town of Leh in July 1865 with permission to go as far north as Ladakh's border with Chinese Turkestan, and not a step further.

At first, Johnson acted accordingly. He and his men marched into the mountains of the Kunlun range, where they saw stunted willows, crippled by cold, on the banks of streams alive with wild trout. Later, where grass would not grow, they saw wild lavender, a staple of the Tibetan antelope on Ladakh's high plains. Towards the end of August, they made camp on the banks of the Karakash river, less than a day's march from the border, where they remained for three weeks. Johnson conducted a survey of the surrounding area, climbing 'three peaks of the Kunlun range which, having no names, are known by us as E57, E58 and E61'. Then, on 6 September, he and his men struck camp, cresting the Yangi Diwan pass and crossing the border into Khotan, the southernmost province of Chinese Turkestan.

Johnson would later claim that, shortly before his departure from Leh, he had received a letter from the Khan of Khotan 'inviting me to enter his territory, as he wished much to see me'. The Khan was apparently aware of the surveyor's previous visits to Ladakh's northern frontier and 'agreed to render me every assistance, and to permit me to return to Leh, after a short stay in his capital Ilchi'. With no time to seek the approval of his superiors, Johnson had decided, on his own initiative, to accept the Khan's invitation.

This was *incredibly* convenient. Johnson had made several formal applications for permission to make a 'scientific exploration' of Chinese Turkestan. All had been rejected. Now this invitation had arrived at the exact moment he was leaving for the border. Moreover, as it later transpired, he had borrowed fifteen thousand rupees – exactly the amount he would need for an expedition of this kind.

If there was to be an inquisition it would have to wait. Johnson's gamble was that he would return from Khotan with such a wealth of intelligence that all sins would be forgiven. Already, coming down out of the mountains on the Khotanese side, he noted down all he saw: the wild senna – valued for its medicinal properties – growing on the hillsides, the wheat and barley cultivated in large quantities on flatter ground. At one village, counting around five hundred houses, the surveyor learned that it was populated by convicts exiled from the cities, 'known by their beards being kept shaved, and their faces branded with round marks'. The inhabitants of the village were, the surveyor noted, 'particularly uncivil to travellers'.

For ten days Johnson continued north. Leaving the Kunlun range behind, he and his men crossed 'an immense plain, sloping gently downwards, watered by numerous small streams and some large rivers'. The surveyor saw how fertile the country was, how fine the cotton and silk, where gold washed down from the mountains so prodigiously that three thousand men worked in the goldfields. Three miles from Khotan's capital, Ilchi, he was met by the Khan's two sons, accompanied by cavalry and infantry under their command. They were his escort into the city, where he was taken directly before their father, the Khan of Khotan.

At eighty years of age, Khan Habīb Allāh cut an impressive figure, six feet tall and 'seen to great advantage' in robes of silk and gold thread. Once a local magistrate, he had come to power following a violent uprising against the ruling Chinese, a bloody massacre in a fort that, it turned out, Johnson now called home. Indeed, after his audience with the Khan, Johnson was taken to his new quarters. Falling asleep that night, above dungeons still containing instruments of torture left behind by the Chinese, he might have noticed the line between hospitality and captivity beginning to blur.

On 1 December 1865, six months after setting out from Leh, a party of weary, weatherbeaten men stumbled into town. Their faces told the story of all they had endured, forcing their way back over the frozen heights of the Karakoram pass in deep midwinter. Of sleepless nights, keeping vigil against Hunza robbers. Of frost biting at their fingers and toes, as the temperature fell below the lower limit of their thermometers. Of icicles, growing in their beards, declining to melt even in direct sunlight.

Their leader, a bedraggled surveyor, might have used those long nights to keep a record of his experiences, except his hands had shaken too much to write, and the ink had frozen between heated inkpot and paper. How many hundreds of miles had he travelled? How many thousands of feet had he climbed? Now he had returned, heartened by the prospect of a hero's welcome.

William Johnson arrived back, some months later than planned, to find that word of his improvised itinerary had travelled on ahead of him. The government was demanding to know what one of its men had been doing venturing deep into Chinese Turkestan, in contravention of direct orders. It fell to the superintendent of the Survey, Colonel James T. Walker, to account for Johnson's actions. Anxious to buy some time, Walker asked that judgement be reserved until the surveyor had been given a chance to explain himself.

That explanation came in the form of a written report, a detailed account of Johnson's expedition to Khotan. In it he recounted the events leading up to his arrival in Ilchi and described how, as had been agreed in advance with Khotan's ruler, he had spent four days touring the country. His report included details of Khotan's military capabilities, describing six thousand infantry, and slightly fewer cavalry, equipped with poor-quality Chinese weapons and an artillery of maybe sixty big guns – that was the army of Khotan. Nor was its ruler under any illusions as to its shortcomings. Johnson brought word that the Khan, fearful of competing rebel rulers in neighbouring provinces, and of Russian forces massing in the north, hoped to bring the region under British protection.

That, according to Johnson, was why the Khan decided not to let him depart from Ilchi after all.

The Khan 'showed me much kindness while in his country', offered Johnson, 'and kept all his promises, with the exception of not allowing me to leave the place'. 'He wished to detain me as a hostage,' he went on, 'until such time as the British Government sent him assistance, in the shape of troops and arms.'

Johnson's residence at the old Chinese fort had become a prison. The Khan had made a point of showing the surveyor the dungeon, containing some of his favourite devices: 'the rack, which is worked by screws; the tread-mill, and another instrument for extorting confession, which consists of a wooden bed covered with sharp stones and gravel, on which a culprit is made to kneel, while a log of wood is laid over the knee-joints, thereby causing excruciating pain.' Meanwhile, on tours of the city, Johnson had seen gallows erected – hanging was the prevailing form of capital punishment, that and 'blowing away from guns'.

Even Khotan's national sport held a mirror up to Johnson's predicament. *Boj-Baji*, translating as 'sheep wager', found horsemen 'racing after one another of their number, and trying to get possession of a sheep which he is carrying. The game carried on until both horses and men are completely exhausted.' Johnson might have felt some affinity with the carcass in question, clung to as he was, just as doggedly, by the Khan of Khotan. He wished 'to keep me with him altogether', wrote the surveyor, 'which he would have done, had I not pointed out to him the uselessness of doing so.' Becoming desperate, Johnson argued that it was futile to detain him, while waiting for the British to intervene. He could do far more for Khotan's cause, insisted the surveyor, if he was permitted to make the case for intervention in person.

The Khan relented. He agreed to let Johnson go, but only once the surveyor had issued a written promise to return – ideally at the head of the entire British army. On 4 October 1865, after a stay of sixteen days, Johnson left Ilchi. He and his men faced uncertain passage through the borderlands to the south, followed by a perilous crossing of the Karakoram pass. Johnson would press for three of his companions – he named them as Nur Bux, Emám Allí and Mátádín – to 'be rewarded with a gratuity of six months' pay'. 'All these men,' he went on, 'had many and trying difficulties to contend with.'

So ran Johnson's report – one that, he believed, ought to earn him and his men a handsome reward. He had delivered a trove of geographical intelligence, bringing word of Khotan's great natural abundance and mineral wealth, all under the protection of a makeshift military and a ruler anxious to do 'business' with the Indian government. This, at a time when the 'Great Game' was at its peak. With Russia and the British vying for control of Central Asia, regional allies were invaluable. Johnson had served one up on a plate.

Colonel Walker was satisfied. He declared Johnson's report 'the most valuable contribution to the geography of Central Asia that has been made for several years'. These sentiments were echoed by Sir Roderick Murchison, who told the Royal Geographical Society he had never read a paper better exemplifying 'the character of a true, bold and scientific manager of an expedition'. The mood at the RGS was that Johnson's initiative exemplified the expansionist aspirations of the British, executed with a professionalism that did his countrymen proud.

Viceroy Sir John Lawrence saw things differently. It had been the cause of considerable embarrassment to the Indian government to learn through a third party that one of its men was in Chinese Turkestan. Lawrence took the view that, if the surveyor had exceeded expectations with the dividend from his latest expedition, it was only because he had exceeded his orders. There would be no reward for Johnson or his assistants, only an official reprimand. The government would cover the cost of his expenses, not a rupee more.

Johnson was furious. He confronted Lawrence in person, with a litany of grievances. He complained about having been repeatedly passed over for promotion, arguing that his orders for 1865 had given him latitude to accept the invitation from the Khan. He changed his story, insisting that he had been relieved of a considerable sum of his own money before being permitted to leave. This, Johnson reasoned, was a legitimate expense – money he could expected to have reimbursed.

It was Colonel Walker's turn to lose his patience. Superintendent of the Survey, he was not about to see the Indian government shaken down by one rogue surveyor, least of all a man lacking 'the benefit of a liberal education'. Walker executed a dramatic *volte face*. He claimed he alone was responsible for all that was good in Johnson's report. It 'would have been ridiculed... had it been published as it came from his pen', insisted Walker. 'His map would have done more harm than good to the cause of Geography.'

The government and the Survey closed ranks. Within months Johnson had resigned – an ignominious end to an industrious career. After everything he had done in service of the Survey, all he would have to show for his time with the Kashmir Series was a gold watch, gifted him by the Royal Geographical Society many years later.

In 1884, a year after Johnson's death, the English mountaineer Douglas Freshfield delivered a paper at the English Alpine Club. Freshfield had been looking over the surveyor's report of his 1865 expedition when he was struck by one detail in particular. Johnson had been camped at Ladakh's northern frontier, shortly before he travelled on to Ilchi, when he 'ascended three peaks of the Kunlun range which, having no names, are known by us as E57, E58 and E61'.

Freshfield consulted the Survey maps of the region to find that Peak E61, sometimes known as Muztagh, rose 23,890 feet above sea level. That, Freshfield realised, would have taken Johnson fifteen hundred feet higher than anybody had ever climbed before. Cross-referencing the surveyor's original report against the version subsequently 'corrected' by General Walker, Freshfield saw that the claim had been redacted. The climb became known as Johnson's 'suppressed ascent' and is still debated to this day.

Presenting his discovery to the Alpine Club, Freshfield was in two minds as to whether Johnson had climbed E61. Johnson and his men 'had carried up a full-sized plane table with its braced tripod stand, both bulky articles, to the summit of the peak,' noted Freshfield. 'The ascent from the camping ground, the survey work on the summit, and the descent had all been accomplished in a single day... without any special effort.'

At the same time, Freshfield was aware of the surveyor's record and reputation. 'Johnson had established an extraordinary number of trigonometrical stations above 20,000 feet and slept at nearly 22,000 feet in the previous year. As to his laying little stress on his exploits, it may be noted that he was a very reserved man and laid little stress on anything he did.'

In the final reckoning, Freshfield considered 'the probabilities... very strongly against Mr Johnson'. The American mountaineer William Hunter Workman shared Freshfield's doubts, suggesting Johnson had misidentified whatever mountain he had climbed, and that the height of E61 had probably not been accurately recorded by the Survey anyway.

Others disagreed. 'It is one thing to say of a "mere mountaineer" that he mistook his position or his peak,' argued Tom Longstaff, 'and quite another to suggest this of a professional surveyor.' Nor could Longstaff see any reason to doubt the height assigned to E61. 'Until the Kuen-Luen Muztagh (E61) is remeasured by some thoroughly competent observer,' he went on, 'I see no way of avoiding the admission of Johnson's ascent in 1865 of a peak 23,890 ft in height.'

Some years later the veteran surveyor and Himalayan historian Kenneth Mason did some detective work of his own. Mason drew on the results of a 1900 expedition led by Sir Aurel Stein, who believed he had identified the location of Johnson's campsite, and observed that an 'ascent from there to E61 or "Muztagh" was an absolute physical impossibility'. Seeing that the path to E61 was every bit as challenging as Stein described, Mason found another mountain for which it could have been mistaken – Zokputaran. 'The climbing of this peak... does not look difficult,' wrote Mason. 'It lies on the same range as E57 and

E58; its height is about 1,000 feet lower than that of E61... it is highly probable that Zokputaran was the actual peak climbed.'

If Mason was right – and he makes a convincing case – Johnson had climbed a peak 22,639 feet in height. That was almost four hundred feet higher than the Schlagintweits on the eastern peak of Ibi Gamin ten years earlier, a world altitude record *and* a world summit record – by far the highest mountain ever climbed to the top.

In *Imperial Eyes: Travel Writing and Transculturation*, Mary Louise Pratt described 'two simultaneous and... intersecting processes' observable in Northern Europe around the turn of the nineteenth century. 'One is the emergence of natural history as a structure of knowledge, the other is the turn towards interior, as opposed to maritime, exploration. These two developments,' offered Pratt, 'register a shift in what can be called European "planetary consciousness".'

Humboldt and Bonpland in 1802, through the brothers Gerard and Schlagintweit, to Godwin-Austen and Johnson more than half a century later: all can be understood as agents of this new way of seeing – and subjugating – the wider world. They sought vantage points and elevated perspectives under the banner of science and surveyance, making the early running in the story of mountaineering's world altitude record; those who, reaching heights of nineteen thousand feet and more, would not have called themselves 'mountaineers'.

But, even as Johnson was going about Company business at the top of what *might* have been Zokputaran, things were about to change. For more than a decade a new pastime had been on the rise in Europe, an outdoor pursuit especially popular with Britain's upwardly mobile middle class. The sport of 'alpinism' would bring a new urgency to the quest for the world's highest peaks, personified by a man whose ego would eventually outgrow the mountains of Europe. He arrived with a bang, and his name was Whymper.

'The Ascent of the Matterhorn, on July 14th 1865: Arrival at the Summit'.
Illustration by Gustave Doré (1865).

PART 2

THE
ALPINISTS
ARRIVE

There would be one last twist – an awkward corner…

...it was inevitable that there would be close shaves...

'Whymper's Fall on the Matterhorn', from *Edward Whymper* by
F. S. Smythe (1940). Illustration by Edward Whymper.

CHAPTER 5

The Golden Age

From Zermatt, anybody looking up at the Matterhorn that day would have seen what they had always seen: the east face of the mountain, a soaring wall of stone under a thin coating of ice and snow, as smooth as it was steep, as blank as it was imposing. Propped up against it, the contorted north face, where the mountain seemed to flinch under its own weight, folding into the hunched back of the precipitous Zmutt Ridge. This was Europe's most iconic mountain at its most arresting, seen from a village where, as of 14 July 1865, the consensus was that it would never be climbed.

For Edward Whymper, one of seven men moving together high on the mountain, the last few hours had been a revelation. The Englishman had been trying to reach the summit of the Matterhorn for five years, but always by the southwest ridge, always on the Italian side. For all that time he had dismissed the east face, seeing how steep it looked, how bare and featureless. Then, starting at dawn from a tent at eleven thousand feet, he and his companions had raced up it. They had found that, owing to the sloping stratification of the rock, the east face formed, in Whymper's own words, 'a huge natural staircase'.

Now, not long before midday, they were closing in on the summit. There would be one last twist – an awkward corner, where they were forced out into a dangerously exposed position. A stiff test for the less experienced members of the party but, with the help of the guides, they passed it safely. Beyond that, no difficulties remained.

The race for the Matterhorn was over. It came down to a straight sprint, as Whymper and the Chamonix guide Michel Croz charged neck and neck up the last two hundred feet of snow. Coming to the summit, Whymper declared it 'a dead heat', happy to share the honours with Croz, and happier still to think that he had beaten Jean-Antoine Carrel, the 'Cock of Valtournenche', to the Alps' most coveted prize. Carrel, a local Italian guide, 'considered the mountain a kind of preserve' and any attempt to climb it 'an act of poaching'. He was somewhere on the Matterhorn that day, still hoping to claim the summit for himself.

Somewhere. A terrible thought occurred to Whymper. He looked along the summit ridge, 'rudely level' and at least 350 feet long. He could not see the other end. *What if Carrel had beaten him to it after all?* What if the Italian party had already come and gone?

Whymper started along the ridge, scanning the snow to the left and right, searching for footprints. He saw nothing. Coming to the end, he felt a surge of relief, a swell of satisfaction. He had done it. No, *they* had done it, there were seven of them at the summit that day. But in his heart, Edward Whymper felt that the victory was his alone. It had been that kind of story, and he was that kind of man.

And where was Carrel's party?

'I peered over the cliff,' recalled Whymper, 'half doubting, half expectant, and I saw them immediately – mere dots on the ridge, at an immense distance below.' The Englishman took off his hat and began waving it in the air, joined by Croz as they shouted themselves hoarse. 'The Italians seemed to regard us – we could not be certain.'

It was not enough for Whymper. He had to be sure.

'I seized a block of rock,' he went on, 'and hurled it down, and called upon my companion, in the name of friendship, to do the same. We drove our sticks in, and prized away the crags, and soon a torrent of stones poured down the cliffs.' So desperate was Whymper to show Carrel that he was beaten, he was ready to bombard his rival with rocks.

'There was no mistake about it this time,' wrote Whymper. 'The Italians turned and fled.'

Climbing in light clothing, heated by the movement of their bodies, the men had felt warm. Now, resting at the summit, they began to cool down. Those with silk handkerchiefs tied them round their necks and buttoned their closely woven tweed jackets to the very top. They turned their plus-fours or breeches down over their knees and tucked them into their socks. If they carried gloves or mittens, they put them on, then, finding a place to sit and rest, gazed out from beneath the narrow brims of stout felt hats.

'The day was one of those superlatively calm and clear ones,' wrote Whymper, 'perfectly still, and free from all clouds or vapours. Mountains fifty – nay, a hundred – miles off, looked sharp and near. All their details – ridge and crag, snow and glacier – stood out with faultless definition. Pleasant thoughts of happy days in bygone years came up unbidden, as we recognized the old, familiar forms. All were revealed – not one of the principal peaks of the Alps was hidden.' All around them was the story of the 'Golden Age of Alpinism', a decade that had seen many of Europe's most famous mountains climbed for the very first time.

At the heart of the Golden Age was a partnership of amateurs and professionals – most of these first ascents had been accomplished by British alpinists climbing with Continental guides. Victorian gentleman arrived in the Alps in need of someone to show them around, to find that the locals could be relied upon as more than just 'porters and pointers of paths'. They were physically strong, could read the changeable Alpine weather and knew their way around the glaciers, able 'to thread their way safely through a maze of crevasses'. 'So there rose, alongside the climbers, a corps of professional guides,' wrote Walt Unsworth. 'The best became superb mountaineers and legends in their own lifetime.' One such immortal, for Unsworth, was the man at Whymper's shoulder at the summit of the Matterhorn – 'the finest Chamonix guide of his generation', Michel Croz.

Born in La Tour, Croz had been 'discovered' by the pioneering English alpinist Alfred Wills in 1859. He and Whymper first climbed together in 1864; together they added to the guide's extraordinary record of first ascents. 'Of all the guides with whom I travelled, Michel Croz was the man most after my own heart,' wrote Whymper. 'It was only when he got above the range of ordinary mortals, and was required to employ his magnificent strength, and to draw upon his unsurpassed knowledge of ice and snow, that he could be said to be really and truly happy.'

Croz was not the only guide at the summit of the Matterhorn that day. Among the seven-strong party were two others, Peter and Peter Taugwalder, *père et fils*. The Taugwalders were in the employment of Lord Francis Douglas, an eighteen-year-old English peer at the start of his alpine career. Douglas had arrived in Zermatt fresh from pioneering a new route up the Gabelhorn, intent on giving the Matterhorn a try. Following a chance encounter with Whymper, the two had agreed to join forces. Whymper was well aware of Douglas's talents, but his true interest was in securing the services of the Taugwalders. Old Peter was one of few guides who believed not only that the Matterhorn could be climbed, but that it could be done from the Swiss side.

The aristocratic Lord Douglas personified the spirit of exceptionalism at the heart of mountaineering's Golden Age, but the fashionable new pastime had taken keenest hold among Britain's upper-middle class. Many of the earliest and most enthusiastic members of the newly formed English Alpine Club were artists and authors, barristers and civil servants, chaplains and clergymen, men whose professions permitted them to spend six weeks of every summer experiencing a world more elemental. Men like the Reverend Charles Hudson.

A vicar from Lancashire, Hudson was a man of seemingly unimpeachable virtue. Known to walk fifty miles just for the exercise, he was handsome and athletic, an adventurous amateur with the best instincts of a professional guide. In 1855, he and T. S. Kennedy had devised a new route up Mont Blanc, the highest mountain in Western Europe, then that same year he had been among an eight-strong party first to the highest peak of the Monte Rosa, the pretender to Mont Blanc's throne.

By the age of thirty-six, Hudson had a reputation as one of the most accomplished climbers of his day.

Hudson had arrived in Zermatt two days earlier, with Croz as his guide. Whymper was having dinner at the Monte Rosa Hotel, ready for a fresh attempt on the Matterhorn, when Hudson marched in. For Whymper, already allied with Lord Douglas and the Taugwalders, here was an opportunity to further strengthen his party, adding one of Britain's most accomplished amateurs and one of Europe's finest guides.

There was one catch – Hudson and Croz were not alone. With them was a nineteen-year-old named Douglas Hadow, a novice mountaineer spending his first season in the Alps. When Whymper questioned whether Hadow was up to the challenge, Hudson vouched for the younger man's incredible fitness, pointing out that together they had completed an ascent of Mont Blanc 'in less time than most men'. That was not the full story – T. S. Kennedy, who had been with them on the day, later attested to the inexperience of Hadow and men like him. 'It is necessary to protest against the practice of inexperienced men ascending difficult peaks,' Kennedy wrote in a letter to *The Times*. 'A man who has spent only three or four years on the Alps is not and cannot be a first-rate mountaineer.'

Hadow, in his own way, was also typical of the age, with an enthusiasm for alpinism exceeding his aptitude and experience. And, if he had the air of a hanger-on, it was well-deserved – he had been hanging on all morning. Where the more experienced men had made light work of the Matterhorn's east face, Hadow had required constant attention from the guides. Yet, with his confidence in retreat, with the going getting more difficult the higher they climbed, he had made it. He had clung on around that final awkward corner, then moved up onto the snow-slope above. He had not sprinted for the summit. He had been thankful to get there at all.

That was behind him now. Hadow might have lacked the pedigree of Hudson, or the natural ability of Douglas, but he was there just the same, a member of the first climbing party to summit the Matterhorn. For that alone, his name would be written in stone.

As the six other men rested on the summit ridge and enjoyed the view, Whymper took out his pencils and began to draw. He had produced hundreds of sketches in the five years he had been visiting the Alps, pictures of the places he had visited, the people he had met, the mountains he had climbed. Now, from the ultimate vantage point, he captured the view he had worked hardest for. The result was not just a drawing. It was the culmination of a vow he had made, in 1861, following his first attempt on the Matterhorn, 'to lay siege to the mountain until one or the other was vanquished'. It was a trophy.

27 January 1855. A fifteen-year-old boy wrote a short entry in his diary, ending it with these three words: 'No news whatever.' It would be a familiar refrain in the pages that followed, as young Edward Whymper dutifully documented his uneventful existence amid the goings-on – or lack of them – in the world at large. 'To read it is a strangely depressing experience,' wrote Frank Smythe, Whymper's biographer. 'It is the story of a boy of quick intelligence and high ambition, tied down to dull and monotonous work.' Exactly the sort of boy who would, at the first opportunity, go out and pick a fight with a mountain.

As a child, reading about the exploits of Britain's polar explorers, Whymper dreamed of following them to the ends of the earth. Instead, apprenticed to his father, an engraver, he faced a life of running errands and 'cutting up wood', leading to what Smythe described as 'an atrophy... of spirit'. Whymper's work did provide a showcase for his artistic talents – in 1860, when he was twenty years old, he attracted the attention of the publisher William Longman. Needing some illustrations of the Alps for a forthcoming book, Longman commissioned Whymper to spend his summer sketching Europe's pre-eminent peaks.

Whymper arrived in the Alps with little experience as a mountaineer. He and his brother had climbed on the chalk cliffs of Dover and, following the death of their mother in 1859, he had lost himself in the pages of *Peaks, Passes and Glaciers*, the journal of the Alpine Club. Now, a guest at the Monte Rosa, he listened as more experienced alpinists held court deep into the night. Taking his small stock of knowledge onto the mountains, he proved himself a natural. 'His frame was light and lissom, yet superlatively wiry and strong,' wrote Smythe. 'He was the perfect build of a mountaineer.'

Whymper was back in the Alps the following year and, after a promising first ascent of the highest peak of Mont Pelvoux, he turned his attention to the Matterhorn. He would try, and fail, to climb the mountain six times in the next four years. Twice, according to Whymper, it was his guides or porters who let him down, losing their nerve in the face of what they deemed insuperable obstacles. Twice the weather thwarted him, storms so wild 'we saw stones as big as a man's fist being blown away horizontally into space'. On one occasion, he and his porter simply climbed into a dead end, 'spread-eagled on the all-but-perpendicular face, unable to advance and barely able to descend'.

For one terrible moment, late in the summer of 1862, Whymper thought he had been beaten to it. Still smarting from his latest failure, he arrived back in the village of Breuil to find Professor John Tyndall, the veteran Irish alpinist, preparing an attempt of his own. All Whymper could do was watch, certain that Tyndall would succeed, as the Irishman started towards the mountain accompanied by three seasoned guides – Jean-Antoine Carrel among them – carrying a ladder to see them over the worst of the difficulties.

Whymper's heart sank when, early the next morning, he heard that a flag had been seen on the summit of the Matterhorn. But when the climbing party returned that afternoon, Whymper saw that their heads were hung low. They had turned back, claimed Tyndall, 'within a stone's throw of the summit'. As far as the Irishman was concerned, the Matterhorn had taken on 'a prestige of invincibility'. He declared that he had given up any hope of climbing it, and that others should do the same.

Whymper was having none of it. He was back, time and again, probing the mountain's defences, searching for the weakness that would allow him to go higher. Spending so much time on its slopes, it was inevitable that there would be close shaves, none closer than the tumble he took,

climbing alone, below the cliffs of the Tête du Lion. He had backed off
in the face of 'inextricable difficulties' when he lost his footing. 'I fell
nearly 200 feet in seven or eight bounds,' wrote Whymper. 'Ten feet
more would have taken me in one gigantic leap of 800 feet on to the
glacier below.' Instead, lying injured on the lip of a precipitous drop, he
listened to the sound of the rocks he had dislodged thudding into the
ice of the Glacier du Lion, which 'told how narrow had been the escape
from utter destruction'.

Then, in 1865, the breakthrough came.

For as long as Whymper had been trying to climb the Matterhorn
the accepted wisdom had been that, if it could be climbed, it was via
the southwest ridge. Seen from any other direction the mountain was a
slanting spire of rock, hopelessly sheer, impossibly smooth. The southwest ridge, by contrast, presented a staccato surge of towers and cliffs,
suggesting 'the possibility of a route', wrote Frank Smythe, 'and the
existence of handholds and footholds, cracks, chimneys, gulleys, ribs,
ridges and buttresses to assist the mountaineer.' For Jean-Antoine Carrel
it had become a point of pride – if the Matterhorn would 'go', it would
be from the Italian side.

Now, after he had failed on the southwest ridge half a dozen times,
Whymper's thoughts turned to a conversation with Sandbach Parker,
one of three brothers who had arrived in Zermatt in 1860. The Parkers
had set out to reconnoitre the east face of the mountain, reaching a
height of around twelve thousand feet. But for 'clouds, a high wind and
want of time', Sandbach told Whymper, they might have gone higher.
The Parkers had not been given much credence at the time, unreputa-
ble alpinists climbing without guides. Now, five years later, Whymper
wondered if they had been onto something.

He had just begun his own first forays up the east face when
he learned that time was against him. An Italian geologist named
Felice Giordano had assembled a party, led by Jean-Antoine Carrel,
intent on claiming the summit for Italy, and from the Italian side.
That was when Lord Douglas and the Taugwalders had arrived in
Zermatt, followed closely by Hudson, Hadow and Croz. Seeing his

opportunity, Whymper had seized the initiative. He had forced the issue. He had won.

As flags go, it lacked a certain dignity. Tied to a tentpole, fluttering over the Matterhorn, the Alps, all the mountaineering world, was the soiled undershirt of Michel Croz. 'It was a poor flag,' conceded Whymper, 'and there was no wind to float it out, yet it was seen all around'.

After an hour at the summit, the time had come to climb down. The last thing Whymper did was to write their names on a piece of paper then, rolling the paper into a tube, he placed it inside a bottle, and the bottle inside a cairn. This would be their 'visiting card', to be discovered by whomever came after.

Whymper and Young Peter were the last to start down. They caught up with the other men at the most difficult part of the descent, the awkward corner where the rock was smooth and glazed with ice. There the mountain sloped sharply downwards then gave way to thousands of feet of vertical ruin, a sheer drop to the head of the glacier below.

Croz went first. He moved downwards until he found a good stance then turned to help Hadow, who followed close behind. Next came Hudson, helping Hadow from above, then behind him Lord Douglas, watched over by Old Peter. Whymper had tied onto the elder Taugwalder and after him came Young Peter, bringing up the rear.

Progress was slow, moving in turn. As they stood, patiently waiting, their minds had time to wander. Down the 'huge natural staircase' of the east face, where they would soon be able to move more freely, with wide shelves of rock to catch them should they fall. Over now-familiar ice and snow, then back along the easy paths, through alpine meadows and pine forest, all the way to Zermatt. There the homely comfort of the Monte Rosa awaited, where these conquerors of the Matterhorn would recount their adventure for the first time. A story they would tell, time and again, for the rest of their long lives.

Then Hadow slipped.

That, at least, was how it looked to Whymper. Croz, who was immediately below Hadow, had just finished helping him. The guide was turning to take his next step down when Hadow, still adjusting to his new position, lost his footing and fell.

Croz should have been the one to 'catch' Hadow. If he had seen the slip happen, he would have tightened his grip on the rope with one hand and taken a firm hold of the rockface with the other. Instead, his back to the danger, he didn't stand a chance. Whymper heard 'one startled exclamation', as the falling Hadow struck Croz between the shoulders, then the guide too began to fall.

Their best chance was Hudson. Hudson, who had vouched for Hadow, who had gambled his life on the younger man and convinced others to do the same. Hudson, who – after Croz – might have been the most capable mountaineer in the party, hugely experienced, famously strong. Hudson, who was pulled clean off the rockface by the weight of the falling men, followed immediately by the helpless Lord Douglas.

More of the men were now falling than not. And, as the rope to Old Peter Taugwalder went taut, it looked for all the world as though the veteran guide was next to go. But this piece of rope was different. Tying onto Douglas, Old Peter had used a length of what was 'little more than a sash-line', lighter and weaker than the manilla rope connecting the men below. Old Peter and Whymper both took a firm hold of the rockface, and the weight of the falling men came onto them as one. The rope tightened.

And snapped.

'For a few seconds we saw our unfortunate companions sliding downwards on their backs, and spreading out their hands, endeavouring to save themselves,' recalled Whymper. 'They passed from our sight uninjured, disappeared one by one, and fell from precipice to precipice on to the Matterhorn glacier below, a distance of nearly 4,000 feet in height. From the moment the rope broke,' he went on, 'it was impossible to help them.'

Whymper clung to the rockface, struggling to make sense of what had just happened. He and the Taugwalders would stay frozen to the spot for the next thirty minutes. Somewhere in the shock, the panic and the fear, he understood that this changed everything. That the Golden Age of Alpinism was over, even if the world didn't know it. Like a body, already falling, but yet to hit the ground.

Croz and Hadow were found a short distance apart, their bodies lying crumpled in blood-stained snow at the foot of the north face. Both were naked, bruised and broken, the clothes torn from them as they fell. Croz was missing the entire top half of his head, and could only be identified by his beard and, later, a rosary cross dug out of his jaw.

Hudson was discovered fifty yards away. A few possessions were scattered around him, among them his prayer book.

Of Lord Douglas they recovered only his gloves, a belt, a boot and a coat sleeve.

'I have seen nothing like it before or since,' wrote Whymper, 'and do not wish to see such a sight again.' He was one of nine men who made their way, two days later, to the head of the Matterhorn glacier. They considered themselves a search party, going in the hope that someone, somehow, might have survived. In the weeks to come, the mother of Lord Douglas would cling to that hope – when she learned that her son's body had not yet been found, she sent a telegram asking, 'is it not possible to seek in the rocks above or to let down food?' But Whymper and those with him were in no doubt. The best Douglas could have hoped for was a quick death. His body was either snagged somewhere on the north face, or it had disintegrated entirely.

As word spread, confusion reigned. The Irish alpinist John Tyndall learned about the accident en route to the mountain. Tyndall was especially disconcerted to learn that the accident had claimed the life of the famous Irish alpinist, Professor John Tyndall. 'I then listened to a somewhat detailed account of my own destruction,' he recalled, 'and soon gathered that, though the details were erroneous, something serious if not shocking had occurred.'

In Britain, the mood darkened. This was not the first fatal accident to occur in the Alps, nor would it be the last – days later a schoolteacher fell and died on the Riffelhorn – but the loss of Lord Douglas, 'one of the best young fellows in the world', drew a scathing reaction from the press. 'Why is the best blood of England to waste itself in scaling hitherto inaccessible peaks?' demanded *The Times*. 'There is use in the feats of sailors, of steeple-climbers, vane-cleaners, chimney sweepers, lovers and other adventurous professions, but in the few short moments a member of the Alpine Club has to survey his life when he finds himself slipping, he has but a sorry account to give of himself.'

It was open season on the Alpine Club. In France, the *Journal Illustre* marvelled at the organisation's very existence, 'the aim of which is to suggest and glorify dangerous attempts at climbing European mountains'. John Ruskin saw little sport in alpinism, thinking it 'more vanity than any other athletic skill', while Charles Dickens complained that climbers 'contributed as much to the advancement of science as would a club of young gentlemen who should undertake to bestride all the weathercocks of all the cathedral spires in the United Kingdom'. 'What is the use of scaling precipitous rocks, and being for half an hour at the top of the terrestrial globe?' rounded *The Times*. 'If it must be so, at all events the Alpine Club, that has proclaimed this crusade, must manage the thing rather better, or it will soon be voted a nuisance.'

Whymper's first instinct was to stay silent but, with the Alpine Club becoming a pariah, its president, Alfred Wills, urged him to speak out. Days later, *The Times* published a letter from Whymper containing a detailed account of the accident, putting the deaths of the four men down to the slip by Hadow. Mindful of the dead men's families and wary of adding to their grief, Whymper stopped short of criticising Hadow directly, though he did make reference to the younger man's 'want of experience'. Whymper declined, too, to lay any blame on the man who, he believed, bore ultimate responsibility – Charles Hudson. It had been Hudson who had vouched for Hadow, Whymper privately observed; it had been Hudson, with all his experience, who ought to have known better.

Whymper's letter had the desired effect. *The Times* softened its rhetoric and the furore died down. As more of the facts became clear, a new question arose: why had Old Peter Taugwalder tied into Lord Douglas with such an inferior piece of rope? In the days after the accident Zermatt had been gripped by rumours that the guide had cut the rope to save his skin. Whymper had been vehement in his defence of the guide. However, even he struggled to explain Old Peter's decision to attach himself to Douglas using a length of the 'stout sash-line', conceding that it 'had a very ugly look for Taugwalder'. Whymper's letter to *The Times* described how father and son had been frozen in fear for a full thirty minutes after the accident, relying on the Englishman to steady their nerves and guide them to safety. Worse still, with the danger behind them, Young Peter was soon laughing, smoking and eating 'as if nothing had happened'. The implication was clear – if there were those in Britain looking for someone to blame, they need look no further than the Taugwalders.

Alfred Wills was satisfied. Whymper had presented 'a clear and manly narrative', wrote Wills, 'told with a candour and honesty which give him an additional claim on the sympathy of every feeling heart'. It was wishful of Wills, however, to claim that Whymper's version of events 'strips the calamity of all mystery and doubt'. Questions dog the accident on the Matterhorn to this day.

It was Whymper, after all, who had allied himself with Hudson, Croz and Hadow, nervous perhaps that if they went alone they might beat him to the summit. The entire climbing party had been a product of Whymper's panic on learning that Carrel was about to make a fresh attempt from the Italian side. The 'sash-line' was Whymper's rope, Whymper's responsibility – he had to have seen Old Peter using it to tie into Lord Douglas. Whymper had been the natural leader of the expedition, with all his experience of the mountain they hoped to climb. Weren't the dead men collateral damage in his combative campaign to climb the Matterhorn, victims of a monomaniacal obsession with being first to its summit?

If there were those who considered Whymper the true author of the accident, he answered them in writing. In 1871 he published *Scrambles Amongst the Alps*, an epic of high adventure brought to life with more than one hundred of his own illustrations. *Scrambles* was a way not just to relive his climbs but to immortalise them, taking control of the narrative and making money in the process. Yes, he was sensationalising – and profiting from – a tragic accident, enhancing his reputation at the expense of others. But he had read the future of mountain literature perfectly. *Scrambles* was a bestseller.

Whymper had come a long way from the young man measuring out his life in the orderly increments of his dreary diary. 'I had ideas floating in my head that I should one day turn out to be some great person, be the person of my day,' he had written, aged seventeen, in a rare moment of honest aspiration. 'Time will tell if they be true or false.' Already, with *Scrambles*, and the events it described, he had written his name into legend; he had shown that climbing mountains could be a thrilling and deadly pursuit. Still, he was not satisfied. Resolving that in future, when he climbed, it would be under the banner of science, Whymper would attempt to summit a mountain once believed to be the highest in the world.

'We knew that the enemy was upon us...'

'Chimborazo from 17,450 feet', from *Edward Whymper*
by F. S. Smythe (1940). Illustration by Edward Whymper.

CHAPTER 6

Mountain Sickness

Long before the likes of the English Alpine Club had descended upon Zermatt and Chamonix, the Alps had been the preserve of naturalists, geologists and physicians, for whom it was unthinkable to climb a mountain in the name of anything but science.

Johann Scheuchzer, a professor of physics from Zurich, made a series of journeys through the range in the early eighteenth century. When he published his findings, alongside his ground-breaking theories of glaciology, he included lavish illustrations of the different species of dragon he had encountered. For Scheuchzer, it was a region 'so well provided with caves that it would be odd *not* to find dragons there'. If science was to draw back the veil of fear and superstition that lay over the mountains of Europe, it would not be happening overnight.

Some of the mythical creatures inhabiting the Alps proved especially difficult to dislodge. In the 1770s a young Swiss aristocrat was on his way to Chamonix when he met a local guide who claimed to have found proof of the existence of fairies and magical spirits. The man said he had seen snakes, sea creatures and all manner of living things turned to stone. The traveller was fascinated but, coming to the place, he saw only fossilised fish and reptiles, with no trace of the supernatural beings said to have enchanted them.

The young aristocrat's name was Horace Bénédict de Saussure. He was twenty years old when he visited Chamonix for the first time, in

1760, sent to collect plants for the Bernese anatomist, physiologist and botanist Albrecht von Haller. Saussure was spellbound by the dramatic physical geography of the Alps, but nothing impressed him more than the highest of the mountains in the range – Mont Blanc. After examining it from a smaller peak nearby, Saussure announced that he would give a reward to the first person to climb it.

Saussure's bounty would not come easy. Unlike the horns, spitzes and needle-like aiguilles that punctuated the skyline of the Alps, Mont Blanc rose in a solemn sweep to a height of 15,774 feet, distinguished by its brooding mass, its aura of invincibility. To climb it meant crossing vast glaciers riven with crevasses, then marching up slopes where the snow lay waist deep. And, as Saussure began to understand, it meant something else. 'The brilliancy of the light, the oppression of the air', he wrote to a friend, 'and possibly moral causes, such as the weariness of a long march on steep snow-slopes and the dread of these immense solitudes, served to dishearten... even in the absence of any real and insurmountable obstacles'.

One party after another failed in their attempts to climb Mont Blanc. In 1785 Saussure tried for himself but, driven back by deep snow, he retreated to Geneva, where he turned his restive mind to the question of whether the mountain might better be ascended by balloon. Then, in September 1786, a Chamoniard named Jacques Balmat appeared on Saussure's doorstep. He had come to collect his reward.

Balmat, a chamois hunter and crystal gatherer, had partnered with a local doctor named Michel-Gabriel Paccard, reaching the summit of Mont Blanc late on 8 August 1786. The two subsequently disagreed on every detail of the climb – who had first approached whom, who had devised the route, who had helped whom up the final stretch – but their ascent of Mont Blanc was not in dispute. They had been seen at the summit by a number of witnesses, Balmat waving his hat and Paccard, in a heavy coat, silhouetted against a clear blue sky. Their differences aside, they had done it. The highest mountain in Western Europe had been climbed.

A year later Saussure would visit the summit of Mont Blanc for himself. He would experience, too, the effort of climbing up the last gentle slope that led to the top. Dizzy and nauseous, he stopped every few steps before his legs gave out, leaning on his stick and gulping down the fresh northern breeze. 'Despite the delight which this superb spectacle gave me', he wrote of the view, 'I felt a painful sense of not being able to draw from it all the profit possible, and that my power of appreciation was limited by my difficulty in breathing. I was like an epicure invited to a splendid festival and prevented from enjoying it by violent nausea.'

Writing about his experience, Saussure brought his powers of deduction to bear on the question of what it was that had affected him. He made a connection with the thinness of the air but reasoned that altitude alone could not explain the phenomenon – balloonists had reached greater heights without experiencing such acute symptoms. Noting that the effects seemed to vary from one individual to another, he concluded that they had been exacerbated by 'the muscular exertion of walking uphill'. Saussure was the first European to attempt such a detailed diagnosis of this affliction. It would come to be known as 'mountain sickness'.

In November 1879 Edward Whymper sailed from England aboard a ship belonging to the Royal Mail Steam Packet Company, bound for Guayaquil. With him was Jean-Antoine Carrel, the 'Cock of Valtournenche', Whymper's fiercest rival for the summit of the Matterhorn all those years ago. They were joined too by Louis Carrel, cousin of Jean-Antoine. Whymper had recruited the cousins to assist him with a programme of scientific research in the Andes mountains of South America.

Whymper was a few months away from turning forty. On top of the Alpine world at twenty-five, engulfed in tragedy a few hours later, he had written a bestselling book by the age of thirty, cementing his reputation as a tenacious mountaineer who 'would, but for one melancholy circumstance', wrote Leslie Stephen in the *Alpine Journal*, 'have been the most triumphant of us all'.

Following the accident on the Matterhorn, Whymper had revisited his childhood dream of becoming a polar explorer, leading two expeditions to Greenland; both had been hamstrung by lack of funding and, unable to explore the inland ice sheet, Whymper considered them failures. Resolving to go back to the mountains, he settled upon a new realm of scientific enquiry – one that required him to climb. Hard at work in his cabin en route to the New World, he was finalising plans for an expedition that would, he hoped, solve the mystery of 'mountain sickness'.

Almost a century had passed since the first ascent of Mont Blanc but, for all those who had since gone to the highest summits in the Alps, opinion was very much divided on the nature – and even the exact symptoms – of mountain sickness. 'The most opposite statements and opinions have been advanced concerning this matter,' wrote Whymper. 'The extremes range from saying that fatal results may occur, and have occurred, from some obscure cause, at comparatively moderate elevations, down to that no effects whatever have been experienced at the greatest heights which have been attained.'

Whymper's own experience – or lack of it – added to the confusion. 'Neither of the two Carrels, nor I myself, had ever experienced the least symptom of mountain-sickness,' wrote the Englishman. 'None of us, however, prior to this journey had been 16,000 feet high.' That was the heart of the problem – that, to be subject to the more acute effects of altitude, it was necessary to venture beyond European shores. Hoping to add to the stock of knowledge on the condition, known in French as *mal des montagnes*, Whymper was en route for the mountains of Ecuador.

As their mail steamer passed through the Panama Canal and emerged into the Pacific Ocean, the Englishman spent more of his time on deck, hoping for a first good look at the Andes. He was searching the skyline for one mountain in particular but, 'although the nearer parts of the outer ranges could be discerned, their tops were in cloud and the great snow-peaks were invisible'. Making port in Guayaquil on 9 December, he climbed a hill at the northern end of the town; still he saw nothing but a mantle of cloud lying low over the mountains to the east.

At Guayaquil, Whymper recruited an Englishman named Perring to be their translator and transport officer, then, with the rainy season about to arrive, started northeast along the River Guayas on the steamer *Quito*. The Europeans found themselves sharing the vessel 'with a large and very miscellaneous freight', including four Italian organs stowed on the upper deck, 'each playing a different tune'. Salvaged from war-torn Peru, these instruments made for a musical distraction much enjoyed by the Ecuadorians on the *Quito*, 'but the alligators in the river seemed more sensitive', wrote Whymper, with a childlike gaze. 'They came up and stared with open mouths, and plunged down again immediately, out of hearing.' Seeing sandbanks carpeted with the animals, Whymper was struck by how untroubled the locals seemed by their close proximity; 'though,' he noted, 'it is admitted they do occasionally chew incautious children'.

That night they disembarked at Bodegas de Babahoyo, 'the entrepôt of Quito', a town upriver where goods were stored en route to the capital. From there they would proceed on horseback, leading a caravan of pack animals and the *arrieros* who drove them. Passing the nights at *tambos*, low-slung huts along the way, the Europeans were grateful for plank beds that lifted them, a few inches at least, above the world of 'scuttling things' that 'ranged the floor and invaded our boots'. Then, each day, they followed the 'Royal Road' to Guaranda, a muddy track churned up under the hooves of mules carrying everything from cases of champagne to huge bales of quinine bark. Through shady jungle and dense forest, over streams and up steepening slopes, the Royal Road grew worse and worse until it had become, wrote Whymper, 'a mere rut', where 'animals dying en route were left to rot'.

Pressing deeper into the Ecuadorean interior, Whymper was following in the footsteps of his celebrated predecessor, Baron Alexander von Humboldt. Famous for reaching a record height on Chimborazo, Humboldt had returned to Europe with lurid descriptions of the toll the ascents had taken on him and his party, recounting how they had suffered, at different times and at different altitudes, from nausea, vomiting, dizziness, shortness of breath and bleeding from the lips and gums. 'All these symptoms vary considerably according to age, constitution, the softness of the skin, and the prior exertion of the muscles,' wrote Humboldt, 'but for single individuals they are a sort of measure of the thinning of the air and the absolute altitude that one has reached.'

Drawing on Saussure's belief that mountain sickness was due, in part, to the rarefaction of the air, Humboldt had deduced that the principal cause was a lack of oxygen in the blood, owing to the diminishing barometric pressure and its effect on the body.

Whymper was well aware of Humboldt's theories about mountain sickness – and the gaps in them. Failing to reach Chimborazo's summit, the Prussian had questioned whether it was humanly possible to climb to the top of such a mountain, fearing that under too little atmospheric pressure 'one's lung vessels could burst… and one could cough up blood'. Now, as his caravan crested a ridge and came within sight of their objective, Whymper meant to settle the matter. In the valley below was Guaranda, his 'base for attack', as he attempted to succeed where Humboldt had failed. There, beyond it, stood Chimborazo.

Not long after their arrival at Guaranda, Whymper was visited by 'the very thin upper crust of the town' – a government official known as the *Jefe-Politico*, accompanied by the chief of police and a local priest. Reasoning that the Europeans could not possibly hope to climb Chimborazo, and must therefore be treasure-hunters, the three had come to negotiate their share. Whymper agreed to give them half of everything he found – on the condition that they cover half the cost of the expedition. The men 'drew long faces, and went away'.

A trove of a different kind awaited the Europeans at Guaranda: more than one thousand pounds of equipment and provisions sent on in advance. This included food for the entire expedition – tinned ox-cheek, mutton, beef and potted ham, along with soup, cocoa, condensed milk and a syrup beef paste called Liebig's Extract, all organised into daily rations, soldered inside waterproof tin boxes. Mindful that symptoms of hunger and fatigue were easily mistaken for those of mountain sickness, Whymper meant to make sure that he and the Carrels were never without a square meal.

His plan was to ascend Chimborazo 'gradually and leisurely, by small stages… by the simplest means that could be devised, and by the easiest routes that could be found'. Here again Whymper's thinking owed something to Humboldt who, after failing to climb Chimborazo, theorised about the possibility of 'building houses in the snow every 150 *toises* [959 feet] where fire and food supplies would be stored'. 'One could seek refuge from one to the other', he went on, 'in case one could not hold out in the highest one'. Outlandish as it seemed, Humboldt's suggestion prefigured the 'siege tactics' Whymper was about to pioneer. Substituting tents for Humboldt's houses, he planned to establish a series of camps on the slopes of Chimborazo, pushing provisions and equipment up the mountain until the summit was within reach.

For Humboldt, one of the advantages of this approach would be to form 'a connection with the inhabited region'. The Prussian had completed what scientific research he could through his day-long attempt on Chimborazo, but he had been short on time, and doubt had since been cast on what measurements he succeeded in taking. Anxious to avoid the same fate, Whymper travelled with two Fortin mercury barometers, two boiling point thermometers and seven aneroid barometers, all for the purpose of measuring altitude. The Fortins – nicknamed 'the babies' – were especially fragile devices, entrusted to Jean-Antoine Carrel. 'Many children would be fortunate indeed', wrote Whymper, 'if they were tended with the loving care which he bestowed upon those mercurial infants'.

With a clear plan of attack and all the preparations complete, Whymper and the Carrels left Guaranda early on the morning of 26 December accompanied by two porters, three arrieros and fourteen mules. Fording the River Chimbo, they climbed up onto the plain above, the Great Arenal. They rode on mules through the midday heat, then watched their shadows lengthen as the sun dipped towards the far horizon. Camping that night on the lowest slopes of the mountain, they woke to find the stream beside their campsite frozen solid. 'The remains of the soup in the cooking utensils were frozen up, cruelly hard,' wrote Whymper, 'but it was harder still to find in the morning that the two coolies and five of our mules had disappeared.'

Anxious not to lose momentum, Whymper reorganised his plans for the day ahead. He sent their remaining mules off early with Jean-Antoine, with orders to establish their next camp. Guide and animals returned a few hours later for a second load, and this time Whymper climbed with them, up the small valley he had named the 'Vallon de Carrel', then east, up the western slopes of the southwest ridge of the mountain. There, below a wall of lava, was their second camp.

'We were all in high spirits,' wrote Whymper, happy to make camp before nightfall. But the work of the last few days was about to tell. The Europeans had passed a bitterly cold night at the camp below, then climbed to an altitude of 16,450 feet – one thousand feet higher than any of them had been before. They had arrived 'in good condition', wrote Whymper, but 'in about an hour I found myself lying on my back, along with both the Carrels, placed *hors de combat*, and incapable of making the least exertion. We knew that the enemy was upon us,' he went on, 'and that we were experiencing our first attack of mountain-sickness.'

'I had never felt disposed to question the *reality* of mountain-sickness,' wrote Whymper, 'and on the contrary had frequently maintained that it is reasonable to expect some effects should be produced upon men who experience much lower atmospheric pressures than those to which they are accustomed.' Now, lying in a tent at 16,450 feet, Whymper confronted that reality for himself. Feverish and gasping for air, his throat bone dry, he struggled to drink or even to talk, managing 'a few words at a time… cut short by irrepressible, spasmodic gulps'. Worse still were the headaches, so intense they made him 'almost frantic or crazy'.

The Carrels were similarly affected. Both were 'habitual consumers of tobacco', wrote Whymper, and 'smoked conscientiously upon every opportunity. When such persons put aside their beloved pipes there is certainly something wrong.' Perring, however, appeared entirely immune. Whymper had observed that their transport officer 'was a rather debilitated man… [who] could scarcely walk on a flat road without desiring to sit down'. With his companions incapacitated, he tended to the fire and melted snow to drink. 'Except for him', wrote Whymper, 'we should have fared badly'.

Three days would pass before they felt ready to resume the climb. On the morning of 31 December, they ventured higher up the south-west ridge of Chimborazo – the same route, Whymper reckoned, that Humboldt's party had followed. Humboldt had known it as the *cuchilla*, the name given to it by his local guides, meaning 'knife edge'. Sure enough, Whymper found that there was barely room to pitch a tent. Eventually, dropping down onto the eastern side of the ridge, they found space for a campsite.

The next day – New Year's Day, 1880 – brought an unsavoury discovery. Breaking the seal on one of their food boxes, 'a most appalling stench rushed out'. 'We found that the ox-cheek had burst its bonds,' wrote Whymper, 'and had not only become putrid itself, but had corroded the other tins and ruined almost the whole of the food itself.' Worse still, further inspection revealed that this was not an isolated incident. 'We found ourselves obliged to hurl over the cliffs a mass of provisions which had cost endless trouble to prepare.'

With the offending items disposed of, the next day was spent transporting food, fuel and equipment up to the third camp. By nightfall they had everything they needed to push higher up the mountain. Whymper was satisfied, too, that they had a practicable line of retreat, with a tent and plenty of firewood at their second camp and the remainder of their supplies at a depot in the mouth of the valley. With Perring and the local porters stationed at the camps below, 'word was given the same afternoon', wrote Whymper, 'that Chimborazo was to be assaulted the next morning'.

Whymper and the Carrels were away at 5.35 a.m., first traversing a series of large snowfields on the western side of the ridge, then climbing up onto its crest. Moving between huge patches of ice and the bare, decaying rock of the ridge itself, the three climbed continuously for two hours, stopping where the ridge terminated, at the foot of the 'Southern

Walls of Chimborazo'. Above rose steep cliffs, insurmountable but for a few snow-filled cracks and gullies. 'Thus far and no further a man may go', wrote Whymper, 'who is not a mountaineer'.

One gully in particular, 'the breach in the walls', rose at an angle of fifty degrees, steep enough that snow 'slid away in streams, or tiny avalanches, down to the less abrupt slopes beneath'. After a day dealing with rancid ox-cheek, a slanting gully was meat and drink to the Carrels, happy to put their talents to use. 'The axes went to work,' wrote Whymper, 'and the cliffs resounded with the strokes of the two powerful cousins.' But, as they cut step after step, they felt the wind rising. Whymper sensed the day turning against them. He shouted to the Carrels that he had decided to turn back.

Lying in their tent that night, ready to go again the following day, Whymper felt confident. That first attack of mountain sickness was behind them and, high on the mountain, but for a tightening of their chests and a shortening of their pace, all had felt strong and ready to go on. The southwest ridge would be familiar ground, the way clear to a height of 18,500 feet or more. It was the first time a party of skilled alpinists had laid siege to a mountain of this size. With one day of good weather, Chimborazo should be theirs.

They had been wading around, up to their necks in snow, for three long hours.

Whymper had thought at first that they had entered a labyrinth of crevasses, only to find that the hollow plateau between Chimborazo's twin summits was a sea of soft snow, twelve feet deep in places. Arriving there not long after eleven, they had imagined it the work of an hour to reach the higher of the two summits. Now, gone two in the afternoon, they were still stumbling around on the snowy plateau. The wind had strengthened and dark clouds blocked out what, hours earlier, had been a brilliantly clear blue sky.

Whymper turned to the Carrels.

'Would you rather turn back,' he asked, 'or go on?'

The cousins conferred for a moment in Italian. 'When you tell us to turn, we will go back,' said Jean-Antoine. 'Until then we go on.'

And that was that. On they went, throwing themselves into the snow and upon it, flattening it down into a crust firm enough to crawl on. Moving, yard by yard, towards the foot of the western summit.

The day had started so well. Away at 5.40 a.m., they had raced up the southwest ridge then, taking advantage of the steps they had cut the day before, completed their ascent of 'the breach' by eight. From there they bore left, zigzagging up a large snowfield then across a glacier. Jean-Antoine led, under orders from Whymper to go steady. Even so, the Englishman noticed that, as the morning advanced, the guide's pace grew shorter, 'until at last the toe of one step almost touched the heel of the next one'.

At 10 a.m. they had passed the last exposed rocks. The weather was still fine, the sun was shining and, as they climbed higher still, they saw the Pacific Ocean, 120 miles away and 20,000 feet below. Turning back to face the mountain, two rounded domes rose ahead. And there, between them, was the summit plateau, a third of a mile across, where they would soon be swimming in deep snow.

Unsure which dome rose higher, Whymper had adjudged it the nearer one. Now, hours later, he and the Carrels reached the place where the plateau ended and the western dome began. Feeling the ground steepen and the snow harden, they trudged upwards, leaden feet growing lighter in anticipation of success. 'We arrived on the top of it about a quarter to four in the afternoon,' wrote Whymper. Three hours of daylight remained – more than enough to take all the measurements they wanted, and to get back to their camp 3,200 feet below.

Except that they were not on top of Chimborazo. Only now, from the crest of the western dome, could they see that they were standing on the lower of the two. There to the east, separated by a third of a mile of deep snow, was the true summit of the mountain.

In that moment, it might have seemed hopeless. But, possessed of the same drive that had taken him to the top of the Matterhorn, Whymper wasted no time canvassing opinion. He and the Carrels were straight back into the thick of the snow, 'to resume the flogging, wading and floundering'.

Their resolve was rewarded. The ground near the eastern dome proved firmer than expected and they were soon pounding up its slopes, shrugging off the northeasterly wind that pulled at their clothing and stung their faces. The day was almost twelve hours long, they had been working hard for all that time, climbing at heights few Europeans had gone to. Again, their steps grew lighter, their lungs relaxed, until all the mountain was beneath their feet.

Whymper savoured the moment. 'We arrived upon the summit of Chimborazo standing upright like men, instead of grovelling, as we had been doing for the previous five hours, like beasts of the field.' But the ascent had taken its toll. 'We were hungry, wet, numbed, and wretched, laden with instruments which could not be used.' Their visit to the western dome had cost precious time and Whymper was anxious to avoid down-climbing 'the breach' – itself fifteen hundred feet below – in darkness.

Still, he insisted on setting up a Fortin barometer, taking the measurements needed to calculate the true height of Chimborazo. 'One man grasped the tripod,' wrote Whymper, 'while another stood to windward holding up a poncho to give a little protection.' By the time the barometer was back in its case, it was almost five thirty. 'Planting our pole with its flag of serge on the very apex of the dome, we turned to depart, enveloped in driving clouds which entirely concealed the surrounding country. Scarcely an hour and a quarter of daylight remained, and we fled across the plateau.'

A disconsolate Perring awaited, tending to the meagre fire that saw the climbers home. Its light guided them down the crest of the southwest ridge, through 'a night so dark that we could neither see our feet nor tell, except by touch, whether we were on rock or snow'. They had passed 'the breach' just as the day's last light was fading, and crawled into their tent a little after 9 p.m., 'having been out nearly sixteen hours, and on foot the whole time'.

'So ended the tussle with Chimborazo,' wrote Frank Smythe. 'The first peak of over 20,000 feet had been climbed, at all events by a European.' Sadly, for Whymper, it was not quite the landmark Smythe described. Haversham Godwin-Austen and William Johnson had taken their survey work to Himalayan summits of 20,000 feet or more. Godwin-Austen had climbed the 20,613-foot Mata Peak in 1862 and Johnson was said to have established triangulation stations as high as 22,300 feet during his controversial career – even before his 'suppressed ascent' of the mountain he knew as E61.

Chimborazo, meanwhile, was about to get a downgrade, courtesy of Whymper himself. In 1802 Humboldt had assigned it a height of 21,425 feet, a figure still widely accepted eighty years later. Whymper, taking a reading from one of his Fortin barometers, got a very different result. He gave the mountain's true height as 20,545 feet – four feet less than the figure of 20,549 feet given to it today.

Whymper's ascent of Chimborazo was, nonetheless, the most famous high-altitude climb of his day. Godwin-Austen and Johnson were obscure figures, their attainments were not widely known. Whymper was a household name. Author of a wildly popular book, synony-mous with the headline-grabbing events it described, he had gone to the top of a mountain once believed the highest in the world. He would return to Europe telling a sensational story, culminating with a singular success.

The results of Whymper's investigation into mountain sickness were more ambiguous. Following the ascent of Chimborazo, he and the Carrels had passed a night on the rim of Cotopaxi – at 19,347 feet, the highest active volcano in the world. Whymper held this 'interesting and unusual experience' up as testament to how well acclimatised he and the Carrels had become, but it typified the anecdotal evidence behind many of his observations, and the vagueness of his ultimate conclusion – 'that those persons in the future, who, either in pursuit of knowledge or in quest of fame, may strive to reach the loftiest summits of the earth, will find themselves confronted by augmenting difficulties which they will have to meet with constantly diminishing powers'.

Whymper, though, was not a scientist in the mould of Humboldt or Saussure – a true Victorian, science was one of many strings to his bow. Through his apprenticeship in engraving, he became an expert draughtsman, whose maps and illustrations brought his books to life. As a writer, though no great stylist, he held the attention of his readers, describing his adventures with pith and poise. For a sportsman he could be incredibly unsportsmanlike, but he was nothing if not competitive. And, though he was no romantic, there was a romance to him. A teen-age boy, who might have stayed hidden in the shadows of his inherited profession, if he had not fallen under the spell of the mountains, and of one mountain in particular – a spell that also proved a curse.

Conqueror of the Matterhorn, first to the summit of Chimborazo, we can only wonder what Whymper might have accomplished had he ever climbed in the Himalaya. Instead, it would fall to another Englishman to bring European alpinism to the world's highest peaks. He was a man more at peace with mountains, and with himself. His name was William Woodman Graham.

The Alpine Club asked two things of prospective members – to have climbed 'a reasonable number of respected peaks', and to be gentlemen.

English barrister and mountaineer William Woodman Graham.
Illustrated by Ruby Light from photograph.

CHAPTER 7

No Higher Purpose

High in the gods of the Mont Blanc massif, Graham felt the icy wind eddy and swirl. It pulled at his jacket and funnelled up his sleeves, chilling the Englishman to his complaining bones. He pressed his body closer to the rockface, a matter of feet below the summit of the towering aiguille. A speck of tweed against the jagged skyline of the Alps, he was in a desperately precarious position.

There, beneath him, was the Frenchman, Alphonse Payot. Graham stood on the broad shoulders of the Chamonix guide, steadying himself with one hand, groping for a handhold with the other. Graham could feel his nailed boots sinking into Payot's flesh; he did not need to look down to know they were drawing blood. Payot did not flinch.

The guide stood, both hands planted on the rock, at one end of a narrow arête. Coated in thick ice, the ridge was flanked on either side by deadly drops, spanning the forty-foot gap between the twin pinnacles of the Giant's Tooth, the *Dent du Géant*. This needle-like spire of rock is one of eleven peaks in the Mont Blanc massif rising to more than thirteen thousand feet. By August 1882, alpinists had summited ten – only the Dent du Géant remained unclimbed. Many considered it the last great Alpine honour waiting to be claimed.

Graham had been in Zermatt when he heard: *the Dent has finally been climbed*. An Italian party led by Alessandro Sella had climbed the southwest pinnacle, naming its summit *Pointe Sella*. Graham quickly

gathered, however, that the Italians had left the higher northeast peak
unclimbed. Moreover, from what he could tell, some of the fixed ropes
used by Sella's party had been left in place. The Englishman, who had
long admired the Dent du Géant, sensed an opportunity to make its
story his own.

Graham went straight to Chamonix where he recruited two French
guides, Alphonse Payot and Auguste Cupelin, and a young porter 'whose
sole name, christian or sur, was Pierre'. At the first sign of good weather
the four made their way to a mountain hut, where they enjoyed a few
hours' sleep. Setting off at two in the morning, they marched through 'a
pitch-dark moonless night, the natural result being that we lost the track
on the Mer de Glace almost immediately'. Owing to the resulting delay,
'and to our taking it very easy', it was eight by the time they reached
a col at the western end of the Rochefort Ridge. There, 'after breakfast
and a rest, we started at nine to attack the mountain'.

The Dent du Géant towered over them, rising at seventy degrees,
eighty in places, accelerating upwards against a stone-washed sky. Earlier,
Pierre had gamely declared that he wished to join the climbing effort
'comme volontaire'. Now, his 'courage evaporated'. The young porter
mumbled his excuses and retreated to the sanctuary of some rocks
nearby, taking their packs and ice-axes with him.

Many of Graham's fellow alpinists might have been surprised to see
him leave his ice-axe behind. Most considered these necessary all the
way to the top of a climb, for cutting steps in ice and snow on steeper
ground. Ice-axes could be unwieldy, though, following a design adapted
from alpenstocks – long wooden poles with iron spike tips carried by
Alpine shepherds since the Middle Ages. And Graham could see, looking
at the bare rockface, that he was not going to be cutting any steps. Sheer
as it was, he would be needing both hands.

He had arrived hoping to make use of Alessandro Sella's fixed ropes,
but he saw no sign of them. Instead, he, Payot and Cupelin started
directly up the rockface, making good progress on a rope of their own.
This, for Graham 'was the hardest climbing, from a muscular point of
view, that I have ever tried' – but the real difficulties were yet to come.

The men had ascended a few hundred feet, almost without stopping, when the character of the rockface changed completely. Where there had been blocks and bulges, now came a wall of bare blank quartz, 'a surface almost as smooth as if it had been planed'. They would be climbing on tiny handholds, frozen fingertips on slender edges, in a wildly exposed position. Here was the reason the Dent du Géant had remained unclimbed for so long.

And there, beneath the summit, was Sella's rope. Two hundred feet of it swayed in the wind, ready to see them up the last hard yards. To reach it, Graham and his guides would have to climb the right-hand corner of the southwest face, then traverse a narrow ledge. The day was clear and crisp, a cold wind sweeping the rockface, as the men edged higher, climbing on what cracks and edges they could find. Finally, they drew level with the rope, separated only by the width of the rockface. 'We crossed very gingerly,' recalled Graham, 'the ledge being very narrow, and in most places there being absolutely no handhold.'

Sella's rope was frozen and frayed, but it proved invaluable. His guides had taken days to find a way up those last few hundred feet and Graham could see why – even with the protection of a rope, it was treacherous climbing. The first hint of the southwest summit was the letter 'M', chiselled into the rock where Sella's guide, Maquignaz, had anchored himself and brought up his client. A little way above that was a pillar of stones, left by the Italians as proof of their ascent – along with a tattered *tricolore*.

Sella's party had stopped there, but the true summit, the northeast pinnacle, rose twenty feet higher, separated by a gap of ninety feet. To reach it would mean crossing a narrow arête, then scaling ten feet of 'perfectly smooth' wall on the other side.

Leaving Cupelin on the southwest pinnacle, Graham and Payot let themselves down onto the intervening ridge. 'This was of rock topped with ice,' wrote Graham, 'and gradually narrowed from a foot to a few inches.' To one side was a slope of seventy degrees plunging down to the Mer de Glace, to the other a vicious overhang. Fall to the right and they would strike nothing before they hit the ground.

The two edged across, until they reached the foot of the opposing rockface, as featureless and sheer as it had first appeared. It was there that we found them, one atop the other, Graham's nailed boots drawing blood from the shoulders of his unflinching guide. Graham felt, by his own admission, 'like a man about to undergo the "long drop"'. But he did not fall. Steadying himself in a small vertical crack, his free hand found a good hold. 'Then with a pull I was up,' wrote Graham, 'and with the aid of the rope raised Payot.'

Graham and Payot stood together at the top of the northeast pinnacle, the first to tread the last unclimbed summit in the Alps. So many others had tried and failed – some of the leading lights of the alpine world. Even the famed English climber Albert Mummery, in his celebrated partnership with the Swiss guide Alexander Burgener, had come up short. Mummery had declared the Dent du Géant 'absolutely inaccessible, by fair means'. Now Graham had claimed the summit, by any means necessary.

Taking their plaudits from the wind, Graham and Payot raised a flag of their own, made from a handkerchief and a piece of flagpole 'borrowed' from the Italians. Then, 'after a dram and a yell', they started to climb down. Behind them, their makeshift beacon of conquest fluttered in the chill breeze, over what is still known today as *Pointe Graham*.

Founded in 1857, the Alpine Club asked two things of 'prospective members' – to have climbed 'a reasonable number of respected peaks', and to be gentlemen. Nominated for membership not long after his pioneering ascent of the Dent du Géant, William Graham had spent several summers in the Alps, with a climbing record to match. When his application was rejected, there could be little doubt which of the criteria he had failed to satisfy.

The members had voted him down by forty-nine votes to seven. No formal reason was given, but it appears they considered it unsportsmanlike of Graham to have used Sella's rope on the Dent du Géant. Graham had made no effort to conceal his actions and was unequivocal about the advantage he had gained. The rope had been 'a great assistance, and indeed in one place necessary', he wrote in the Club's own *Alpine Journal*. Graham, a qualified barrister, might have argued his case, but he was done with the Alps and done with the Alpine Club. Before the dust had settled, he had sailed for Bombay.

Graham was accompanied by Joseph Imboden, a Swiss guide who had climbed with him on several occasions. The two pulled into Darjeeling on the newly constructed hill railway late one evening in early March. 'That night', wrote Graham, 'I could not sleep a wink. Before dawn I was up and hastened to call Imboden, whom I found in precisely the same state of excitement.' They rushed out onto the streets just in time to see the sun rise. 'Suddenly, far away in the dark and yet incredibly high in the sky, a pale rosy pinnacle stole into light. It was the summit of Kanchinjanga' – the third-highest mountain in the world. They watched as the first light caught the summit, fifty miles to the north, then lit up the mighty ridges that fell from Kangchenjunga to the east, west and south, 'tipping the peaks in succession with a golden glory'. It was a 'superb panorama', wrote Graham, a sight to 'fill the mind with a sense of beauty mixed with awe'.

As the light settled, Graham and Imboden made out the finer detail of the mountains. That first burst of exhilaration passed and they were soon weighing the range through the eyes of mountaineers. They saw great couloirs, 'the tracks down which sweep volleys of stones, the climber's deadliest enemy. Those dark transverse arcs across the glacier tell him of huge chasms yawning for the unwary footstep; those scarcely visible bands of purest white warn him of the more treacherous foe, the covered crevasse.' They saw towering ice-walls and broken seracs – big blocks or columns of ice, carved apart by intersecting crevasses. 'A hundred phenomena', wrote Graham, 'to the average spectator only so many added glories, to the mountaineer are written symbols. They constitute a book whose characters he alone can read, and in whose every syllable lies a warning and a threat.'

Graham, who had arrived in March 'hoping to test the so-called winter season', immediately set about recruiting some local porters and guides. As a private traveller he would pay these men the going rate, but the sums involved would not have troubled the Englishman, independently wealthy and travelling light. He was more anxious to secure the services of willing and able-bodied men, and was delighted to find that they 'could carry anything and… simply laughed at the 60 lbs per man we weighed out for them'.

Within a fortnight they were camped on the glacier running south from Kangchenjunga, 'in one of the grandest amphitheatres imaginable'. They were surrounded by Himalayan giants, mountains twice the size of their Alpine counterparts, coated in thick winter snows. And, if the mountains soared by a new order of magnitude, so too the temperatures plunged.

It was cold. Deathly cold. Not the snap of bitter wind, or the chill of deep snow, but a cold that numbed the spirit and dulled the mind. In the last throes of a Himalayan winter, it was their constant companion, marching beside them in the daytime, stealing into their sleeping bags at night. It robbed the heat from their campfires and sapped the warmth from their clothes. It was cold in the sunlight, colder still in the shade. And when they climbed, the mercury continued to fall.

The porters felt it too. These were local men, but they were not as well equipped as the Europeans, wearing everyday clothes and shoes, sleeping sheltered only by rocks. Normally they would not have gone further north than Jongri, the last village before the mountains. But they had taken Graham's money and, short of abandoning him and Imboden completely, they could only count the hours until he realised his mistake.

Graham would not turn back. Day upon day the party kept moving, crossing glaciers and passes, completing an exhaustive reconnaissance of Kangchenjunga and the peaks around it. It was only when he began to see cases of frostbite and snow-blindness among the porters that he considered retreat. Then, in his own words, 'a straw turned the balance'. One of the men, 'half asleep from cold, burned my climbing boots, which I had given him to dry'.

By Graham's account, the incineration of his boots was an innocent mistake. Given all the porters had gone through, it might not have been quite the careless moment he describes. The outcome was the same, 'a retreat almost as precipitate as our advance'. The men turned their back on the Sikkim Himalaya and marched south, arriving back in Darjeeling on 10 April.

If Graham felt chastened by this first abortive foray, it had done nothing to discourage him. On the contrary, summer was coming. Now the serious climbing could begin.

Nanda Devi, 'the Bliss-Giving Goddess', is a mountain steeped in Indian folklore, said to be the last refuge of a beautiful princess who dared to rebuff the advances of a Rohilla prince. The young man did not take rejection well and waged war against her father, the king, defeating him on the battlefield. With no alternative but to run and hide, the princess, Nanda, fled to the highest reaches of the mountain, retreating into the rock itself. Thus, she became the mountain, its *Devi*, or patron-goddess, and it her eternal sanctuary.

And what a sanctuary. The mountain 'rises from the centre of two concentric amphitheatres, resembling two horseshoes placed one within the other and touching each other at the toe,' wrote the English mountaineer Tom Longstaff. 'The outer amphitheatre, or horseshoe, measures seventy miles in circumference and from its crest rise a dozen peaks of over 20,000 feet, including Trisul and Dunagiri as well as Nanda Devi East.'

Graham arrived in the vicinity of Nanda Devi in July. Joseph Imboden was not with him; the guide had returned to Europe, leaving the Englishman in need of a replacement. Graham had sent a telegram to the Grindelwald climber Emil Boss, who, unable to find anybody suitable, travelled out to India himself, accompanied by his hometown guide Ulrich Kaufmann. The three met up at the hill station of Nainital towards the end of June and together they made their way up into the mountains of the Garhwal Himalaya.

Planning to first attempt Nanda Devi itself, the men started out of the tiny hamlet of Rini, following the course of a dramatic river-cut gorge, the Rishi Ganga. They had gone just four miles when they found their path blocked by a deep ravine, formed where a glacier had once flowed from a nearby peak. 'Worn to impassable smoothness', it was 'a mighty moat of Nature's own digging,' wrote Graham, 'to guard her virgin fortresses'. Then, 'we gave it up, and returned rather disconsolately to Rini.'

That night they held a 'council of war'. Thinking Nanda Devi 'rather a tough nut', they turned their attention to Dunagiri, a 23,186-foot peak rising over the Rishi Ganga to the north. Facing Trisul to the south, Dunagiri was not the tallest mountain in the range, but it was the most accessible. And, if they were to reach its summit, it would be the highest ascent on record.

Taking seven porters carrying provisions for ten days, the Europeans set out the next morning along the north branch of the Dhauli river. Marching through the day, they drank from a spring bubbling with naturally carbonated water, passed wild fruit trees – apricot, peach and plum – and visited a tiny village called Tolam 'supporting more bees to the square foot than any place I ever saw. The inhabitants,' wrote Graham, 'live chiefly on their honey.' Beyond Tolam there was little trace of a path, but following the bank of the river they moved upwards towards Dunagiri, camping that night 'on a beautiful little ledge some seven feet wide, a cliff above and a cliff below'.

The next day started badly; their path blocked by 'an immense rocky rib… falling sheer into the water'. Determined to find a way through, they climbed for several hours up the steep valley wall, then scrambled down the other side, 'to find to our disgust that we had only gained about a quarter mile in actual distance, though we had a most fatiguing and prolonged day'. Graham was starting to realise that 'these difficulties in the valleys, before you can get near the peaks, are among the most formidable obstacles to Himalayan exploration'.

The Europeans' fortunes were about to change. That evening, settling in at their campsite, they heard a shout and saw a man approaching. They had been tracked by a *shikari*, a local hunter, named Bhop Chand. He had heard about the expedition in Tolam and had followed their trail, hoping they would employ him as their guide. Gathering that Chand could lead them onto the slopes of Dunagiri, Graham agreed terms.

Chand was soon earning his money. First thing the next day he led them up a narrow gully, missed completely by the Europeans, 'in many places a most broken slope of rock and grass, with a precipice above and another below; places where we had to hang on all we knew'. This led to the ridge above, where they could see their way clear onto Dunagiri itself. 'Right in front of us rose the western face of the peak like a wall,' wrote Graham. He informed Chand and the porters that this was as high as he would ask them to go. 'Their faces brightened when we told them that they might go down,' wrote Graham, 'only to fall again when we added that they must come up again to meet us the next day.'

That night, bivouacking in 'a beautiful hole' just above the snowline, Graham took in his surroundings and steadied his thoughts. 'We were at last where I had so ardently desired to be, at the foot of the great giants against whom I had so long desired to measure myself.' Finding something 'in the intense silence of this height… which almost appalled, and which forbade speech', Graham and his companions dispensed with conversation. Instead, they contented themselves with a pipe, a nip of whisky and 'the sleep of the just'.

The next day dawned clear but a cold wind blew, slowing the men as they battled to light a fire and boil some water. They finally got going at 5 a.m., with fourteen hours of daylight to climb – and descend – almost five thousand feet. That was a leisurely day out in the mountains of Europe, but on Dunagiri they were already breathing less than half the oxygen available at sea level and the air was only going to get thinner.

For three hours they attacked a steep spur leading directly towards the summit. Gradually this narrowed into an awkward arête, watched over by an arresting snow-capped *gendarme*, a pinnacle of rock rising out of the ridge ahead. The conditions began to tell. 'The sun had come out, and now beat upon us with a furnace heat,' wrote Graham. 'The reflection from the snow was very painful; we literally panted for breath, and I thought I was going to faint.'

It proved too much for Kaufmann. He had been out of sorts all morning but had kept quiet, hoping to climb it off. Instead, his condition had deteriorated and he was unable to go on. Graham and Boss had no desire to abandon him but nor were they ready to give up on Dunagiri. Leaving Kaufmann in the shade with the last of the whisky, they carried on towards the summit, no more than two thousand feet above.

Step followed step followed step, as Graham and Boss cut footholds in the snow-slope, climbing into a thick canopy of cloud. Rising at fifty degrees now, the ice-wall was steep, but with Boss working 'at great pace' they were gaining height fast. For three hours they climbed, nothing to see but the ice-wall in front of them, then the mist parted and the sun poured through. There was the black rock of the mountaintop. Turning away they saw another peak, one they recognised from their charts. With its summit two hundred feet beneath them, there could be no more than five hundred feet of Dunagiri left to climb. 'In an hour,' cried Boss, 'we shall be there!'

It was not to be. As quickly as it had cleared, the mist rolled back in, wrapping them in darkness 'like a cold shroud'. 'It began to snow and hail very fast,' wrote Graham, 'whilst a wind rose that chilled us to the marrow.' They stopped to confer, but there was little to discuss. Moments earlier Boss had felt success within their grasp; now, with visibility down to nothing, they could have the summit if they wanted, but only for a grave.

Graham and Boss started to climb downwards. It was gone two in the afternoon, leaving three hours of daylight in which to find their way back to their bivouac, collecting Kaufmann along the way. 'How we came down those ice slopes I shall never know,' wrote Graham. 'It was a place where no single man could have held up another, and I was moving mechanically, like a man in a dream, almost crying with vexation and disappointment.'

Kaufmann sat waiting where they had left him. He tied onto their rope and the three descended together, taking tentative steps in worsening conditions. Blinded by hail and snow, they came to a small couloir, a steep chute of ice. Halfway across, Graham, mind wracked by failure, body by fatigue, lost his footing. With the Dunagiri glacier a thousand feet below, he began to fall.

Boss felt the rope tighten. It was no accident that Graham had been put in the lead; this gave Boss, with all his experience, a chance to secure his position and catch the Englishman's fall. His best hope was to dig his feet in and plant his ice-axe as quickly as possible, but he was tired, his reactions were slow, and his foothold gave way. Even as Boss fell, he already knew that it would be too much for Kaufmann. Sure enough, the guide was pulled from his stance. All were now falling together, nothing between them and a bone-splitting, breakneck plunge to the glacier below.

Nothing, besides a small protrusion of rock, sticking out of the snow. It caught Graham in the ribs and stopped him dead. Boss landed hard on top of him, and the two lay there, hardly able to believe their luck. It had the feel of a divine intervention on 'the Divine Mountain', as Dunagiri interceded to spare their lives. Such intercessions can seem uncanny, until you remember that only those who live ever tell the tale.

Their ordeal was not over. Graham had dropped his axe and they were forced to wait as Kaufmann recovered it. By now they had lost their bearings, 'suddenly on the brink of a terrific void'. They retraced their steps until, by chance, they stumbled on a woollen jumper discarded that morning. 'Finally, after many slips and mistakes, we reached our hole,' wrote Graham, 'stumbling over the boulders in the dark, very tired and wet, and, if the truth must be told, in a very bad temper.'

The men had been on the go for fourteen hours: time enough for snow to drift into every crease of their bivouac and belongings. Everything was soaked through and Graham had just a few matches, carefully preserved in a waterproof box. 'The wind was very high, and the sleet lashed us like a whip, go where we would, and one by one the matches failed to strike or the wood to catch. Finally we came to the last match. I could not help thinking what a picture we should have made then, cowering in a little hole, and dependent on one tiny piece of wood for food, comfort, and perhaps life itself. It burnt, and the kerosene caught fire.'

Their joy was short-lived. The wind rallied, and surged, and snuffed out the tiny argument of flame. Gone was their last chance of anything for dinner but whisky and raw flour.

No surprise, perhaps, that tempers flared. Graham and Boss were astonished, however, when Kaufmann took such exception to one remark that he announced he would find somewhere else to sleep. The men had fought their way back to this small sanctuary on the mountain, a hole in which to huddle until the sun rose. Now Kaufmann meant to seek shelter elsewhere. His companions watched him gather up his few possessions and disappear into the darkness of the mountain night.

Graham and Boss were left alone. The Englishman, exhausted, was desperate to sleep, but Boss kept shaking him awake, insisting that they fight slumber off until dawn. 'Although I was very angry at the time, I was afterwards very thankful,' wrote Graham, 'as I really believe that sleep in that weather at that height would have been "the sleep that knows no waking".'

Dawn broke to the east, ushering away the longest night of William Graham's young life. The skies were clear and he felt a surge of confidence that they would now escape the mountain. Reunited with Kaufmann, who had seen out the night huddled around his own hot temper, the men picked their way down to the glacier, met there by Bhop Chand and the porters. 'We promptly transferred our loads and made on for the lower camp,' wrote Graham. 'Once there, what a feed we did make! Was ever cold meat so tender and juicy? Were chupatties ever so hot and muffiny?' Days earlier, Graham had complained about the porters making a fortnight's rations last five days. Now it was the Europeans' turn to put away, at one sitting, a week's worth of food.

They had been defeated on Dunagiri, but there was much to encourage them. 'Boss and I ascended certainly to 22,700 feet,' wrote Graham, who knew now how it felt to climb at heights he and his companions had only previously imagined. For more than a century, scientists had been investigating the effects of altitude, using their bodies as instruments.

Now Graham had shown – in keeping with his overtly unscientific expedition – that if the body was an instrument, it was a singularly unreliable one. 'I had never believed in the impossibility of breathing at these great heights, else I should not have been foolish enough ever to attempt them, but when one reads so many accounts of bleeding at the nose, panting for breath, etc. one is obliged to pay some credence to them. All such symptoms were conspicuous only by their absence.'

For alpinists everywhere Graham's message was clear – that 'the air, or the want of it, will prove no obstacle to the ascent of the very highest peaks in the world'. Climbers, though, deal in summits. Everything Graham had accomplished on Dunagiri was enclosed in the parentheses of failure. His visit to the Garhwal region of the Himalaya had been 'a pleasant, if not very successful, trip', but he was not finished there. He was going back to the peaks of the Sikkim, for 'what we intended to be our *pièce de résistance*'.

'I am perfectly aware that it was a most hazardous proceeding,'
wrote Graham, 'and in cold blood, I should not try it again.'

Illustration from 'Up in the Himalayas', an article by W. W. Graham appearing
in the monthly periodical *Good Words* (1885). Illustrator unknown.

CHAPTER 8

The Climber's Flower

They stood at the foot of the great east face of Kabru, three specks of ambition gazing up into the mist and snow. This would be the closing chapter of Graham's year in the Himalaya. The last hurrah. The grand finale.

To Graham it was just 'Kabru'. Today we know it as Kabru North and Kabru South, two peaks each a little over 24,000 feet in height. Prominent against the crowded skyline of the Sikkim, Kabru was one of the mountains Graham had seen from Darjeeling all those months ago, rushing out of their hotel to feel the breath stolen from him.

He had taken a good look at it on that first foray into the mountains, before the winter conditions had driven him back to Darjeeling. Things were different now, as he returned with Boss and Kaufmann, bringing the benefit of all they had learned since. It had been an eventful six months, and now once again the seasons were about to change. This would be Graham's last chance – on this expedition at least – to reach the summit of a first-class Himalayan peak.

With eight thousand feet of mountain above, they knew fresh snow would make for slow going in the morning. The men crawled into their tents, to get what sleep they could.

*

The final instalment of Graham's 1883 expedition had begun in late August, starting out of Darjeeling under lingering monsoon rains. They marched north through lower-lying valleys, where leeches carpeted the hill-tracks, oozing into action at the first hint of a square meal. Besides the mosquitoes and bamboo ticks, the true insecta non grata was a tiny dipterous fly called a peepsa. Its bites proved a source of intense and lasting irritation; the only deterrent they had found was to douse themselves in kerosene.

Making their way north, they left the heady humidity of the jungle for more temperate terrain. The bamboos and creepers were replaced with walnuts and beeches, then fir trees and pines, thronging with lush rhododendrons, explosions of colour bursting out of the undergrowth. The rain was relentless and, by the time they emerged onto broad, rolling plateaux, they were caught in a violent snowstorm. The entire expedition took shelter in the only building available – a small stone hut, home to a young yak-herd and his goitrous grandmother.

At the first sign of better weather, Graham set his mind on the summit of a nearby peak named Jubonu. It was small by Himalayan standards but proved the most technical ascent of the whole expedition. He, Boss and Kaufmann climbed couloirs and chimneys, braved bergschrunds – gaping cracks between glacier and mountainside – and steep fields of soft, crystalline snow. These were obstacles they knew from the Alps, but on a scale it would have been impossible to imagine from the low-ceilinged *salle à manger* of the Monte Rosa Hotel.

The climb served its purpose, a chance to warm their muscles and sharpen their nerves, and they found the snow in good condition, auguring well for what was to come. Nor was this the last good omen. As they approached the east face of Kabru on 6 October the men were delighted to see edelweiss growing on the banks of the glacier. 'Edelweiss', wrote Graham, 'the climber's flower. Success was prophesied accordingly.'

Graham planned to establish a camp at around nineteen thousand feet, then to go for the summit in a single day. It was what they had tried – and failed – on Dunagiri, but the weather had been against them and Kaufmann had not been well. Now they woke to clear skies over Kabru and were soon at the foot of a towering buttress beneath the mountain's southeast ridge. Seeing two routes they could follow, Boss favoured the south side, up an 'easy couloir' towards the ridge above. Graham's first instinct was to attempt the more difficult north side, bringing them to the same ridge at a more advanced position. Kaufmann had the casting vote but, with the old guide staying quiet, Graham gave way to Boss. The south side it was.

The couloir went easily, just as Boss had said. By noon they were on top of the buttress, where they expected to join Kabru's southeast ridge. Here their luck ran out. They were standing on the lip of a precipitous drop, 'cut off from the true peak by a chasm in the arête'.

Thinking there must be a way forward, Kaufmann edged down to investigate. Graham and Boss watched as the guide disappeared out of view. They saw nothing for a moment, then a burst of loose rocks, looking on in horror as the salvo of stones cascaded down onto the glacier below. They had seen nothing of their friend, had heard nothing. Granted Kaufmann was the strong, silent type, but surely even he would have offered some kind of utterance, falling to his death.

The last of the rockfall left a stony silence behind. Boss finally spoke, calling for his friend and guide. For a moment nothing, then came something by reply. It was muffled, indistinguishable, but yes, it was Kaufmann. The guide's head bobbed into view. Climbing back up to join them, he explained that a rock had given way beneath him, but he had seized the nearest piece of mountainside and managed to hang on.

There was, Kaufmann confirmed, no way forward.

With no alternative but retreat, the men climbed back down, rejoining their guides and porters near the foot of the buttress. They found a ledge wide enough for a tent and settled in for the night, at a height of around 18,500 feet. This would be their high camp. To rush Kabru's summit they would need to gain more than five thousand feet in a single day.

So much for edelweiss.

*

It was a mild night, and a short one. By four in the morning, the climbers were roped together and moving up the north side of the buttress. 'The very first thing was the worst,' wrote Graham, 'a long couloir like a half-funnel, crowned with rocks, had to be passed. The snow was lying loose, just ready to slide, and the greatest possible care had to be taken to avoid an avalanche.' This brought them to the foot of a steep ice-wall. Kaufmann, according to Graham, was 'one of the fastest step-cutters living', but the grizzled guide needed two long hours to see them up the wall, edging higher until they stood at last on Kabru's southeast ridge.

After the hard grind of the early morning, now was a chance to find a climber's rhythm, as they raced up '1,000 feet of most delightful rock-work, forming a perfect staircase'. By 10 a.m. they were just two thousand feet below the summit of Kabru. 'A short halt for food', recalled Graham, 'and then came the tug of war'. Ahead loomed a slope of pure ice, at an angle of forty-five to sixty degrees. 'Under ordinary circumstances', wrote Graham, 'step-cutting up this would have occupied many hours'. That was time they didn't have, but they were in luck: the ice was coated in a layer of snow, three or four inches deep, frozen hard in the searing cold. Kaufmann cut quick little notches in it, just enough to take each man's weight. 'I am perfectly aware that it was a most hazardous proceeding,' wrote Graham, 'and in cold blood, I should not try it again.'

Up they went. Whatever occupied the thoughts of the men, minds addled by altitude, hamstrung by cold, all that mattered was to climb. There were only feet gained and minutes lost, measured in tiny notches chiselled into the mountainside. It was gone midday by the time the gradient began to ease, as they approached the top of the ice-slope. Kaufmann, at almost forty years of age, had led the whole way.

One test remained. The true summit of Kabru stood three hundred feet above, at the top of a slanting arête. It was 'the steepest ice I have ever seen', wrote Graham. 'From my left hand I could have dropped a pebble down the most terrific slopes to the glacier ten thousand feet below; from my right down a steep slope for a hundred feet, and then over what we had seen from below to be a rock cliff of many thousand feet.' The slightest breeze would have put an end to it, but the day was perfectly still, perfectly clear. Slowly, very slowly, they climbed.

The ice was rock solid. It took an age to cut each step, with time against them, where one false move promised to send them tumbling into the void. Just those few hundred feet took another hour and a half.

A little before 2 p.m. the climbers cut their last step. Now, for the first time, they could see the summit ahead. They took the remaining few paces and found what shelter they could. Kabru, all 24,015 feet of it, stood beneath them.

Well, almost all of it.

'The absolute summit', wrote Graham, 'was little more than a pillar of ice'. It rose a further thirty to forty feet, but he understood that they would not be able to climb it. 'Independently of the extreme difficulty and danger of attempting it', he explained, 'we had no time.'

It must have been a torturous moment. They had far surpassed any reasonable expectation of what they might achieve; the first European alpinists to tackle a mountain of this size. A summit, though, is a summit. Something absolute, something indivisible, the simple binary of a mountain climbed. And the summit of Kabru – the *true* summit – was just out of reach.

Graham surveyed the lecture theatre to see an audience of men twice, three times his age. Naturalists and navigators, geographers and generals, the great and the good of the Royal Geographical Society, they had gathered for a paper by one of the youngest speakers ever to address the RGS.

He had accepted their invitation, Graham began, 'with considerable apprehension, and that on many grounds. First on the score of my youth and total inexperience in addressing such an audience; again, because to my shame perhaps, I went to India more for sport and adventures than for the advancement of scientific knowledge; and last – by no means least – I am painfully conscious that there are many now present who know much more about the subject than I can hope to tell them.'

It was an unassuming opening from the young barrister. He had read his audience well, many of whom would have wondered what they could possibly hope to learn from a mere 'sportsman'. The Hungarian mountaineer Maurice de Déchy had summed up the prevailing attitude towards climbing in the Himalaya in the *Alpine Journal* in 1880. Déchy had gone there in 1879, though he contracted malaria a few days out of Darjeeling and never made it to the mountains. 'Although in the Alps I admit mountaineering as a sufficient object in itself', wrote Déchy, 'yet I hold that the climber who turns his steps towards distant lands, still little visited and difficult of access, and offering a field for geographical discovery, should also give his attention to the advancement of scientific knowledge'.

Déchy's view chimed with the mood at the RGS, where India was considered off-limits to the amateur. Yes, sportsmen had visited the Himalaya, but they were soldiers on hunting expeditions, drawn into the mountains in search of more exotic prey. Take Clement Smith of the 1st Bengal Cavalry, recounting his own 'sporting tour' in 1867. By the end of the first page Smith had fallen out of a tree while hunting a tiger, then been thrown from a mail cart, breaking his arm. This was sport as the members of the RGS liked to imagine it – ambulant anecdotes, gamely recollected.

Graham's talk was something different. He described climbing mountains in a language some of his audience barely understood. He spoke of couloirs and crevasses, bergschrunds and bridges, as if they were something to be savoured and enjoyed. He described going higher than anybody had ever been before, higher than the soldiers and surveyors who had been driven back time and again by the freezing cold and the rarity of the air. Graham had surpassed them all and, in his own words, with 'no more difficulty in breathing... than if [we] had been 10,000 feet below'.

In the process, Graham had put the maps of the Survey of India under newfound scrutiny. 'I am sorry to have to criticise any work of members of a body from whom I received so much valuable aid and kindness,' said the Englishman, 'but what can I say when we found one whole range omitted, glaciers portrayed where trees of four feet thickness are growing, and the hill shading generally entirely imaginary.' The maps, rounded Graham, were 'highly inaccurate'.

At the end of the talk the floor was given over to the members. One veteran of India, Sir Richard Temple, thanked Graham for educating them on the value of 'icemanship' and for demonstrating 'that the highest peaks could be ascended by men of strong heart... with much less physical danger than had hitherto been supposed'. Another, Sir Joseph Hooker, spoke of the hardships he had encountered in the Himalaya, suggesting that 'there must be some superiority in Mr Graham's organisation... upon which I congratulate him'. There was talk of Survey men being accompanied by trained mountaineers, since 'they would accomplish a great deal under the training of men like Graham, Boss and Kaufmann'.

It was too much for General James T. Walker. Only a few months into his retirement, Walker had given the best part of his life to the Survey of India. Appointed superintendent of the Great Trigonometrical Survey in 1860, he had cultivated the talents of men like Haversham Godwin-Austen and William Henry Johnson, gifted surveyors who had unlocked so many secrets of the Karakoram and Kunlun mountain ranges. In 1878, after eighteen years of service, Walker had been appointed surveyor-general of India, the position from which he had only recently retired.

Listening that evening, it might have felt as though the work of his long career was unravelling around him. Graham had trampled all over it, in front of an audience of peers and contemporaries whose respect Walker had laboured all those years to command. *Highly inaccurate. Entirely imaginary.* And from a young man who had gone to the Himalaya, by his own admission, *for sport and adventures.* For more than a century the Survey had been the ultimate authority on India, a yardstick of imperial rule. With Graham's critique, Walker saw that grip begin to loosen.

Taking the floor, Walker chose his words carefully. If the work of the Survey resulted in 'rough generalisation', he began, it was not for want of 'icemanship', or on account of its officers 'shrinking at any physical difficulty', but because they 'looked for returns... proportional to the cost'. 'If a party of Survey officers with a detachment of mountaineers from Switzerland travelled in the mountains for eight or nine months', he went on, warming to his theme, 'they might bring back tales of hardy exploits which would be most interesting to the Alpine Club and to the Geographical Society, but if they did nothing more, and brought back no topography and only a few barometric measurements of differential heights, he was afraid that the Government of India would not be altogether satisfied with the result'. The work of the Survey was serious business, argued Walker, not to be confused with the playful distractions of sporting mountaineers.

That might have been an end to it. Walker had mounted a stout defence, in the face of a young sportsman who had only really argued that, if it was not possible to map an area accurately, it might be better not to map it at all. Except, looking back over more than a century of intervening history, there was a greater significance to Graham's presence at the RGS. He was an outrider for the future, who had gone to the Himalaya not in the name of Empire or Company, Survey or Government, but in the service of an idea: that men and women should climb mountains for pleasure and enjoyment. The threat he posed to Walker and his kind – those who had long exercised a monopoly on the icebound extremities of the British Empire – was an existential one.

So yes, that might have been an end to it. But it was not.

Six weeks later an article appeared in *The Pioneer Mail*, an Anglo-Indian daily newspaper. Its author had chosen to remain anonymous, describing himself as 'for nearly 30 years a wanderer in the Himalayas'. He became known as the 'Wanderer' (which, we might note, is another word for 'Walker').

Graham's account of his ascent of Kabru had 'called forth various expressions of incredulity at Darjeeling', wrote the Wanderer, 'especially on the part of those who have been engaged in the survey of Sikkim for the last four or five years'. The south side of Kabru 'presents a series of rugged ridges of ragged rock, irregularly radiating from the craggy crest of the mountain, not one of which is practicable. No amount of skill or experience can avert the almost certain consequences of an attempt to clamber over sharp ledges of rock, and of the yielding of the snow-coating that covers over a concealed crevasse.'

Drawing on the dubious testimony of unnamed local guides, the Wanderer argued one moment that Graham's party had misidentified the mountain they were climbing, the next that their barometers had been at fault. For Graham to have been certain of anything at all would have involved, the Wanderer maintained, 'more trouble than unscientific travellers are willing to bestow'.

It did not need a fine legal mind to pull apart the Wanderer's arguments, but it got one. Not Graham himself, but Douglas Freshfield: lawyer, mountaineer and for eight years the editor of the *Alpine Journal*. Freshfield took to its pages to mount his defence, understanding that there was more at stake than the good name of one young mountaineer. Graham had shown that the Himalaya was the next great frontier for Europe's alpinists; a slight to his reputation was a slur on them all.

All the Wanderer had shown, wrote Freshfield, was that 'there are in India "mountaineers" of thirty years standing who know less of mountaineering than Europeans did fifty years ago. Had we not long ago learnt how to "avoid the consequences" of concealed crevasses the whole Alpine Club would by this time be descending the Alps at the rate of a few inches a day, and in the condition of frozen meat!'

'It is insufferable', Freshfield went on, 'that private travellers should not be able to mountaineer in the Himalaya without being hailed on their arrival as fools and on their departure as knaves'. Here was a climbing party consisting of 'a young Oxonian, an officer in the Swiss army, and a guide of high repute'. Its leader had 'examined the mountain on every side and ascended many points in the vicinity'. It was one thing, argued Freshfield, for members of the RGS to contrast Graham's experiences of high altitude with their own, or to suppose his barometric measurements might have been awry. It was another altogether to suggest that he and his companions had not climbed Kabru at all, mistaking it for another, smaller mountain. 'Mistakes in detail the climbers may have fallen into.

To accuracy in measurements they have made no pretensions. But that they should have honestly mistaken their mountain seems to me altogether beyond the bounds of reasonable hypothesis.'

Freshfield had done his work, turning the Wanderer's arguments against him. Controversy, though, is tenacious – its roots snake back into an un-editable past. However false the Wanderer's assertions, however muddled his reasoning, the article in the *Pioneer* found its mark. A cloud of uncertainty fell over all Graham had achieved in the Himalaya. His ascent of Kabru is still disputed to this day.

Amid the celebrations, Bruce was thinking bigger.

'Climbing Party of Goorkhas' from *Twenty Years in the Himalaya* by
Bruce, Major The Hon. C. G. (1910). Photographer unknown.

CHAPTER 9

Friction

In 1890, as was their annual tradition, the troops of the North West Frontier Province gathered for a regimental games. Events included the hundred-yard dash, wrestling and the shot put, all routinely dominated by the powerful Punjab troops. The Gurkhas, of a slighter build, had come to be regarded as the whipping boys – so much so they had, in the opinion of Lieutenant Charles Bruce, developed something of an inferiority complex.

Bruce decided this year would be different. He had recently taken a post with the 5th Gurkha Rifles at Abbottabad, and spied a chance to earn his men some bragging rights. Bruce was an avid fell runner and had kept it up through military college. He arrived at Abbottabad an accomplished athlete, yet when out drilling his men, he found 'any ordinary Gurkha could easily leave me behind on the hill'. One fellow officer described the sight of the Gurkhas running down almost vertical hillside as like 'raindrops falling down a window-pane'.

Bruce saw to it that a new event was added to the athletics programme for that year – a hill race, or *khud*. Then, with the blessing of his commanding officer, he got his men into training. Bruce knew the Gurkhas' potential, but even he was surprised when the race was run and all but one of the first thirty finishers were from his regiment.

Amid the celebrations, Bruce was thinking bigger. He saw hill running as a way to raise the morale of his men *and* to improve them as soldiers.

His first regiment, the Oxford and Buckinghamshire Light Infantry, had been ahead of the times with the emphasis it placed on 'handling of country as an art'. With the right training Bruce believed his men would make better scouts, spotting for their battalions from nature's vantage points and outmanoeuvring the enemy on the most adverse terrain.

In the summer of 1890 Bruce travelled to the nearby Kaghan valley with 'one servant and one Gurkha, a length of cotton rope about 40 ft. and one axe which had been sent out to me from England as a present and which I did not know how to use properly'. There, leading a bold attempt on the valley's main peak, Bruce slipped and lost his footing, dragging the roped-up Gurkha down a steep snow-slope, only narrowly avoiding a deep crevasse.

Bruce was smitten. His 'training exercises' in the Kaghan became a regular fixture, but it was only a matter of time before he engineered an opportunity to explore the Greater Himalaya. His moment came in 1891, over the umpteenth course of 'an excellent lunch'. Bruce got wind of an expedition planned by the English mountain-explorer Martin Conway. Flushed with liquid daring, he applied there and then for permission to join.

Conway arrived in Abbottabad in late February 1892 at the head of what was 'very much more in reality an exploring expedition,' noted Bruce, 'than a mountaineering one'. Conway was a familiar face at the Royal Geographical Society and knew how divisive William Graham's 'sporting' expedition had been. General Strachey had summed up the mood when he advised anyone going to the Himalaya 'to get icemanship if possible, and to have a strong heart, but above all things to take with them the lamp of science, which would intensify all their enjoyments, and enable them to understand what they saw'.

Conway had taken heed. He had secured generous grants from the RGS, the Royal Society and the British Association, all on the condition he put survey work and scientific investigation at the centre of his plans. Twenty years a climber, Conway was also a proficient surveyor, who 'saw the Alpine Club as a kind of mountaineering wing of the Royal Geographical Society'. Taking his inspiration from Edward Whymper, he devised an expedition doing important work, he hoped, en route to a new world altitude record.

Soldiers, surveyors, scientists and sportsmen had already gone to the Himalaya; Conway's would be the first expedition to include all four. Oscar Eckenstein, like Conway, was more than just a mountaineer. Employed as a railway engineer, he was an accomplished chemist and mathematician with a reputation as a problem-solver. He was the one to recommend the Swiss guide Matthias Zurbriggen, a professional mountaineer with a portfolio of other talents. 'He could turn his hand to anything,' wrote Bruce, 'mending an ice axe, carpentering or cobbling, and besides was a blacksmith by trade.' They were joined by Jack Roudebush, a young familiar of Conway's who liked nothing more than to hunt game, and his friend, the artist A. D. McCormick. There was a long tradition of Himalayan explorers bringing their artistic talents to the mountains; Conway would be the first to have his own artist-in-residence.

Bruce was to act as transport officer, but only when the expedition reached Abbottabad would he understand what he had signed up for. Conway had assembled 'the first carefully prepared expedition that went to India,' wrote Bruce, 'both in the matter of carefully selected stores and scientific arrangements of all kinds'. It was, if anything, 'considerably over-stored and over-equipped', he went on, though this was at least 'a fault on the right side'.

Bruce brought four Gurkha deputies, hand-picked from his regiment: Parbir Thapa, Harkabir Thapa, Amar Sing Thapa and Karbir Burathoki. These men were valuable go-betweens where the Balti porters were concerned, able to make themselves understood in both English and Hindustani, but they were along as more than just intermediaries. The Gurkhas would climb with the Europeans, becoming the first indigenous Asians to join a European-led expedition in the capacity of trained mountaineers. Parbir had accompanied Bruce on his recent trip to Europe, allowing the two to climb together in the Alps. He was 'an excellent companion,' wrote Bruce, 'a fine hill runner and a good man in camp, afflicted by a prodigious sense of the fun and the ludicrous'.

It remained to be seen whether Conway would achieve the lofty objectives he had claimed for what was already, by its very make-up, a pioneering expedition. His backers demanded results – intrepid exploration to fill in the blanks on British maps – and, where the climbing portion was concerned, Conway had talked up the possibility of attempting K2. But, whatever the outcome, the Englishman had already accomplished more than he knew. He had assembled an expedition destined to shape the future of Himalayan mountaineering.

The expedition left Abbottabad in mid-March 1892, riding north in small horse-drawn carts, then at Wular Lake they took to the water, first to Srinagar then Bandipora, where they recruited one hundred local porters. With so many men to manage, Bruce proved indispensable. He had long held 'that all soldiers one had to deal with in the British Army are exactly the same as oneself, with the exception that they have not had equal advantages'. He extended the same equanimity to the porters, arguing 'that to get the best work out of men who cannot be expected to go, as a body, anything but most unwillingly, requires tact, sympathy, and understanding kindness towards them'.

Not everybody took the same view. Tasked with leading a detachment of porters, Eckenstein found 'the amount of profanity required… was really tremendous; I calculated afterwards that it must have taken something like ten thousand curses to get them over that pass, not to speak of a considerable amount of personal violence'. Eckenstein, though, was not all bad news for the Baltis. Known as 'Dr Sahib', he converted his tent into an open surgery, dispensing medicine for a wide variety of complaints. 'Quinine, which they all know, is very much prized by them. There is also a strong run on cocaine.' Eckenstein issued this to be rubbed on the gums in cases of tooth decay, a common affliction among the men. Treatment of symptom rather than cause perhaps, but quite the pick-me-up for a tired, hungry porter.

Eckenstein, the son of a Jewish socialist who had fled Germany following the failed revolution of 1848, had inherited his father's rebellious instincts. Argumentative and fiercely individualistic, he was, according to Walt Unsworth, 'in perpetual revolt against the well-ordered Victorian society of his day, though he lacked the moral fibre to do anything about it'. He had a correspondingly distrustful demeanour, eyes less inquisitive than inquisitional, thunder forever rolling across a hardened brow.

Eckenstein's scepticism could be an asset when applied to his great passion – alpinism. He interrogated every aspect of the sport, searching for new problems to solve, and new methods for solving them. Like many British climbers, he did not confine himself to the Alps, taking the same intrepid instincts out onto the bare rock peaks and crags of Wales, Scotland and the Lake District. There, with little ice or snow to cut steps in, climbers trusted their weight to handholds – what was known as 'grip climbing' – aided by whatever the rock would afford their feet. In time, out of this emerged 'balance climbing', 'a system of continuous compensation,' wrote Geoffrey Winthrop Young in *Mountain Craft*, 'partly drawn from the rhythmic balance of the moving body, partly from a corrective choice of succeeding holds.' Eckenstein was the first great advocate of balance climbing. It was the inception of rock climbing as we know it today.

Eckenstein was interested in more than just the mechanics of the human body. He experimented with new and different knots, and developed light, shorter-handled ice-axes designed to be held in one hand. But his most famous innovation was a modification to the design of climbing-irons, better known as crampons. At the time few alpinists made use of the bladed-boot attachments, preferring regular boots with nails driven through the soles. Today, no serious mountaineer would attempt steep ice or snow without crampons derived from Eckenstein's ground-breaking ten-pointed design.

Out on the mountains of the Alps, Eckenstein put his inventions to work. Fluent in German, he climbed with some of the biggest names in alpinism, completing a string of first ascents and gaining a reputation as a gifted mountaineer. On merit alone, he would have been a shoo-in for the Alpine Club, but Eckenstein would never join. Jewish and of German descent, he was seen as an outsider and an iconoclast by the Club's increasingly conservative membership, at a time when anti-Semitism was rife among Britain's upper-middle class.

For Conway, looking for an expert climber to join his expedition, Eckenstein presented a challenge. On the one hand, he was a difficult character, opinionated and potentially divisive in any setting. On the other, he was a scientist, joining an expedition defined by its scientific aims. He was an innovator, hoping to climb mountains the technical difficulties of which were not yet understood. And he was a pioneer, alive to the intractable pull of the Karakoram's unclimbed peaks. The question was whether a man of such singular powers was willing to be led – and, more specifically, whether Conway was the man to lead him.

At the beginning of June, two months after leaving Srinagar, the expedition passed through the Hunza then the Nagar valleys, deep in the Karakoram. For Bruce, this was a chance to inspect the work of British regiments who had 'pacified' the region in a series of operations he had been unhappy to miss out on. Conway, meanwhile, drank up the fact that the local people believed themselves the descendants of Alexander the Great. Conway climbed nothing if not society, and doubtless relished the idea of keeping such distinguished company.

Eckenstein cut a more dejected figure. He had been struggling to adapt to the change of diet and when his 'inner works went wrong' – as seemed to happen often – his first instinct was to look around for someone to blame. He complained about the food, poured scorn on their equipment, and picked holes in every aspect of the expedition's leadership. 'I am pretty fly-hardened,' he wrote. 'Conway, however, I regret to say, is different; Flies settling on him irritate him fearfully, and so he suffers.' Eckenstein, meanwhile, was becoming a cloud of flies of his own, a source of growing irritation to those who came within his sphere.

The deeper they went into the mountains, the worse it became. Eckenstein's grievances coalesced into one overarching complaint – that, allowing for unseasonable weather, 'we could have ascended two or three decent peaks in the last fortnight or so, instead of doing practically nothing whatsoever'. He began to question Conway's desire to test himself as a mountaineer; the further they advanced into the Karakoram, noted Eckenstein, the less inclined Conway seemed to be to climb.

At Hispar, Conway contrived to rid himself of Eckenstein, for the time being at least. They were nearing the foot of the Hispar glacier which, Conway believed, joined the Biafo to form a single glacial system more than seventy miles long. He hoped to make a pioneering traverse of the two glaciers, but Eckenstein would not be going with him. Instead, the expedition would divide. Bruce and Eckenstein would take a different route to their rendezvous at the village of Askole. They would attempt to become the first Europeans to cross a 17,000-foot pass south of the Hispar glacier – the Nushik La.

It had taken a series of hard marches, 'amid the very finest, roughest, and in parts ugliest scenery imaginable', just to be at its foot. They had crossed mountainsides scored by mudslides, where melting snow gathered up soil and tore down into the dried-up valleys below. There had been whole days marching on nothing but moraine, the rock debris carpeting the surface of the glaciers and heaped along their sides.

Coming within sight of the pass, their eyes went on ahead, up the soaring ramp of 45-degree ice-slopes, riven with crevasses and crowded with toppling seracs. Among the porters they had recruited at Hispar was an old man named Shersé. He claimed to have crossed the Nushik La many years earlier and insisted that pack animals had been taken across it. Seeing the pass for himself, Bruce had his doubts.

They sheltered for the night in some small stone huts, the ceilings only three feet clear of the ground. 'Eckenstein and myself occupied a stone box with holes in it,' wrote Bruce, 'of the tightest description'. They had been short of food from the outset and woke the next morning to find their reserves dangerously low. 'There was nothing for it but to cross or starve,' wrote Bruce, 'so off we set.'

The climbing party consisted of Bruce, Eckenstein, Parbir and Amar Sing, accompanied by Shersé and six other Hispar men. With them too was a Balti *wasir* named Nazar Ali, a wise man who 'was supposed to know everything', wrote Bruce, 'though in fact he knew nothing'. Ali brought an air of ceremony as they started to climb, opening his umbrella and, in the absence of three Balti 'boys' who normally attended him, carrying his own sword.

The day was clear and fine, and cold enough that the snow felt firm beneath their feet. Zigzagging upwards, they climbed the steepening snow-slopes, passing beneath a series of small hanging glaciers. The higher they went, the more crevasses they found until, coming to a daunting drop, they were forced onto a steep wall of rotten snow. Beyond the wall was a couloir leading to the crest of the pass, but the wall itself was a fearful obstacle. 'A slip on this, if unchecked, would certainly have been fatal,' wrote Eckenstein, 'as further down, right under this spot, was an ice precipice'. Bruce argued for turning back and finding another route. Eckenstein persuaded him to wait a moment, to see what the Hispar men would do.

Shersé stepped forward. Eckenstein watched, fascinated, as the old man tied a length of goat-hair rope around his waist 'in true orthodox style'. Then, borrowing Bruce's ice-axe, he worked his way up the slope, cutting tidy little steps as he went. Meanwhile, a second man had driven Eckenstein's axe into the snow, with the rope looped twice around it. It was 'a really capital arrangement', wrote Eckenstein, 'one that not every Swiss guide would care to imitate under similar conditions'.

Eckenstein was the first European to describe people indigenous to the Himalaya using such sophisticated mountaineering techniques; there was perhaps no European better qualified to evaluate what he had seen. Eckenstein would have no qualms about puncturing European pride, taking satisfaction from the fact that here, on an expedition led by a champion of the Alpine Club, he and Bruce were being schooled in mountaincraft by local villagers. For western observers, one of the true revelations of the Conway expedition would be that these men, living deep in the mountains of the Karakoram, included skilled climbers of their own.

With Shersé and the Hispar men across the ice-wall, the Gurkhas and the Europeans followed, gaining the couloir then moving diagonally upwards towards 'an unpleasantly unstable-looking cornice' – an overhanging crust of snow on the crest of the pass. Bruce was alarmed to see the Hispar men stop and say their prayers, then they started along the steep slope, looking for the place where the cornice was thinnest. Finding a suitable spot, Parbir and Amar Sing dug upwards into the roof of snow, hoping not to dislodge the whole thing in the process.

One by one they emerged onto the sunlit crest of the Nushik La. Even the caustic Eckenstein seemed genuinely moved by what awaited, a view that was 'truly splendid. Never before have I seen mountains that gave such an impression of vastness, while the clearness of the air was something marvellous'. For Bruce it was 'wonderful beyond description', as they became two of the first Europeans to see the Karakoram from such a heightened perspective. They had completed, he went on, 'our first piece of real independent exploration'.

The ascent of the Nushik La was behind them, but still they faced a long and difficult march to the next village, on tired legs and empty stomachs. 'We had a gorgeous lunch of 1½ inch of something or other on the summit,' wrote Bruce. 'Still we were ready for our allowance of about ¾ inch of what was left, mixed up in water for dinner.' Here Bruce and Eckenstein found a common cause: neither did well without food. 'Nothing makes me so wild as not having enough to eat,' wrote Bruce. 'Before we arrived at our journey's end we understood the hollowness of life.' 'The principle that nature abhors a vacuum had never before been so forcibly impressed upon my mind and stomach,' agreed Eckenstein. 'This was indeed a hollow world, and... I was a sample of it.'

Late the next day they reached Arandu, having eaten their last scraps that morning. Their first taste of civilisation escalated into 'a gargantuan feast', as Bruce unleashed 'an appetite that it was a pleasure and a pride to own'. Written inventory was kept, in the form of the bill, taking full account of all they had eaten – three whole sheep, the same number of chickens, fifty-three eggs, ten pounds of butter, two gallons of milk and seventy-two pounds of flour.

Now they could relax and enjoy the onward journey to Askole. Eckenstein had exhausted his supply of tobacco, so made do with the local equivalent, which 'had a rather curious but not at all unpleasant flavour, due to the admixture of a little Indian hemp; but this I did not mind at all. In fact, I very soon began to consider it an improvement.'

At Skardu they met the first Englishman they had come across in some time, one Captain Townshend, stationed there in charge of some local troops. He welcomed them with an impromptu *tamasha*, playing the banjo and singing some 'very comic songs'. 'Bruce and I are not of much use in the singing line,' wrote Eckenstein, 'but in the drinking department we were "all there," and strictly stuck to business'.

Reaching Askole in mid-July, they found no sign of Conway. Bruce disappeared into the mountains on a four-day hunting trip. Eckenstein, ensconced on his veranda, whiled away the hours smoking his new favourite blend. He was discovering the pleasures of the *hubblebub*, 'a native pipe... with the smoke passing through water', over what, as it turned out, were his last days as a member of the Conway expedition.

Flushed with success, Conway marched into Askole on 26 July. He and his party had completed a pioneering seventy-mile traverse of the Hispar and Biafo glaciers, expertly guided by Matthias Zurbriggen and, it is fair to assume, their own contingent of local men. Conway had confirmed the existence of the longest glacial system outside polar regions and, in doing so, assured himself a place in the pantheon of Himalayan exploration.

Conway's first act upon reaching Askole was to call 'a sort of a general meeting', where it was agreed that Eckenstein's time with the expedition was over. Conway had too keen a sense of propriety to go into the reasons for this, offering only that Eckenstein 'had never been well since reaching Gilgit'. Bruce concurred, noting that the engineer 'had many of the qualifications of a mountain explorer highly developed, but... one small weakness which is a terrible handicap in that part of the world, and that is a delicate interior'. In a letter to his father, Bruce was more forthright – Eckenstein was 'a useless burden to the party; expensive and incapable'.

Eckenstein's own verdict was that they 'had now been some two and a half months in the mountains without making a single ascent of importance'. Moreover, 'there had been a good deal of friction from time to time'. That, he maintained, was the reason he had decided to leave the expedition.

The next day Conway and the others moved on, leaving Eckenstein at Askole. He stayed a few days, then started back along the valley. Enjoying his newfound independence, he was free to climb as much as he liked and, discovering plenty of boulders at the villages along the way, he found the locals keen to get involved. Eager 'to see how these natives compare with Swiss guides', he began setting challenges. 'The best man I found would beat the best guide I have ever seen with the greatest ease,' he observed, 'over any kind of rocks.' Learning that there were better climbers further along the valley, Eckenstein organised a competition, with a grand prize of one rupee. 'Men had come from far and wide in order to show their climbing powers and gain unheard-of wealth; no doubt many had also come to gaze upon the strange, very strange white sahib who took an interest in such things.'

Which feels like an apposite moment to part ways with Oscar Eckenstein, huffing on a hubblebub in the shadow of a boulder, having, by his own account, 'a high old time'. He was finished with Martin Conway and his meandering expedition. To the Karakoram, however, Eckenstein would assuredly return.

With what energy he had left, and what time there
was available, Conway set up the plane table...

'On the Top of Pioneer Peak' from *Climbing and Exploration*
in the Karakoram-Himalayas by William Martin Conway
(1894). Illustration by A. D. McCormick (1892).

CHAPTER 10

Pioneer Pique

The boy, seven years old, felt lost in the throng of horses and donkeys outside the inn door. Their heavy breath clouded the crisp morning air and their hooves stamped hard on the cold grey cobblestones. His family gathered around, parents, aunts and uncles attended by servants and butlers, until a crowd had formed. Then they were away, following the mule road out of Llanberis, as the sun rose over the cloud-capped peaks of Snowdonia. 'I went off proudly on my two legs,' he later recalled, 'holding my father's hand.'

He didn't remember much about the climb, only the moment when, to his impossible delight, he saw that they were walking in a cloud. Real clouds, clouds that had always seemed to him part of 'the other world', distant and unobtainable. Yet now he moved through the middle of one, under his own steam.

They had not gone much further when one of the adults remarked that the boy looked tired. Before he knew it, he was being hoisted up onto a horse ridden by one of his aunts. He remembered it vividly, the ignominy of it, arriving at the top on horseback, arms tight around her waist. Finally, she let him down so that he could go and place a stone on the cairn at the mountain's summit. He wasn't quite tall enough, so a butler stepped forward and did it for him.

Snowdon was not the first summit visited by young Martin Conway. That mark of distinction belonged to the Worcester Beacon, a 1,394-foot hilltop in the Malvern Hills. He had climbed 'right to the very top', he wrote in a letter to his grandfather, where on a clear day you could see three different cathedrals and thirteen different counties of England and Wales. Later in life he still remembered 'as though it were yesterday the great flat, extending world that... called to be wandered over and possessed by wandering'.

Young Conway also discovered the pleasure of smaller summits. He and his friends had long weaved their make-believe in and out of caves near a sandstone boulder in Tunbridge Wells known as 'The Toad'. One day he decided to try the boulder itself and discovered that 'with a stretch and kick it was possible to scramble up his back and so climb on top of him. One or two rivals appeared,' he recalled, 'and our frequent ascents soon wore convenient footholds in the soft rock, whereupon the climb became popular. The same development on a bigger scale happened on the Matterhorn,' quipped Conway, 'and that scramble also lost its glory.'

Snowdon, the Worcester Beacon, 'The Toad' at Tunbridge Wells: Conway's earliest 'mountain memories', published when he was seventy-four, in 1920, in a book of the same name. Knighted in 1895, president of the English Alpine Club from 1902 to 1904, awarded the Founder's Medal of the Royal Geographical Society in 1905 and elected to Parliament in 1918, Conway was one of the pre-eminent mountain-explorers of his day. These wistful recollections of a self-described 'old-stager' neatly foreshadowed that future, but could they be trusted? Conway, if he was anything, was a romantic. He could barely trust himself.

Marching east out of Askole, Martin Conway must have been happy to see the back of Oscar Eckenstein. For six long months since sailing from Dover they had been living at close quarters, whether crammed into their cabins on the *Ocampo* or cheek by jowl in their tents on the long march into Gilgit-Baltistan. Worse was to come, Conway could be certain of that, but at least he would not have Eckenstein sniping from the rear.

Conway had shown what he could accomplish with that burden removed. While Bruce and Eckenstein became the first Europeans to cross the Nushik La, he had led his half of the expedition in a traverse of the Hispar and Biafo glaciers. His backers had demanded pioneering exploration as a return on their investment. Conway had delivered.

The Survey maps he had with him showed only the foot of the Hispar and, eighty miles away, the bottom of the Biafo, both fading into the blankness of unexplored territory. Now Conway had shown that the two glaciers were connected, forming a single continuous system. To map a place was to take notional possession of it, for himself and those whose approval he craved. He had done the thing most prized by geographers at the time – he had filled in a blank.

But Conway had done more than that. He had surveyed hundreds of square miles of uncharted territory, fixing the heights and positions of the surrounding mountains. He had been helped by Harkabir Thapa, who had 'taught himself, by mere observation, how to set up, level and orient the table, and the tricks of the various cameras'. While others were resting at the crest of a saddle or the top of a pass, Harkabir would be searching for a level surface for the plane table, while Conway readied his instruments. More than once the Balti porters, eager to reach journey's end, had marched on too far before making camp. Each time Conway and Harkabir had awoken the next day and trudged back up the glacier, retracing their steps in order to complete the work. Harkabir 'possessed a fund of quiet good sense and excellent feeling, rare among men of any nationality,' wrote Conway. The two had become, according to the Englishman, 'the best and most inseparable of friends'.

The resulting map would deliver the scientific dividends of his expedition. It would be years before anyone could critically evaluate their work – Conway was now a singular authority on all he had 'discovered'. The map, though, was only half the story, and Conway knew it. Marching east, he was leading them towards another of the Karakoram's great glaciers – the Baltoro. Encircled by several of the world's highest mountains, there would be no escaping the other objective he had claimed for his expedition: to climb to a record-breaking altitude on a first-class Himalayan peak.

That was how the expedition had begun – with a plan to climb the world's third-highest mountain, Kangchenjunga. Dreamed up by Conway and the English mountaineer Douglas Freshfield, it had quickly garnered the support of the Alpine Club and the RGS. Conway had all the right connections and, in Freshfield, a partner held in high enough regard that their plan, however ambitious, was taken seriously.

Their prospects looked more promising still when they roped in Albert Mummery, an accomplished alpinist with Himalayan ambitions of his own. The three met in London in April 1891 and fixed plans to lead an expedition out of Darjeeling the following year. With Mummery on board, the British would be sending their brightest and best to take on the challenge of the Himalaya. Then, within just a few weeks, it began to unravel.

First, tragedy struck. Freshfield's fourteen-year-old son fell ill and died. Freshfield withdrew immediately. Conway and Mummery pressed ahead, climbing together that summer in the Graian Alps. Then Mummery announced that he too was backing out.

It was the right decision. Mummery had made his reputation with fearless first ascents, climbing some of the most famous peaks in the Alps by ever more difficult routes. Conway, by contrast, was a nervous character, who had described feeling something 'more than terror' while out in the mountains. He had been descending a snowfield on Piz Morteratsch when he saw a crack appear, watching 'as in a dream,' wrote Conway, 'not doubting but that a catastrophe would soon happen and we should be flying downwards in a chaos of tumbling snow'. Conway might have raced up and down the well-trodden slopes of the Matterhorn, but he had completed few first ascents of any distinction and seemed happier researching and writing his *Zermatt Pocket Book*, a definitive list of all the routes so far climbed in the Alps.

Conway intended the book to be used by those wanting to avoid repeating established routes. Instead, he found it was being snapped up by novice climbers hoping to emulate alpinists they had read about in the pages of the *Alpine Journal*. Seeing that he was onto something, Conway wrote a pioneering series of guidebooks, making a name for himself as an authority on the accomplishments of others. He was a modern figure in that respect, a different kind of mountaineering celebrity. It did not matter that the books celebrated those with more backbone than him – his was the name on the spine.

Not everybody was fooled. Manton Marble, Conway's father-in-law, was a wealthy media magnate who had made a fortune from his critical disposition. Conway passed himself off as a Renaissance man, an athlete and an aesthete with a professorship at Liverpool University. Marble knew better. Conway's professorship had been expensive – Marble had paid for it – and his lectures were so poorly attended he often abandoned them. Moreover, Conway's book on the woodcutters of the Netherlands had enjoyed neither critical nor commercial success, selling fewer copies than his curious little climbing guides.

Conway had gone to Marble for funding when he began planning his expedition to High Asia. Marble was unconvinced at first, but later relented on condition that Conway secured the sponsorship of *The Times* newspaper and of the RGS. Perhaps somewhere in Marble's thinking was the notion that his son-in-law would either come back a hero or die trying, and that either option was better than a long slow trudge into academic obscurity.

Now here was Conway, many months later, about to lead his expedition onto the Baltoro. This was the glacier Haversham Godwin-Austen had explored more than thirty years earlier, making his 'stiff pull' up one of Masherbrum's northern spurs to steal a first good look at K2. Conway had met Godwin-Austen before leaving England, had studied his maps and read his reports. He knew the Baltoro as an enclave of ice within a gauntlet of stone, thirty-nine miles of glacier surrounded by some of the world's most remote and unassailable mountains. 'If only we can find an easy peak and climb higher than men have previously done,' he wrote in a letter home, 'the whole expedition will have been a great success.'

At the foot of the Baltoro glacier, they moved onto an ocean of stone. 'This glacier far surpasses in discomfort, and in the size of its mounds, both the Hispar and the Biafo,' wrote Conway. 'They are a Piccadilly promenade to it. There can scarcely be in the world anything more loathsomely monotonous and fatiguing to travel over. And what made matters worse was that, when we had climbed to the top of an exceptionally high mound, and could see from it about two days' journey up the glacier, there was still nothing but stones in sight, so that the hope of better things deserted us.'

Rocks of all different shapes and sizes waited impassively for the first careless footstep. McCormick described watching 'in a peculiarly cold and curious mood' as Bruce moved up one stone-covered slope. 'There was a crash like a bomb exploding; the whole thing seemed to burst and go rattling down together – he had stepped on the keystone of the lot. I saw him lying at the bottom of the hill he had so carefully climbed, on top of the offending rock, embracing it with his arms, and hammering it with his fists.'

As they advanced up the Baltoro, Conway lavished names on the landscape. In 1892 it was accepted that geographers should try to identify local names for peaks, passes and glaciers before dreaming up those of their own. Opinions varied, however, on how much due diligence this demanded. Satisfied that the glaciers flowing into the Upper Baltoro were fair game, he named one after Francis Younghusband, another after Haversham Godwin-Austen, a third after Godfrey Vigne. Conway was, at least, showing the fealty of a gentleman explorer, acknowledging his predecessors and paying tribute to them.

On 9 August, after three days of wind, rain and interminable moraine, they established a camp near where the Baltoro skewed south. 'Weary of trough wandering' and with the weather showing signs of improvement, Conway decided to climb a small peak to the north. At three o'clock the next morning he, Bruce, Zurbriggen, Harkabir, Parbir and Amar Sing started up the foot of a rock rib to the north. Karbir remained in camp 'to cook provisions for his companions. He was the only bachelor among the Gurkhas,' wrote Conway, 'and they have some superstition about cooking being done by an unmarried man.'

They scrambled for an hour up 'a steep slope of large debris', then turned to find the view already 'greatly developed'. There, bathed in moonlight, was a vast amphitheatre, the ice-streaked heart of the Baltoro, where tributary glaciers flowed from between the surrounding peaks, frozen affluents converging from every direction. All around were mountains, silhouettes of brooding shadow, the sun only a rumour in the moonlit sky.

Eager to see more, the men kept climbing. They moved onto firmer ground, the dark granite that gave the Karakoram – meaning 'black rock' – its name. 'Sometimes we scrambled along knife-edges,' wrote Conway, 'sometimes we went over the very top of jutting pinnacles, sometimes we were forced on to the steep face… and clambered along little ledges till we could get into a gully and climb back by it to the arête again.' As they gained height, the light rose with them, until, reaching the summit, they saw the extent of their surroundings.

'Name of a Brigand', said Zurbriggen. 'They don't know what mountains are in Switzerland.' The men were thousands of feet above the highest summits of the Alps, and still mountains loomed over them in every direction. More than mountains, these were hulking massifs, where crowded peaks vied for supremacy. There was Gasherbrum to the east, Masherbrum to the south and there, visible over the intervening mountains to the north, K2. 'We were simply surrounded by giants of the first magnitude,' wrote Bruce, 'an ice world where everything was on a gigantic scale'.

To climb any one of these mountains would have given them a new world altitude record with thousands of feet to spare, but there was no thought of trying to do so. 'Zurbriggen declared,' noted Bruce, 'that it frightened him to look at them'. Even the 'smaller' peaks seemed to warn them away. The men saw for the first time the 'Mustagh Tower', a little under 24,000 feet in height, 'whose parallel among mountains', wrote Bruce, 'I have never seen since'. 'Built along lines of the Matterhorn, but infinitely more grand', it was 'an absolute pinnacle, its steepness inconceivable and almost indescribable'.

And there, at the head of the Upper Baltoro, appeared 'the most brilliant of all the mountains we saw, that had been rising into view with our ascent'. Ten miles southeast, its rounded slopes rose gradually upwards, snow-covered to its summit, seeming 'friendly', offered Bruce, 'among savage surroundings'. It was 'a pure snow peak', wrote Conway, 'a *Jungfrau*, of infinite beauty of outline and quite alone in its character, for the general character of these mountains is so rocky and precipitous as to be almost appalling to the imaginative mind.'

The mountain's name was Baltoro Kangri, but Conway would give it a name of his own – the 'Golden Throne'. This, he believed, was his 'easy peak'. 'We were captive to its charms, and our choice was made,' wrote Conway, seeing the sunlit mountain in a halcyon light. 'With one consent we cried out, "That is the peak for us; we will go that way and no other."'

Forty miles from civilisation, at the end of a fragile supply line stretching back to Askole, they had travelled deeper into the Karakoram than any European expedition before. Now the climbing effort began.

For Bruce, the pressure was on. Zurbriggen was a professional guide who had grown up within sight of the Monte Rosa. The Swiss ought to have been partnered in the vanguard by Oscar Eckenstein, who had joined the expedition on the basis of his own elite climbing credentials. Instead, Bruce would have to step up, drawing on all he had learned over a few haphazard forays into the foothills of the Himalaya. Bruce, though, was his own brand of problem-solver, engendering a spirit of can-do conviviality in the men serving under him. Like Zurbriggen, he could be a boisterous *bon viveur*, but was quick to roll his sleeves up if there was work to be done.

And there *was* work to be done. On the evening of 12 August, they made their camp at the foot of a giant icefall, where ice and snow cascaded down Baltoro Kangri into the glacier below. Their first task was to find a way through this mercurial maze, up onto gentler slopes that appeared, from a distance, to lead to the top of the mountain. There would be no rushing the mountain Alpine-style, up couloirs and rockface. They would not be back, summit in their pocket, in time for afternoon tea.

They entered the icefall on the morning of the thirteenth, swallowed up immediately by a strange new world. Dark crevasses leered up at them and twisted seracs loomed overhead. Looking always forward, always upward, they searched for a way through, even as the icefall worked against them. Its movement might be imperceptible, signalled by the creaks and groans below, or the crash of a serac collapsing nearby, but it flowed forever downwards, a ceaseless convulsion of nature, one frozen wave crashing down upon another.

They gained twelve hundred feet on that first day. In the Alps that was a poor return, but Bruce and Zurbriggen felt pleased. They had cut steps in some of the steepest places and had cached provisions and equipment high inside the icefall. It was only when they returned the next morning that they understood what they were up against. Heavy snow had fallen overnight, erasing the work of the previous day. Many of the crevasses now lay hidden, the snow-bridges that spanned them almost impossible to find. With snow continuing to fall, and food and fuel running short, they retreated down the glacier to the camp below.

By now they had been living on the Baltoro for almost a fortnight. For all that time it had been a struggle to eat, to sleep, to keep warm, before they even thought about trying to climb mountains. Life was especially tough for the porters, who suffered badly, sleeping in the open with only blankets for protection. In his journal Conway describes how Harkabir appeared one afternoon 'and took away our mackintosh floors'. The Gurkha had helped the Baltis build little stone huts for themselves and needed material for roofing. 'We had to sleep on carpets of broken stones,' wrote Conway, 'like a new-made road over the ice. I don't know how the others found it, but I slept comfortably enough.'

Bruce and Zurbriggen arrived famished, wolfing down their lunch even as they made plans for a fresh push. For all they were up against – the ever-changing icefall, the execrable weather, the porters at breaking point – they had no intention of giving up. They were away again the next morning, leading a band of men back to the foot of the icefall, 'carrying plenty of self-cooking tins and other provisions'. As far as they were concerned, the siege of Baltoro Kangri had just begun.

The elements were kinder this time. After a day cutting steps the temperature plummeted overnight, and they returned the next morning to find them frozen solid, scored into the ice as if carved from stone. With the good weather holding, the way was clear to press higher.

Now Bruce witnessed a masterclass from Zurbriggen, as the Swiss drew on all his experience to lead them almost to the top of the icefall. 'Bruce,' wrote Conway, 'describes Zurbriggen's performance as incredible.' 'He says he never conceived that it was possible for a man to do the things Zurbriggen did. He describes him as having, on more than one occasion, jumped across a great chasm and stuck on a steep face of thinly covered ice on the far side.' All day Zurbriggen led and the others followed, until only one obstacle remained. Like the rearguard of a retreating army, a last line of seracs stood between the climbing party and the plateau above.

The men trudged back to camp that evening knowing a single night of heavy snowfall might sweep away all their hard-fought gains. They arrived at their tents to find Conway and McCormick waiting, meaning the camp was now home to four Europeans, four Gurkhas and a large group of Balti porters. With the expedition looking dangerously top-heavy, the pressure was on. They were back in the icefall the next morning, searching for a way through, but it was a day of lost causes and dead ends, followed by another night crammed together at their highest camp.

Then, on 21 August, more than a week after Bruce and Zurbriggen had entered the icefall, the breakthrough came. Following a well-trodden path, Zurbriggen bore right where they had always previously gone left. Crossing a sturdy-looking snow-bridge, they moved up into the tangle of seracs, emerging onto a small slope at the top of the icefall. There, at last, was the mountain above.

This was the site of 'Serac Camp'. At an altitude of 18,200 feet, it was 'a mere open snowfield', where 'snow insisted upon creeping into the tent and making everything damp. Our store of provisions was scanty, and there was nothing to drink but snow that refused to melt.' Moreover, 'the weather was not good,' noted Conway, 'and looked as if it meant to become worse'. None of the men planned to stay a minute longer than necessary at Serac Camp.

Nor would they have to. The light had barely broken before Bruce and Zurbriggen were away again, establishing 'Lower Plateau Camp' at a height of nineteen thousand feet. The next day they went higher still, to 'Upper Plateau Camp', at twenty thousand feet. With Bruce and the four Gurkhas working to keep them provisioned with 'needful things', and even their artist-in-residence, McCormick, lending his weight to the climbing effort, only Conway remained behind. He worked on his journal, and kept a record of his scientific observations, even as his companions were giving their all in his 'playground for the spirit of man'.

It would be Conway's only night at Upper Plateau Camp. He, Zurbriggen and McCormick woke on 25 August crammed into a single tent. They had not slept well – barely at all – and their senses were that bit blunter for an impromptu 'beano' the night before, following the discovery of a quarter-bottle of 'the finest liqueur brandy'. McCormick was feeling especially done in, having suffered from violent headaches and toothache for several days now. He would not be joining the climbing party on what Conway was calling 'summit day'.

Not long after they awoke Bruce appeared, accompanied by Parbir, Harkabir and Amar Sing. They had passed the night at the camp below and were raring to go. They arrived to find Conway greasing his legs with marmot fat to protect them against the cold, while Zurbriggen knelt patiently over the stove, 'with indifferent spirit to burn'. Pulling his boots on, Conway found 'every movement was a toil. After lacing a boot, one had to lie down and take a breath before one could lace the next.'

At 6 a.m. they said farewell to McCormick and started up the long snow-slope behind Upper Plateau Camp. The sun had risen, but the men were still mired in shadow, climbing on little more than a few sips of hot chocolate. As they 'plodded steadily upwards in the bitter cold', Conway felt himself losing all sensation in his feet. Fearing frostbite, Zurbriggen hauled off the Englishman's boots – the same boots he had laboured so long and hard to pull on – and rubbed his feet, hoping to restore circulation. Frostbite 'would, indeed, have been a melancholy contingency', wrote Zurbriggen, 'for there were no doctors within 1,200 miles.'

When sensation returned, they were off again, moving out of the shadow and into the glare of the sun. They joined a ridge, following it for a quarter of an hour to the first of several pinnacles. There they stopped again, 'to read the barometer and take some photographs of the glorious scenery by which we were surrounded,' wrote Conway, 'especially striking, as it appeared in the early morning, with the blue shadows filling all the hollows of the hills'. At around 20,700 feet they ate a breakfast of kola biscuits and chocolate, the only food they had. 'All began to suffer from thirst,' he went on, 'but as yet the sun was not powerful enough to melt snow for our drinking'.

Moving off again, the men faced 'a rather difficult rock-scramble' down the crest of a narrow ridge. 'Here the climbing-irons were of the greatest assistance,' noted Conway, 'for the rocks were fissured over with tiny cracks, too small to catch boot-nails, but affording securest anchorage for the steel-pointed claws'. This was the first expedition to make use of crampons in the Himalaya, which had only been brought along at the insistence of Oscar Eckenstein; he considered them indispensable, and so they proved. Where it was necessary to cut steps, 'small steps sufficed,' wrote Conway, 'but if we had been without climbing-irons, very large ones would have been necessary for safety. As it was, Zurbriggen found the labour of step-cutting, severe at any time, incomparably more fatiguing than at the ordinary Swiss levels.'

Climbing-irons or not, their situation was dangerously exposed, with the narrow ridge falling away steeply on both sides. 'Sometimes I would picture the frail ice-steps giving way,' wrote Conway, 'and the whole party falling down the precipitous slope. I asked myself upon which of the rocks projecting below should we meet our final smash; and I inspected the schrunds for the one that might be our last not-unwelcome resting place.' Fear drove Conway to distraction, just as it had on Piz Morteratsch all those years ago, as he pictured their ruined bodies thousands of feet below.

Stopping at a second pinnacle, they saw that Amar Sing was not well. It was nearly noon and they were climbing under 'the terrible heat which the burning rays of the sun poured upon our heads... in the midst of utter aerial stagnation'. The intensity of the heat, the stillness of the air, it was a recipe for mountain sickness. Amar Sing had worked day upon day to get them so high on the mountain, but he could not go on. They left him 'in a sheltered nook, and, after a tolerably long halt, continued our upward way'.

And then they were five. Zurbriggen took the lead, and for two and three-quarter hours they climbed. All around 'mountain masses of extraordinary grandeur were showing over the cols', wrote Conway, who remained 'dimly conscious of a vast depth down below on the right, filled with tortured glacier and gaping crevasses of monstrous size'. Coming to a third peak along the crest of the ridge, Zurbriggen cut his way up an awkward cornice then, reaching the top, anchored himself in a cradle of snow and brought the other men up behind him. One after another they arrived at the top. One after another, they saw the world fall away beneath. The ridge ended there.

'Beyond it was a deep depression,' wrote Conway, 'on the other side of which a long face of snow led up the south ridge of the Golden Throne'. None of this had been visible until now – the ridge had always appeared to rise in a single movement all the way to the top of Baltoro Kangri. Now Conway saw that 'ours was a separate mountain, a satellite of its greater neighbour, whose summit still looked down upon us from a height of 1,000 feet'.

Conway understood that this was it. They would go no further. 'If we could have had tents and warm wraps and spent the night at this point, we might perhaps have been able to restore our forces,' he later wrote, 'but I doubt it. We were all weakened, not so much by the work of the previous hours as by the continued strain of the last three weeks.' The men were showing tell-tale signs of sustained exertion at high altitude, struggling to digest their food – what food they had – and growing weaker under the warring attentions of cold and sun. 'We had all,' Conway went on, 'reached the limit of our powers'.

With what energy he had left, and what time there was available, Conway photographed the surrounding panorama. He set up the plane table, and 'was able to sketch an important addition to the glacier survey'. Then he turned to his barometer. Was this the 'easy peak' that would give him and his companions a new world altitude record?

'It stood at 13.30 inches,' wrote Conway, 'which gave our altitude at 22,600 feet.'

Was it enough? It put them higher than the 22,259 feet recorded by Adolph and Robert Schlagintweit on Ibi Gamin. Yes, there were the disputed ascents of William Graham and William Johnson, but they were exactly that – *disputed*. Besides, to Conway's eye, they couldn't be more than one thousand feet below the summit of Baltoro Kangri. That put their true height, to his reckoning, at 'over 23,000 feet'.

Conway was satisfied. He would claim a new world altitude record.

Few – for the time being – would argue with him.

They stayed until four o'clock, 'for it was hard to give over repose', wrote Conway, 'and harder still to tear ourselves away from a scene so magnificent and rare'. To the south stood mountains no European had set eyes on, then as they looked west, and northwest, they retraced the path they had followed, a journey of several months, into the heart of the Karakoram. 'This incomparable view was before us during all our descent,' wrote Conway, 'with evening lights waxing in brilliancy upon it, and the veil of air becoming warmer over it. The high clouds that overhung it became golden as the sun went down, and every grade of pearly mystery, changing from moment to moment, enwrapped the marshalled mountain ranges that formed the piled centre of Asia and send their waters to the remotest seas.'

Conway dined out on his Himalayan exploits for years to come. Returning to London, he embarked on a nationwide lecture tour, recounting his ascent of 'Pioneer Peak' – that was what he named it – at the many meals and receptions held in his honour. In 1894 he published *Climbing and Exploration in the Karakoram-Himalayas*, a florid account of their long season in the mountains, to popular and critical acclaim.

Amid all the talks, toasts and gushing reviews, it was left to a lone voice in the *National Observer* to offer a counterpoint – that 'in spite of armies of coolies, drafts of Ghoorkas, Swiss guides, the aid of the Royal Society, the Geographical Society and the British Association, [Conway] succeeded only in getting up a single second-rate peak of a paltry 22,000 feet or so, from which he surveyed the real Himalayas [...] very much as we may gaze at the Matterhorn from the top of the Riffelhorn.'

When Oscar Eckenstein's account of the expedition was published, he offered his own take on proceedings. Conway's party 'had attempted the ascent of one of the larger peaks of the Baltoro glacier,' wrote Eckenstein in *The Karakorams and Kashmir; an Account of a Journey*, 'but luck had been against them, and they had only succeeded in reaching a minor point on one of its ridges'. Manton Marble was likewise unimpressed. When Conway suggested taking his lecture tour to America, his father-in-law warned him against it. Marble anticipated little interest in an expedition that had simply passed within sight of the world's second-highest mountain.

In time Conway himself would come to question his achievements as a mountaineer. He stopped one day, while travelling in the Andes, to inspect a rock of unusual colour. 'The notion came into my head that the big mountain behind was just another stone such as I held in my hand, only bigger, and that in actual fact I might as well labour to set down on paper the shape of the one as of the other.' 'That realisation,' wrote Conway, 'ended my mountaineering career.'

All of Conway is contained in this moment. Was it the epiphany he describes? Or was it a moment of pique from a man who felt his mythos fading? His energy and industriousness had taken him far, had seen him stand in the reflected glory of the greatest mountain range on earth. Still, he had come up short.

Yet, whatever Conway's doubt about his individual accomplishments, there is no questioning the significance of his 1892 expedition. He would not return to the Himalaya, but this was just a first taste of the world's highest mountains for Charlie Bruce, whose climbing career would lead him and men from his regiment, thirty years later, onto the slopes of Everest. Matthias Zurbriggen would be back in the Karakoram, on the way to becoming the most decorated mountain guide of his day. And Oscar Eckenstein, who had turned back at Askole, would yet march up the Baltoro, en route to K2.

And there were the 'nearly men'. Douglas Freshfield, key to the inception of the expedition, would fulfil his ambition to visit India in 1899, leading a party once round Kangchenjunga with 'a plodding worthiness', wrote Walt Unsworth, 'which does nothing to fire the spirit'.

First, though, came Albert Mummery. With spirit to burn.

He had come to the Himalaya to climb, and only to climb.

English mountaineer Albert 'Fred' Mummery from *My Climbs in the Alps and the Caucasus* by A. F. Mummery (1895). Photographer unknown.

CHAPTER 11

World of Giants

The monsoon was breaking over the Vale of Kashmir. A thunderstorm raged, leaving the road to Baramulla in a parlous condition. Boulders, dislodged by torrential rain, thundered down the mountainside, some coming to rest in the middle of the road, others tearing it clean away. In places, the mountainside itself was moving, taking the road with it, sliding downwards into the foaming waters of the Jhelum river.

Under a canopy of leaden cloud, through a gloom pierced only by the occasional bolt of lightning, a convoy of *tongas* – sturdy horse-drawn carriages – made slow progress on their 170-mile journey from Rawalpindi. The men inside had sailed on the SS *Caledonia* a fortnight earlier, en route for the westernmost mountains of the Himalaya. Now their progress had come to an abrupt halt. Ahead stood the ruins of a bridge, all that had been spared by the surging river. For the trio of Englishmen, the time had come to get out and push.

Geoffrey Hastings had the frame of somebody built to wrestle a recalcitrant tonga across a swollen river. He was the bulkiest and most powerful of the men, a business owner from Bradford credited with some famous first ascents in the English Lake District. Of a narrower build was John 'Norman' Collie, a rangy figure who worked as an assistant in the chemistry department at University College London. Like Hastings, Collie had been climbing for over ten years, pioneering routes on Scafell, Ben Nevis and the Isle of Skye.

Then there was Mummery. A slighter fellow still, with shrinking features and bespectacled face, he was acutely short-sighted and moved awkwardly over flat terrain. Nobody would have thought so to look at him, but Albert Frederick Mummery had led the way up some of the most difficult ascents in the European Alps. Now, declaring the mountains of Europe 'overcrowded', he was upping the ante. He, Collie and Hastings had come to India to climb the world's ninth-highest mountain.

Barely three years had passed since the Conway expedition but, for Charlie Bruce, the Karakoram was a distant memory. Taking a month's leave from his regimental duties, he was spending April 1895 exploring the Kaghan valley. The Alpine-style peaks were not in the same class as the mountains of the Karakoram but, for Bruce, the valley was 'a playground and a training-ground'. He had visited several times in recent years, but this trip was different. Along with four men from his regiment – among them Harkabir Thapa and Karbir Burathoki, two veterans of the Conway expedition – Bruce was accompanied by Finetta, his wife of five months. This was the closest they would come to a honeymoon and, for Bruce, hunkered down in a branch valley, theirs was 'a most comfortable camp' – though 'on this point,' he noted, 'my wife and I hold different opinions'.

Part of the charm of the Kaghan was that, though encamped on the northwest frontier of British-administered India, they were still within reach of civilisation. Not long after they arrived, a letter found them, a message from the English mountaineer Albert Mummery. He was writing to advise Bruce of his imminent arrival in India, and to invite the young lieutenant to join his expedition.

Only two weeks remained of Bruce's regimental leave. But this was Mummery. Coming to the Himalaya. Bruce had crossed the Nushik La with Oscar Eckenstein, had climbed the icefall on Baltoro Kangri with Matthias Zurbriggen. Now here was a chance to continue his extraordinary apprenticeship, tackling one of the biggest mountains on earth with three leading lights of the European alpine scene.

The next day, he and two of the Gurkhas were off, over the mountains, bound for Bandipora, where Bruce meant to arrange all the porters and ponies Mummery could need. Finetta was left to make her own way back to Abbottabad, accompanied by the other two men. Her honeymoon – such as it was – was over.

Their base camp in the Rupal valley was pitched on a gently sloping bank of grass, in the shade of some large willow trees. Already they had collected a generous supply of firewood from the surrounding thicket and there was 'a babbling stream', wrote Collie, 'within a stone's-throw of our tents'. They could buy fresh provisions at the village of Tarshing, a few miles down the valley, where they could also recruit porters and local guides.

Arriving on 16 July, they gave themselves a rest day, passing the time 'in blissful laziness'. Occasionally a rope on one of the tents might need tightening, later perhaps a little loosening, but for the most part they lay in gentle repose, listening as the willows whispered sweet nothings on the breeze, beneath the chatter of cuckoos and skylarks. The men might have imagined themselves back in the English countryside they knew so well and loved so much, until they happened to angle their gaze upwards, to be reminded that they had lately wandered into a world of giants.

There, blocking out an ocean of blue sky, was the southeast face of Nanga Parbat. The ninth-highest mountain in the world, its summit was just two miles northwest of their campsite but three vertical miles above it. Tracing their eyes across the vast, bewildering extent of it, the men could see that its name, Sanskrit for 'Naked Mountain', was well-deserved – they were looking at a wall of looming precipices and hanging glaciers, much of the soaring southeast face so steep that snow would not settle there. 'It was huge, immense,' wrote Collie. 'Instinctively we took off our hats in order to show that we approached in a proper spirit.'

There are fourteen mountains of eight thousand metres or more in the world – that's roughly 26,250 feet in old money – all in Central Asia. Most are found along a 300-mile stretch of Nepal's border with

Tibet where the Himalaya is at its highest, or jostling for position in the crowded confines of the Karakoram. Everest and Lhotse are part of a single massif, so too are Broad Peak, Gasherbrum I and Gasherbrum II, folded into one another where the very surface of the earth strains upwards, forty million years in the making.

Nanga Parbat is different. It stands apart, at the westernmost end of the Himalaya. A few minor peaks are dotted around it, but all shrink away in the presence of its brute size. Its 26,660-foot summit is the highest point along a mountain ridge stretching twenty miles from southwest to northeast; for fifteen of those miles, it remains above a height of twenty thousand feet. From the twin Chongra Peaks in the northeast, through Rakhiot Peak and the summit itself, to the two Mazeno Peaks in the west, all join forces to create the immutable wall of rock that is the Nanga Parbat massif.

This was the mountain Mummery hoped to climb. He had come to the Himalaya to climb, and *only* to climb. Mummery was not like Conway; he had no interest in currying favour with the Royal Geographical Society. 'To tell the truth', he wrote, 'I have only the vaguest ideas about theodolites, and as for plane tables, their very name is an abomination.'

The differences between the two did not stop there. Conway was handsome, physically fit, bristling with confidence. Mummery cut an awkward figure. He had developed a deformity of the spine at a young age and – perhaps owing to his frailty – his father had chosen not to send him away to public school. Instead, he had received a sheltered upbringing and even now, at the age of thirty-nine, hated to be photographed, all too aware of his physical disadvantages.

If Conway was, in the words of the historians Maurice Isserman and Stewart Weaver, the 'consummate insider', Mummery was his polar opposite. From a middle-class background – his family owned a leather tannery in Dover – he was a political economist of a strongly socialist persuasion. He brought the same intellectual rigour to alpinism, believing its essence lay 'not in ascending a peak, but in struggling with and overcoming difficulties'. He was happy climbing without professional guides and, more scandalously still, sometimes with *women*. It was no

coincidence Mummery had given his name to perhaps the most noto-
rious 'pitch' in the Alps – a flake of rock still known as the 'Mummery
Crack'. Forever drawn to the route of most resistance, he was seeing and
shaping the future of the sport.

Mummery's single-mindedness came at a price. The RGS and *The
Times* newspaper had happily given their patronage to Conway's lofty
scientific agenda but they had no interest in financing an expedition
undertaken purely for sport. Mummery, Collie and Hastings were paying
their own way and this, more than anything, was why they had chosen
Nanga Parbat. Easy to reach from Rawalpindi, it had much to commend
it, for a party climbing less on a rope than a shoestring.

Now, however, face to towering face with the 'Naked Mountain', the
implications of that decision – to Norman Collie at least – were all too
clear. 'Eagerly we scanned every ridge and glacier,' wrote Collie, 'as naturally we preferred to attack the peak if possible from the well-provisioned
and hospitable Rupal nullah'. His prognosis was bleak. 'Precipice towered
above precipice', he went on. 'Hanging glaciers seemed to be perched
in all the most inconvenient places.'

Mummery took a more positive view. Writing to his wife Mary, he
described the campsite, enthusing about all that was going on around
him. 'If you could only be transported here without the labour of the
journey,' wrote Mummery, 'you would like it no end'. As for the climbing, he was feeling confident. 'I don't think there will be any serious
mountaineering difficulties on Nanga,' he wrote. 'I fancy the ascent will
mainly be a question of endurance.'

Charlie Bruce, Raghubir Thapa and Goman Singh arrived to find the
campsite all but empty. A few locals were there, watching over equipment
and livestock. Mummery, Collie and Hastings were nowhere to be seen.

Bruce soon gathered that they had gone off exploring and were
expected back at any time. Not one for idling in the shade of a willow,
he led the two Gurkhas up into the seracs of a glacier flowing down
from Nanga Parbat. Bruce knew the south face from afar but, playing

among the icefalls of the Rupal glacier, this was his first opportunity to 'see and take in the prodigious scale'.

Bruce had not stopped moving for the past two weeks. He had completed 'a most sporting march' to Bandipora, where he had made all the arrangements he usefully could. He then hurried back to regimental headquarters in Abbottabad, already rehearsing the conversation he was going to have with his commanding officer. He applied for permission to join Mummery's party the moment he got there. Permission – in the form of an additional month's leave – was granted.

Within forty-eight hours Bruce, Raghubir and Goman Singh were racing north. 'To show how light our outfit was,' wrote Bruce, 'I may mention that myself, Goorkhas, and luggage all fitted into one tonga. From Bandipora we marched by the usual route as hard as we could go, and arrived in Astor on the fourth day.' Two days later, less than a week out of Abbottabad, they wandered into Mummery's base camp in the Rupal valley.

That evening there was still no sign of the three Englishmen; it was deep into the next day before a small band of porters drifted into camp. These men expected to find Mummery, Collie and Hastings there ahead of them, and were disconcerted to discover that this was not the case. The Englishmen had tried to go, explained the porters, 'where there was no road at all'.

Concerned about the whereabouts of his fellow countrymen, Bruce took a stroll. Wearing nothing but a native cloak called a *choga*, he set off alone up the Rupal valley, savouring the coolness of the evening and the beauty of the setting. 'I had gone about a mile before I espied a weary figure coming towards me,' wrote Bruce. 'It turned out to be Collie.'

Bruce could see Collie was exhausted. Learning that Mummery and Hastings might still be some miles behind, he hurried back to camp and organised some men with ponies to go out and meet them. By nightfall they too had arrived in camp. Both looked, Bruce reckoned, 'pretty well done up'.

That night, drinking Bass pale ale – 'a priceless treasure in these parts' – around a roaring campfire, Mummery, Collie and Hastings apprised Bruce of all they had seen and done. After a few days in the Rupal valley they had agreed that 'to get ourselves into proper training, a walk around to the other side of Nanga Parbat was in order'. Their so-called 'walk' turned into a week-long epic, as they came to understand the true size and scale of the Nanga Parbat massif.

They took three days just to reach the other side. Hard days, in the scorching sun, grinding up long stretches of moraine, over what they knew as the Mazeno pass. It was the first time the trio of Englishmen had attempted anything of that kind, but for Bruce it would have been all too familiar. He had 'moraine-hopped' for days on end in 1892; 'one of the finest trials to the temper that exists,' he had written, which 'as a destroyer of respectable language, beats golf hollow'.

Their reward was to look at the northwest face of the mountain. Seen from the Diamirai valley it was not as sheer as the Rupal side but, in its own way, every bit as foreboding. But there, between the bulwarks and buttresses, the shoulders and spurs, up a series of three slanting ribs at the head of the Diamirai glacier, was a line that caught Mummery's eye – an Alpine-style climb of Himalayan proportions – leading up to a vast sloping snowfield above. That, adjudged Mummery, was their route to the summit.

His mind made up to attempt the mountain from that side, there was nothing to do but move their camp round from the Rupal valley. The return journey had not gone well – Mummery had tried to lead them on a 'shortcut', forcing them to march the last twenty-five miles on a few sticks of chocolate – but now at least they had their new arrivals to help them. Bruce would not have relished the prospect of many days of moraine-hopping, but Mummery had the answer. It was another shortcut, one demanding an explosive burst of climbing. This time, he assured them, it would not backfire.

Norman Collie sat on a rock. Looking back, he saw Raghubir a few hundred yards away, lying in a crumpled heap. Behind the Gurkha stood the Mazeno pass, and beyond that, somewhere, were Bruce, Hastings and Mummery. It was still many miles to Lubar, the tiny hamlet on the north side of Nanga Parbat, and Collie could barely stand.

The Englishman struck a match and lit his pipe.

Mummery's latest shortcut had not been a success. Sending Goman Singh and a detachment of porters the long way round, Mummery, Collie, Hastings, Bruce and Raghubir had hoped to cut the ultimate corner, crossing the ridge west of Nanga Parbat at a height of around 21,000 feet. Starting out under darkness, they had worked their way up steep moraine to the side of an icefall, then up a long glacier that seemed to go on forever. Next came a stone-swept couloir, leading to an arête beneath the great west ridge. At 5 p.m. they checked their barometer to see they had gained seven thousand feet in a single push. It had been a heroic effort. It would not be enough.

Collie already knew they would fail. The point where Mummery hoped to cross the ridge was more than a thousand feet above, and Collie – only Collie – had ventured far enough up the Diamirai glacier to see that, even if they made it over, there was no easy way down on the northern side. He had put his faith in Mummery but, facing the prospect of a night high on the mountain, he let his misgivings be known. They should use what daylight remained to climb down towards the Mazeno glacier, to see out the night in 'a less exalted position'.

Mummery 'would not hear of beating a retreat this early', wrote Collie. Instead, he and Hastings carried on up towards the main ridge, hoping 'for a full moon and the possibility of climbing on during the night'. Meanwhile Bruce, Collie and Raghubir searched for a way down, contemplating an awkward descent in the failing light. At a height of twenty thousand feet, with darkness falling, the climbing party was divided and in disarray.

It was a long, cold night on the mountain. Collie, Bruce and Raghubir managed to climb down a little, where they found a flat stone wedged into a crack, large enough – just – for the three to sit on. 'A stone thrown out on either side of our small perch would have fallen many hundreds of feet before hitting anything,' recalled Collie, 'so we did not take off the rope, but huddled together as best we could to keep warm'.

Late in the evening they heard voices above. It was Mummery and Hastings. Fearful of venturing too far into the unknown, they had turned back short of the top. Now they were within sight of the three men's lantern-light and were searching for somewhere to pass the night. 'With leaden feet the night paced tardily on,' wrote Collie. 'Let any one who may be curious on the subject of a night out on a rock ridge at 19,000 feet try it; but he must place himself in such a position that, twist and turn as he may, he still encounters the cold, jagged rocks with every part of his body, and though he shelter himself ever so wisely, he must feel the wind steadily blowing beneath his shirt.'

First light brought a long, slow descent to the Mazeno glacier, where Bruce, Mummery and Hastings curled up on some flat stone slabs and slept. Collie, haunted by the possibility of another night without food or shelter, struck out for Lubar, with Raghubir for company. They had not gone far when the Gurkha too lay down on the ground, unable to go on.

This was the sequence of events that found Collie alone with his pipe in the sprawling shadow of Nanga Parbat. He had reasoned that if he alone made it to Lubar, it might be possible to send back men, food, perhaps even ponies. Still able to walk, he felt torn between staying with Raghubir and going for help. Logic dictated that he go on, but instead he sat there, alone on his rock, breathing clouds of thick smoke into the crisp Himalayan air.

Collie had known the company of the countryside from a young age. For much of his youth he and his older brother had occupied themselves roaming the hills and valleys of Deeside. The two brothers loved to fish and also 'birdsnested', poaching eggs from the tops of trees, as Collie indulged his natural curiosity about the world, cultivating powers of observation that stayed with him for the rest of his life.

Privately tutored, he had shown an aptitude for academia, winning a scholarship in chemistry at University College, Bristol, before graduating to a teaching position. He became known for his 'salutary sarcasm', fond of telling his students about the chemist Robert Bunsen, who became so engrossed in his laboratory he missed his own wedding. Collie believed it was necessary to know a man before you could hope to understand his work.

'Remember too', Collie would tell his students, 'that friendship is always founded on common interests and happy is he whose life is enriched by the possession of many friends.' It was through climbing that Collie forged his most enduring relationships. His first outings were in the Cuillin Mountains of Skye, accompanied by a local man, John MacKenzie, a lifelong friend. Later Collie travelled to Chamonix, part of, as Walt Unsworth put it, 'that immortal quartet – Mummery, Slingsby, Collie and Hastings – who put modern climbing on its feet.' Their partnership had taken them to the summits of some of the Alps' most iconic peaks, and by the most adventurous routes, and now it had brought them here.

Collie had left his friends asleep on the other side of the Mazeno pass. Now, looking back the way he had come, something caught his eye. Three tiny black dots, on the crest of the pass, growing larger all the time.

Collie waited.

Soon he made out the figures of Mummery, Hastings and Bruce, approaching the stricken form of Raghubir Thapa. Drawing level, Bruce urged the Gurkha to his feet, using a combination of kind words and an ice-axe. Collie, sensing redemption, found his stock of energy renewed.

The sun was setting by the time they reached Lubar. Mummery and Collie were last in, arriving to find Bruce wafting the liver of a freshly butchered sheep in the vague direction of a flame. The five men fell upon the animal, leaving barely enough for breakfast, then fell to the ground and slept.

Mummery had seen it first. Only Mummery, perhaps, was ever going to see it. 'An absolutely safe way up Nanga', he wrote in a letter to Mary. 'Easy glacier, up which coolies can carry our camp, and thence onward, a broad snow and rock ridge right up to the top.' Three slanting bands of rock formed a single continuous climb of more than five thousand feet, still known today as the 'Mummery Rib'.

The route was Mummery to a tee, rising with a forbidding directness up the Diamir face. The going would be tough, but the climbers could gain height quickly with little need for tiring, time-consuming step-cutting. 'I think we are bound to have the summit still,' he told Mary, flushed with confidence. 'It is merely a matter of steady training to get our wind into order.'

Whatever awaited on the mountain, Geoffrey Hastings would have no part in it. He had injured his leg and, though nobody had the heart to say it, he was not capable of serious climbing. Worse still, the expedition was also about to lose Charlie Bruce. His month's leave had flown by and he faced a 250-mile march back to Abbottabad. Raghubir and Goman Singh, however, would remain with the expedition. They were important intermediaries where the porters were concerned and Raghubir had proven 'a first-rate climber', so much so that when Mummery set out to push provisions and equipment up the first two ribs on 7 August, it was the Gurkha who went with him.

Arriving at the foot of the first rib, Mummery and Raghubir left Collie and Goman Singh to explore the Diama glacier to the east, and started to climb. That first day, according to Mummery, was 'magnificent climbing'. The rib was a towering rockface flanked by dangerous chutes and couloirs but, moving between large patches of ice and snow, the men found good hand and footholds. Climbing in wildly exposed positions, as much a test of nerve as technique, the crux came at the top. Here they faced a mad dash across a couloir raked by rockfall. Both crossed it smartly enough, rewarded with more pitches of pure rockwork, up steep slabs and soaring buttresses.

Early that afternoon they reached the top of the second rib, at a height of around 17,500 feet. Mummery was delighted. He and Raghubir had shown that thousands of feet could be gained at short order, climbing in an Alpine style. It was as high as they would go – they were not equipped to pass a night on the mountain – but Mummery was happy to note that there was room enough to pitch a tent. Satisfied that their reconnaissance had been a success, they left a waterproof knapsack filled with biscuits, soup and chocolate, and started down.

That night the heavens opened, and the men woke the next day to find the Diamir face caked in snow. They watched as avalanches poured down the couloirs either side of the three ribs, swallowing up the mountainside in giant clouds of powder snow. *An absolutely safe way up Nanga.* Whatever he had told Mary, Mummery's route was fraught with danger. To attempt it now would be suicide.

No, they would have to wait for the snow to melt, but that did not mean giving up all thought of climbing. Instead, they turned their attention to a smaller peak south of their camp, linked to the massif by one of its northern spurs. Diamirai Peak was not the mountain the Englishman had come for, but if they were to reach the top it would be the highest any of them had climbed. 'By this time we had learned that the ascent of any peak 20,000 feet high', wrote Collie, 'was a laborious undertaking'.

Goman Singh had gone with Hastings to retrieve fresh supplies from the Rupal valley, so it was Mummery, Collie and Raghubir who started out on the morning of 11 August, accompanied by one other man – a shikari named Lor Khan from the village of Lubar. They scrambled up a gully to gain a ridge where the snow lay firm enough to walk on. Before long, however, the crust began to give way, forcing them to wade knee-deep through the snow. Higher up they found crevasses, and the ridge grew dramatically steeper. Mummery decided he no longer trusted it, and led them out onto an ice-slope to the left.

Their situation, to Collie's eye, was 'a sensational one – we were crossing the steepest ice slope of any great size I had ever been on; below us it shot straight down some 2,000 feet without a break'. Mummery, leading the party, was not looking downwards. He had just made another course correction when Collie, third on the rope behind Raghubir, looked back to see Lor Khan following too closely behind. A loop of rope had formed between them – this would allow the shikari to build up too much speed if he fell. Collie barked instructions to Lor Khan, who slowed his pace

The Schlagintweits and indigenous assistants camped within sight of the Kunlun mountains, the vast natural frontier separating British-administered India from the forbidden territory of Chinese Turkestan.

'There, with not a particle of cloud to hide it, stood the great Peak K2, on the watershed of Asia!' Henry 'Haversham' Godwin-Austen sketches his first good look at the world's second-highest mountain.

3

English mountaineer Edward Whymper, aged twenty-five. 'His frame was light and lissom, yet superlatively wiry and strong,' wrote biographer Frank Smythe: 'the perfect build of a mountaineer.'

4

5

English art critic, mountaineer and explorer Sir William 'Martin' Conway. Twenty years a climber, Conway was a proficient surveyor, who 'saw the Alpine Club as a kind of mountaineering wing of the Royal Geographical Society'.

Edward Whymper was one of seven to first ascend the Matterhorn in 1865; the first descent made the headlines: 'From the moment the rope broke,' wrote Whymper, 'it was impossible to help them.'

6

Oscar Eckenstein (*seated, second from left*) – one of mountaineering's first great innovators. He championed 'balance climbing' and revolutionised ice-axes and 'climbing-irons', today's crampons.

Conway's 1892 expedition to the Karakoram included four Gurkha soldiers: (*clockwise, from left*) Karbir Burathoki, Harkabir Thapa, Amar Sing Thapa and Parbir Thapa. Two Gurkhas were among the party of five at the top of 'Pioneer Peak'.

Albert 'Fred' Mummery (*right*) and Charles 'Charlie' Bruce (*centre*) on the Nanga Parbat expedition of 1895. Mummery led the first attempt to climb an 8,000-metre mountain, heading an expedition 'not much further furnished,' wrote Bruce, 'than a shooting party'.

The globetrotting Swiss guide Matthias Zurbriggen (*left*) and client Edward Fitzgerald (*second from left*) in New Zealand's Southern Alps in 1895, ready to steal some 'virgin' peaks from under the noses of local mountaineers.

(*Left*) American alpinist, explorer and travel writer Fanny Bullock Workman, who became one of the most accomplished Himalayan mountaineers of her day.

(*Right*) 'Eckenstein recognized from the first the value of my natural instincts for mountaineering,' wrote poet and occultist Edward Alexander 'Aleister' Crowley, 'and also that I was one of the silliest young asses alive.'

12

1902 saw the largest party of European alpinists yet to arrive in the Himalaya – (*left to right*) Viktor Wessely, Oscar Eckenstein, Dr Jules Jacot-Guillarmod, Aleister Crowley, Heinrich Pfannl and Guy Knowles – with an objective to match: K2.

13

Fanny Bullock Workman (*centre*) and husband Dr William 'Hunter' Workman (*left*) having dinner at 'Riffel Camp' overlooking the Chogo Lungma glacier, waited on by a Balti tent servant.

14

The 1907 Trisul expedition. Front row: (*left to right, standing*) Dina; Moritz Inderbinen; (*seated*) Charlie Bruce; Karbir Burathoki; Dr Tom Longstaff; Dhan Lal; Alexis Brocherel. Second row: Jeman Sing; Kal Bahadur; Pahal Sing; Buddhi Chand; Damar Sing; Henri Brocherel; three porters; and (*on extreme right*) Seban Sing.

15

16

(*Left*) Italian mountain guides Henri (*left*) and Alexis Brocherel (*centre*), and Gurkha mountaineer Karbir Burathoki (*right*), on the summit ridge of Trisul, the first 7,000-metre mountain climbed to the top.

(*Right*) Italian mountaineer and explorer Prince Luigi Amedeo Giuseppe Maria Ferdinando Francesco di Savoia-Aosta, Duke of the Abruzzi. Following his ascent of Mount Saint Elias in 1897, the Duke was the envy of royal houses everywhere, a paragon of aristocratic exceptionalism.

17

The Italian K2 expedition of 1909 is remembered for – and through – the photography of the legendary Vittorio Sella, but this picture of the northeast face of K2 was taken by the Duke himself.

18

19

(*Above*) The Duke of the Abruzzi and two guides in the icefall at the head of the Upper Baltoro glacier. He believed that to reach the Chogolisa saddle at the top would be 'the work of two days at most'.

(*Right*) Besides the loss of Mallory and Irvine, the 1924 Everest expedition claimed the lives of Lance-Naik Shamsherpun of the 6th Gurkhas, who suffered a brain haemorrhage, and Man Bahadur, assistant bootmaker, who died of pneumonia. They were among thirteen men lost in 1921, 1922 and 1924.

a little, letting the rope go taut. It was a timely intervention from the Englishman. Moments later, the shikari – who wore nothing more than a few strips of leather on his feet – slipped and fell.

Collie was ready. Hearing 'a startled exclamation', he jammed the point of his axe into the ice and wheeled around to see the empty space where Lor Khan had been standing. The shikari fell five or six feet before his weight came onto Collie, who braced himself and hoped his stance would hold. Mummery and Raghubir dug in their axes, but Collie was their best hope.

Lor Khan swung like a pendulum, as the snow he dislodged fanned out into a full-blown avalanche. He might have panicked and struggled, might have pulled them all from the mountainside. Instead, he showed a veteran's temperament, calmly cutting himself a step and waiting as Collie and Raghubir hoisted him up.

Senses sharpened by their narrow escape, they carried on. Mummery led the way, until, within half an hour, they arrived on the summit of Diamirai Peak.

With plenty of time left in the day, Mummery and Collie could take a moment to enjoy their first Himalayan summit. For Collie, however, satisfaction was tinged with disillusionment. Nanga Parbat was hidden by a wall of mist and cloud, but he saw clearly now the challenge it presented. At twenty thousand feet above sea level, he was already feeling the rarity of the air – 'my headache', he wrote, 'was by no means a negligible quantity'. He pointed out to Mummery that, to climb Nanga Parbat, they would need to go several thousand feet higher. 'How should we feel', he went on, 'if we ever ascended to 26,000 feet?'

'It was no good', wrote Collie. 'Mummery only laughed at me.'

As the days went by, conditions improved. The men were able to resume pushing provisions and equipment up the ribs of Nanga Parbat. On 15 August, Mummery, Raghubir and Lor Khan passed a night in a tent on top of the second rib. The next day they deposited a knapsack of food a thousand feet higher. Then the rains came back in.

The climbers arrived back in camp utterly soaked through. Mummery regaled Collie with stories of the ice world above, alive with avalanches sweeping its near-vertical slopes. He was sure they had found a way to the top of the third rib, and to the snowfield above.

That night, with the men asking new questions of the mountain, Collie imagined he heard it answering back. 'About midnight, gusts of cold wind began to moan amongst the stunted pines that surrounded our tents; then, gathering in force, this demon of the mountain howled round our tents, and snow came down in driven sheets. The anger of the spirits that inhabited the mountain had been roused.'

The men woke to find the landscape flattened. The rhododendron bushes growing in such abundance around their campsite had disappeared completely, buried beneath a carpet of snow. The sun was shining brightly though, and did its work, melting away any trace of the blizzard from the night before. Under a cloudless sky, with a cold wind blowing in from the south, everything was set for a fresh attempt on the mountain.

But not for Collie. Waking early the next morning, camped at the foot of the first rib, he let Mummery know that he was not fit to go on. 'Flour that is largely composed of grindstone is apt to upset one's digestion,' offered Collie, whose diet over the past few weeks had taken its toll. In truth, however, he had always seemed more of a passenger, a check to Mummery's relentless drive. There is an unmistakable sense, reading Collie's account of the expedition, that his heart was no longer in it.

Collie settled himself on the rocks and watched as Mummery and Raghubir began to climb. All day he followed their progress up the first rib, then the second, losing them occasionally, only to see them reappear after a little while, higher up the mountain. Midway through the afternoon a great avalanche fell, thundering down an adjacent couloir, swallowing up the climbers in a huge cloud that drifted across the rockface. Collie watched, and waited, and sure enough the tiny figures reappeared, climbing ever higher. Then, towards the end of the afternoon, he could see them no more.

All Collie could do was go back to base camp. The next morning, Hastings returned, leading a band of porters laden with provisions, carried all the way from Astor. Ordinarily, the arrival of fresh food and Kashmiri wine would have precipitated a proper old 'beano'; for now, the festivities were on hold, as they waited to learn the fate of their friends.

They would not have to wait long.

Leaving Collie seated on the rocks below, Mummery and Raghubir climbed. By mid-afternoon they were closing in on the top of the second rib, where they would pass a night before tackling the third rib the next day. All went to plan, and on 20 August they started out before daylight from a height of 17,150 feet.

The climbing on the third rib was more difficult than anything so far. It was colder, the air was thinner, more of the rockface was coated in ice and snow. All day avalanches raked the couloirs either side – most barely troubled the climbers, but later in the day a larger one formed. Mummery and Raghubir watched as it thundered down the mountainside, sweeping away the tent they had left standing on the rocks below. Hours earlier they had been asleep in that tent. Now it – and the knapsack of provisions inside – was gone. Still, they climbed, fighting their way up to 21,000 feet, a little way short of the great snowfield. Then Raghubir collapsed.

The Gurkha was alive, but there was no question of him going any higher. His strength had completely deserted him. Bruce later suggested that Raghubir had not been eating properly, but the climbers carried plenty of food. More likely, the sheer effort had done for him – they had ascended six thousand feet of steep rockface in a little over twenty-four hours, a nerve-shredding climb. The man had simply reached his limit.

They had stopped almost at the top of the third rib, with the first slopes of the snowfield a little way above. One more night on the mountain, Mummery felt certain, and the summit would be theirs. Others were not so sure. For Bruce, 'the remaining climb of 6,000 and more feet, and especially over unexamined ground, would have been much too severe'. But Mummery believed the summit within their grasp and rued the loss of Collie and Hastings to illness and injury. He might have been up there

with two experienced alpinists. Instead, he and his climbing partner did
not even have a language in common.

They faced an exacting retreat. It took several hours to descend the
three ribs and would be late that evening by the time they stumbled
back into camp where, warmed by a fire, hot food and a plentiful supply
of Kashmiri wine, Mummery recounted the events of the climb. Collie
saw that his friend was finally coming to terms with the reality of what
they were attempting. 'There is no doubt the air affects us when we get
beyond 18,000 ft,' wrote Mummery. 'Nanga on this side is 12,000 ft. of
rock and ice as steep and difficult as a series of Matterhorns and Mont
Blancs piled one on the other.'

Peaking at around 21,000 feet, Mummery and Raghubir had not
gone to a record-breaking height. The world altitude record, though,
was not the right yardstick for what they had done. They had made the
first concerted attempt to climb an 8,000-metre mountain, tackling a
Himalayan giant in an Alpine style. That, from an expedition 'not much
further furnished,' wrote Bruce, 'than a shooting party'.

And still Mummery would not give up.

Three days later, Mummery was ready to go again. 'Tomorrow I cross a
high pass with the Gurkhas to the Rakhiot Nullah,' he wrote in a letter
to Mary. 'If the NW. side of Nanga is easy we may yet pull it off.'

Mummery wanted to inspect the northwest face of the mountain,
in search of an easier route to the summit. That meant a move to the
Rakhiot valley and, ever averse to long trudges, Mummery had devised
yet another shortcut. He would lead Raghubir and Goman Singh
over the Diama pass, dropping into the valley beyond. Collie – who,
with Hastings, would be leading the porters the long way round –
warned his friend to be careful. Mummery shrugged it off. 'Don't
worry,' he told Collie, 'I'm not going to risk anything for the sake of
an ordinary pass.'

Collie arrived on the Rakhiot side three days later to find that
Mummery, Raghubir and Goman Singh were nowhere to be seen.

Looking to the pass, he saw a sheer wall of ice and snow where they would have had to climb down. 'It seemed to us quite hopeless. I spent about half an hour looking through a powerful telescope for any traces of steps cut down the only ridge that looked at all feasible. I could see none.'

Collie reasoned that Mummery must have turned back. But when Hastings returned to the place the three men had last been seen, he found no trace. Mummery had left a store of provisions on that side of the pass, anticipating the possibility that they might be forced to retreat. Hastings found it untouched.

Mummery, Raghubir and Goman Singh were gone.

As days turned to weeks, search parties were organised in villages around Nanga Parbat, but for Collie 'the mountains amongst which we had spent so many pleasant days together no longer were the same. The sunshine and the beauty were gone; savage, cruel, and inhospitable the black pinnacles of the ridges and the overhanging glaciers of cold ice filled my mind with only one thought.' 'Some catastrophe must have overtaken them,' he went on, 'during their attempt to climb over the pass'.

For Charlie Bruce, the only explanation was that they had been caught in an avalanche. 'A slip is out of the question,' he wrote, loyal to the last. 'Mummery was one of possibly the most accomplished amateurs there have ever been, and both the Goorkas were first-rate on their legs.' First-rate perhaps, but the chilling east face of the Diama pass would have tested the most experienced mountaineer. Might one of them have slipped, as Lor Khan had on the Diamirai Peak, without Collie there to read the danger? 'In that vast ice world the dangers are so many,' wrote Collie, 'that any suggestion must necessarily be the merest guessing, and what happened we shall never know'.

Mummery, Raghubir and Goman Singh were the first to die in the quest for a Himalayan giant. It was said Collie was so affected by Mummery's death that he never spoke of it again. Privately, however, he did address the matter. In a letter written forty years later he acknowledged that, though he recognised Mummery's qualities as a climber, he doubted his instincts as a mountaineer. 'He was not good in knowing what was the best way up a mountain or the safest,' wrote Collie. 'Once he was started on a route it was almost impossible to get him to turn back from difficulties and dangers.'

Which is why it feels wrong to lionise Mummery, to romanticise his death, as many have done. Mummery, who described mountains as 'the very breath of life to his being'. 'The faithful climber gains a knowledge of himself,' he wrote, 'a love of all that is most beautiful in nature, and an outlet such as no other sport affords for the stirring energies of youth; gains for which no price is, perhaps, too high.' Mummery was ready to give his life in the pursuit of mountaineering greatness. Raghubir Thapa and Goman Singh may not have felt quite the same way.

'In a Crevasse at Snow Lake' from *Ice World of the Himalaya* by Fanny Bullock Workman (1900). Illustration by Arthur Cooke (1900).

PART 3

AMATEUR HOUR

*The greatest excitement came when Fanny
fell into a concealed crevasse.*

*He had taken one especially big fall on Mount
Sefton, his life hanging by a literal thread.*

'The Accident on Sefton' from *Climbs in the New Zealand Alps* by
Edward Fitzgerald (1896). Illustration by H. G. Willink.

CHAPTER 12

Lord of the East Face

Zurbriggen looked on as three hundred third-class passengers boarded the ship, en route to a new life in the Americas. It would be a long voyage from Lisbon to Buenos Aires, longer still travelling in steerage; the Swiss guide lamented 'these poor wretches who could hope for nothing better than to feel a little less hungry in the land discovered by Columbus'. Yet, it might once have been his own story. Ten years earlier he had been ready to travel to the New World in search of work. Now, late in 1896, he went there as the 'Lord of the East Face', holding court among five Swiss porters with whom he played cards and told stories to pass the time.

Zurbriggen had learned at a young age that life hung by a slender thread. Swiss by birth, he was five when his father died, succumbing to injuries sustained in a mining accident. With his mother struggling to raise seven children on a meagre income, Matthias earned what he could looking after their neighbour's cattle, then at twelve he left their home in the Piedmontese mountain village of Macugnaga in search of proper work.

It was eleven hard, haphazard years before he saw his hometown again. Zurbriggen's quest for work took him from the silver mines of Chandolin to the manufacturing towns of Northern Italy, through the ranks of the Italian military and deep into the Algerian desert. When he eventually returned to Macugnaga, in 1884, it was to bid farewell to his family – he intended to emigrate to South America, where there was great demand for skilled labourers. His mother had other ideas. She convinced him to stay and become a shopkeeper.

Zurbriggen settled down to a humdrum life in the shadow of the second-highest mountain in the Alps – the Monte Rosa. With four conjoined peaks all over fifteen thousand feet in height, it was a massif first made famous by Horace Bénédict de Saussure, the Swiss aristocrat who had put a bounty on the summit of Mont Blanc almost a century earlier. Saussure's visit to Macugnaga had not been an unqualified success. Though 'charmed with the situation of the village', he declared himself 'ill-satisfied with the hospitality of the natives'. He found the innkeepers of Macugnaga gravely suspicious of strangers and reluctant – contrary to the guiding principles of innkeeping – to give them shelter. Saussure likewise found it difficult to procure a satisfactory meal, in a village that had not yet discovered the potato. 'The inhabitants of Macugnaga – including the parish-priest himself – live on milk-food,' wrote Saussure, 'and rye-bread which is made six months or a year in advance and can only be cut with a hatchet.'

Saussure did not let the inhospitality of the Macugnagans deter him. Intent on taking a closer look at the Monte Rosa, he climbed to the top of a smaller mountain nearby. From there he studied the detail of the massif's mighty east face, steep and snow-clad in the lee of the four peaks. A hundred years later, Zurbriggen felt his eyes drawn to the same east wall, to the same summits above. 'When I reflected that these peaks had been climbed and, in fancy, saw myself pioneering some foreign visitor through their difficulties,' wrote the young shopkeeper, 'my blood danced in my veins.'

Eyeing a change of career, Zurbriggen put in a word with some local hoteliers. He began escorting tourists to some of the nearer summits but his heart 'yearned for higher peaks'. Then, in 1885, two visitors from Trieste engaged him to guide them up the Monte Rosa. It was a huge gamble – he had never climbed the mountain – but he had studied the route and knew what to expect from the weather. Two days later he was looking down on his hometown from his first major summit. 'No pen can describe the beauty of our surroundings,' he wrote. 'It seemed as if we had left the world below to enter paradise itself.'

By the end of that summer Zurbriggen had repeated the ascent several times, as well as climbing a number of other prized peaks. He appeared so at home on the Monte Rosa his fellow guides nicknamed him 'Lord of the East Face' and, as his pocketbook filled with glowing testimonials, he found himself much in demand. But Zurbriggen had to be careful. There was a risk associated with taking every offer of work that came along, as he was about to find out.

Early in the season of 1889 a member of the English Alpine Club named E. H. Fison engaged Zurbriggen to guide him up the Matterhorn. They made a bright start under a cloudless sky and all morning it remained fine but, as they were closing in on the summit, the weather turned. A strong wind rose, whipping freshly fallen snow into a thick mist. Within a matter of minutes, visibility was reduced to nothing.

With other parties turning back, the two pressed on, climbing in a full-blown hurricane. Zurbriggen allowed them a few minutes at the summit then, as they began to descend, he was dismayed to see his client slowing down. They had gone a short distance when, numb with cold and 'done up' by fatigue, Fison stopped and lay down in the snow, begging to be allowed to rest.

Zurbriggen had to get Fison moving. He propped him up and fed him cognac, urging him to his feet. When that failed, he tried rolling the Englishman down the mountain, then pulling him with a rope. 'I now began to fear for my employer's life,' recalled Zurbriggen. 'My heart beat with feverish energy and I felt a terrible cold pierce my very marrow.' Soon he would have no choice but to leave Fison on the mountain, or to lie down next to him and guide him on the greatest adventure of all.

Growing desperate, Zurbriggen resorted to violence. He had done so once before, reviving some fellow guides by 'belabouring them soundly'; it was another matter altogether to inflict a beating on a paying client. It worked. Fison 'was immediately on his feet', recalled Zurbriggen. He 'felt the blood coursing through his veins, heaped a torrent of abuse on me, saying that I had ceased to act as his guide, and threatened to report me for ill-treatment'. On his feet, however, the Englishman stayed, all the way back to Zermatt. The next morning Zurbriggen was delighted to find Fison nothing but grateful, offering a generous *pourboire* as a supplement to the full payment of his fee.

Zurbriggen's star was in the ascendancy. He climbed with some of the most respected figures in the alpine world, among them Oscar Eckenstein, who in turn introduced him to Martin Conway. Conway was so impressed he invited Zurbriggen to join his 1892 expedition to the Karakoram, where the guide got his first taste of the Himalaya.

And it would be Conway who, in the summer of 1894, introduced Zurbriggen to an American named Edward Fitzgerald. The two hit it off immediately. Zurbriggen was, in Conway's words, 'lusty, extravagant and overflowing'; in Fitzgerald he had found a client to match. The American was a cocksure young epicure keenly possessed by the pull of the unattainable – in time he would gain a reputation for taking an unwholesome interest in other men's wives. For now, in his early twenties, Fitzgerald devoted his time – and considerable fortune – to mountaineering.

Fitzgerald recruited Zurbriggen to act as his guide for the next five years. Their first expedition was to New Zealand's Southern Alps, where they stole some 'virgin' peaks from under the noses of the local mountaineers, then in 1896 Fitzgerald made plans for a second expedition, to South America. So it was that late in the year Zurbriggen boarded a ship bound for Argentina. There he and his client hoped to make a first ascent of the highest mountain anywhere outside Central Asia – Aconcagua.

Edward Fitzgerald was not the first European to lead an attempt on Aconcagua. Thirteen years earlier, in 1883, a German alpinist named Dr Paul Güssfeldt had ventured high into the Principal Cordillera, the band of Andean mountains along the Argentina–Chile border. Guided by Chilean *huasos*, local horsemen unaccustomed to mountain work,

Güssfeldt had reached a point thirteen hundred feet below Aconcagua's 22,837-foot summit. There he and the man with him had been driven back, by the thinness of the air, and the searing cold.

Fitzgerald had studied Güssfeldt's itinerary and his description of Aconcagua. The German, though, had approached from the northwest, travelling through Chile, whereas Fitzgerald would come from the east, on the Argentinian side. His party – including a naturalist, two topographers and an English climber named Stuart Vines – made port at Buenos Aires on 29 November. They stopped for a week in Mendoza to recruit mules and muleteers, and then were back aboard the Transandine Railway, riding on a platform in front of the engine, enjoying 'a perfect view of the scenery without annoyance from cinders'.

'Twenty miles from Mendoza we left the plains, almost without warning,' wrote Fitzgerald, 'and plunged in among the mountains'. They wound their way up the Rio Mendoza gorge, over high bridges and through short tunnels, then as the valley widened, they got a clear look at the Principal Cordillera. Anxious for a first glimpse of Aconcagua, Fitzgerald quizzed his fellow passengers on the whereabouts of his prized peak. 'None of them ever seemed to have seen it at all. Mystery and uncertainty hung over the great mountain.'

The train took them to Punta de las Vacas, a tiny village high in the Andes. Nobody there confessed to knowing anything of Aconcagua. 'Not until afterwards', wrote Fitzgerald, 'did we learn something of the almost superstitious dread with which every native of these passes shrinks from admitting that Aconcagua is ever visible to the human eye.' Fitzgerald was quick to ascribe the reticence of the locals to superstition. Hard lessons of history, however, had taught them not to trust visitors from Europe with the keys to their lands.

Fitzgerald and Zurbriggen understood they would have to find their mountain for themselves. Waking the next day, they left Vines in charge and rode up the Vacas valley, guided by a local arriero. Mountains rose either side but they could see nothing fitting the description of Aconcagua and, when they cross-examined the muleteer, 'he told us he believed that there was once a man who had been up in these parts,' wrote Fitzgerald, 'who had come back and told his wife's uncle that he had seen a high spur which might possibly be part of the mountain, but he could not say for certain'.

All day the men rode up the valley, crossing and recrossing the river torrent. They had not brought a tent, so spent a night sheltering under a large overhanging rock, then the next day Zurbriggen left Fitzgerald and rode on ahead, accompanied by the muleteer. Reappearing at dusk, Zurbriggen described how he had gone to the top of the valley and had seen 'a great peak' away to his left, but 'the arriero had assured him that it was not Aconcagua, and, in fact, nowhere near it'. 'Whatever it was', wrote Fitzgerald, 'he thought that it did not look very accessible from this side, so I determined to go down, rejoin our party, and try the next valley – that of the Horcones.'

Riding back down the Vacas valley, Fitzgerald had his suspicions. The 'great peak' sounded like Aconcagua, and it was exactly where they would have expected to find it. If the arriero was wrong – and the arriero *was* wrong – Zurbriggen had stolen a first good look at the mountain they had come all this way to climb.

On the morning of 18 December, Zurbriggen started up the Horcones valley. He was accompanied by an arriero, but the next day he sent the young man back and rode on alone. Seeing a mountain – the same 'great peak' he had glimpsed at the top of the Vacas valley – Zurbriggen felt sure he was looking at Aconcagua. At first, all that rose ahead of him was 'a precipice about eight or nine thousand English feet high', but when he reached the head of the valley Zurbriggen saw 'a place from which I could swear that it was possible to go up Aconcagua without too much difficulty'.

He might have turned back there and then. Instead, retreating as far as his tent, he slept for a few hours, ate a little food, then at two in the morning rode back up to the head of the valley. Tethering his horse at the bottom of a steep gully, Zurbriggen began to climb. For six hours he picked his way 'over rubbish and detritus of rocks', until 'I reached the summit of an eminence,' wrote the guide, 'from which I saw, stretched out before me to the north, the valley that leads into Chile'.

Consulting a barometer, Zurbriggen reckoned he was standing at around nineteen thousand feet. A few hours after first setting foot on Aconcagua, he was less than four thousand feet below its summit.

It was late in the day so, noting that the slopes above 'did not look at all difficult to ascend', he scrambled down the gully to where his horse was waiting. With the light beginning to fail he rode back down the valley until, coming to a place where an avalanche had fallen, he and his mount were forced up onto the steep valley sides. Picking their way across the debris, the horse lost its footing. It stumbled, and fell.

Zurbriggen tried to jump clear, but his foot was caught in one of the stirrups. The horse rolled over and over, and Zurbriggen – alone, without food or a tent, several miles from his camp, further still from his friends – rolled with it.

Edward Fitzgerald woke on 22 December feeling concerned. Four days had passed since he had last seen Zurbriggen – four days and four bitterly cold nights – and he had begun to wonder what had become of his friend and guide.

Fitzgerald knew this was not country to be trifled with. Besides reading what Güssfeldt had written, he was familiar with the work of Élisée Reclus, a French geographer who had explored the area around Aconcagua. Reclus had described a chaos of rugged spurs and winding gorges surrounding the mountain, where 'we had to contend against temperatures and conditions that ranged between a Sudan campaign and an Arctic expedition'. He had found that higher up the air grew thin, the temperature dropped further still and the storms became blizzards, shutting off any prospect of retreat. This was what Zurbriggen had ventured into, alone, but for his horse.

Fearing for Zurbriggen's safety, Fitzgerald asked Vines if he would go in search of their guide. Saddling a horse, Vines rode through the grass-covered dunes at the mouth of the Horcones valley, up over marshy pastures and round a lake 'in whose waters are vividly reflected the great white walls of Aconcagua fifteen miles away'. He had been riding for two hours when he saw a figure, on foot, leading a horse down the valley towards him.

Zurbriggen had been lucky. Rolling under the weight of his mount, he could so easily have broken a leg. As it was, he had suffered nothing worse than a few cuts and bruises. The fall, though, had lamed the horse. It had taken two long days to lead it down the valley from there.

Now, reunited with Vines, Zurbriggen learned that events had moved ahead of them. While he had been away, Fitzgerald had received a telegram. A ten-strong expedition mounted by the German Athletic Club in Santiago was en route to Aconcagua. Approaching on the Chilean side, the Germans hoped to claim the summit in honour of Güssfeldt. From what Fitzgerald could tell, they might be less than a week away.

Realising they were now in a race, Zurbriggen hurried back 'to lay before Mr Fitzgerald the results of all my exploration'. Fitzgerald's relief turned to resolve when he gathered that Zurbriggen had climbed, with seeming ease, to nineteen thousand feet. The Swiss was confident, too, that it would take the German party many days to reach the same position, coming from the north. But Fitzgerald was not taking any chances. Their attempt on Aconcagua would begin the next day.

Only Zurbriggen knew what to expect. Not because he had scouted ahead, but because four years earlier, as a member of the Conway expedition, he had spent months in the Karakoram living at high altitude. Only he had sampled air so thin, in conditions so extreme. Only he had any idea how his body – and his mind – would react.

None of the other members of the party had gone higher than the summit of Mont Blanc. Fitzgerald and Vines had travelled to Switzerland earlier that year 'with the intention of camping as high up as possible on the Dom, the highest mountain there'. Owing to a spell of bad weather, they made their highest camp at around thirteen thousand feet. 'Here Vines and I spent a night in a storm, which, at the time we thought unpleasant,' wrote Fitzgerald. 'It was hardly even a suggestion of what we were to suffer later on in the Andes through wind and snow.'

Now, as Fitzgerald and four porters followed Zurbriggen up the Horcones valley, they rode into the unknown. Through landscape 'exceedingly wild and picturesque', they approached the mountain, where 'the giant cliffs and crags of Aconcagua towered above us to the east... like the battlements of some stupendous castle.' Leaving their horses, they climbed to sixteen thousand feet where, as the sun set, the scales fell from Fitzgerald's eyes.

'The cold was intense as soon as the sun went down, and being much fatigued, we decided not to pitch our tent, but simply to crawl into our sleeping-bags.' They huddled together, sharing what warmth they could, but none slept more than a few minutes at a time. As soon as the sun tipped the peaks of the mountains opposite, they were up, gathered around their stove, trying to heat some water. 'It was with great difficulty that we managed to melt some snow,' wrote Fitzgerald, 'and prepare a lukewarm beverage we called coffee.'

Feeling weak and ill, the porters started up the scree-slope above. Burdened with heavy loads, they trudged through the sloping sea of loose stones, each man taking a different line towards the saddle above. Fitzgerald watched in dismay as the men slipped back with every step, swimming against a vertical tide. Then, as darkness fell, they hurried to pitch a tent, anxious to avoid another night out in the open. Instead, packed together like sardines, starved of oxygen and numb with cold, the men writhed around under canvas, gasping for air.

It was Christmas Day. Now the stove would not light at all, so for breakfast the men ate Irish stew straight from the tin, 'slowly melting the lumps of white frozen grease in our mouths, and then swallowing them'. Fitzgerald's spirits reached a new low. 'One man made a feeble attempt to greet me with a "Merry Christmas". I replied that to my mind it was not a merry Christmas, and that was the last word upon the subject.'

*

Zurbriggen was standing, he reckoned, at around 21,000 feet. It was Boxing Day and once again the guide had struck out alone, leaving Fitzgerald and the four porters pitching a tent on the saddle below.

He had stopped to inspect a small heap of stones 'that had the appearance', he wrote, 'of having been piled up by human hands'. Removing a few from the top, he saw a flash of metal – a tin box. Prising it open, Zurbriggen found a 'visiting card', the kind left by European climbers. It was signed 'Dr Paul Güssfeldt'. 'It was at this point', he went on, 'that the great explorer had been obliged to return, in order to save himself and his companions from freezing to death'. All alone on the mountainside, Zurbriggen felt heartened by this discovery, a small scrap of humanity left by the only other European to have gone so high on Aconcagua.

Satisfied with his reconnaissance, late that evening Zurbriggen rejoined the rest of the party at the camp below. They, like him, were completely done in. It had taken all day to move everything up to 18,700 feet, where the tent now stood in a hollow beneath the saddle, sheltered from the worst of the wind. There was no escaping the cold though. The moment the sun set, the temperature plunged, driving them into the tent, into their sleeping bags and still it came for them. 'I have seen the men actually sit down and cry like children,' wrote Fitzgerald, 'so discouraged were they by this intense cold.'

Fitzgerald had once imagined that, with a camp at this height, their only thought would be for the summit. Instead, they spent the days to come fetching wood, blankets and whatever provisions they could from the camps below. Finding that the wood burned indifferently, they experimented with putting cotton in their cooking furnace, soaked in spirits of wine. 'The result, as might have been expected, was a tremendous explosion... Zurbriggen got the lion's share of the scalding,' noted Fitzgerald, 'and was proportionately furious'.

On 31 December they at last turned their thoughts to the slopes above. 'The day looked promising,' wrote Fitzgerald, 'and as the dawn came we were all quite cheerful, feeling certain of success... the summit looked so very near'. As they began to climb, however, they found the 'reefs of solid rock' above their camp replaced by 'a great and steep slope of loose rolling stones'. Like on the scree-slopes further down the mountain, they slid back with every step, making a treadmill of the mountainside.

Seeing one of the porters 'turning a sickly greenish hue', Fitzgerald felt the wind rising, conjuring up tiny particles of rock that tore at their skin and threatened to blind them. They took shelter and ate lunch – 'cold soup in the form of an almost frozen jelly' – then tried to push higher, but with a gale blowing, they felt the breath sucked out of them. By two in the afternoon Zurbriggen agreed the summit was beyond them. Facing a gruelling descent against a wind 'now risen almost to hurricane force', they started down.

That night, with no furnace, they went supperless to bed. To bed, but not to sleep – they lay awake rubbing each other's hands to fend off frostbite. Feeling the bodies shifting around him, listening to the rasping breaths, Fitzgerald wondered how much more they could take. In this godforsaken place, where hunger weighed on them constantly, where the cold stole through their veins, even the American, whose resolve had never faltered, found himself starting to unravel. 'At times', he wrote, 'I felt almost as if I should go out of my mind.'

Waking on 2 January, Fitzgerald was sure the German expedition had reached the mountain by now. Who knew how high they had climbed, how close they were to claiming the summit for themselves? But it was no good. With his men at their wits' end, he gave the order to retreat. He could take comfort, at least, in the knowledge that the Germans would find the mountain no less forbidding. That they too would have to contend with the searing cold. That they too would have to live on the thin gruel of such impoverished air.

Fitzgerald rang the changes. He gave up on cooking equipment – they would rely instead on firewood, a light pine found to burn well at altitude. This would ensure a ready supply of hot food, and of the right kind. Tins had not been a success, so they would stick to hot soup, eggs and fresh vegetables. He arranged for fresh butter to be sent by rail from

Buenos Aires along with port wine and, in anticipation of their success, a bottle of champagne.

After months of planning, Fitzgerald was adapting his ideas, working to find whatever edge he could ahead of going back onto the mountain. He had shown, climbing in New Zealand, that he was willing to put everything on the line. He had taken one especially big fall on Mount Sefton, his life hanging by a literal thread – two of the three strands of the rope had broken, in his narrowest escape yet. Even then he and Zurbriggen had pressed on to the summit, where they had enjoyed a bottle of claret and their customary cigar.

Aconcagua, though, was not like Mount Sefton. It would not be overcome by coolness, courage and acrobatics. It demanded tireless resolve. Once they were back on its punishing upper reaches, would their minds hold together? Would their bodies see them through?

Climbing back up to their high camp, 'the men all seemed in excellent condition,' wrote Fitzgerald, 'laughing and joking with one another over their pipes until sunset'. Thinking they might at last be acclimatising, he gave them the next day to rest. But, after two 'unspeakably long' nights, 'hour after hour… panting and struggling for breath', Fitzgerald realised his mistake. 'Every day spent at this height makes one the weaker,' rued the American. 'We should have pushed on at once.'

Starting out on the twelfth, they were soon in trouble. 'I had barely reached 20,000 feet, when I was obliged to throw myself on the ground,' wrote Fitzgerald, 'overcome by acute pains and nausea'. Seeing his client stricken, Zurbriggen would not let the day go to waste. He climbed on alone, depositing a rucksack higher up the mountain. In it, among other things, was the bottle of champagne.

The next day they tried again, going a few hundred feet higher before Fitzgerald tripped and fell. 'I did not really hurt myself,' he wrote, 'but the fall seemed to completely shatter me, and in a few moments I was again desperately sick. I rested here for over an hour, but it was no use, and at an altitude of a little under 21,000 feet, we all turned back.'

The fourteenth dawned calm, clear, with the cold seeming a little less severe. Fitzgerald felt good – he knew he might never get a better chance to summit Aconcagua. They made a fast start, reaching Güssfeldt's cairn in under three hours, where they stopped to make a fire and heat some soup. One of the porters went to retrieve the rucksack Zurbriggen had stowed. By the time the man returned, the situation had changed.

'Up to this moment I had been feeling strong,' wrote Fitzgerald, 'and indeed certain of success, but during our stay here, my old symptoms of nausea gradually came on'. Within half an hour the American felt it would be impossible for him to go on. When the climbers discovered that the bottle of champagne had burst, their spirits sank lower. 'Though we might have known this would happen,' he went on, 'yet – so much importance can trifles assume – it discouraged us greatly'.

Fitzgerald had a decision to make. Twice already Zurbriggen had stopped short of Aconcagua's summit for the sake of his client. Now the American's hopes of climbing the mountain had been thwarted once again. 'Of my disappointment I need not write,' he continued, 'but the object of my expedition was to conquer Aconcagua. I therefore sent Zurbriggen on to complete the ascent.'

Fitzgerald rested for an hour, thinking he might yet resume the climb. The summit he had crossed the world to tread was less than one thousand feet above him, along a route free from any conspicuous difficulties, but he was powerless to proceed. Instead, all he could do was watch as Zurbriggen went on ahead. 'I saw him four hundred feet above me, going across the face of the big stone slope on the way to the saddle between the two peaks. Then for the first time the bitter feeling came over me that I was being left behind, just beneath the summit of the great mountain I had so long been thinking about, talking about, and working for.'

It was as much as Fitzgerald could do to make it back down the mountain. 'I had the greatest difficulty in crawling down; my knees were so weak that I repeatedly fell, cutting myself with the sharp stones that covered the mountain-side. I crawled along in this miserable plight, steering for a big patch of snow. Here, unable to stand any longer from sheer exhaustion, I was obliged to lie down and roll down the mountain-side.' When Fitzgerald made it back to camp, still his ordeal was not over.

He was tormented by 'one of the most severe headaches I have ever in my life experienced'. And by the knowledge that, four thousand feet above him, Zurbriggen was making Aconcagua his own.

Carrying on towards the summit, Matthias Zurbriggen could take a moment to reflect on how far he had come. He had guided countless clients to the tops of the highest mountains in Western Europe, had been the driving force behind Martin Conway's climbing effort in the Himalaya, had helped Edward Fitzgerald rewrite the record books on the Southern Alps of New Zealand. Now he was closing in on the summit of the highest peak in the Americas – a new altitude record in both the Southern and Western Hemispheres.

Late in the afternoon, he arrived alone on the small square summit plateau, where he stood and surveyed the continent below. 'My joy at standing thereon is better imagined than described,' wrote Zurbriggen. 'The view from there was indeed a marvellous one: I saw the whole of South America extended below me, with its seas, mountains and plains, covered with villages and cities that looked like little specks. Ah! How deeply is one impressed, on such heights by the marvellous works of the Creator!'

At 22,837 feet, Zurbriggen's ascent of Aconcagua was a new world *summit* record – the highest mountain ever climbed to the top. It put him at the top, too, of the alpine world: a defining moment for the man from Macugnaga, who had climbed out of poverty to mountaineering supremacy. Carving the date into the handle of Fitzgerald's ice-axe and fixing it to a freshly constructed cairn, Zurbriggen inscribed his own name into the record books.

Nothing remained but to climb down. Back to their high camp, where Fitzgerald would be waiting, ready to greet the bittersweet news that Aconcagua had fallen. Back to their hotel in Puente del Inca, for the first of many champagne receptions – it would take Zurbriggen two days to recover from the celebrations. Back to Europe, whiling away the long sea voyage over a collection of newspaper clippings, articles about the conqueror of Aconcagua, a prodigious professional guide who was 'highly valued, esteemed, liked and also feared'. And, before too long, back to the Himalaya. This time in the service of a new employer – one who, brandishing her signature pistol and whip, knew all too well what it meant to be feared.

It was, he offered in closing, 'almost impassable to a woman'.

Cover of *Journal des Voyages* No. 686, 23 January 1910.
Illustration by F. Conrad.

CHAPTER 13

Nature at Her Wildest

"Begin at the beginning," said Bess, "tell me what has upset you today."

"The truth is," replied Maud, "I am tired of this sort of life. English country life may be charming to some, I must confess I am weary of it. I should like of all places to be among the old Alps, with only transient visitors for companions, and honey and goat's milk for food. How I could read, sketch and enjoy nature."

So begin the fictional adventures of Maud Alton, a debutante who leaves behind her aunt's stately home in Dorsetdale, England to travel to the Wengernalp in Switzerland. There, where she hopes to find 'nature at her wildest', Maud meets a handsome young American and falls in love.

The setting for Maud's adventure was one the author of *A Vacation Episode* knew well. The American heiress Fanny Bullock Workman was seventeen when her parents sent her to Europe to finish her education. They hoped she would acquire a respectable European husband but instead Fanny fell for the place itself, and its mountains in particular, adopting them as the setting for her short stories. Another of her heroines, a peasant girl named Adèle, finds star-crossed love in the arms of an English aristocrat, Lord Harcourt, who confesses his feelings as they sit together at the top of a celebrated local peak, the Donnerkönig, or 'Thunder King'. In Fanny's eyes, mountains were a

185

place of romance and adventure. At a mountain's summit, anything was possible.

Returning home three years later, Fanny felt stifled by society life in Massachusetts. She escaped by hiking in the surrounding hills, or by disappearing into the books of famous mountaineers like Edward Whymper and Martin Conway. Then she met Hunter.

Dr William Hunter Workman was not in the mould of the polished paramours from Fanny's short stories. A Harvard-educated doctor twelve years her senior, he could hardly have been a more suitable match. For the fiercely independent Fanny, however, in an age of patriarchy and male social privilege, Hunter had one truly distinguishing characteristic. Recognising that Fanny was more ambitious than him, more astute and more athletic, he was happy for her to be the driving force behind everything they did.

Together, Fanny and Hunter explored the White Mountains of New Hampshire, going several times to the top of Mount Washington. It was always Fanny, the stronger climber, who arrived at the windswept summit first, there to be greeted by an extraordinary panorama. To the north was Canada, to the south Massachusetts, to the east lay the sprawling Atlantic Ocean, to the west the Adirondack Mountains of Upstate New York. And, if she cared to angle her gaze downwards, she might see Hunter, labouring up the mountain behind her.

In June 1882, a year after they married, Fanny and Hunter inherited sizeable family estates. Free to do as they pleased, they continued to climb in the White Mountains, but Fanny dreamed of loftier heights. Within a few years the Workmans had moved to Dresden, Germany, where, living in a city she knew from her student days, Fanny was within a few hours of the Alps.

In the summer of 1891, she and Hunter climbed Mont Blanc, the highest mountain in Western Europe. In 1892 it was the Matterhorn. Fanny reached the summit at first light on the last day of August, closely followed by Hunter, just as the icy wind that had troubled them all morning fell suddenly away. As the skies cleared, the Workmans watched a golden sunrise through a moment of stillness and calm.

They stayed long enough to have their picture taken, then started down.

Fanny and Hunter's visits to the Alps were a chance to exercise their other great love – their 'safety bicycles'. A newly invented alternative to the high-wheeled penny-farthing, the chain-driven design is instantly recognisable as the model on which modern bicycles are based. The Workmans cycled to and from the mountains in 1892, and the following year they completed a two-month tour of Italy, cycling up to eighty miles a day loaded with twenty pounds of luggage. Then, on their arrival back in Dresden, tragedy struck.

The Workmans had two children. Their daughter, Rachel, had been born in 1884. Eight years old, she had grown up in the care of nurse-maids, governesses and schoolteachers. She had been joined, in 1889, by Siegfried. By the age of three he was, in Hunter's words, 'of a rare beauty of form and face, and of a disposition amiable and playful to a degree I have never seen engaged in a child'.

Within days of their return from Italy, Siegfried fell ill. After a bout of influenza, pneumonia took hold. He became weaker and weaker, until Fanny and Hunter could see the end was near. 'His eyes closed half turned upwards and outwards,' wrote Hunter, 'a peaceful look came over his face. His breath suddenly stopped as gently as possible; not a moment indicated that he had suffered. Not a muscle stirred. Our Siegfried was no more.'

Siegfried was buried in Worcester Rural Cemetery alongside his grandparents. Fanny and Hunter observed a period of mourning but after losing Siegfried, more than ever, they lived life on the hoof. Within months of his death, they embarked on a cycling tour of Algeria. On the boat from Marseilles, the ship's captain advised them to travel around North Africa by train, enjoying the comfort and security of a first-class carriage. Instead, they cycled hundreds of miles across the Atlas mountains and into the Sahara, pedalling through remote and unforgiving country with nothing to protect them but Fanny's dog-whip and revolver. If grief rode along with them, it was to places promising no end of distraction.

This was the life Fanny had dreamed of as a young woman, person-ified by the audacious protagonists of her stories. Now she put pen to paper once again. Published in 1895, *Algerian Memories: A Bicycle Tour over the Atlas to the Sahara* was the first of her travel books, followed two years later by *Sketches Awheel in Modern Iberia*. Fanny hoped that, by combining lavish, lyrical descriptions with robust scientific obser-vations, her books would appeal to the broadest possible audience. As it was, they enjoyed moderate success, neither substantive enough for the high minds of the Royal Geographical Society, nor frivolous enough for the masses.

Sketches Awheel was published early in 1897, just as Fanny's thoughts turned to the east. By the end of the year, she and Hunter had arrived at the port of Colombo in Ceylon, with plans to spend two and a half years cycling through India and Indochina. From Tuticorin in the south up to Srinagar in Kashmir, they followed a meandering route across more than four thousand miles of the subcontinent. Accompanied at first by an English valet, they dispensed with his services after he cycled off a cliff in the thick of a torrential downpour, narrowly escaping with his life. After that it was just the two of them, riding north into the foothills of the Himalaya, escaping the intensifying heat of a summer on the plains.

There, in the mountains, Fanny found a world still waiting to be discovered, everything she needed to hold audiences rapt, from the RGS to Madison Square Garden. There, in the Himalaya, she would climb higher than any woman had gone before.

The political officer was in no doubt whatsoever. He had crossed the pass in question and knew 'a good deal about the difficulties of the route, of the density of the rhododendron forests beyond the Guicha La, of the obstruction caused by rivers, of steep and slippery paths'. They would be marching through country home to tigers and wild elephants, where the jungle teemed with parasitic ticks and leeches eager to grow fat on foreign blood. It was, he offered in closing, 'almost impassable to a woman'.

He was the latest local official to question the wisdom of Fanny and Hunter's plans. They had already met with the deputy-commissioner but had found him quite useless. He and his *sirdars* – tribal chiefs or head-men – 'had never been within miles of the places we were inquiring about', wrote Fanny, 'and, when questioned respecting these, the principal sirdar would place one hand over his heart and raise the other aloft, turning up his eyes at the same time with a pathetic expression, which seemed to say, "What you wish to do is beyond the range of human possibility."'

Fanny was having none of it. She and Hunter were in Darjeeling in September 1898, leading the best-equipped Himalayan mountaineering expedition since Conway's six years earlier. They had ordered tents, clothing, equipment and provisions in from London, and now needed porters to carry it. By the time the meeting was over, the political officer had agreed to provide the Workmans with a sirdar, sixty local porters, a cook, an interpreter and a *munshi* – a go-between to act on their behalf in local markets.

On the morning of 11 October, they left Chia Banjan, the last village on the Singalila Ridge, and started north. Fanny and Hunter went on ahead, accompanied by their Swiss guide, Rudolph Taugwalder, marching through lush, luxuriant jungle thronged with tree ferns and bamboo thickets. Between the trailing creepers, 'that hang in long festoons from the tall trees and darken the forest with their tangled masses', they stole glimpses of the mountains ahead, where 'the towering white god of snow seemed to float upward from a billowy world of mauve vapour'. All morning they marched until, at eleven, it seemed prudent to stop, to allow the porters to catch up.

The Workmans waited three hours before, with no sign of the porters, they saw no alternative but to turn back. They retraced their steps for more than an hour before they came at last upon two men, who explained that the rest of their number were some way behind. Retreating further, they met the sirdar, coming along with those men who had not already deserted them. 'He said they could go no further that day,' wrote Fanny, 'and we therefore encamped for the night in a thistle-covered field, five miles from Chia Banjan.'

So began a battle of wills. The Workmans woke early the next day keen to make up for lost time. Instead, they found the porters 'leisurely cooking huge portions of rice and chillis, tea, etc. The sirdar was told to hurry them up,' wrote Fanny, 'but he did nothing, remarking they could not march until they had eaten.' The sirdar informed the Workmans that the porters would not march at all unless a ration of curry was included in their evening meal. 'How curry was to be obtained in this wilderness,' wrote Fanny, 'he did not explain. After a while he said, if they could have an ox at Jongri, they would go on.'

Such was the pattern over the days to come. Fanny and Hunter were soon pitching their own tents, gathering their own firewood and preparing their own food. As far as Fanny was concerned, their cook 'never showed the least knowledge of the simplest elements of cookery. He never succeeded in boiling an egg properly... and could never even start a fire with any certainty.'

At the end of the fourth day a storm broke over the Sikkim. Taking shelter in some shepherds' huts, all they could do was wait. More porters abandoned them and others burned their clothes in protest. Finding the sirdar unrepentant, Fanny and Hunter saw no way to proceed. Twenty miles out of Chia Banjan, at an altitude of fourteen thousand feet, one week into a two-month itinerary, their first Himalayan expedition was at an end.

For the Workmans, all their problems owed to the bad faith of the local men. From the political officer and the deputy-commissioner to the cook, sirdar and munshi, everywhere they looked they saw themselves deceived and taken advantage of. If Fanny and Hunter had taken this moment to interrogate their assumptions, to notice the futility of their ultimatums, to recognise that all the money in the world would not buy the allegiance of hungry men, they might have put their 'porter problems' behind them. They did not.

Abandoned after a few days, the Workman expedition of 1898 had been an abject failure. Fanny, though, believed she had the answer.

She and Hunter had been guided up the Matterhorn by a man who had been to the Himalaya, and to other places besides. When they returned to India the following year, it was in the company of Matthias Zurbriggen.

A photograph taken early in the 1899 expedition shows Zurbriggen being helped out of a shadowy crevasse. The faces of a dozen Balti porters are visible, witnessing the rescue of a wayward sheep. Here was Zurbriggen doing what he did best – a feat of icemanship making a resounding appeal to the hearts, minds and stomachs of the local men.

As a veteran of the Conway expedition, Zurbriggen was the only European guide with first-hand experience of the Karakoram. Now he led Fanny and Hunter along the 42-mile length of the Biafo glacier, following a route he and Conway had pioneered. Passing stone cairns left behind in 1892, they chanced on a bundle of firewood at one of their old camps. The greatest excitement came when Fanny fell into a concealed crevasse. The moment is captured in an illustration showing her up to her shoulders in ice, as Zurbriggen prepares to haul her back to safety. The anxious faces of the Balti porters are, on this occasion, conspicuous by their absence.

It was all well and good, following in Conway's footsteps, but by August the Workmans were ready to pioneer some peaks of their own. They struck out west, up the valley of the Braldoh river then along the lateral moraine of the Skoro La glacier all the way to its head, 'that swept down in a chaos of dazzling seracs from the circle of peaks above'. All around were mountains – unclimbed mountains – rising to heights of eighteen thousand feet and more. It was two years since the American adventurer Annie Smith Peck had summited Mexico's 18,491-foot Pico de Orizaba – the highest point known to have been reached by a woman. Now, as Fanny's eye settled on 'a beautiful silvery horn' directly east of the Skoro La, she fixed her mind on claiming that record for herself.

The Workmans passed a night at Avalanche Camp, 'where the silence was broken only by the music of the ice streams and the roar of the avalanche', then early the next morning Zurbriggen led them across the Skoro La glacier. 'An ordinary Swiss guide would... doubtless have lost some hours finding his path through the labyrinth of seracs and crevasses that confronted us,' wrote Fanny. 'Not so Zurbriggen. He led us in and out, over and around them, as if a path existed and was not for the first time being trodden out. Mountain instinct seemed to lead him... and, before we thought it possible, we had passed the seracs and were taking a light breakfast on a sloping snow plateau.'

Accompanying the Workmans and Zurbriggen were two Baltis, tasked with carrying the food, camera and scientific instruments. Fanny and Hunter were unusual among Himalayan explorers in expecting local porters to go as high as they did. The Baltis were guided by instincts of a different kind. One of the men 'chattered and gesticulated', wrote Fanny, 'and did his best to show us, we were on, what he thought was, the wrong road'. The cause of the porter's consternation soon became clear – it had not occurred to him that the Europeans intended to go to the top of the mountain, rather than trying to find a way around it.

Back at Avalanche Camp the rest of the porters watched, across the icebound auditorium of the Skoro La, as five black specks moved up the mountain's snow-covered slopes. Seen from a distance, the climbers drew diagonal lines up the steepening snow, then disappeared against a series of large slabs of rock. The day stayed beautifully calm and clear, and by eleven they could be seen just below the mountain's summit.

With thirty feet of snow-slope left to climb, the two porters 'threw down their loads, and went to sleep on the rocks'. Now Fanny led the way, up onto the snowy cornice of the mountaintop. Arriving at the summit, all eyes were on their barometers. Taking the average of the two, they saw they were 18,600 feet above sea level. That was around one hundred feet higher than Annie Smith Peck's mark on Pico de Orizaba. Fanny, hoping to do just enough to make the record her own, had judged it to perfection.

'We named the mountain the Siegfriedhorn,' wrote Fanny. 'There were two reasons for giving it this name. The first was a personal one...

the second, that... *Sieg* or success had crowned our efforts, and there was *Friede*, peace, at the summit in the windless sun-warmed silence, that reigned throughout those upper regions on that day.'

At the summit of the Siegfriedhorn the climbing party had seen heavy clouds rolling in from the south. They broke that night over the Skoro La. Waking next morning under a thick carpet of fresh snow, the Workmans would be hemmed in at Avalanche Camp for the next two days.

It was a new experience for Fanny and Hunter to kill time at sixteen thousand feet, where the only exercise was clambering on moraine or 'pottering about' among the crevasses and seracs. If they were lucky a glorious sunset might cause them 'to forget cold feet and cheerless sur- roundings, in temporary enthusiasm over ice-world beauties', but in the darkness to follow there was little to do except retreat to 'the solace of a sleeping bag'. 'Such is life in a camp higher than the summit of Mount Blanc,' wrote Fanny, 'when the elements are warring'.

By 10 August they were climbing again, up towards a second, higher peak to the north of Avalanche Camp. Their route took them up a huge bank of scree, 'one of the most disagreeable places of its kind we have contended with', wrote Fanny, 'piled together at as steep an angle as the stuff will lie'. Halfway up, the porters decided they had gone quite far enough, so set down their loads and refused to go on. Hunter's solution, as cruel as it was undignified, was to pelt them with small stones until they resumed the climb.

After a night at a high camp the same five climbers set out for the summit, roped together this time. 'It was far from pleasant... to hear Zurbriggen calling to the stupid fellows to move with care, and keep the rope taut between them,' wrote Fanny, with her usual invective, 'adding each time, that if one mis-step were to be made, we should all perish'. The Workmans fancied they were educating the Baltis in 'mountaincraft', but the local men had their own cause for concern, finding their fates bound to three tightly wound westerners, so intent on putting them- selves in harm's way.

All morning they climbed. Zurbriggen led, cutting steps as they zigzagged up two thousand feet of steep snowfields and crevassed ice-slopes. The ascent was not especially difficult, being on the shady side of the mountain, but they suffered bitterly in the cold. When the sun finally found them, it was at the foot of a final arête, four hundred feet of steep ice at an angle of around sixty degrees. One last push, and at ten o'clock they gained the summit of what Fanny christened 'Mount Bullock Workman'.

On the Siegfriedhorn, Fanny had improved on Annie Peck's record by a little over one hundred feet. Four days later, she stood at what their aneroid barometers gave as 19,450 feet. She had not only broken her own record, she had put one thousand feet of daylight between her and her closest rival.

The time had come to move on from Avalanche Camp. Within days the expedition had crossed the Skoro La into the Shigar valley, as the Workmans attempted one last mountain. It was the highest peak of a massif at the northernmost end of the range and, unlike the Siegfriedhorn or Mount Bullock Workman, it already had a name. It was called Koser Gunge.

Zurbriggen was left to reconnoitre their route up the mountain, while Fanny and Hunter scoured the surrounding villages for porters and provisions. Word went out that only the youngest and strongest men should come forward but 'when the applicants for loads appeared', wrote Fanny, 'several centenarians were found well to the front'. Fanny was pleasantly surprised, though, to find that these men 'did as good a work as the younger coolies'. The Workmans soon had a camp at 17,900 feet, confident that if the fine weather held, they could summit the next day.

The ascents of the Siegfriedhorn and Mount Bullock Workman had been mainly over ice and snow. Starting out on 25 August, however, the Workmans were met by 'rock scrambling *de premier ordre*'. They crawled along narrow ledges and forced their way up slippery chimneys, intricate rockwork demanding climbing of a more gymnastic kind. They gained height fast and, after an entertaining two and a half hours, hauled themselves over the lip of a large snow-filled basin.

They had hoped they might see the summit. Instead, all that stood ahead was a ridge disappearing into oncoming cloud. Starting upwards, they felt a cold wind. The snow lay deeper beneath their feet and the heat of the sun was soon a distant memory. 'The clouds had by now covered most of the distant peaks, and the outlook was for storm, but no one spoke of retreat; we had worked too hard to do that unless absolutely driven to it. And still no peak.'

By noon they had reached a height of around twenty thousand feet. Winds of twenty-five miles an hour swirled around as they waited for Zurbriggen to tread down each new step in the slanting snow. Fanny started shouting at the guide, her words lost in the storm, telling him she could not feel her ice-axe. Hearing her at last, Zurbriggen stopped and rubbed her hands until circulation was restored. When she was able to resume the climb Fanny looked up and saw an end in sight. There, still some distance away, was the summit of Koser Gunge.

This was it. The first female mountaineer above twenty thousand feet, Fanny was contending with conditions as bad as anything Zurbriggen had encountered in the Karakoram. Their situation was made more urgent when, as they zigzagged up a steep ice slant leading to the massif's highest peak, one of the porters lost heart. Reaching his limit somewhere in the thick of the storm, he turned his back on his fellow climbers, and sat down in the snow.

One by one, the Europeans felt a dead weight come onto the rope. Turning to see what was going on, Zurbriggen, wild-eyed, waved his hands in the air and bellowed profanities. His message got through – the man must get to his feet or remove himself from the rope. The others waited, resting on their ice-axes, as the porter slowly untied himself, then began to trudge back down the mountainside.

One more push, and at three o'clock they were standing on a cornice of blue ice at the summit of Koser Gunge. 'All the four winds of heaven seemed to be holding a *tamasha*,' wrote Fanny. 'It was no place for us, weak and frozen to the last enduring point, to stop to make careful observations or to try to leave any record. There was not even a pipe for Zurbriggen, and we were quite ready, after stamping our feet for a few minutes on the ice at the highest point, to start down again.'

By going to the 20,997-foot summit of Koser Gunge, Fanny had done more than just cement her hold on the women's altitude record. She had gone shoulder-to-shoulder with the likes of Martin Conway and Albert Mummery, seasoned alpinists who had led their expeditions to similar heights. She would return to Europe one of the most decorated Himalayan mountaineers – man or woman – of her day.

Eckenstein woke to find a uniformed police officer sitting at the foot of his bed.

English mountaineer Oscar Eckenstein.
Illustrator unknown.

CHAPTER 14

Rough Diamonds

In 1892 Oscar Eckenstein had offered a withering verdict on the small horse-drawn carts used by Conway's party en route to the Karakoram. 'An "ekka" is an invention of the devil,' he had written, 'a two-wheeled contrivance devoid of any kind of apology for springs.' He continued, 'Stability is chiefly distinguished by its absence. What with jolting and the uncomfortable position one is screwed into, it is far and away the worst means of progression that I have ever attempted.'

Ten years later Eckenstein was back in Punjab at the head of an expedition of his own. He and his party were bound for Srinagar, but all was not going to plan. Coming to Rawalpindi, they found roadworthy ekkas in short supply. Now it was Guy Knowles, a young friend of Eckenstein's, who came to know the truth of this particular mode of conveyance. 'Never travel in an ekka,' ran a local saying, noted down in his journal, 'with less than one wheel.'

The Europeans left Rawalpindi six hours behind schedule, covering twenty-five miles before they stopped for the night at the village of Tret. There, at the dawn of the next day, came a startling new development. Eckenstein woke to find a uniformed police officer sitting at the foot of his bed. The young man informed Eckenstein that he and his companions were being detained pending the arrival of Rawalpindi's deputy-commissioner.

When the deputy-commissioner appeared, he revealed that Eckenstein had been refused permission to enter Kashmir. Eckenstein demanded to know why, but, offered nothing by way of an explanation, all he could do was send Knowles and the others on ahead. He instructed them to go as far as Srinagar then to await him there, while he went back to Rawalpindi – all the way to government headquarters at Delhi if necessary – to find out what the devil was going on.

Guy Knowles was the obvious choice to deputise for Eckenstein. The 22-year-old had taken a leading role in financing the expedition and had worked for months preparing for their departure from England. Instead, as they carried on to Srinagar, it was another member of the party who took the lead.

Eckenstein had been at Wasdale Head four years earlier when he first met Aleister Crowley, then just twenty-three years old. Crowley had been climbing since the age of sixteen and was ready for a mentor like Eckenstein, who brought a physical and intellectual rigour to alpinism, along with stories of his travels in the mystical East. 'Eckenstein recognized from the first the value of my natural instincts for mountaineering,' wrote Crowley, 'and also that I was one of the silliest young asses alive'.

The two spent a summer climbing together in the Alps, then met up in Mexico in 1900 to attempt a number of the country's larger volcanoes. For three weeks they explored the sheer ice-walls and precipices of Iztaccihuatl, surviving the final few days on nothing but champagne and Danish butter. Later they travelled to Guadalajara, where they were forced to abandon a climb when the soles of their shoes began to melt. Finally, they trudged up steep slopes of loose volcanic debris to claim the 17,694-foot summit of Popocatépetl, following in the centuries-old footsteps of Diego de Ordaz, the Spanish conquistador who had all but climbed the mountain in 1519.

Finding they could comfortably withstand altitudes of seventeen thousand feet or more, Eckenstein and Crowley turned their thoughts to the Himalaya. Crowley travelled on from Mexico to Asia, while Eckenstein returned to London, where he had lunch with Knowles. The two had climbed together in the Alps and, though Knowles had nothing of Eckenstein's experience or Crowley's raw talent, he was keen, capable and extremely wealthy. By December 1901 Eckenstein and Knowles had rented a workshop, where they packed provisions and equipment for transportation to Bombay.

At the same time, Eckenstein looked for others to join them, searching for a particular kind of mountaineer. At the heart of his partnership with Crowley was their belief in 'guideless climbing'. The two did not subscribe to the orthodoxy of the time: that the correct way for a gentleman to climb a mountain was in the company of a professional guide. 'The average Alpine clubman qualifies by paying guides to haul him up a few hackneyed peaks,' wrote Crowley. 'Mountaineering differs from other sports in one important respect. A man cannot obtain a reputation at cricket or football by hiring professionals to play for him.'

Of course, where the Himalaya was concerned, there were no professional guides to speak of, not in a mould any European would recognise. In their absence, a good French or Swiss man was thought better than nothing. William Graham, Martin Conway, Fanny Bullock Workman – all had travelled to India accompanied by Alpine guides and had been more successful for it. Only Mummery had attempted a guideless ascent in the Himalaya. To those who argued against dispensing with the services of trained professionals, Mummery's fateful exploits were a case in point.

Eckenstein had been surprised, however, by how difficult he had found it to recruit fellow mountaineers. Among the members of the Alpine Club – even those known to favour climbing without guides – he had drawn a complete blank. Widening his search, he managed to enlist the two Austrians, Heinrich Pfannl and Viktor Wessely, with an ascent of Mont Blanc among their impressive record of guideless climbs. They were joined by Dr Jules Jacot-Guillarmod, a Swiss army officer who had bagged a number of notable peaks, among them the Dom and the Monte Rosa, all without professional help.

Now, arriving at Srinagar, the five Europeans who made up the expedition were doing without more than just guides. They had lost their leader and, though Crowley had assumed the role with characteristic swagger, they would not be going any further until they received word from Eckenstein himself. Knowles used the time to make what preparations he could, while Crowley looked into Eckenstein's detention for himself. 'We pumped the bigwigs of Kashmir, and we sifted the rumours of the Bazaar,' wrote Crowley, 'but beyond learning that Eckenstein was a Prussian spy and a cold-blooded murderer, we obtained little information of importance.'

Turned back at Tret, Oscar Eckenstein returned to Rawalpindi in search of answers. He interrogated every official he could find, pressing them on why he had been denied permission to enter Kashmir, to no avail. The rank of the officials rose, but their answer remained the same – the Englishman had been detained on 'Government orders'.

Eckenstein travelled from one place to another until, on a train from Calcutta to Simla, he found he was sharing a carriage with a high-ranking member of the Indian government. He learned that an allegation had been made against him – 'that he had misbehaved at Gilgit and in Kashmir in 1893'. The year *after* the Conway expedition.

Eckenstein had wasted enough time. He went directly to Delhi and confronted the Viceroy of India, Lord Curzon himself. Eckenstein pointed out that he had been living in South Hampstead at the time of the alleged transgression, to which his mother would willingly attest. This left Curzon with no alternative but to rescind the restrictions; to the question of who had made the accusation against Eckenstein, the Viceroy remained tight-lipped.

Crowley had a theory of his own. 'We could not but connect it with Eckenstein's quarrel with Conway in 1892,' he wrote, convinced Conway had been the source of whatever allegations had been made. 'I remain unrepentant that the incident was the result of the unmanly jealousy and petty intrigues of the insects who envied him, complicated by official muddle.'

Conway had motive. He had once talked up his prospects of attempting K2, the world's second-highest mountain, but had been forced to settle for 'Pioneer Peak' – or, as Eckenstein put it, 'a minor point' on one of Baltoro Kangri's ridges. Now Eckenstein was back in the Karakoram, at the head of the largest European climbing party yet to travel to India, with an objective to match. He intended to climb K2.

Eckenstein raced north, reaching Srinagar to find the expedition almost ready to depart. All their provisions and equipment had been loaded into *kiltas*, lightweight lidded wicker baskets, and 150 Balti porters had been recruited to shoulder them. All that remained was to collect their *parwana*, a letter giving them authority to requisition fresh porters and food at villages along the way. Then, a fortnight behind schedule, they started north.

Eckenstein knew how difficult it would be to keep track of the porters and their loads, so arranged for numbers to be painted on the kiltas and tickets issued to the bearers, who were only to be paid once their load had been delivered and inspected. 'This involved a considerable amount of work with a hundred and odd loads,' wrote Knowles, 'but amply repaid itself in that we had no difficulties of any kind with our men who were all willing and contented.'

Eckenstein knew, too, how important it was to look after the porters themselves. He had run what passed for a surgery on the Conway expedition and now it was Jacot-Guillarmod, a qualified physician, who tended to the men. The Swiss proved himself a true devotee of the Hippocratic oath, operating an open clinic at every village they came to, treating whatever injuries or afflictions were brought before him. Knowles described how at one village a dropsical man was carried to the doctor and, after a short operation, 'walked away on his own legs. To the natives the thing was incredible: without doubt it appeared a miracle to them.'

Jacot-Guillarmod was more than just a medic. An avid photographer, he had brought his new Vérascope stereoscopic camera with him – it was in action from the moment they made port at Bombay. And, just as Jacot-Guillarmod was keeping a pictorial record of their travels, Knowles showed a corresponding devotion to his journal. The villages they came to along the Indus valley were 'miracles of fertility', wrote Knowles, describing how the Europeans were welcomed with gifts of tea, cakes and dried apricots, and festooned with wildflowers when they left.

If there was a fault in Knowles's account of the expedition, it lay on the side of omission. Nowhere in his journal do we find reference to the beatings Aleister Crowley routinely inflicted on the Balti porters. It was left to Crowley himself to boast about it, describing how he grabbed men by the beard – a grievous insult to a Muslim – then whipped them with his belt. 'The result was that I never had the slightest difficulties with natives in India ever afterwards,' wrote Crowley. 'I had forced them to respect us, which, with an Indian, is the first step to acquiring his love.'

Avoiding this unpleasantness, Knowles exercised the discretion of a true English 'gentleman', reserving his harshest language for the local tea. Brewed using butter and salt, it was 'what one would expect train oil to taste like,' he wrote, 'after it had trickled through a farmyard'. Even then, he was soon drinking it daily.

At the end of May they reached Askole, the last village in the Braldu valley, visited by Adolph Schlagintweit, Haversham Godwin-Austen, the Conway expedition and the Workmans before them. 'North, South, and East are big mountains and the ice,' wrote Knowles, who thought it 'a very world's end of a place'.

Ten years after turning back at the gateway to the most extraordinary mountain system on earth, Eckenstein had returned at the head of an expedition that appeared to be dealing well with the rigours of Himalayan travel. He was so pleased with the performance of the porters he made them a gift of two sheep. 'They made a regular *tamasha* of it,' wrote Knowles, 'and the rest of the village joined in and sang far into the night.'

Only the Austrians were giving Eckenstein cause for concern. Pfannl and Wessely had been racing ahead from the moment they left Srinagar, 'always boiling over', wrote Crowley, 'to exhibit their prowess'. They would march on together then, when the others caught up, make a great show of announcing how long they had been waiting. Even at Askole, where the Europeans had the opportunity to rest for a few days, Pfannl and Wessely were off racing up nearby peaks. They returned from one outing brimming with excitement, having stolen a first glimpse of K2. 'Such a big fellow', said Pfannl, 'that the others scarcely reach his waist'.

Pfannl claimed he and Wessely were just maintaining their fitness ahead of everything to come – an essential part of the process of acclimatisation. Others were not so sure. Crowley doubted whether Europeans could ever truly 'acclimatise' in the Himalaya, climbing to heights where their brains were starved of oxygen and their bodies crippled by cold. 'To talk of acclimatisation is to adopt the psychology of the man who trained his horse gradually to live on a single straw a day,' wrote Crowley, 'and would have revolutionised our system of nutrition, if the balky brute had not been aggravating enough to die.'

For Crowley, all the Austrians would achieve was to make themselves unwell. To his mind, the secret to climbing a mountain like K2 was timing. 'The only thing you can do is to lay in a stock of energy... and jump back out of its reach, so to speak, before it can take its revenge.' Happily, a fresh stock of energy had lately presented itself, in the form of a colony of blue rock pigeons nesting in the rockface near Askole. This 'afforded us some sport in the mornings and evenings', wrote Knowles, 'and gave us a change in the menu from the eternal mutton and chicken'. They were right to make the most of it – Askole was the last place they could expect to eat well. All their food would be carried from there.

With porterage at a premium, Eckenstein limited the Europeans to forty pounds of personal possessions. Crowley pushed back. He had brought several large volumes of poetry with him – vellum-bound to protect them from the elements – and insisted they go as high on K2 as he did. This maddened Eckenstein, who appealed to his friend to see reason. 'I would rather bear physical starvation than intellectual starvation,' responded Crowley, with a preening pomposity almost to be admired. 'Either I take my books with me or I leave the expedition.'

His bluff called, Eckenstein backed down. They were about to
enter a decisive phase of the expedition and Crowley had an important part to play. He would be leading the first of three parties up
the Baltoro glacier, twenty-two Baltis carrying everything needed to
establish a camp at the foot of K2. A day behind him would be sixty
more porters led by Pfannl and Wessely, and a day behind them,
Jacot-Guillarmod and Knowles with fifty-eight men. It was masterful
man-management from Eckenstein, who knew Crowley would see
hell freeze over before he allowed the Austrians to catch him, and that
Knowles would strain every sinew to keep pace. Eckenstein would
remain at Askole, following behind once he received word that all
was proceeding as planned.

Crowley left Askole on the ninth of June, the Austrians on the tenth,
and behind came Knowles and Jacot-Guillarmod, facing ten marches
to the foot of K2. Ten days, venturing deeper into the ice world of the
Karakoram. At first, they marched under rain, sleet and snow, everything
lost in a mantle of cloud. All they could see was the glacier ahead, covered
by an undulating expanse of broken stone. It stretched away 'as far as
the eye can reach', wrote Knowles, 'like a series of waves thrown up by
a boiling rapid'. Jacot-Guillarmod's photographs showed them adrift on
this ocean of stone, picking their way from rock to rock, from campsite
to campsite, the porters a blur.

Then came the mornings when they woke to find the sky brilliantly
clear and saw the mountains towering above. They got their first view
of 'the giants' – Gasherbrum, 'towering up majestically at the end of
the glacier', Broad Peak beside it, and Masherbrum, 'a wonderful maze
of hanging glacier and rock ridge with a snow capped rocky summit'.
Further up, they saw the Mustagh Tower, spiry and spectacular, and
Mitre Peak, 'made of a wedge so thin', wrote Knowles, 'at every gust of
wind one unconsciously expects it to topple over'. They were nearing
'Concordia', the junction of the Baltoro and Godwin-Austen glaciers.
To the southeast was Conway's 'Golden Throne' then, as they rounded
a spur of rock on the north side of the Baltoro, 'so gradually did the
monster Chogo-Ri appear'.

'Chogo-Ri' was, the European members of the expedition had dis-covered, what the Baltis called K2. Crowley embraced the name. It symbolised the perverse affinity he felt with the local men – when he wasn't seizing their beards and beating them – and his corresponding disdain for the various institutions of the British government. The joke, though, was on him. *Chogo* was the Balti word for 'mountain', and *ri* meant 'big'. When asked, 'What is that?', the porters were giving a literal answer to what, from their perspective, probably seemed like a rather stupid question.

And it *was* a big mountain. Ten miles distant, 'radiant and resplendent in the clear morning air', it formed a colossal pyramid of ice and stone. Knowles and Jacot-Guillarmod would be two days marching up the Godwin-Austen Glacier towards it. Then, on the morning of 20 June, they saw some small shapes ahead, tiny triangles of shadow with figures moving between them. They had done it. There, among the tents, they found Crowley waiting, Pfannl and Wessely too. And there, towering over them all, was the southeast face of K2.

The snow fell. It fell during the daytime, a fine snow that soaked them through the moment they stepped outside. It fell at night, swirled around by fierce winds, invading their tents when the flaps came loose. It fell until avalanches thundered, one after another, down the valley sides; until all they could hope for was 'to keep as warm as possible in one's sleeping bag and sally forth for food in the lulls of the storm'. And even then, sheltering in their tents, as night fell and the temperature dropped, the moisture in the men's breath condensed and froze, and gathered on the canvas overhead. Until, *inside* their tents, the snow fell.

Very occasionally there came a tantalising interlude, as the clouds parted and the sun's rays poured through. They rushed outside to arrange their sodden clothes in these precious pockets of sunlight, only for the clouds to close back up again and the snow-filled heavens to reopen. Back inside their tents, they lay for hours reading or playing chess, the warmth seeping from their bodies, melting the ground below. Soon they

were lying in pools of freezing water, unable to reposition themselves –
or their tents, so long as the snowstorm raged.

Technically speaking, this was 'Camp X', the tenth camp out of Askole.
They knew it as 'Camp Misery'. Crowley had situated it in the middle
of the glacier because it put them a safe distance from the avalanches
raking the steep valley sides, but it left them brutally exposed. Now,
caught in a snowstorm that began almost the moment they arrived, all
they could do was await Eckenstein, at what would be their base camp
for the climbing effort to come.

On 27 June, more than a week after Crowley had established Camp
X, Eckenstein arrived. He had been bringing up the rear all the way
from Askole, coordinating an endless relay of porters and supplies. His
progress had been slowed by the same foul weather, but he had taken
advantage of a break in the storm to complete the last march up the
Godwin-Austen glacier. Now, with his arrival at Camp X and the good
weather holding, they could contemplate a first push up K2.

For Crowley, it was not a moment too soon. Hemmed in at Camp X,
he had found what he believed was the best route to K2's summit. He
favoured an ascent by the southeast ridge, up a giant spur that loomed
large over their tiny camp on the glacier. He was convinced the ridge
would 'go' and that it offered by far the most direct route to the upper
reaches of K2.

A meeting was held and, with Eckenstein feeling unwell, it was proposed that Crowley, Pfannl and Jacot-Guillarmod should go – a fitting
vanguard for the most international Himalayan climbing expedition
yet. 'At this point', wrote Knowles, 'Wessely made some remarks at
his non-inclusion… as unreasonable as they were unsportsmanlike.'
Wessely evidently believed he and Pfannl made up the expedition's
strongest rope, and was not afraid to say so. For Crowley, it was 'an
intolerably bad piece of sportsmanship', from a man to whom he had
taken a visceral dislike. 'None of us had ever seen such a perfect pig,'
wrote Crowley. 'He was very greedy and very myopic. Explorers are
not squeamish, but we had to turn our heads away when Wessely
started to eat.'

With the men at loggerheads, the elements intervened; it began snowing again. The most they would accomplish over the days to come was to explore the upper reaches of the glacier on skis. Pfannl, Wessely and Jacot-Guillarmod ventured up to the head of the valley, where they took a first proper look at the northeast ridge of K2, rising from a col they named 'Windy Gap'. They returned speaking of a 'gentle snow slope' on the northeast side, suggesting an easier path to the mountain's summit. All preferred it to Crowley's spur, which menaced Camp X with its hulking shadow.

Eckenstein agreed. Early on 1 July, with the snow in good condition, Pfannl and Wessely set off for Windy Gap, accompanied by a small team of porters. That evening the four Europeans left at Camp X threw a party. It was Guy Knowles's twenty-third birthday, so to celebrate they enjoyed a meal of soup, sausages and biscuits, washed down with a bottle of whisky. For Crowley, they were also celebrating being 'rid of the Austrians'. In reality, the expedition was now riven in two.

Two days later a porter arrived at Camp X, one of Pfannl and Wessely's men sent down with a note. The Austrians had established Camp XI at a height of around twenty thousand feet. Then came a bombshell. They had seen immense difficulties waiting higher up the mountain – more than the porters would be able to overcome. They were all for giving up any thought of K2's summit, ready to settle for a new world altitude record instead.

Crowley had long been convinced that the Austrians were 'totally incapable of realising the magnitude of the task we had set out to perform', so it came as little surprise to find them baulking at the reality. He made preparations to set off for Camp XI immediately. He wanted to see for himself what lay ahead.

Then, just as he was about to depart, it began to snow.

Camp XI might have afforded Pfannl and Wessely a little more shelter, but the storm hit hard just the same. As the wind strengthened, it whipped the snow up into a gale-force blizzard, blowing all through 'an abominable night' and deep into the next day. The Austrians knew that, with so much fresh snow on the mountain, it would be days before it was safe to climb. They were in for a long wait.

It was fine. The two men had climbed many mountains together, had waited out many storms. They were, at least, spared the endless barbs of Aleister Crowley. From what they had seen, he was an intensely unkind man, finding the tiniest faults in others, then prising them open with his crowbar of a tongue.

Their note to the camp below had been clear enough. Yes, it would have been a fine thing to return to Europe with K2 in their pockets, but the men had now seen the mountain for themselves. They might be able to climb the northeast ridge, but the porters would not stand a chance. No porters meant no food or equipment beyond what the Europeans could carry. Instead, Pfannl and Wessely had now set their minds on climbing a few thousand feet higher, to claim the record – not just for the expedition but for themselves.

At last, the storm passed and the snow hardened. On 10 July, ten days after the Austrians had struck out by themselves, Crowley and Jacot-Guillarmod joined them at Camp XI – Crowley dubbed it 'Camp Despair' – followed a day later by Eckenstein and Knowles. On the morning of 12 July, the six Europeans awoke together at Camp XI. It was the last night they would spend together on the mountain.

First thing the next morning, Pfannl and Wessely were off again, taking porters, a tent and some provisions, and disappearing up a side valley. Later that day they established Camp XII, at a height of around 21,000 feet, only for the 'execrable weather' to return. Hemmed in once again, they could only wait.

After a further two days, a porter arrived at Camp XI with a note from the Austrians. It took the form of a shopping list – they were demanding twenty-two different foodstuffs, many of them things that would have to be retrieved from the camp below.

But, even as those at Camp XI were digesting this extraordinary request, a second note arrived. It was from Wessely. Pfannl, all of a sudden, had fallen seriously ill.

Dr Jacot-Guillarmod was the first up to Camp XII, but it was Crowley who saved Heinrich Pfannl's life.

Crowley had been right to warn the Austrians about the dangers of overtraining. He had been right, too, about the impossibility of ever fully acclimatising – it is accepted today that above 26,000 feet the human body will eventually die. (He had been right about situating Camp X out of the reach of avalanches and, though it would be half a century before anybody proved it, he was right about the most viable route to K2's summit.) When Jacot-Guillarmod arrived back at Camp XI with the stricken Pfannl, it was Crowley who diagnosed pulmonary edema.

The Austrian was moving under his own steam, but with fluid filling his lungs, preventing him from obtaining sufficient oxygen. A more obvious diagnosis would have been pneumonia. 'Many climbers have died because the drugs used against pneumonia did absolutely nothing for pulmonary edema,' wrote the mountaineer Galen Roswell. 'Crowley's group did exactly the right thing by removing Pfannl immediately to lower elevation. The isolation of edema from pneumonia in Crowley's account was long before its time and one of the earliest ever recorded.' Crowley understood that the best thing for the Austrian was to get him down to a lower altitude as quickly as possible, so after a short rest Pfannl, Wessely and Jacot-Guillarmod carried on down to the lower camps.

This left Eckenstein, Crowley and Knowles with the mountain to themselves. Free to contemplate their own attempt on K2, they cast their eyes up the southeast ridge, thinking they would go for the record. One constant, however, was the abysmal weather. In came the snow once again. With the end of July looming and the monsoon perhaps only days away, their last window of opportunity began to close.

Driven back into their tents, Crowley took a turn for the worse. He had contracted malaria some months earlier and relapsed into a deep and prolonged fever. Confined to the tent he shared with Guy Knowles, Crowley was caught in the throes of some wild hallucinations. All of a sudden, he pulled a gun on his young tent-mate.

History does not record why Crowley felt the need to draw his revolver. Knowles, discreet to a fault, does not mention the incident in his journal. He would only speak about it later on in life, describing how he disarmed Crowley with a knee to the groin, then took possession of the gun. The incident was over as quickly as it had begun, but it would take on a strange significance – the defining moment of an expedition remembered as one of the more sensational failures in the history of Himalayan mountaineering.

And a failure it was. Jacot-Guillarmod would claim an altitude record, insisting he and Wessely had reconnoitred as high as 23,000 feet. The details he provides, however, are vague and no more credible than the ascent he conspicuously discounts; that of William Graham, to nearer 24,000 feet, on Kabru in 1883. Not to be outdone, Crowley staked a claim on a record of his own. 'I had been altogether sixty-eight days on the glacier,' he wrote, 'two days longer than any other member of the party. It was another world's record,' he went on. 'I hope I may be allowed to die in peace with it.'

Eckenstein, by this point, had accepted defeat, even before he received word of a cholera epidemic in the Braldu valley. Their best line of retreat now lay over a treacherous 18,000-foot pass. They would face a stiff test just to make it home in one piece.

Along the way, the expedition would divide and divide again. First it was Pfannl and Wessely being formally ejected 'for sundry reasons', namely that they had stolen and eaten two whole sheep, in what Knowles described as 'a stupendous performance'. At Askole the rump of the expedition divided again. Crowley and Jacot-Guillarmod went on ahead, rafting along the river then carrying on back to Srinagar. Eckenstein and Knowles followed, their temperance tested when they arrived at the Wular Lake to find that their friends had commandeered both the vessels ordered for the expedition. They were left camped on the shore, eaten alive by mosquitoes as they awaited boats of their own.

Finally, on 7 September, Eckenstein and Knowles walked the last four miles into Srinagar. They remained there for the rest of the month, idly touring the markets, an unassuming partnership finishing the expedition as it had begun. They had travelled a long way together since those busy months packing cases in a borrowed workshop. Now it was souvenirs and keepsakes they were packing, ready for the journey home.

More than half a century would pass before, in 1960, a man named David Dean visited Guy Knowles, now almost eighty years old, at his home in London. Dean, a librarian at the Royal Commonwealth Society, was researching an article for the *Alpine Journal* – a retrospective of the life and climbing career of Oscar Eckenstein. The writer had been struck by the fact that no obituary had appeared following Eckenstein's death in 1921 and that so little was known about this influential figure.

Dean described entering 'a house full of treasures; a Degas bronze, two Rodins, ten Whistlers, and a magnificent Guardi sketch'. Knowles recalled being with his father when he had bought the Guardi, and a Titian, for twelve shillings and sixpence apiece. Had he looked carefully Dean might also have noticed an old Colt revolver on Knowles's mantelpiece – the same gun that had once belonged to Aleister Crowley.

'Mr Knowles, whose father used to shoot snipe on Chelsea marshes and whose great-aunt Carrie danced at the Waterloo Ball, was the source of some entertaining personal detail about Eckenstein,' wrote Dean. As he spoke, Knowles addressed the question of why Eckenstein had been refused permission to enter Kashmir, casting new light on the controversy that had hamstrung the 1902 expedition at the outset. 'His view of it, though more temperately expressed, inclined towards that of Crowley,' wrote Dean. 'That Conway, by this time president of the Alpine Club, interposed to put obstacles in Eckenstein's way, and that Curzon… did not relent until faced with a threat to expose the whole story to the *Daily Telegraph*.'

If Conway had been afraid of what the Eckenstein expedition might mean for his Himalayan legacy, he was right to be. Knowles, marching up the Baltoro glacier, had been struck by the many errors contained on Conway's map. 'The more I see of the country', wrote Knowles, 'the less I think of this map which is intended to represent it. The inaccuracies are great: far greater indeed than those in the Indian Survey map which it aspires to improve upon.' Likewise, it was Knowles who had learned that some of their men were veterans of the 1892 expedition. Conway's porters had 'suffered rather severely from cold and insufficient food arrangements', wrote Knowles. 'One or two died and many were badly frostbitten.'

But Conway's worst fear, surely, was that Eckenstein would succeed where he had failed, by reaching a record-breaking height on K2. And on that count, looking at the lead-up to the 1902 expedition, Conway dealt a telling blow.

Eckenstein had known he would need the help of other mountaineers if he was to have any hope of success. Pfannl and Wessely had not been his first choice, far from it. The Austrians were fine alpinists, but Eckenstein would have preferred for Englishmen to make up the party. And yet, whoever he approached, nobody was interested.

Looking back, it is easy to see the hand of Conway in this – the new president of the Alpine Club, warning its members away. Eckenstein and Crowley were seen as mavericks at the club, but they were also respected for their talents. Tom Longstaff, a future Himalayan legend, considered Eckenstein 'a rough diamond, but a diamond nonetheless'; for Longstaff, Crowley was 'a fine climber, if an unconventional one'. Norman Collie, veteran of the 1895 Nanga Parbat expedition, had climbed with both men. Had Eckenstein talked either into joining them, who knows how high they might have gone up the slopes of K2?

Higher, in any event, than the camp above Windy Gap where Pfannl and Wessely's hopes had been extinguished, and with them those of the expedition as a whole. An expedition that had demonstrated Eckenstein's formidable powers of problem-solving and organisation, Crowley's uncanny ability to read a mountain and the dangers it posed, the climbing prowess of the two Austrians, the myriad talents of Jacot-Guillarmod, the inexhaustible good nature of young Guy Knowles. But that, owing to the meddling of Martin Conway, never exceeded the sum of its individualistic parts.

Zurbriggen was 'a fool about taking care of himself',
Fanny went on, 'and an ass in most respects'.

'Two Record Climbers', from *Ice World of the Himalaya* by Fanny Bullock
Workman (1900), showing Swiss guide Matthias Zurbriggen and American
mountaineer Fanny Bullock Workman. Illustrator unknown.

CHAPTER 15

Monarchs of a Void

A lone black bird waited at the site of Foggy Camp when the expedition first arrived. It was the only sign of life at the head of the Chogo Lungma glacier, making, wrote Fanny Bullock Workman, 'an uncanny impression on our minds', that 'served to accentuate the almost terrifying desolation and loneliness of the place'. Moments earlier an avalanche had thundered across the glacier behind them, 'with a roar such as might be produced by fifty trains running abreast at high speed, leaving in its path a chaos that must be seen to be appreciated'. This was a place of dark omens and devastating forces.

It was 1902, and Fanny and Hunter were back in the Karakoram. They had returned at the head of a new expedition and, for all the acrimony of 1899, Matthias Zurbriggen was with them. An Italian, Giuseppe Muller, was acting as their porter and a fifth European had joined the party – the topographer Dr Karl Oestreich. The Workmans had engaged Oestreich to help make the case for themselves as serious geographers, doing work of real scientific value. The task at hand? To produce a comprehensive map of the Chogo Lungma glacier.

Unlike the various glaciers mapped and made famous by Conway in 1892, the Chogo Lungma was still largely unexplored. In 1861 Haversham Godwin-Austen had ventured a few miles along its left bank then, two years later, an Englishman named Frederick Drew claimed to have marched fifteen miles up the ice, searching for minerals on behalf of the Maharajah of Kashmir. The Chogo Lungma, though, stretched to almost twice that length, lying twenty-seven miles from foot to head. When the Workmans arrived in 1902, at least half of it – and, to their minds, the more interesting half – lay unexplored.

A photograph of Foggy Camp, taken on Fanny's beloved Kodak camera, shows three small tents pitched in a swirl of grey and shape-less isolation. Arriving there, the Workmans had completed their main objective – to explore the length of the glacier. Now they could turn their attention to its various tributaries, flowing from among the surrounding peaks. At the head of one of those – they named it Basin Glacier – was the Bhayakara Col.

The Bhayakara Col was not a mountain; it was a saddle along the eastern ridge of a mountain that 'might afford a view,' Fanny wrote, 'of what lay beyond'. At an altitude of 19,260 feet, it did not rise to a record-breaking height; Fanny had twice gone higher in 1899, first on Mount Bullock Workman then, days later, on Koser Gunge. The ascent of the Bhayakara Col would, however, take Fanny and Hunter to new heights of danger. It would test them, like no other climb, as mountaineers.

They set out at daybreak on 21 August, with Zurbriggen and the porter Muller making up a party of four. Zurbriggen guided them through a maze of crevasses, then up 'the still steeper debris of a recently fallen avalanche', until they arrived at 'a wide bergschrund, over which only a single insecure snow-bridge was found'. The night had been cold and clear and, as they started up the steep 'avalanche-scored' ice-wall, they found the snow frozen hard and in good condition.

For three hours they climbed. Zurbriggen led, cutting steps in the ice, except where they were able to take to small patches of bare rock. They moved in long zigzags, coming to a final sixty-degree incline of smooth, solid ice, angling upwards against the vertical rock ridge above. They had hoped the rock would afford a few good handholds, but it was the worst kind of sandstone. Weather-worn and badly decayed, it was separated from the ice by an awkward gap.

To reach the col the climbers faced a long traverse to the left. 'It was exceedingly dangerous and slow,' wrote Fanny, 'and Zurbriggen feared starting an avalanche.' All the time, there beneath was 'a sheer sweep of almost 2,000 feet of precipitous wall'. 'To anyone inclined to vertigo', she went on, 'the downward view… would have been appalling.'

At one o'clock, six hours after starting out, they gained the crest of the col. The view was a disappointment – 'a vast trefoil basin, surrounded by massive, jagged mountains, which cut off all view beyond' – and, with 'barely standing room' at the top of the saddle, they did not stay long.

'We returned slowly and painfully along the treacherous edge in the pitiless heat,' wrote Fanny. It was only as they began to move down the ice-wall that they understood how dangerous their situation had become. In a heat that was 'almost unendurable', the steps Zurbriggen had cut that morning were being turned to mush. He was the first to speak.

'This is a joke,' said Zurbriggen. 'We are not getting down today.'

'I never before saw him thrown off his balance,' Hunter wrote of Zurbriggen's outburst. The guide knew, though, that there was no question of staying where they were, crowded together on the ice-wall, the mountainside melting beneath their feet. So, after some kola biscuit and a short rest, they resumed their descent.

Zurbriggen had read the danger well. They had gone a few steps when Giuseppe Muller slipped and fell.

Zurbriggen was ready. Last on the rope, he already had the shaft of his ice-axe buried in a crevasse, the rope looped twice around it. It was as good an anchor as he could have hoped, but if the Workmans were pulled free by Muller there was no guarantee it would hold.

It did not come to that. Hunter, seeing Muller slip, took hold of 'a small ice projection'. He felt the porter's weight come onto the rope. His feet held.

Muller took a moment to recover his footing. Then, to Hunter's relief, he felt a little slack come onto the rope.

It was understandable that Muller had fallen, but he would not be spared a volley of abuse from Zurbriggen. 'We went on,' wrote Fanny, 'but the feeling of danger was tremendous'.

The descent took five hours. The way Hunter told it, it was only *todesmut* – a German word describing anything from 'true heroism' to 'a total disregard for one's safety' – that had seen them down alive. He might have given a little more credit to Zurbriggen. The guide had called on all his experience to get them back to their tents at Crevasse Camp, 'none the worse for the climb, except bruised hands and burned faces'.

'Thus ended this adventurous ascent to a col,' Hunter wrote in his journal, 'which we named the Bhayakara Col, from the Sanskrit word for perilous; Zurbriggen called it the most dangerous one he had ever made.'

The members of the Eckenstein expedition were elsewhere in the Karakoram that year, failing in their attempt to climb K2, hamstrung by the same awful weather that limited the Workmans' ambitions. Besides their ascent of the Bhayakara Col, Fanny and Hunter summited four minor peaks, none over eighteen thousand feet. 'Cornice Peak' was the pick, named after the overhanging edge of snow at its summit. The ascent was 'worth the candle', wrote Fanny, 'in spite of the fact that its technical difficulties had proved greater than its height'. Even before the season was over, Fanny was making plans to return the next year. From Cornice Peak, she and Hunter had looked northwest to see three larger peaks towering over the head of the Chogo Lungma. Arriving back in Srinagar in 1903, they were intent on climbing them.

Zurbriggen would not be joining them. The Workmans had employed him for two seasons of Himalayan travel and, for all they had accomplished, things had not been easy. Fanny was too 'proper' a person to share her feelings about him in her books; all her vitriol was reserved for the local men. Leaf through her expedition journals, however, and a different picture emerges. At the first sign of disagreement Zurbriggen would unleash 'a torrent of abuse... lots of vile talk perfectly uncalled for'. He would go off 'on long tirades as to how satisfied everyone including the King of Italy had been with him,' wrote Fanny 'and what a great guide he was'. Zurbriggen was 'a fool about taking care of himself', she went on, 'and an ass in most respects'.

In Zurbriggen's place were two Courmayeur guides, Cyprien Savoye and Joseph Petigax, with Petigax's son, Laurent, along as porter. Savoye had just returned from a three-year expedition to the North Pole led by Prince Luigi Amedeo di Savoia, Duke of the Abruzzi. Three men were lost and several others had given up their extremities to frostbite, among them the Duke himself, who returned at the cost of one finger. Savoye, for his part, was fully intact, and the experience had prepared him well for the worst excesses of Himalayan exploration.

Fanny's itinerary for the 1903 season took them back to the foot of the Chogo Lungma glacier then along its north side to 'Riffel Camp', their main base in 1902. The camp took its name from the peak looming over it, which reminded the Workmans of the Riffelhorn of Zermatt. Situated above an encirclement of broken and jagged seracs overlooking the main junction of the glacier, it was 'a kind of Brunnhildaberg', wrote Fanny, 'that we were the first to storm'.

The Workmans were not the first visitors to the Himalaya to style themselves the conquerors of its ice and stone. There was a singular bloody-mindedness, however, about the way they bent the wilderness to their will. They insisted their tents be pitched on flat ground, even where that meant cutting terraces into the hillside. One photograph shows a chain of fifty porters passing flat stones up from a dry river-bed, so that the ground where the Workmans slept could be paved and insulated with rocks.

Another picture shows Fanny and Hunter taking their lunch seated at a table overlooking the bewildering vastness of the Chogo Lungma glacier. A servant waits on them, standing close by. 'The meals,' wrote Fanny, 'would not have tempted an epicure. Chops were singed and blackened by the smoky flame… and the custard pudding was of swimming consistency, because it refused to bake over the miserable nomad-fireplace.' This, at a time when the stock of grain was so low it had 'nearly caused a famine' among the porters.

Fancying themselves the rulers of this frozen fiefdom, the Workmans were ugly extensions of British colonial rule. 'Mrs Workman's conspicuous contempt for Baltis and other "Orientals" demonstrates the pervasive extent of Orientalism,' notes the geographer Kenneth Iain MacDonald. 'Women could be equal to men, but the Oriental could never be equal to the Caucasian.' Fanny herself, in her written account of the expedition, laid her prejudices bare. 'The Himalayan shepherd is the personification of primitive and unintelligent man,' she wrote, 'scarcely higher in his habits than the animals under his care.'

And, as their journals filled with complaints about the Baltis, about how they stole from dwindling supplies and feigned illness to avoid work, worse was to come. With the arrival of fresh grain and the promise of good weather, Fanny was ready to attempt one of the peaks at the head of the glacier. Now relations between the Workmans and the indigenous members of the expedition would come under greater strain, as the climbing effort began.

The party leaving Riffel Camp early on 9 August was as large as it was ungainly. Savoye led them out, followed by the Petigaxes, Fanny and Hunter, twenty-two Balti porters and a tent servant. Only with so many men could the Workmans transport all they deemed necessary to live, at their highest camps, in the manner to which they were accustomed.

They made camp early that afternoon at 16,350 feet, but the next day the going was more difficult, as they climbed a series of uneven ice-slopes. The Baltis 'wished to rest all too often', wrote Fanny. 'We urged them constantly, telling them it was necessary to cover as much as ground as possible before the snow softened, when work for all would become more difficult. This information did not appear to stimulate their climbing ardour.' Sure enough, as the Europeans pressed on, buoyed by the 'great assistance' of their snowshoes, the porters sank deeper into the melting snow, weighed down by heavy loads.

It was only owing to Savoye that the porters made it to their camp at all. Leaving the Petigaxes stamping out steps for Fanny and Hunter, he brought up the rear, shouting encouragement and urging them on. He stayed with them up a 'long, wearisome arête' until they came at last to 'gentler inclines' where, on a small plateau, the Workmans sat waiting. Fanny, who 'had wished to push on up another high ridge before camping', considered it an act of kindness to stop there. 'The last loiterers arrived,' she wrote, 'throwing themselves down in various attitudes of distress, some nursing their feet, others holding their heads'. The Baltis had been climbing, without snowshoes or warm clothing, for seven and a half hours.

With the porters treading down the snow at what became Intermediate Camp, the Workmans took in the view. 'The site was magnificent,' wrote Fanny, 'commanding, in addition to a view of the great peaks around, a coup d'oeil of more than twenty miles down the majestic sweep of the Chogo Lungma, banded with the snaky curves of its giant medial moraines, above which soared a vista of peaks stretching in tortuous ranges into the dim distance.'

Day three got off to an inauspicious start. The porters had passed the night crammed into a tent of their own. The tent servant, sent to wake them at 4 a.m., returned with word that they refused to get up. Anxious to make a start, Hunter and Savoye circled the Baltis' tent then, 'without any ceremony', wrote Fanny, 'the tent-pins were pulled up, and, as the coolies crawled out from under the prostrate canvas, they were commanded to put on their boots and get ready to march.'

Savoye once again brought up the rear, joined by Hunter, but as the ground grew steeper, where the snow lay knee-deep, the Baltis fell behind. By nine in the morning a gap of five hundred feet had opened up between them and the vanguard. Then, as Joseph Petigax was cutting steps up an especially steep wall, 'an imperative call' came from below.

Turning to look downwards, Fanny saw several of the porters 'lying prone in the snow'. She called down, asking what the trouble was – 'the answer rang through the limpid air, that some were mountain-sick and others refused to advance.'

'Offer them *Bakshish* and tell them the road is good,' shouted Fanny. Bakshish – meaning, broadly speaking, a tip – was the Workmans' answer to everything. The Baltis were unmoved. 'There being no hope,' wrote Fanny, 'the advance party descended from the well-earned wall and rejoined the caravan.'

Fanny's verdict was scathing. 'Bawling and unendurable', she noted in her journal that evening, 'and only a few really ill. Have spoiled a splendid day and chance of reaching first peak.' These were men who had carried heavy loads to near twenty thousand feet, overcoming deep crevasses and vast snowfields to get there. Men who did not have the warm clothes of the Europeans, the snowshoes, the full stomachs. It was an amazing effort from the Baltis and it was at an end. The Workmans were brought to understand that no promise of reward, no amount of bakshish, would persuade their porters to go a step further.

Fanny and Hunter did not sleep well. Woken by their own rasping breaths, they gave up long before the night was over. Outside they found it still and clear, a gentle breeze blowing down the mountainside. This was Highest Camp, at an altitude of 19,350 feet.

The tall, white peak loomed over them, under a veil of moonlight. The night before, the Baltis had been as one that they would climb no higher, but the Europeans had succeeded in persuading two men – their names are not a matter of record – to join them. Together they made up a climbing party of seven, pushing for a summit two thousand feet above.

They roped up and began to climb, finding the going easy until, higher up, they traversed a slanting face of ice and snow, where 'an appalling precipice of 2,000 feet fell away'. 'As we went higher in the waning moonlight,' wrote Fanny, 'great peaks rose on every side, sharp in outline but ghastly in tone.' Then, to the east, dawn began to break. 'At last King Sol came, flinging his rays aslant one great summit, then another… flooding the endless sea of peaks with gold. This was sunrise at 21,000 feet.'

With the mountains of the Karakoram lighting up around them, the seven 'climbed the last zigzag of the glittering cone, and at 7.15 stood on the summit, 21,500 feet above sea level'. It was four years since Fanny had gone to the top of the 20,997-foot Koser Gunge. Now she had improved on her record once again.

The climbing party stopped for a little breakfast atop what the Workmans named 'Mount Chogo'. Then, looking to the northeast, to the summit of a second, higher mountain, they prepared to go on. 'The day was still young, and we were still fit,' wrote Fanny. 'Why not have that peak too?'

'It was a day in a thousand. Not a cloud crossed the blue firmament, and the air was still.' Looking back the way they had come, Fanny could see footsteps snaking down the crest of the ridge, back to where they had stood on top of Mount Chogo. Now, three hours later, they were closing in on their second peak of the day.

Twenty minutes later, Fanny arrived at the top of what she named Mount Lungma, with Laurent Petigax a few steps behind her. She already knew, looking back at Mount Chogo, that this was the higher of the two. It was only when she consulted a barometer, however, that she understood the true significance of the climb. At 22,568 feet above sea level, it was more than just a new record. It was one of the highest known ascents to any mountain's summit, by woman or man.

Fanny and the young porter settled down to a lunch of meat, kola biscuits and milk chocolate, resting on the corniced summit of Mount Lungma. For Fanny it was a chance to rest, too, on the laurels of mountaineering distinction. And to watch Hunter. He and the two guides were moving across a broad snow-plateau below, towards what they had dubbed 'Pyramid Peak'. Hunter was not resting on anything.

'The pyramid peak', wrote Fanny, 'as seen from where our party separated, was entirely snow-bound, its apex being formed by a pointed, sharply-defined cornice, which soared into the deep-blue sky like the curling crest of a mighty wave about to break'. 'Probably in the course of the afternoon the top might have been reached,' she went on, 'but the peak would have become the mausoleum of the party, for camp could not have been regained that night, and a night in the open at that altitude would have meant certain death.'

Instead, Hunter and the two guides were intent on reaching a point along the arête leading to the summit. Not long after midday, 'after some stiff work', they arrived there. From the average of his two barometers,

Hunter put their position at 23,394 feet above sea level. That, he believed, gave him a claim on a record of his own.

But, for the moment, Hunter permitted himself to enjoy the view. 'Over a space of three-quarters of a circle countless thousands of spires of every size and shape shot up in the air as far as the eye could reach,' he wrote in his journal. 'One could see from the immense mass of Nanga Parbat, bounding the horizon sixty miles to the southwest, around to Masherbrum, the Golden Throne, Gusherbrum, and K2, ninety to a hundred miles to the east.' It was 'such a view as in long mountain experience none of the party had ever seen before – the one view of a lifetime'.

For only the second time in its 75-year history, a woman was speaking at the Royal Geographical Society. The British explorer, writer, photographer and naturalist Isabella Bird had been the first, delivering a talk in 1897 about her travels through the Sichuan province of Southwest China. Now, on 20 November 1905, came Fanny Bullock Workman.

Fanny began with a description of the glacial exploration she had completed over her 1902 and 1903 seasons in the Karakoram. She moved on to an account of 'Two Pioneer Ascents in the Himalaya', describing how she had climbed Mount Chogo and Mount Lungma. She made observations about her experiences of high altitude, the possibility of acclimatisation and the suitability of certain foods. And, of course, she moaned about the porters. 'Obdurate' and 'demoralised', they 'complained and floundered in the soft snow', declared Fanny, 'quite unfit to endure the strain, that we Europeans undergo'.

Fanny's remarks were not universally well-received. Sir Francis Younghusband, one of the first Europeans to explore the Karakoram, congratulated Fanny on her 'brilliant achievements' and for overcoming the challenges of Himalayan travel 'with the utmost determination'. Then Younghusband came to the defence of the Baltis, who, he reminded her, 'are not really mountaineers. They live in the bottom of the valleys, they do very little in the way of climbing, and, I am sure, of their own accord they never venture on these horrible glaciers.' 'I placed myself entirely in their hands,' he said of his own travels in the region. 'My experience was that there are amongst them many excellent men.'

Another member, Colonel Rawling, echoed these sentiments. 'The little experience I have had,' Rawling said of the Baltis, 'tends to show they have always done excellent work'.

Yet, whatever their misgivings about Fanny's attitude toward the Baltis, Younghusband and Rawling were in no doubt that there before them was a record-breaking mountaineer. In 1905 few at the RGS would have imagined that Inca women – and perhaps even children – had once gone to heights of 22,000 feet and more. Fanny's closest rival for the women's world altitude record was Annie Smith Peck, who had visited the 18,491-foot summit of Mexico's Pico de Orizaba in 1897. Fanny's credentials as a geographer and humanitarian might have been somewhat suspect, but no woman alive had a mountaineering record like hers.

Hunter Workman was another matter. Six months earlier he had delivered a paper of his own at the English Alpine Club, entitled *Some Obstacles to Himalayan Mountaineering and the History of a Record Ascent*. The 'record ascent' in question was, he claimed, his own, to a height of 23,394 feet on 'Pyramid Peak'. In an endnote to the paper, Hunter argued that William Graham's 1883 ascent to 24,000 feet was 'so strongly disputed that it must be regarded as far from proved'. The world altitude record therefore belonged to Matthias Zurbriggen, reasoned Hunter, for his 1896 ascent of Aconcagua, 'till the above described ascent in 1903'.

Graham had since emigrated to the Americas, but two English mountaineers came to his defence. Norman Collie, who had been with Mummery on Nanga Parbat in 1895, argued against such a summary dismissal of Graham's ascent of Kabru. Likewise, Edmund Garwood, who had explored the Himalaya without ever climbing especially high, argued that the record belonged to Graham. Hunter responded, the debate playing out in the pages of the *Alpine Journal*, until the editor – seeing that it was going nowhere – declared he would be publishing no further correspondence on the subject.

History was on Collie and Garwood's side. While the case for Graham has only strengthened, Hunter's claim on the record would collapse. Some years later, Karl Oestreich – the topographer who had accompanied the Workmans in 1902 – identified 'Pyramid Peak' as a mountain named Yengutz Har. Known today as Spantik, it reaches a height of just 23,056 feet. Hunter, who had stopped well below its summit, had no claim on a record of any kind.

Looking at the maps available today, it is clear the Workmans were climbing along the crest of the mountain ridge running east of Spantik, where the summits of Mount Chogo and Mount Lungma are clearly shown. The heights of those peaks is not a matter of record, but it is evident the Workmans' barometers were inaccurate and Hunter's plane table measurements just plain wrong.

Knowing this, we can reappraise what, in Hunter's words, had been a 'red letter day for all'. They had not reached quite the heights they described and, if there was a standout performance, it came from a member of the climbing party who barely received mention.

In her account of the expedition Fanny made passing reference to the two Balti porters who joined the Europeans that day. She mentioned that they had left the first of them, 'who here gave out', at the summit of Mount Chogo. She then described how only she and Laurent Petigax had gone to the summit of Mount Lungma. It followed, then, that whatever height Hunter and the two guides reached on Pyramid Peak, they were matched by an unnamed Balti porter. Less well-fed, less well-clothed and less well-rested than his European counterparts, tasked with carrying Hunter's heavy instruments, he had stayed with them foot for foot and step for step.

*Few Europeans had ever passed a night at such
a height, in such an exposed position.*

Italian guides Alexis and Henri Brocherel on Nanda Devi Saddle,
8 June 1905. Photograph by Dr Tom Longstaff (1905).

CHAPTER 16

Baptism of Ice

Born in the dying days of the eighteenth century, George Dixon Longstaff still remembered the moment he heard Wellington had won the day at Waterloo. 'As the coach drove into York the guard discharged his blunderbuss from the roof,' he told an audience of grandchildren. 'His voice was very hoarse from shouting again and again "Wellington has defeated Boney at Waterloo"; then all the people cheered and tar barrels were lit in the streets.' It was a story George's grandson, Tom, never tired of hearing, told by a man who, in his eyes, could never grow old.

The Battle of Waterloo brought an end to the Napoleonic Wars, a victory owing, in part, to the supremacy of British sea power. Now, in peacetime, the Royal Navy found itself with ships and men to spare. John Barrow, Second Secretary to the Admiralty, struck upon the ruse of using those same vessels – and their restive captains – to usher in a new era of overseas exploration. In the decades to come, British officers would be sent to investigate the last blank spaces on Admiralty charts and maps, venturing up the great rivers of the continent of Africa, discovering the very existence of Antarctica and unpicking the closest secrets of the Arctic, as they searched for a navigable sea lane connecting the Atlantic and Pacific Oceans – the so-called Northwest Passage.

For young Tom Longstaff, whiling away rainy days in his grandfather's library, the books and magazines it contained were a repository of dark adventure. He could read about Captain James Kingston Tuckey, who sailed two hundred miles up the River Congo, into a hotbed of pestilence and disease. 'Never were the results of an expedition,' wrote Barrow, 'more melancholy or disastrous.' Or there was 'the man who ate his boots', Captain John Franklin, sent overland to map the north coast of Canada. He returned, 5,500 miles later, amid claims of murder and cannibalism. The same Franklin sailed north, twenty-five years on, in command of the *Erebus* and *Terror*. Both ships were lost to the Arctic night, along with Franklin himself. More boots were eaten, and more people.

All this was required reading for any ten-year-old boy, but in 1885 these were stories from the past, the former triumphs and tragedies – mainly tragedies – of men guided by a heady mix of duty and ambition. Leafing through the *Illustrated London News* and *Punch Magazine*, Tom could see that the world had moved on. Adventure was no longer the exclusive domain of men with rank and reputation. It was a plaything, a pursuit, personified by the hero of the story that lived in Tom's imagination like no other.

He came across it in an 1885 edition of a literary periodical called *Good Words*, an account of an expedition to the Himalaya written by a man named William Woodman Graham. 'It was the first time I had read anything about mountaineering,' Longstaff recalled, 'and I never forgot the story; but it did not occur to me to ask any questions about mountaineering; that was all quite obvious and natural. I had already seen mountains spread calmly in the sunlight inviting me to walk over them in complete freedom of body and spirit, and I knew far more about that than any grown-up.'

Longstaff's first experiences as a climber came on the sea-cliffs of Devon. There, he and his cousins designed long horizontal traverses that could only be tackled when the tide was low. By the age of fifteen he had set his mind on becoming a mountaineer, but his father insisted he have a real profession to fall back on. In 1894, at the age of nineteen, he enrolled at Oxford as a student of medicine. Three years later, shortly after graduating with a third-class degree in physiology, he set off for his first proper season in the Alps.

Longstaff arrived in the mountains ready 'to learn something of mountaineering' and set about trying to recruit 'a really first-rate guide'. They were few and far between, the best men often booked well in advance, 'but I had luck,' wrote Longstaff. 'Christian Kaufmann was then a young guide, very handsome, refined, and of quick intelligence.' Longstaff and Kaufmann embarked on a spectacular season of big-ticket climbs, starting with traverses of the Mönch, Finsteraarhorn and Schreckhorn. Then, leaving the Oberland for Valais, they walked up the Saas valley from the railway station at Stalden, where Longstaff scandalised the local villagers with the shortness of his trousers.

His learning curve was steep, at times precipitous. On the Aiguille Verte, he, Kaufmann and a porter named Ulrich were reversing a 150-foot ice traverse when Longstaff informed his guide that he had little confidence in the foot and handholds they had cut that morning. Kaufmann overruled him and sent Ulrich on ahead, with Longstaff next on the rope and the guide bringing up the rear. Longstaff had just passed a bulge in the ice-wall when he looked ahead to see Ulrich hesitate, then, in agonisingly slow motion, fall backwards.

A strange eternity enveloped Longstaff. He shouted to alert Kaufmann, but he already knew it was pointless. The guide would have committed to the traverse and, just as Longstaff had no hope of catching Ulrich's fall, there was no way Kaufmann would catch the weight of two men. Instead, he too would be pulled from the ice-wall, taking all three into freefall. Sure enough, Ulrich's weight caught Longstaff like a blow to the midriff. He too was soon falling to what, he found a moment to notice, was certain death.

'It was all so unnecessary,' thought Longstaff. 'It would mean the awful disgrace of a search party. "Comes of taking a guide who does not know our mountains," the Chamonix men would say. And then, of course, "it was the amateur who had slipped". If we finished up in a crevasse our bodies would never be found. It would be a horrid shock to my mother and father. And all my fault. I *knew* that traverse would not do on the descent. I was furious with myself for having given way to Christian, and furious with Christian for rejecting my warning.' Such was the kaleidoscope of emotions experienced by Longstaff as he fell a distance of thirty feet.

This warping of time was a trick being played in Longstaff's brain. His overriding emotion was fear – when a person is scared, activity increases in a part of the brain called the amygdala. All the time he was falling, Longstaff's amygdala was laying down an additional set of memories, leaving him with a richer sense of the experience, more readily recalled. He was not the first mountaineer to experience this phenomenon, nor would he be the last. It was, he later wrote, 'an experiment with time'.

The rope went taut. Longstaff felt the weight of Ulrich, sucking the wind out of him. It took him a moment to notice that he was no longer falling, that he was not going to die. He steadied himself on the rope, then looked up to see the beaming face of Kaufmann. The guide had taken heed of Longstaff's concerns after all, and had followed along the ridge above. Seeing Ulrich slip, he had let himself drop down the other side, creating the counterweight that saved their lives.

Longstaff hurried back to Zermatt, happy to have a story that would pass muster in the smoke-filled *salle à manger* of the Monte Rosa, where British alpinists gathered in the evenings to relive one another's near misses and narrow escapes. So many famous names were in the Alps that summer, veterans of the Himalaya like Norman Collie and Charlie Bruce. Longstaff even found time to take a lesson in the use of crampons from 'that enigmatic couple', Oscar Eckenstein and Aleister Crowley. His Alpine apprenticeship complete, he was beginning to imagine a place for himself in this world of giants.

Longstaff was in the audience when, years earlier, the English mountaineer Clinton Dent had visited Eton College to speak. He remembered Dent, 'his face like Odysseus', describing his travels in the Caucasus, a range of mountains forming a natural barrier between Eastern Europe and Western Asia. It might have sounded like a schoolboy boast when Longstaff rose to his feet and announced that, one day, he would go there himself. Yet here he was, in 1903, progressing from the playground of the Alps to the rugged spine of Europe's eastern frontier.

Longstaff rode into the mountains accompanied by his friend L. W. Rolleston, with local horsemen as their guides. Opinion was divided on the question of their safety in the Caucasus, a region ruled by competing tribal factions. The Russians maintained that the mountainous regions should be avoided at all costs, but the British and American consuls took a more diplomatic position, saying Longstaff and Rollaston would be safe enough if they gave the borders with Turkey and Persia a wide berth.

Some dangers rode along with them. One of their local guides, a man named Gramiton, stirred up trouble at every opportunity. He eventually succeeded in bringing proceedings to a complete halt, insisting that he and the other horsemen would go no further unless their pay was doubled. The Englishmen refused, prompting Gramiton to lay his hand on his pistol. 'I hitched forward in my saddle exposing my holster,' recalled Longstaff, 'but did not move my hand towards the revolver, for it is a fool's trick to draw unless you are prepared to shoot at once and take the consequences'. His bluff called, Gramiton rode away, seen off by Longstaff with 'the insulting phrase a Russian would use to a dog'.

Journeying deeper into the wild, Longstaff and Rolleston passed through settlements unlike anything they had seen before. The houses were built on strong stone towers, 'like the castle of a bandit', with the entrances twenty feet above the ground. 'These fortified houses have an aspect of grim readiness,' wrote Longstaff. 'They are not set too close together, so that your neighbour cannot get too easy a shot at you, but near enough to support each other if the village is attacked.'

By the beginning of August, they were at the 15,267-foot summit of a peak named Tikhtengeni, after Rollaston had forced his way along a 'vicious curving ice ridge'. 'My companion was in his element,' wrote Longstaff, 'for he is a dominating personality on steep ice'. The two then climbed Tenuldi, a 'great pyramid' 15,918 feet in height, higher than Mont Blanc and 'a far finer peak, rising as an isolated cone rather than as the culminating point of a great massif'. Then came Shkhara. At

16,592 feet it was the highest of all their Caucasian peaks; for Longstaff, 'the finest climb I ever had'.

Longstaff was thriving on mountains that were a step up from what he knew, relishing his partnership with Rollaston, whose 'confident resolution… kept me going, for I hate and fear bad weather on a high peak'. Longstaff knew, however, that these were still mountains of European proportions, under seventeen thousand feet in height and surmountable in a single day. Climbing at 'about the limit for alpine standards', the worst he and Rollaston would experience in the way of mountain sickness was 'the curious feeling of aloofness from the world below'.

In the evenings Longstaff relaxed around the fire, eating shashlik kebab and grazing on the works of Shelley 'like a good Victorian'. The Caucasus had given him a taste of a world beyond the Alps, of remotely situated peaks about which little was known. He felt ready for more but – as he was about to find out – nothing could prepare him for the mountains of the Himalaya. There, at seventeen thousand feet, the hard work was just beginning.

'When in 1905 I first went to the Himalaya,' wrote Longstaff, 'my objective had been determined years beforehand'. As a boy he had dreamed of following in William Graham's footsteps, picturing Graham, Boss and Kaufmann as they tried to force a way up the Rishi Gorge into the 'inner sanctuary' of Nanda Devi. Longstaff had known even then where his own Himalayan adventures would begin.

Nanda Devi was 'the most romantic mountain in the world', wrote Longstaff, 'surrounded by a legend of inaccessibility… doubly barred from the outer world by a wall within a wall'. He planned to approach the mountain following the same route as Graham but, not long after he arrived in India, his plans changed. Longstaff met Charles Sherring, deputy-commissioner of Almora, who was preparing to embark on a trade mission to Tibet. Sherring invited Longstaff to join him.

Longstaff knew this was too good an opportunity to miss, a chance to climb mountains few westerners had ever seen, deep inside territory he was otherwise forbidden from entering. Better still, the journey to Tibet would take them within the vicinity of Nanda Devi. Longstaff would still have a few weeks to explore the mountain on its eastern side.

Like Graham before him, Longstaff had travelled to India accompanied by a guide and a porter – two brothers from Courmayeur, Alexis and Henri Brocherel. The three made their base camp at the village of Ganaghar, to the east of Nanda Devi, on 27 May. Longstaff promptly disappeared up the opposite side of the valley to get a better look at the mountain's outer wall, while Alexis Brocherel borrowed the Englishman's rifle, aiming to make sure they had plenty of meat for their 'flesh-pots'. He returned boasting that he had killed three *burrhal* with a single shot, firing at a ram and killing a ewe in lamb with the same bullet. 'Peasant economy', scoffed Longstaff, happy to fill up on mutton ahead of all to come.

That night, following his reconnaissance, Longstaff shared his plan with the Brocherels. From what he had seen – and judging by the Survey maps at his disposal – if they could reach the col at the head of the Panchu glacier they would be at a place where Nanda Devi's two outer walls merged into one. There, he hoped to command a view of the mountain's inner sanctuary, a lost world he and the Brocherels would be the first Europeans – perhaps the first human beings – ever to see.

Longstaff looked down at the map, then up at the landscape in front of him. He and the Brocherels ought to have been looking down on glaciers flowing around the base of Nanda Devi. Instead, all they could see was another larger mountain wall rising ahead. It was the same map Graham had used, produced by the Survey of India around the middle of the nineteenth century. Graham's misgivings were well documented – he had returned to England complaining that it was, in places, 'entirely imaginary'. Longstaff had not imagined, however, that the surveyors who made it would have rolled two such enormous ridges, situated almost a mile apart, into one.

It had taken three days to reach their current vantage point, such as it was. The first of those had been spent marching to the head of the Panchu glacier, where Longstaff had sent the Bhotia porters back, then they had lost twenty-four hours waiting out a storm. At the first sign of better weather, they had shouldered their packs and climbed the rotten crumbling rockface at the head of the glacier, under a scorching sun. Now, seeing nothing but this new obstacle, all they had to look forward to was a long and wearisome retreat.

Three days later they tried again. Longstaff had seen another col, at the head of the Lwanl glacier; he settled on this as their next objective. Leaving their Bhotia porters at the top of the glacier, they started alone up the gully ahead. By five in the afternoon, they came to a good place for a bivouac, on a small rock platform at around 17,400 feet.

They woke the next day facing a climb of two thousand feet up to the col above, up thin rock ribs and long snow-filled gullies. A cold wind was blowing, whipping the snow up into their faces, at a height where the thinness of the air began to tell. 'The guides were grand,' wrote Longstaff, 'cutting steps in turn, though we had often to pause for breath'. It was 'very laborious work for heavily-laden men', he went on, describing how in places they hauled their fifty-pound loads up on the end of a rope, before the last man followed after.

At three-thirty that afternoon, after eight hours of continuous climbing, they crested the col. 'The tracks of a snow-leopard showed that we were not the first visitors,' wrote Longstaff, 'but we were the first human beings to stand on the rim of the Inner Sanctuary: the first to look down into it'. Clouds concealed much of what lay below, but Longstaff could see glaciers and, to the northwest, the foot of Nanda Devi itself. Longstaff named it the Nanda Devi pass, but on a map produced a few years later it had become 'Longstaff's Col'.

How quickly the summit of one ambition becomes a staging point for the next. Longstaff had fulfilled Graham's dream of looking into Nanda Devi's mythic interior but there, to the north, stood Nanda Devi East. Longstaff had thought, from the col, they might prospect a route up the 24,390-foot peak. All felt strong, with Henri seemingly impervious to the effects of altitude. Thinking the summit within reach, they looked around for somewhere to sleep.

The ridge was too narrow to pitch a tent, so the Brocherels did what they could to enlarge it, taking the rest of the afternoon to construct an impressive stone platform. One of Longstaff's photographs shows the sturdy silhouettes of the two brothers, dark shadows against the hulking backdrop of Nanda Devi East, preparing for a night at 19,200 feet. Few Europeans had ever passed a night at such a height, in such an exposed position. Packed into a small tent, perched on their makeshift platform, they got what rest they could.

It was a cold night, as cold as any of them had known. All they had to look forward to in the morning was a little lukewarm tea – Longstaff spilt some and it froze instantly. Pulling on his frozen boots – he had used them as a pillow – he felt signs of frostbite in two of his toes, so was forced to yank them back off, rubbing his feet to restore circulation. They finally made it away shortly before sunrise, taking what provisions they could but leaving the tent and sleeping bags behind.

A sleepless night had given Longstaff plenty of time to weigh their prospects for the day ahead. The summit of Nanda Devi East was four miles away and five thousand feet above. To have any hope of reaching it and getting back to their tent before nightfall they needed to make quick progress along the ridge ahead. It was with a heavy heart then, that, a little way above their bivouac, they came face to face with a towering *gendarme* – a steep pinnacle of rock, obstructing the way forward.

Climbing on decaying rock, careful to test each handhold before they trusted it with their weight, the men lost precious time overcoming that first gendarme. When they did so, it was only to see another, then another, each larger and more awkward than the last. For three hours they grappled with them, trusting their lives to the cold caprice of these crumbling upper ramparts, until they cleared the last of the pinnacles. Now, for the first time, Longstaff had an unobstructed view of the ridge ahead. 'I think it was about 10 o'clock,' he wrote, 'that the utter impossibility of reaching the summit that day was borne upon me.'

Longstaff checked his barometer and his heart sank further still – they had gained just a few hundred feet. The Brocherels wanted to press on but both understood it would mean a night in the snow, perhaps two, with no sleeping bag or tent. 'The risk of frostbite was more than I could face,' wrote Longstaff, 'so to the unconcealed chagrin of the guides I gave it up and we turned back at noon.'

With time for one last climb before they were due to join up with Charles Sherring's diplomatic mission, Longstaff and the Brocherels scoured the skyline for another objective. They settled on a peak called Nanda Kot.

Several miles apart from Nanda Devi's outer wall, Nanda Kot might have seemed like an easier proposition, disentangled from the maze of peaks and glaciers to the west. The mountain, though, carried a certain menace. Seen from the southeast, its summit ridge was drawn across the skyline like a blade, earning it the nickname of *Kulhari*, meaning 'The Hatchet'. Moreover, at 22,530 feet in height, it was no pushover; if they were successful, it would be the highest undisputed ascent of any Himalayan peak.

With the help of five Bhotias, they established a camp at sixteen thousand feet, then got away the next day at 3.45 a.m. By mid-morning they had joined the northeast ridge, moving up the right-hand side of the mountain's imposing north face. 'A sea of mountains was visible in all directions,' wrote Longstaff, 'but the most impressive sight of all was Nanda Devi, its twin peaks being seen to better advantage from here than from any other viewpoint: they rose magnificent above the saddle which we had left only two days before.'

All three men felt good. The altitude did not seem to be affecting them and, gaining height fast, they felt 'confident of success'. As they climbed, though, the ridge narrowed and steepened, flanked to the left by an 'appalling' drop down the sheer north face. Finally, at around 21,000 feet, with the summit visible above, Alexis stopped. The guide was worried about the condition of the snow. He thought it looked unstable. He was wary of going on.

Reaching down, Longstaff took up a handful of snow. He compacted it into a ball and tossed it onto the slope ahead. All three watched as 'a hissing baby avalanche formed', wrote the Englishman, 'and started down that horrible north face'.

The peaks of this region of the Himalaya had been in Tom Longstaff's thoughts ever since he was a young boy. All that time he had wondered what it would be like to claim one for himself. Now one of those fabled summits was there in front of him, a childhood dream almost come to fruition. Enough, surely, to play tricks with reason and restraint.

But Longstaff held himself to a higher standard. As a mountaineer he did not prize fearlessness, but from the capacity to know fear, to harness it, to see through it with clarity. He understood, too, that courage sometimes needed to be contained; that, in his own words, it was 'safe to tackle any climb as soon as you have learned when to turn back'. This was mountain leadership as Longstaff saw it. This was what he knew as keeping one's nerve. So, for the second time in four days, he signalled retreat.

Their time was up. As they trudged down to their campsite, it was a chance for Longstaff to reflect on two weeks of climbing in the mountains of India. 'I was beginning to realise', he wrote, 'that success on any big Himalayan peak was unlikely if we confined ourselves to rush-tactics suitable for the Alps or Caucasus'.

'Furthermore', Longstaff went on, 'owing to the horrible effects of high-altitude, success is only to be attained through endurance of the greatest physical discomfort and by such concentrated mental resolve that little spiritual energy remains for the pure enjoyment of living through such days.' The Englishman was changing, in his own words, 'from the esoteric mountain climber into the epicurean explorer. In the Himalaya, with its manifold diversities of attraction,' he wrote, 'the change is almost inevitable.'

His timing was impeccable. Many miles lay ahead as he and the Brocherels raced to meet Sherring, then travelled deep into Tibet. This would be the perfect proving ground for this emerging ethos, along a route weaving through the valleys of Kumaon, to Askot, then along the course of the Kali river.

And yet, even with these revelations fresh as falling snow, Longstaff would soon be working again to bag a summit and claim a record. He would not admit as much, but that splinter of ambition was there, lodged deep in his mind. He took it with him into Tibet on what, he later wrote, 'might well have proved my last adventure'.

*'On looking at the mountain I had
instinctively chosen the easiest way to go up...'*

'A Perilous Crossing', from *Tibet and Nepal* by A. Henry Savage Landor
(1905), showing English writer and explorer Arnold Henry Savage Landor
and his Tibetan guides. Illustration by A. Henry Savage Landor.

CHAPTER 17

Because I Must

When, in 1899, the British explorer Arnold Henry Savage Landor crossed the Kali river and entered Nepal, rumours were rife that he was mounting a full-scale invasion.

Landor's reputation preceded him. Two years earlier, on his first visit to the Himalaya, he had displayed a wilful disregard for Nepal's territorial sovereignty, leading to his capture, imprisonment, torture and release. Now, returning at the head of twenty indigenous guides and porters, he and his men were armed to the teeth. They carried 'several rifles and double-barrelled guns,' wrote Landor, 'a revolver, eight thousand rounds of ammunition, and ten pounds of gunpowder,' and each man had also been given a large Gurkha *kukri* – a short sword with a recurved blade – 'for his own protection'. That, led by a man who travelled so light he wore, 'in any country and in any climate… no underwear'.

Landor ventured into Nepalese territory with one mode of conquest very much in mind. 'It was my intention to do a considerable amount of mountaineering *en route*,' he wrote, 'and I did it.' He was not your typical mountaineer. He eschewed climbing equipment, declining even to use a rope, and sported 'clothes of the thinnest tropical material, no underclothing to speak of, a straw hat, and a small bamboo stick in my hand'. Mountaineering was 'a delightful amusement, and possibly the pleasantest, healthiest, and most instructive exercise in existence'. Woe betide, however, the school of alpinists who set out 'to climb mountains by impracticable ways'. 'In plain words', wrote Landor, 'any man who tries to go up a mountain by any but the easiest way is an idiot, and should be confined to a lunatic asylum.'

Landor was soon putting his methods to the test. Nearing what he called the 'Lumpa Peaks' he resolved to climb one, starting out from a camp at 13,600 feet accompanied by a dozen local porters and guides. His account incorporates all the signature ingredients of an epic Himalayan climb. The climbing party crossed 'huge and tortuous crevasses', and were bombarded with falling rocks. They witnessed 'the birth of an avalanche', then crossed a deadly arête, featured in one of Landor's lavish illustrations. The picture shows the Englishman striding, unroped, across the narrow crest of the ridge, straw hat on his head, bamboo cane in his hand. 'On looking at the mountain I had instinctively chosen the easiest way to go up,' he wrote, pictured a few pages later at its dizzying summit.

Landor put his success down, in part, to his consumption of concentrated meat lozenges – 'each one was supposed to be as a good as a meal', he wrote, 'and I ate at least fifty in the space of eight hours and a half'. 'I think it was partly due to the constant nourishment... that I was able to break the world's record in mountaineering, going several hundred feet higher than other mountaineers, with comparative ease. Had the peak which we climbed been higher,' he went on, 'I could have gone even higher and reached a considerably greater elevation. But perhaps Nature gave me quite an abnormal constitution for work of that kind, as people who know me can testify.'

Landor made the most of his time at the summit. He oversaw the construction of a cairn, a lasting record of their ascent, and took 'all the necessary observations'. Then, after consuming 'two whole pounds of chocolate', he led his party back down the mountain.

Arriving back at their camp on the glacier, Landor had completed a truly abnormal performance. He had measured the summit of Mount Lumpa at a record-breaking 23,490 feet; he and his party had gained – then lost – almost 10,000 feet of elevation in a single day. All without climbing equipment of any kind and in boots 'such as I would wear in London on a wet day', noted Landor, a man 'who made no difference between going up on a world's record breaking expedition and taking a stroll down Piccadilly'.

Six years after Landor's adventure, in 1905, Longstaff and the Brocherels crossed the Kali river and entered Nepal. Landor's book, *Tibet and Nepal*, had come out earlier that year. Seeing an opportunity to investigate his predecessor's claim on the world altitude record – which he considered 'all very intriguing' – Longstaff was lucky enough to encounter some of the men who had acted as Landor's porters and guides. They led him first to Landor's highest camp, at 13,600 feet, then to the crest of a spur running down from a peak which itself rose no higher than 20,000 feet. 'The mystery was cleared up,' wrote Longstaff, 'when we were shown Landor's cairn and assured that no-one had ever been any further.' Longstaff measured the altitude of the cairn at 'around 16,500 feet'.

Satisfied they had laid bare the truth of Landor's dubious attainments, Longstaff and the Brocherels resumed their journey north, meeting up with Charles Sherring at Askot then carrying on to the Tibetan townlet of Taklakot. Longstaff had little interest in the diplomatic affairs of the British, so at the first opportunity he and the Brocherels abandoned Sherring's trade mission and struck out in the direction of an isolated mountain massif named Gurla Mandhata. Leaving on the morning of 18 July, Longstaff agreed to rendezvous with Sherring six days later at a camping ground named Baldak. This lay west of the mountain and was en route for Sherring's party as they continued north. Longstaff knew there was every chance he and the Brocherels would be delayed on the mountain, so he told Sherring to be prepared to wait at Baldak for at least five days.

Little was known about Gurla Mandhata. 'Its name is mentioned in the narratives of several British travellers of the last century,' noted Longstaff, but 'political difficulties of access rather than physical ones have led to its neglect.' It had never been examined by skilled mountaineers practising, as Sherring put it, 'approved modern methods', but the Survey of India had observed and triangulated the massif's four main peaks, measuring the highest at 25,243 feet. To reach its summit, Longstaff knew, would be to stand atop by far the highest mountain yet climbed.

Longstaff, the Brocherels and six Bhotias made for the foot of one of its western spurs. 'From noon to 6 p.m. we toiled up the interminable stony slopes of the buttress making for the snow-line, our only source of water.' At around eighteen thousand feet, with a few patches of snow appearing on the mountainside, Longstaff told the Bhotias 'to dump their loads, descend at once and not return to look for us till after two nights had passed'.

Longstaff woke the next day feeling unwell. Seeing clouds coming in over the ridge above, he took the decision to rest. That evening the clouds lifted, the skies cleared and the men got underway shortly after midnight, under a moon so bright they had no need of lanterns. As they climbed their eyes adjusted to the conditions and they made out 'another great shoulder of our peak', the mountain's main western ridge, separated by 'a profound pit of darkness' where the Gurla glacier lay. Approaching twenty thousand feet, Longstaff was forming a clearer picture of the western side of the mountain. Nothing, though, prepared him for what he was about to see. When dawn came, it was a revelation.

'Suddenly, far away to the southeast a great peak in Nepal caught the first rays of the sun, flaming red,' wrote Longstaff. 'It was surely Dhaolagiri (26,826 feet) 180 miles away, the Hill of Flame. It overtopped all its neighbours of the mighty and seemingly continuous Himalaya of central Nepal. We were like Cortez seeing the Pacific for the first time; for no other eyes had seen these peaks from such a height spread as a continuous range. I was more elated by this enormous vista of the unknown than by any other discovery or ascent that I have accomplished.'

Longstaff's elation was short-lived. He and the Brocherels had been climbing for several hours, roped together on steep snow, 'but on gaining the first snowy top of our ridge, a great disappointment awaited us. We now saw a tremendous drop effectively cutting us off from the main peak,' wrote Longstaff. 'Unable to reconnoitre properly we had committed ourselves to a route which was quite impracticable.'

Even as the men prepared to turn back, Longstaff looked to the great western ridge above the intervening Gurla glacier. Clearer than ever in the light of a new day, it formed an uninterrupted path all the way to the summit. That, Longstaff decided, was the route they must follow.

They started afresh at eight o'clock the following morning. The three Europeans and five Bhotias left their camp at fifteen thousand feet and started up the loose stone of the main western ridge. They climbed for seven hours to a height of nineteen thousand feet then, just as before, Longstaff sent the porters back, with orders not to expect them for at least three days.

That first day took its toll on Longstaff, who woke the following morning feeling 'very feeble'. Wanting to travel as light as possible – and with no Bhotias to help – they left their tent standing, with three eiderdown sleeping bags inside. All they carried was 'a few extra clothes and two days' food'.

Longstaff found the ridge 'quite easy, the snow in condition and the weather fine', and as the day advanced, he started to feel better, able to keep pace with the younger, fitter Brocherels. At 2 p.m. they stopped to rest on a shoulder of the mountain, where Longstaff – who had broken his barometer some weeks earlier – tried to gauge their height. Several peaks of the surrounding massif had been triangulated by the Survey of India and, judging their position in relation to one, he put them at 'about 23,000 feet'. Longstaff knew, though, that the best way to be certain of their altitude was to reach the top of Gurla Mandhata. And that, he could plainly see, was still 'a long way off'.

A long way off and under darkening skies. They were facing a night on the mountain. Nobody was known to have ever passed a night at such a height. They would be doing so without tent or sleeping bags.

Longstaff consulted the Brocherels and found them divided. Henri was for carrying on and digging a good '*maison de neige*' at the next depression. Alexis, who had spotted a rocky outcrop a little way down on the south side of the ridge, argued for seeking whatever shelter that might afford. With the casting vote, Longstaff sided with Alexis and the men began lowering themselves, rope-length by rope-length, down the snow-slope below.

'At first all went well and we descended a hundred feet down snow that seemed good,' wrote Longstaff. 'I had just steadied Alexis down the full length of the rope while Henri anchored me from above. Just as I was turning to gather in the slack of Henri's rope I heard his warning cry and a hissing sound – *shshshshshshsh* – like the surge of a spent wave up a smooth shore.' Longstaff turned to see an avalanche forming. There, at the centre of it, was Henri Brocherel.

Longstaff felt the snow beneath him start to move, even before Henri crashed into him, sweeping the Englishman clean off his feet. The two hurtled towards Alexis, a tangle of men, rope and snow.

Alexis was all that stood between his companions and the Gurla glacier thousands of feet below. He seized Longstaff's jacket and tried to hold him, but the force was too much. He, too, was jolted off his feet. Now all three men fell together.

If the avalanche had been formed of powder snow it would have quickly engulfed them. Instead, they were carried down the mountainside on 'a moving bed of snow, heavy and wettish… pushing the surface layers into motion ahead of us'. The avalanche was gathering pace, gathering size, and they were at its heart, ensnared in their own ropes, clawing helplessly at the mountainside with their ice-axes.

Longstaff noticed something, a familiar feeling. That was it – he was about to die. 'My mind seemed quite clear,' he noted, 'but curious about the end rather than terrified. Thoughts passed at incredible speed, while bodily sensation was blotted out.' He had time to take in his surroundings, time to notice the glacier below rushing towards them, 'its crevasses widening and widening just as the engine of a passing express train seems to grow higher and higher as it rushes towards the platform'.

'*À droite! À droite!*' shouted Alexis. The guide had seen that they were going to collide with some rocks below and hoped to direct them towards a snow-filled gully to the right. They tried to steer themselves using the picks of their ice-axes, but it was as much as they could do to stay on top of the avalanching snow.

They bounced over a first small outcrop of rock. Then came a larger one.

'This must be the finish,' thought Longstaff.

'A longish drop and then – blank.'

'The next thing I remember', wrote Longstaff, 'was intense surprise at feeling the rope tight around my chest. I was stopped with a jerk that squeezed all the breath out of my body.' Trying not to panic, he groped around for his knife and, finding it, cut the rope. Air flooded back into his lungs.

Struggling to his knees, he saw that the avalanche was over. Coming to where the mountainside grew gentler, it had slowed and stopped. He saw, too, just how far it had taken them. It was extraordinary. 'We had fallen some 3,000 feet,' wrote Longstaff, 'in a minute or two.'

But for 'a few cuts', he was completely unharmed.

Longstaff was the lightest of the three men and had been carried the furthest. Looking back up the mountainside, he spotted the bodies of the Brocherels, half-buried in the snow. They lay motionless. Longstaff called up to them. Relief washed over him as one, then the other, began to move.

Alexis was the first to speak.

He wanted to know what *on earth* had possessed Longstaff to cut his favourite rope.

High on the mountain, with the light beginning to fail, Longstaff took stock. He was still trembling, sometime later – 'from shock, for I had experienced no feeling of fear, anxiety or pain. The two Piedmontese showed no concern at all'. Nobody was seriously injured, but the avalanche had exacted a significant toll. 'Each of the men had broken a crampon. We had lost our three hats and worst of all our ice-axes.'

The Brocherels started back up the mountain in search of the ice-axes, while Longstaff descended to the Gurla glacier below. Finding a spot to shelter in, he started building a small stone wall. Three hours later the Brocherels appeared. They had climbed over one thousand feet, recovering all three of the axes. Their reward was a dinner of four sardines each, followed by a small piece of chocolate, then the men set about making themselves as comfortable as possible. They wrapped their feet in dry socks and stuffed them inside their rucksacks, huddling together in the lee of Longstaff's wall.

Shivering in the darkness, Longstaff had plenty to think about. The next day was 24 July. In a few hours Sherring was due to meet them at the camping ground at Baldak, a few miles from their base camp at the foot of the Gurla glacier.

They had been climbing for two long days. They had gone to a height of 23,000 feet, had been swept away by an avalanche, had fallen three thousand feet in under a minute. They had endured two nights at an altitude of nineteen thousand feet or more, one with no tent or sleeping bags. They were running dangerously low on food. If they turned and walked away from the mountain, they could hold their heads high. They would be lucky to be walking away at all.

But Longstaff had told Sherring to wait five days at Baldak for a reason. If they had no food and fuel, no tent or sleeping bags, that was less to carry. They had recovered their ice-axes. The mountain was right there, waiting. He was determined to give it one more go.

The Brocherels did not need convincing. Alexis had said from the outset that the Gurla glacier might be their best route up the mountain. Now it was in front of them, a mazy mess of gaping crevasses, crumbling snow-bridges and tottering seracs. Long before sunrise they were up. The elder Brocherel took the lead, guiding them through, zigzagging up towards the glacier's far-off head. There they would try to rejoin the ridge leading to the mountain's summit.

As the day advanced the sun came overhead. The Brocherels had lost their hats in the avalanche, so instead of wide-brimmed solar topees they had only handkerchiefs to protect them. By midday, moving in the hollows of the glacier, they were climbing in a furnace heat. Alexis had shown extraordinary strength and resilience from the moment they arrived in the Himalaya, but by mid-afternoon it was all too much. He collapsed.

Longstaff and Henri hauled him into the shade of a small serac and let him rest. His decline was a bellwether for what was to come – a sign, if one were needed, that Gurla Mandhata had gained the upper hand. Longstaff and Henri considered pressing on to the summit, thinking they could find their way back to Alexis, by lantern light if necessary. But to leave him there, stricken, waiting who knew how long? Longstaff would not consider it. Instead, he sat, breathless and running on empty, as Henri, seemingly unaffected by the punishing conditions, dug a first-rate hole.

It was their third night on the mountain, at around 23,000 feet. 'I dreamed that Sherring had sent a square khaki-coloured water-cart full of warm wraps up the glacier to us,' wrote Longstaff, 'but when it arrived it contained only Jaeger stockings, and the driver, in spite of my violent abuse, insisted that we were only entitled to one pair each.' It must have been a strange awakening for the Englishman, at around two in the morning, struggling to judge where these frantic imaginings ended and their torturous predicament began.

Alexis, better for a few hours' rest, felt ready to go on. 'We started off by lantern light at two-thirty on the 25th,' wrote Longstaff, 'threading our way up the final icefall among big crevasses'. After an hour they came to the bergschrund – a giant crevasse separating the Gurla glacier from the mountain itself. They tried to cross in two places, but the gap was too wide. They would have to wait for daylight if they were to find a way over.

It had been one thing to climb, warmed by their own perpetual motion. Now, forced to sit and await the sunrise, Longstaff began to suffer. 'I got so cold that I felt incapable of climbing another step and through chattering teeth I told the men I would give in.'

Henri Brocherel, adamant they were less than one thousand feet from the summit, urged his client on.

'If you turn back now,' he told the Englishman, 'you'll regret it very much when you get down into the valley.'

'If I don't turn back now,' replied Longstaff, 'I will not be returning to the valley at all.'

Growing desperate, Henri asked permission to carry on alone. Longstaff refused. He knew how dangerous it would be for the younger Brocherel to strike out for the summit by himself, 'and could not contemplate his descending alone through the crevasses in the afternoon'.

It was four in the morning. Longstaff and the Brocherels had been at an altitude of twenty thousand feet or more for three days. They had slept at 23,000 feet with nothing but rucksacks for sleeping bags. They were standing, Longstaff reckoned, at what 'may have been over 24,000 feet'. That put them shoulder to shoulder with William Graham, Longstaff's great inspiration. They had given Gurla Mandhata their all. Still, it had defeated them.

Staring downwards, it was a relief just to be moving again. They went quickly, over frozen snow and soon felt the warmth returning to their bodies.

They believed, for all the world, that the worst was behind them.

Down they went.

Down the Gurla glacier, through the maze of seracs and crevasses, its secrets unlocked.

Down, on cold ground that was firm underfoot, then, when the glacier's surface became too icy and rough, down the rocks to the right, a long lateral moraine leading all the way to its snout. Down, to where 'the bare ice became worn into the most fantastic pinnacles, fretted by the power of the sun and by radiation and evaporation into the thin dry air'.

'We began to find a few small flowers,' recalled Longstaff, 'the first vegetation of any sort we had seen for three days'. The Englishman, a devoted botanist, 'collected some specimens and a few seeds'. Alexis, meanwhile, was struggling, falling further behind. Still, they pressed on, anxious to reach their old camp, where they expected to find the porters waiting. They arrived at half three in the afternoon. The Bhotias were nowhere to be seen.

Longstaff and the Brocherels were running on empty. They had finished the last of their food that morning, confident that before the day was over they would be sitting down to a square meal. Now, with no sight of the Bhotias, they faced a gruelling march to the camping ground at Baldak, where Sherring should be waiting. 'I found a finger of chocolate in my pocket and divided it,' wrote Longstaff. That was the end of it. He and Henri struck out, with Alexis following as best he could.

Time ticked by and their path stretched out ahead, but there was still time to make it to Baldak. Still time to rendezvous with Sherring, with all the pleasures that would bring. Sherring, who was all too aware how little food they had. Who understood how important it was to meet with the men as agreed. Longstaff had left no room for confusion. He had left no room for doubt.

Baldak was deserted. Sherring was nowhere to be seen.

All was not lost. There was a second camping ground nearby, a place called Sekung. So, on they trudged, through the failing light, 'very much chagrined' that Sherring had not posted someone at Baldak to meet them. It was three long hours, their strength beginning to fail, before they reached Sekung.

There, once again, they saw no trace of human life.

Night was falling over the patch of bare, flat ground, and over the three hangdog men standing, bewildered, at its centre. Hungry, tired, dismayed and downright confused, they lay down in the dust, and slept.

Where the hell was Sherring?

Had he never left Taklakot? Was it possible illness or some other emergency had detained him? Or had he carried on north over the Gurla pass, all the way to the shores of Lake Manasarovar? If so, to catch him would mean a march of many miles, taking them deeper into the wild, with no food to sustain them. Abandoned without explanation, ravenous without respite, Longstaff now saw that their troubles might be far from over.

Hunger was not the only thing they had to worry about. They woke at Sekung to find a Tibetan tent pitched nearby, with sheep grazing around it. Dogs appeared and started barking loudly and the Europeans were forced to defend themselves with the tips of their ice-axes. Alerted by the noise, a man emerged, 'with long straight sword, red cloak, long loose hair, bare breast, and magnificent carriage'. He was a *jykpa* – a Tibetan highwayman.

The Europeans watched the jykpa weighing up what to do with them. 'To give him time and show we weren't afraid of him,' wrote Longstaff, 'I admired the coral-studded pommel of his sword.' Then a second man emerged. A shepherd trader, he spoke a few words of Hindustani and 'excitedly told us to be off, evidently afraid of what the Jykpa might do'.

Longstaff could see that the jykpa was dangerous. But the Europeans were in a desperate situation. They could not afford to walk away.

Longstaff chose his next words carefully. He asked the shepherd trader if he had seen the 'Pombo', meaning Sherring. The man said no. Then Longstaff asked for food. The man offered him some strips of raw yak skin. Remembering that Henri had two four-anna pieces, Longstaff exchanged one for two handfuls of coarse flour. All the time the jykpa stood in silence, eyeballing the Europeans. Longstaff was happy when they were finally able to back away.

The men choked on the dry flour, so they mixed it with some water from a nearby stream and found the paste a little more palatable. As they knelt there, slaking the worst of their hunger, they noticed something. 'Across the stream was an obvious track,' wrote Longstaff, 'and the guides said they recognised the boot-marks of Sherring's police escort.' Taking this as evidence Sherring had passed that way, the Brocherels reasoned he must be waiting on the shores of Lake Manasarovar.

Longstaff was unconvinced. He felt certain Sherring must have been held up at Taklakot, 'by illness or some other unforeseen cause'. 'I could not believe he could have been so rash as to go on so far with no news of us,' he wrote, 'knowing that our food must be exhausted'. But the Brocherels were adamant the boot-prints belonged to Sherring's escort. So, after a pitiable breakfast, they started north.

They had not gone far before Alexis and Henri's strength began to fail. Toiling up the 'unending slopes of gravel' leading to the Gurla pass, the

Brocherels, 'in spite of my urging them on', wrote Longstaff, 'sat down to rest at more and more frequent intervals'. Finally, they lay down, one and then the other, unable to go a step further.

'How can you carry on without food?' Alexis demanded.

'Because I must,' Longstaff replied.

A cairn awaited Longstaff at the top of the Gurla pass, a stone for every Bhotia or Tibetan who had ever gone by. The devout would be careful to pass on the left, so that the short prayer they uttered would not be in vain. Longstaff had plenty to pray for, cresting the pass alone, exhausted, uncertain of what he would find on the other side. But he had not yet put his fate in the hands of the gods.

For all his fear and frustration, he 'couldn't help feeling pleased' that he had outlasted the Brocherels. He put it down to his size – 'it was probably their great weight against my light weight that told against them'. Now, stopping at the top of the pass, Longstaff had a difficult decision to make. Looking ahead, he could see the shores of Lake Manasarovar, still several miles away. Though much of the view was obscured by a large spur of rock, he could see no trace of Sherring, no sign of his camp. Was he going in the wrong direction? Had Sherring never left Taklakot after all?

If he turned back now, at least he had a chance – a good chance – of making it back to Taklakot. There, he could be certain of finding someone willing to help. It was a long way back, to where he had left his guides, to the camping grounds at Selduk and Baldak, then to Taklakot itself, but at least he would be striking out in certainty, rather than supposition.

And if he went on. He would be going deeper into the unknown, perhaps without the strength to return. He would be at the mercy of the elements. He would be alone.

Longstaff took a last look at Lake Manasarovar. Then he turned and started back the way he had come, down the long ramp of gravel leading south from the Gurla pass.

*

Longstaff found the Brocherels where he had left them, resting at the trackside. They still maintained Sherring must be ahead but accepted the logic of returning to Taklakot. 'So we retraced our steps to Baldak, and a terrible walk it was,' wrote Longstaff. 'My reserve of strength was nearly exhausted and I began to lose courage.'

They arrived back at the camping ground at Baldak at six in the evening, twenty-four hours after first finding it empty.

This time it was not.

A Tibetan shepherd was there, with his family, some sheep and some donkeys. He understood a little Hindustani, enough to confirm that Sherring's party had passed that way, going in the direction of the Gurla pass and Lake Manasarovar. He was willing, too, to sell Longstaff one of his sheep, on the promise payment would be waiting at Taklakot. 'The guides killed it at once,' wrote Longstaff, 'and cut out the liver: on a fire of twigs and yak dung we singed and ate pieces of it; and then we fried slabs of the carcass and felt better.' Five days since their last proper meal, the men ate as much as they could stomach, then curled up underneath 'the fly of an old tent' – a gift from the Tibetans – and fell fast asleep.

The Brocherels staged a miracle recovery. After a rolling mutton buffet and a good night's sleep, they were off up the mountain to retrieve their tent, sleeping bags and cooking equipment from the camp they had left at twenty thousand feet. But, though Alexis and Henri were back to their brute-strong selves, Longstaff was an altogether diminished proposition. Played out by the sheer physical strain, he was almost blind from the dust and glare of the bare sandy gravel lying everywhere in that part of Tibet. All he could do was lie with a wet handkerchief over his eyes, 'feeling very done now that the strain was over'.

Longstaff's first thought was to send a note to Sherring, 'telling him that we were too done to catch him up and asking him to send my servants and camp back to Taklakot, whence I would make my way back to India alone. This shows,' wrote Longstaff, 'that I'd got pretty low'. But, when the Brocherels returned with some of the Bhotia men, who had gone up to the high camp in search of them, Longstaff rallied enough to drag his broken body up the Gurla pass once more. He fuelled himself with *goor* – 'brown, semi-liquid sugar, which I ate with the greatest relish' – and wore, in lieu of a hat, a pair of white flannel rowing shorts on his head.

History does not record the content of Longstaff's exchange with Charles Sherring when he finally tracked down his elusive fellow countryman. There was much he might have demanded an explanation for, but none of the details found their way into Longstaff's account of the expedition. All we know is that the two men parted ways at Lake Manasarovar and that before he and the Brocherels left, they bathed in its sacred waters. 'Manasarovar,' wrote Longstaff, 'the Lake created from the Mind of Brahma is the holiest in the world. Bathe in it and all your sins are forgiven.'

Longstaff marched south for Taklakot, making his final crossing of the Gurla pass. As he did so, he took one last look at Gurla Mandhata. It was the same mountain he had seen for the first time less than a month ago, but now its ridges and spurs told the story of his 'greatest adventure yet'. Nor would it be long before he was back in High Asia, striving for the Himalayan summit that had so far eluded him.

But, even as Longstaff and the Brocherels withdrew, another veteran of the Himalaya was back for more. He was hunkered down at that very moment in a hotel in Darjeeling. And, this time, Aleister Crowley would be taking orders from nobody.

With ten thousand feet of mountain still above them,
how long would they call Camp IV home?

Camp IV on Kangchenjunga, August 1905.
Photograph by Dr Jules Jacot-Guillarmod (1905).

CHAPTER 18

Five Brothers

For Dr Jules Jacot-Guillarmod, veteran of the Eckenstein expedition of 1902, failure on K2 had brought success of its own. On his return to Switzerland, he was inundated with opportunities to lecture on his experiences. Nobody before him had photographed the Karakoram so intimately. His pictures opened a window into the heart of High Asia and, in his heart, he longed to return there.

In April 1905 Jacot-Guillarmod visited Aleister Crowley at Boleskine Manor, Crowley's home overlooking Loch Ness. The Swiss presented his host with a copy of *Six Mois dans L'Himalaya*, his written account of the 1902 expedition, then revealed his intention to return to India that summer. He was planning an attempt on the summit of another Himalayan giant, and had travelled to Scotland to persuade Crowley to join him.

If Jacot-Guillarmod hoped to pique Crowley's interest, he could hardly have picked a better mountain to do it. Kangchenjunga was the most sacred of the 'eight-thousanders', a peak steeped in religious belief and local legend. One Tibetan translation of its name, 'Five Brothers of Great Snow', referred to five brothers who guarded treasures – gold, silver, precious stones, grains and sacred scriptures – hidden at its five summits. The mountain was likewise said to be home to *Dzö-nga*, the 'Demon of Kangchenjunga'. Anybody trespassing on its highest slopes could expect to draw the demon's ire.

The mountain had come to life for Jacot-Guillarmod on the pages of *Round Kangchenjunga*, Douglas Freshfield's account of his 1899 expedition to the Sikkim. Faced with abysmal weather, Freshfield had led his party on a reconnaissance of the mountain, through the maze of giant peaks surrounding it. It was not Freshfield's words that had inspired Jacot-Guillarmod, however, so much as Vittorio Sella's pictures. Sella's photographs of the Sikkim Himalaya are among his most famous work.

Freshfield, a seasoned mountaineer, could see the challenge Kangchenjunga presented. 'The whole face of the mountain might... have been constructed by the Demon of Kangchenjunga,' he wrote, 'for the express purpose of defence against human assault'. But, for Crowley, here was the perfect opportunity to demonstrate his superior talents as a mountaineer. He would lock horns with Freshfield's demon. He would claim the five treasures of the high snow for himself.

Crowley agreed to join forces with Jacot-Guillarmod, but on one condition: he alone must lead the expedition once it reached the foot of the mountain. Crowley went as far as to put his demand in writing, drafting an agreement giving him sole authority over the climbing effort, a document he and the doctor signed. Then, with no time to waste, Jacot-Guillarmod left Boleskine to return to Switzerland.

A week later Crowley boarded a train for London. Before he left Scotland, however, he had one last item of paperwork to attend to.

He drew up a will.

Aleister Crowley was fourteen years old when he resolved to settle the question of whether a cat has nine lives. 'I therefore caught a cat,' he recalled, 'and having administered a large dose of arsenic, I chloroformed it, hanged it above the gas jet, stabbed it, cut his throat, smashed its skull and, when it had been pretty thoroughly burnt, drowned it and threw it out of the window that the fall might remove the ninth life.' Crowley described feeling genuinely sorry for the animal, insisting he had only carried out the experiment in the name of science. 'In fact, the operation was successful,' came his conclusion. 'I had killed the cat.'

It is easy to see why his mother, Emily, took to calling him 'The Great Beast'. She and Edward Crowley were members of a religious sect called the Plymouth Brethren, preaching the literal truth of the Bible and the imminence of the Second Coming. Both exerted a huge influence on their son but not, perhaps, in quite the way they intended. Crowley believed in God – as recently as 1902 he had witnessed, in the Karakoram, 'the awful desert of stones, God's rubbish heap, the waste material left over from the stately masterpiece, Creation'. But, as Emily Crowley was one of the first to see, he would follow a distinctly wayward path. 'I simply went over to Satan's side,' wrote Crowley, 'and to this hour I cannot tell why.'

As a climber Crowley was correspondingly unorthodox. His first ascents were on Skye and around Langdale when he was sixteen years old, and on the chalk cliffs at Beachy Head, where he climbed one especially treacherous line known as 'The Devil's Chimney'. The climbing community didn't agree about much, but all were of one accord that climbing on chalk was as disagreeable as it was deadly, a view Crowley endorsed. 'Chalk is probably the most dangerous and difficult of all kinds of rock,' he wrote, 'its condition varies at every step. One does not climb the cliffs. One hardly even crawls. Trickles or oozes would perhaps be the ideal verbs.'

Taking his maverick talents to the Alps, Crowley gained a reputation as 'a fine climber, if an unconventional one. I have seen him go up the dangerous and difficult right side of the great icefall of the *Mer de Glace*,' wrote Tom Longstaff, 'just for the promenade. Probably the first and perhaps the only time this mad, dangerous and difficult route had been taken.' Crowley's devil-may-care attitude was one of the things that attracted the interest of his mentor, Oscar Eckenstein, when the two met in 1898. The resulting partnership took them up the volcanoes of Mexico then, in 1902, onto the slopes of K2.

Now Crowley was going back to the Himalaya, with a point to prove. The Eckenstein expedition had been, by any reasonable definition of the term, a failure, riven with disagreement before retreating in disarray. This time around, Crowley would be leading the climbing effort, attempting to summit the third-highest mountain in the world – Kangchenjunga. With him in charge, he felt certain, it would be a different story.

Indeed, it would. The 1905 Kangchenjunga expedition would be more than just a failure. It would be a complete disaster.

Alcesti C. Rigo De Righi, manager of Darjeeling's Drum Druid Hotel, had a reputation for being as accommodating as the building itself. Baroness Mary Victoria Curzon of Kedleston had found the young Italian at 'the greatest pains to see that everything was nice', and Charlie Bruce – veteran of the Conway and Mummery expeditions – vouched that De Righi was 'always ready to assist any traveller to the upper ranges'.

Now, in July 1905, the Italian was once again going out of his way for one of his guests. Aleister Crowley, who was staying at the Drum Druid while he awaited the arrival of the other members of his expedition, had amassed over eight thousand pounds of provisions and equipment. He had roped in the ever-willing De Righi to help as he prepared everything for transportation fifty miles north into the Sikkim Himalaya.

When he wasn't packing crates and sealing boxes Crowley sat writing on his veranda. Surrounded by tins, sacks and paraffin bottles, he composed poetry to the staccato rhythm of the rain that clattered against the rooftops and poured through Darjeeling's sluiced passageways. Crowley was convinced he would one day be celebrated as one of the great poets of his age, but since arriving in Darjeeling he had been writing more than just verse. He had agreed to author a series of articles for *The Pioneer*, one of India's most popular English-language newspapers, correspondence that would be syndicated in the *Daily Mail*. Crowley promised to take readers inside the expedition, bringing news of its progress to British breakfast tables even as the climbers were getting to grips with the mountain itself.

For the majority of his readers, in India and beyond, Himalayan mountaineering was a new and altogether foreign concept. Martin Conway had led the most famous expedition to date, but that owed mainly to the popularity of his book. Mummery, whom many considered the most gifted climber of his generation, was likewise known for going to the Himalaya, if only to die there. British alpinists had, for the most part, confined themselves to the Alps, the accepted crucible for this haphazard pursuit.

Crowley, of course, had Himalayan pedigree of his own, but the Eckenstein expedition had been starved of publicity before it had failed, and ridiculed thereafter. He had seen how the 'pusillanimous braggarts' of the Alpine Club had maligned his friend, aided by the geographical establishment and the British press. Now Crowley meant to ensure that he would not suffer the same fate. He was taking control of the narrative, just as he was indulging his great love of the sound of his own voice.

In the first of his articles, Crowley described the preparations he was making as he awaited the rest of the party. 'Calculations, lengthy bargainings, careful weighings, more careful inspections, occupied days and nights... lists, labellings, numberings, cross-checkings, weighings – where is Romance gone now?' But, with the work almost complete, he was growing impatient. 'I wish the rest of the party would turn up,' he wrote, 'but they have been shipwrecked in the Gulf of Suez – which is undignified'.

'Shipwrecked' was an exaggeration. The vessel in question had run aground and quickly been refloated. This, though, was just the first of the delays Dr Jules Jacot-Guillarmod, Charles-Adolphe Reymond and Alexis Pache would encounter en route to Darjeeling. They steamed into the worst of the monsoon on their way across the Indian Ocean, then were further held up at Bombay as they brought all their supplies and equipment ashore.

Finally, on 1 August, the Swiss pulled into Darjeeling on the 'Lilliputian' hill railway. Crowley was on the platform waiting. He hadn't met Reymond and Pache before, nor did he know them – as mountaineers – by reputation. They, like Jacot-Guillarmod, were officers in the Swiss army and, while Reymond had completed his fair share of climbs, Pache was a total novice. Crowley, though, was in no position to complain. He had tried to recruit Guy Knowles before leaving England, but the young veteran of the Eckenstein expedition had declined, recalling

perhaps a little too vividly the experience of having a loaded gun lev-
elled on him at nineteen thousand feet. Crowley had likewise failed in
his efforts to recruit Eckenstein himself, who confided in a friend that
he lacked confidence in the expedition and in Crowley's ability to lead
it. Writing years later, Crowley acknowledged his disappointment. 'I
should have preferred it vastly,' he wrote, 'if he had accepted.'

Now, almost ready to leave Darjeeling, they had one more vacancy
to fill. The expedition needed a 'transport officer', somebody able to
combine the roles of quartermaster and translator – fluent, ideally, in
both Hindustani and Tibetan. Crowley believed he had found just the
man – heading, albeit, a shortlist of one. The more he had seen of De
Righi, the more impressed he had been – the Italian, he had written
to Jacot-Guillarmod, was 'a prince in disguise'. Crowley and De Righi
agreed that he would join them as the fifth European member of the
party, keeping discipline among the porters 'and keeping their price
down, even if he never does any heroic exploits'.

For De Righi, here was a chance to join a prestigious Himalayan expedition led by seasoned mountaineers. Crowley and Jacot-Guillarmod had
failed in their efforts to climb K2, but the two men thought enough of
one another to reprise a partnership forged in the Karakoram. Crowley
could be hugely charismatic, Jacot-Guillarmod famously good-natured.
De Righi had no way of knowing how fragile their association would
ultimately prove.

Two weeks out of Darjeeling the expedition descended on the last village
before Kangchenjunga, a tiny hamlet called Tseram. 'It consists of two
miserable cottages,' wrote Jacot-Guillarmod, 'and its entire population
comprises one family; children, parents, grandparents, a dozen people
in all.' Tseram would be their base camp as they pressed north up the
Yalung glacier, then up the southwest face of the mountain.

Crowley was the first of the Europeans to start up the glacier. He and
a small team of porters established Camp I at its foot, then pushed up
to Camp II on a small grassy spur on the right bank. Camp III, situated

across the glacier high on its left bank, was 'no place for a golf course', wrote Crowley, but had the advantage of being 'a perfect Pisgah' – a natural vantage point, with a clear line of sight all the way to the foot of Kangchenjunga, now just two miles away.

By the morning of 25 August, Jacot-Guillarmod and Reymond had also made it up to Camp III. Crowley struck out early the next day, leading porters across the broken surface of the glacier then up some 'easy slabs' to gain the crest of a ridge. There, a thousand feet above the glacier, on 'a broad level plateau of loose stones', he established Camp IV. He had left Jacot-Guillarmod and Reymond to follow with a larger group of porters and, 'having carefully pointed out to the Doctor and Reymond the route to be followed', wrote Crowley, 'I thought I was safe in going on ahead'.

Standing at Camp IV, looking back across the glacier, Crowley felt his heart 'uplifted by the excellence of our prospects'. Barely a fortnight out of Darjeeling they had reached nineteen thousand feet and, for all the rain they had endured on their march into the mountains, the weather was 'looking better all the time'. As to his own form, he was 'fresh as paint and as fit as a fiddle. I had never felt better in my life', purred Crowley. 'I was in perfect condition in every respect.'

The one thing troubling him was that he could not be in two places at once. De Righi had stayed back in Tseram, tasked with sending up provisions as per Crowley's written instructions, but the flow of food and fuel was proving erratic. Crowley was beginning to suspect that the Italian was out of his depth. Nor, for that matter, did he have any great confidence in the other European members of the party. Pache, at least, had the good grace to admit his total ignorance of all matters mountaineering; he was 'a simple unassuming gentleman', noted Crowley, 'in a state to acquire information by the use of his eyes rather than of his ears'. But, besides the dour and dependable Reymond, that left Jacot-Guillarmod – 'a cheerful ass', wrote Crowley, who 'I liked so well, personally, that I unconsciously minimised his imbecility'.

Crowley, then, had plenty to think about, standing on his small plateau at Camp IV, watching as the party led by Jacot-Guillarmod and

Reymond attempted to follow his trail across the glacier below. Watching, as they took one wrong turn after another, becoming helplessly lost in its labyrinthine interior. Watching, to his utter exasperation, as they gave up trying to find their way up to the ridge above, dumped their loads on the ice below and began pitching their tents.

No, Crowley could not be in two places at once. But, as he raced down the mountainside towards them, 'in a mood to ice-axe the lot', he was giving it his very best shot.

It had been a trying few days.

It began with a full-blown argument. Crowley had hurried down to find Jacot-Guillarmod and Reymond at their wits' end, after several hours trying to decipher a glacier more tangled and broken than anything they had ever known. Crowley had no sympathy and started tearing out their tent-pegs, insisting they carry on up to his camp on the ridge above. But the men were exhausted and, in the face of Jacot-Guillarmod's outright refusal go a step further, Crowley gave way.

The acrimony rumbled on into the next day. It was a long slog up to Camp IV, where Jacot-Guillarmod and Reymond arrived to find a handful of tents pitched on the slender crest of the ridge. One of Jacot-Guillarmod's photographs captures the scene, tentpoles and canvas slanting this way and that, sorry-looking men slumped in between. With ten thousand feet of mountain still above, how long would they call Camp IV home? This place, where the real climbing began, amid a chaos of provisions and personnel barely clinging to the mountainside.

Jacot-Guillarmod and Reymond were already suffering badly from mountain sickness. The more they saw of the route Crowley meant to follow, the queasier they became. They let their misgivings be known, pointing out that the entire southwest face of the mountain was being swept by avalanches. 'I can see well the avalanche danger,' Crowley flashed back, 'but this is not Switzerland. The obstacles and the dangers are three times greater. Therefore you need to be three times as audacious.'

Crowley was more worried about the camps below. The expedition was now strung over a distance of several miles, all resting on the narrow shoulders of their transport officer, De Righi. Crowley was sending back notes telling the Italian what was needed; instructions that, as far as he was concerned, could not have been clearer. But, for reasons he could not understand, they were not being followed. The 'mean and suspicious' De Righi, Crowley would later write, 'who ran his hotel by hectoring the men under him, finding himself for the first time in his life in a position of real responsibility... was utterly at sea.'

On 29 August it became clear how chaotic things had become. Midway through the afternoon Alexis Pache appeared in Camp IV despite – according to Crowley – being given clear instructions not to do so. 'It was becoming increasingly evident', wrote Crowley, 'that my comrades were too ignorant to understand that any instructions I gave were for the good of all'. To make matters worse, Pache could not account for all the porters in his charge. Several had apparently deserted, taking – much to Pache's chagrin – his 'sleeping valise' with them.

Seeing the expedition starting to unravel, Crowley drafted a note to De Righi, putting the blame for their problems squarely on him. Jacot-Guillarmod was to be the messenger, sent down to restore order. 'The doctor had recovered his health and his good humour,' wrote Crowley, 'and we had none of us a moment's doubt that he would put the fear of God into Righi.' Then, satisfied it was all in hand, Crowley turned his mind back to the ascent of Kangchenjunga.

At thirty-one, Alexis Pache had seen enough adventure to last a lifetime. A dragoon lieutenant in the Swiss army, he had fought against the British in the Boer War, becoming something of a celebrity after his exploits were serialised in the *Gazette de Lausanne*. He had accepted Jacot-Guillarmod's invitation to travel to the Himalaya mainly as an opportunity to hunt game; Pache made no claim to be a climber of any kind. On the contrary, noted Crowley, 'he was perfectly aware of his own inexperience on mountains'.

Crowley needed all the help he could get. To have any hope of climbing Kangchenjunga they would have to find a way up the steep slopes above Camp IV, cutting steps and fixing ropes so others could follow. Up ice-walls streaked with bare black granite, past teetering seracs clinging drunkenly to the mountainside, on ground softened by the sun and ready to avalanche. 'These slopes', wrote Crowley, 'were the critical point of the passage.'

Pache could take comfort from the fact that Crowley, for all his faults, appeared to know what he was doing, and that Reymond brought a serviceable climbing record of his own. They were joined by Salama, one of the three Kashmiris, veterans of the Eckenstein expedition. Salama did not have the alpine experience of the Europeans but Crowley rated him highly, enough that he trusted him with his life.

Pache would have been heartened, too, by the progress they made, setting out early on the thirtieth and climbing for three hours. By noon they had established Camp V in a snowy hump on the main ridge, at a height of around 20,350 feet. For Pache, it might as well have been the top of the world.

The next day they pushed higher still. Salama took the lead, cutting steps up several hundred feet of steep ground. 'We advanced very rapidly,' wrote Crowley. 'I have never seen a man ply an ice-axe faster than Salama did that day.' But, as the hours passed, their progress slowed, until they were climbing on snow 'lying thin on hard blue ice at an angle of 50 degrees or more'.

With Salama, Reymond and Pache in the vanguard, Crowley followed behind, leading a team of six Lepcha porters. Roped together, they used ice-axes and shovels to enlarge Salama's steps, paving the way for others to follow. They were midway up a steep couloir when Crowley heard a sound coming from above, 'the gentle purring hiss, rather like a tea kettle beginning to sing, which tells one that loose snow is beginning to move'. Looking up, he saw that an avalanche had formed, snow dislodged by the men above.

Crowley barked instructions at the Lepchas, warning them to brace themselves. They were roped together and firmly anchored, but Crowley saw that a man named Gali was trying to untie himself. He shouted again then, seeing that his words had no effect, raised his ice-axe and swung it, striking Gali with the flat side, leaving the porter momentarily stunned.

By the time Gali had gathered his senses the avalanche had passed. So too the danger. Crowley, seeing all the men were shaken, signalled retreat, congratulating himself for administering the 'sharp tap' to Gali that had 'probably saved his life'. Only a sharp tap, perhaps, but, where the fate of the expedition was concerned, it would make a lasting impression.

Jacot-Guillarmod had found Pache's sleeping valise. It was lying at the foot of a 1,500-foot drop, next to the mutilated body of the young Lepcha porter who had been carrying it. He was one of the men said to have 'deserted' Pache – Jacot-Guillarmod now understood that the porter had not abandoned the expedition at all. Far from it, he had gone back on his own initiative, alone, to bring up Pache's personal effects. He had hoped, by doing so, to cover for another of the porters, his ailing father.

Seeing the corpse of the young Lepcha, understanding that their expedition had come at the price of a human life, Jacot-Guillarmod's doubts and fears began to crystallise. In recent days he had grown increasingly concerned about the Lepcha porters, about the insufficiency of their clothing and equipment, about their poor treatment at the hands of Aleister Crowley.

Weeks earlier, seeing them marching through the jungle barefoot, Jacot-Guillarmod had accepted Crowley's assurances that they were saving their boots for mountain-work – Crowley had been responsible for clothing and equipping the men, with money set aside to do so. But, even on the glacier and the mountain, Jacot-Guillarmod had noticed that many of the porters still wore only rags around their feet.

Sure enough, making routine examinations, Jacot-Guillarmod had seen the Lepchas' health beginning to suffer. He recorded cases of ophthalmia – inflammation of the eyes, where some had not been given snow-goggles – and mountain sickness. Morale was low, meaning porters 'would exaggerate their maladies, so as not to go back to higher camps. They were men,' wrote the doctor, 'who could no longer be relied upon.'

And there were the beatings. Jacot-Guillarmod had always favoured 'persuasion and kindness' as the best way to motivate local men. Crowley, from what the doctor could see, preferred the point of an ice-axe and 'the toe of his well shod boot'.

Jacot-Guillarmod had been sent down to 'put the fear of God' into De Righi. Instead, meeting the Italian coming up from one of the camps below, he voiced his concerns. Even as they spoke, fresh 'deserters' arrived, those who had fled Camp V after the avalanche earlier that day. 'Complaining that they had been roughed up and beaten', they insisted that the climbing above Camp V was just too dangerous.

Jacot-Guillarmod had heard enough. As darkness fell, he settled on a new course of action. He and De Righi would be going back up the mountain first thing the next day.

Crowley woke at their highest camp on the first day of September still believing the summit of Kangchenjunga within his grasp. Believing that, if they could just make it to the great snow-basin above, the worst of the difficulties would be behind them. So, once again, he gave Salama the lead, detailing Reymond and Pache to go with him, renewing their attack on the ice. As before, Crowley followed behind, accompanied by the three remaining Lepchas.

This time, coming to where the snow had avalanched, it held fast. Unfortunately, such was Salama, Reymond and Pache's momentum that, when they should have been stopping to help Crowley's party up behind them, they simply carried on up the mountain. Crowley watched in astonishment as they disappeared out of sight, taking the only rope with them.

Crowley could not believe it. Without a rope of his own, he and the three Lepchas were stranded, unable either to follow the men above or to retreat to the camp below.

Four hours passed.

For all that time Crowley had no way of knowing what was going on higher up the mountain. All he could cling to was the knowledge that Salama, Reymond and Pache would come back that way sooner or later – assuming, of course, they came back at all.

And yet, as it turned out, salvation came from below. Deep into the afternoon Crowley looked down to see a large group of men arriving in Camp V. Seeing Jacot-Guillarmod and, inexplicably, De Righi, accompanied by more than a dozen Lepcha porters, Crowley shouted down for a rope. Within thirty minutes his party was safely down.

Jacot-Guillarmod got straight to the point. He informed Crowley that he had lost confidence in him and was assuming leadership of the expedition. His first act was to bring it to an immediate end.

Crowley was furious. He refused to make way, insisting that there was no provision for it in their agreement. He grew angrier still when Jacot-Guillarmod claimed that any contract between them was annulled – that he was past worrying about what, as far as he was concerned, was 'only a piece of paper'.

It was now that Salama, Reymond and Pache climbed back down into view. Flushed with success, they had climbed more than one thousand feet up the mountain. All of a sudden, they were being asked to pick sides in the turmoil engulfing Camp V. With the afternoon well advanced, Jacot-Guillarmod announced that he would lead all the men willing to follow him down to Camp IV before darkness fell.

For Alexis Pache the decision was an easy one. The day's climbing had taken him to a height of 22,000 feet or more – an amazing achievement for a novice mountaineer. He decided his time on Kangchenjunga was over. He would quit while he was ahead.

With Crowley's authority ebbing away, Jacot-Guillarmod asked Reymond to stay overnight at Camp V, so that Crowley was not the only European left behind. Reymond agreed and, even as Crowley continued to protest, Jacot-Guillarmod prepared to lead the other men down.

Crowley urged Pache not to go, telling him it was too late in the day, that the snow would not be safe. He warned him against putting his trust in Jacot-Guillarmod, a man capable of 'producing accidents out of the most unpromising material'. 'If you go now,' Crowley told Pache, 'you'll be dead within ten minutes.' But Pache had made his decision. As he prepared to leave, Crowley shook him by the hand. He told him he hoped to see him again, but did not expect to do so.

A party of seventeen Lepcha porters were the first to leave, making it down to Camp IV without ropes, ice-axes or crampons. It took fifteen minutes. Behind came Jacot-Guillarmod, De Righi and Pache. They followed the same route, accompanied by two porters and one of the Kashmiris, Ramzana. He, like the Europeans, had an ice-axe and wore crampons. All were connected by one hundred feet of rope.

Just a little way below Camp V came the steepest part of the descent. Jacot-Guillarmod and De Righi led the way, followed by the two porters. Then came Pache, then Ramzana.

Fifth on the rope, Pache was well placed to see what happened next. One minute, the two Lepchas were moving down; the next, one lost his footing and fell. He slid to where the ground dropped sharply away, then disappeared over the lip of the snow-slope.

The rope to the second porter went taut, then he too was pulled from his feet. 'No,' said Pache, understanding what was about to happen. 'We've only just begun!'

The weight of both men came onto him.

Jacot-Guillarmod and De Righi turned to see the two Lepcha porters, Pache and Ramzana careering downwards. They dug in their ice-axes and braced themselves. For a moment they thought they had done enough, that the ground beneath them was going to hold.

Then the mountain itself seemed to move away.

Reymond had done everything asked of him from the moment they left Darjeeling. He had marched wherever he had been asked to march, he had carried whatever he had been asked to carry, he had climbed whenever he had been asked to climb. So, when he heard his companions calling for help, their panicked shouts rising up the darkening slopes, there was no question of whether he would go to their aid. He rushed out of the tent to find out what was going on.

The first thing he heard was the voice of Jacot-Guillarmod, fraught and faint from below. 'Help!' called the doctor. 'Reymond, help! There's been an avalanche!'

Reymond moved to the edge of the slope and peered downwards. The light had begun to fail, but he saw immediately where the snow had given way. Following it downwards, there at the foot of the slope were Jacot-Guillarmod and De Righi. Both were still tied into the rope and were pulling at it frantically, where it disappeared into the ground at their feet.

Reymond understood right away what had happened. The avalanche had poured into a crevasse, carrying four men – Pache, Ramzana and the two porters – in with it.

Reymond ducked into the tent and told Crowley what he had seen. Then, without waiting for 'orders', he threw a few items into a rucksack, put on his crampons and started down.

He reached the foot of the slope to find Jacot-Guillarmod and De Righi clawing at the snow with their bare hands. They had lost their ice-axes, but Reymond had recovered them on his way down and the three men used them to dig. But, as deep as they went, the rope went deeper. There was no trace of the four men.

Night was falling. Under a pall of darkness, they gave up the search.

Their companions were dead.

Crowley pulled on his boots and stepped outside to savour the day's dying light, seen from the rarefied heights of Camp V.

He had warned them. He had told them how dangerous it was to descend the mountain so late in the day. They had chosen to ignore him. They had usurped his leadership and sabotaged the climbing effort. They had taken their lives into their own hands. So no, he had not gone to help. Theirs were just the cries of men who, as far as Crowley was concerned, had 'been yelling all day'.

Now, seeing the beauty of the Sikkim, Crowley began to soften. 'It was night,' he wrote, 'and the finest and loveliest sunset I had ever seen in these parts.' He had not gone as high as he hoped on Kangchenjunga, but he accepted now that his attempt on the mountain was over. 'The mighty masses of ice and rock behind me, lit by the last reflection of the day, stood up reproachfully, like lovers detached, as if they knew that I could do no more.'

Even in the face of failure – and the wake of tragedy – Crowley was there at the centre of his own universe, watched over by the enlarging eyes of mountain gods.

Crowley and Salama descended to Camp III early the next day. Crowley described seeing debris from 'a small avalanche' on his way down. Only now did he learn that it had claimed four lives.

He started issuing orders. He instructed one group of porters to fetch his possessions from the higher camps. He told another to go and dig up the dead men's bodies. Then, at eleven in the morning, he, Salama and a detachment of porters took up their loads and left.

That was it. Crowley had gone.

They found Alexis Pache later that day. He was buried, upside down, beneath ten feet of snow. One of Jacot-Guillarmod's photographs shows Pache's body, a look of staid solemnity on his ashen face. He lies flat on his back, arms bent, palms closed, hands lifted just a couple of inches above his waist. You can almost see the rope clenched between his fingers, almost feel the panic in his chest, before the cold numbed his senses, as he suffocated to death.

Reymond took three days to chisel a headstone. It, and a crude wooden cross, marked the place where they laid his friend to rest. A hillock, where the Yalung glacier meets the foot of Kangchenjunga, is still known today as 'Pache's Grave'.

Three weeks later, on 20 September, Jacot-Guillarmod, Reymond and De Righi marched back into Darjeeling. That same day, an article appeared in *The Pioneer*. It professed to describe all that had happened since the expedition had begun, in the eyes – and words – of Aleister Crowley. The three men were 'struck dumb' by what it contained.

Crowley had stolen a march on his companions. He had rushed back to civilisation, then rushed out his side of the story, in an article embroidered with wit, self-deprecation and lyrical verve. He was 'the miserably soaked Crowley that squatted, in spite of the arthritis in his left knee, under a rock', as they made their rainswept way into the mountains. His were the 'words of gentle admonition' reserved for porters 'over whose proceedings I will draw a veil'. He alone had shouldered the burden of leadership, giving 'the most necessary orders... construed as brutal tyrannies', to safeguard 'the lives of men as dear to me as my own'. Lives 'wantonly sacrificed to stupidity, obstinacy and ignorance'.

'It may yet take generations to teach people that mountain accidents are always the result of incompetence,' Crowley went on, painting a picture of an expedition hamstrung by 'comrades... too ignorant to understand that any instructions I gave were for the good of all'. Crowley blamed De Righi, a man 'full of petty personal pique', for failing to keep the higher camps properly supplied with food and fuel. He blamed Pache for the death of the young porter who 'went off somewhere on his own account, fell and was killed'. And he blamed Jacot-Guillarmod for 'the folly of attempting to descend to Camp III... ignorant or careless of the commonest precautions for securing the safety of the men'. This, he was clear, had led to the loss of four lives. 'A mountain "accident" of this sort,' rounded Crowley, 'is one of the things for which I have no sympathy whatsoever.'

Reading the article, Jacot-Guillarmod understood that events had moved ahead of him. He sent an urgent message to Crowley. Within days the two met face-to-face. The Swiss was conciliatory, apologetic even, ascribing his behaviour to deficiencies in his health and state of mind. They had disagreed over money but now that was resolved, signified by the return of some pornographic poetry Jacot-Guillarmod had been holding as collateral. To Crowley's mind, it was an end to the matter, concluding his dealings with a man whom he considered 'simply a fool but incapable of malice or treachery'.

And yet, even as Jacot-Guillarmod parleyed with Crowley, the next day's *Pioneer* was going to print. It contained an item of correspondence attributed to De Righi, undersigned by Jacot-Guillarmod and Reymond. Addressed 'To The Editor', it purported to correct 'mis-statements' in Crowley's account of the expedition. De Righi was no match for Crowley as a writer and rhetorician, nor did he claim any great authority as a mountaineer. He was, however, ready to get his hands dirty. 'I will give the true version,' pledged the Italian, 'of what really occurred.'

De Righi rebutted Crowley's accusations, one after another. He denied any suggestion the party had 'starved', describing how he had arrived at Camp V to find it well stocked with raw mutton. He denounced Crowley's claim to have only once struck a porter, the 'sharp tap' that 'probably saved his life'. De Righi cited a beating Crowley had inflicted on an elderly porter named Thenduck, 'so severe that Mr Reymond made a note of it in his journal… he noticed that the man lay down and received several kicks from Mr Crowley's well-nailed boots. Mr Pache was near but, according to Mr Reymond, apparently so disgusted with this proceeding that he turned his back on it.'

'To come to the accident and its probable causes,' wrote De Righi, 'I shall confine myself to the opinions expressed by the Doctor and Mr Reymond as Alpinists of experience.' De Righi noted that both men had questioned Crowley's favoured route up the mountain. He challenged any suggestion the avalanche was a 'small' one, arguing that it had fallen a distance of one hundred and fifty metres and buried its victims in up to ten feet of snow. To the question of whether he and Jacot-Guillarmod had cut the rope connecting them to the stricken men – a serious charge in mountaineering – De Righi was at pains to explain that he had slipped out of the rope in order to dig for his companions and that it had only been cut some ninety minutes later so that they could use it to descend safely to Camp III.

De Righi had done enough to ensure that the argument would rumble on, revisited by Crowley in the pages of the *Pioneer* and, months later, by Jacot-Guillarmod and Reymond in the *Gazette de Lausanne*. The facts of the accident were in Crowley's favour – his companions *had* taken their lives in their hands by descending from Camp V so late in the day. But history had other plans for Aleister Crowley. He would soon be more famous as an occultist and black magician than he had ever been as a mountaineer; the accident, an early cameo from the so-called 'wickedest man in the world'.

A man who – by his own admission – had made a matter of principle out of what, for four of his comrades on Kangchenjunga, had been a matter of life and death.

A photograph, taken in the days after Pache's death – and Crowley's subsequent departure – shows Jacot-Guillarmod, Reymond and De Righi crouching together outside one of their tents. Something burns in their eyes, the common understanding of men whose proximity with death has given them an urgent sense of what it means to be alive. Here, perhaps, is a glimpse of a bond that formed between the men Crowley had abandoned.

Crowley had been right – just as he was on K2 – about the route, the same one taken by the team of mountaineers who became the first to summit Kangchenjunga half a century later. He was right, too, when he had insisted that climbers in the Himalaya needed to show a greater measure of enterprise and ambition than their counterparts in the European Alps.

And, to give him his due, climbers would one day summit the world's highest mountains armed with little more than an ice-axe, crampons and their own bloody-minded individualism. Crowley was about seventy years ahead of his time.

But, in 1905, if you hoped to tread the summit of a true mountain giant, you had to take others with you. Success, at best, you might earn a share of. Crowley's failure on Kangchenjunga was his to own.

*She had claimed a record even Fanny, with all
her ambition, could not have imagined.*

American mountaineer Fanny Bullock Workman at the summit of Pinnacle
Peak, from a 1906 edition of *Le Petit Journal*. Illustrator unknown.

CHAPTER 19

Camp America

In June 1906 Fanny and Hunter Workman arrived in Srinagar for what would be their fifth summer season in the Himalaya. They had achieved a great deal in years gone by, but too much time, to their minds, had been spent 'sitting on cold snow-slopes awaiting the snail-like approach of unwilling coolies, and at snow-camps hearing their wailing complaints and refusals to march'. The Workmans had finally accepted that they might *never* be able to rely on local porters and guides pressed into their service as they quested for mountaintops.

Their solution was simple – this year's expedition would be a distinctly European affair. The Workmans had retained the services of Cyprien Savoye, the seasoned Italian guide who had been with them on the Chogo Lungma glacier in 1903, and had instructed him to bring six compatriots to work as high-altitude porters. These would be the men on whom the Workmans would depend to see them and all their creature comforts to the highest camps.

Fanny had asked Savoye to ensure that among these men was a cook. The Workmans had been deeply dissatisfied with their Kashmiri *khansamahs*, who had prepared food 'in an improper and unappetising manner'. Savoye's man, by contrast, was 'the proud possessor of several medals from Italian cooking-societies', wrote Fanny. 'He was seen an hour after the arrival of the party in Srinagar, with shirtsleeves rolled above the elbows, preparing fifteen pounds of mutton over a native fire, as if he had done nothing else in his life.'

The Workmans likewise broke with tradition in their choice of transport officer. Dispensing with the services of the Kashmiri who had filled the position in the past, they recruited an Englishman from Calcutta, a former policeman named Hogg who spoke fluent Hindustani. 'He was decidedly on the shady side of sixty,' wrote Fanny, 'but he was energetic, accustomed to plenty of exercise, and, best of all, enthusiastic in his desire to go with us.'

Ten Europeans, then, made up the colonial contingent of 1906, more than any Himalayan expedition of the past. They were far outnumbered by local porters – the Workmans would recruit more than two hundred men to carry provisions and equipment – under the orders of two Gurkha soldiers, detailed to help Hogg with the transport effort. Taken together all would comprise 'one of the largest private explorers' caravans ever made up'.

Their objective was a mountain massif the Workmans had sighted eight years earlier, travelling back from Ladakh in 1898. They had been coming down the Rangdum valley when they saw to the west that 'several dazzling white snow and rock-peaks lifted their heads high above the neighbouring mountains, surrounded by a multitude of sheer rock-aiguilles with tops dashed with snow, which, tinged by the red afterglow at evening, shot up into the cold grey sky like prongs of flame'. They were looking at the Nun Kun, a group of mountains on the border of Kashmir and Ladakh, 160 miles east of Srinagar.

Here, again, the Workmans hoped to make life a little easier for themselves. Set apart from the higher ranges to the north, the Nun Kun was – by Himalayan standards – reasonably accessible. Popular with game hunters and army officers leading training exercises, it had twice been visited by Arthur Neve, an English missionary and mountaineer, who had climbed to a height of around eighteen thousand feet. The Dutch mountaineer Henrik Sillem had gone there in 1902 and was said to have gone higher still. For Fanny and Hunter, 'the rugged, savage beauty of the group and the evident complexity of its formation proclaimed it a most alluring field for investigation'.

And yet, with all the changes to the expedition personnel, with all the promise of this new objective, it was somehow inevitable things would not run smooth – this, after all, was a Workman expedition. Fanny and Hunter were about to discover that, where the exploration of the high Himalaya was concerned, there was no such thing as low-hanging fruit.

The note arrived 'like a thunderbolt from a clear sky'. It was from Hogg, the transport officer, who had gone on ahead with two *dungas* – four-wheeled carts – loaded with provisions. At Islamabad he had divided it into loads and recruited more than two hundred local porters to carry it. Now he sent word that, within days, 150 of those had deserted him. They had disappeared into the surrounding country, wrote Hogg, taking almost a ton of grain with them.

This was grave news. Crops had failed that year in Suru, meaning the Workmans had to carry all their food with them, and ponies were proving difficult to come by, so everything had to be transported on two legs rather than four. More porters meant more grain, and more grain meant more porters, 'and so on in a diminishing ratio', wrote Fanny, 'until the problem assumed proportions that fairly staggered one's power of calculation'. Now it was apparent many of the porters, coming from villages facing starvation, had made a simple calculation of their own.

There was no time for recriminations. 'We had more important work on hand just then,' wrote Fanny, 'than collecting evidence and conducting a criminal suit.' She and Hunter were about to set off themselves, accompanied by the seven Italians and the remaining local porters, facing a dull trudge up the Sind valley then a difficult crossing of the rainswept Zoji La. Now progress would be slower still, stopping in every village to recruit what additional porters they could.

At Suru they agreed that Savoye and two of his men would go on ahead, with Fanny and Hunter following a few days behind at the head of an unwieldy caravan of men and livestock. It ought to have been a dozen marches to the Nun Kun. But Savoye, finding the Ramdung river impossible to ford, was forced to march for an additional two days up the valley then, when he found a place to cross, two days back. Fanny and Hunter, and all the men with them, would have to do the same.

After two long and exacting weeks the Workmans were reunited with Savoye, high on the Shafat glacier, where the world of trees and rivers gave way to the frozen ramparts of the Nun Kun. They completed the final scramble up a steep spur to find their base camp waiting, at a height of around fifteen thousand feet, with terraces for their tents already carved into the hillside. 'All were now keen for snow-work,' wrote Fanny. 'Ice-axes were tested and polished, and thick clothing was stowed in our clothes-bags in place of thinner garments heretofore worn. Extra mountain-boots were brought out and oiled, and those already in use re-nailed and repaired where necessary. The sound of pounding was heard for hours, for the porters were expert cobblers as well as cooks.'

For Savoye, this was the cue to press further ahead, prospecting a route to the higher reaches of the Nun Kun. He and his men established a camp at the head of the Shafat glacier, at a height of almost eighteen thousand feet, then crossed the ridge above onto a second glacier, lying perpendicular to the first. Theirs would be the untold story of the expedition – like so many professional guides, Savoye left no written account of his experiences. The only record was a trail of boot-prints and scuff marks, punctuated by the occasional tin can or empty bottle, a story swept into the margins as it was being written.

Fanny and Hunter, by contrast, filled their journals with descriptions of their time in the 'untrodden maze' of the Nun Kun, following in the literal footsteps of their guides. For the Workmans the puzzles were already solved, the path stamped down, the steps cut. And even then, they understood that 'having accepted the challenge thrown down by the Nun Kun, we have rugged work before us'. So up they went. Up the ice-slants and snow-slopes, through the tangle of crevasses and bergschrunds, until late on 25 July they saw 'what is seldom seen ahead at near 20,000 feet in Himalaya, refuge huts, three tiny green tents with bags stacked beside them'.

They had arrived at 'White Needle Camp', towered over by the spectacular snow-covered aiguille from which it took its name. A porter was waiting, and a tent-servant. Food was being prepared and water boiled. Able to stop and appreciate the view, Fanny found it 'grand and entrancingly beautiful'. All around her she saw 'a chaos of broken ice-walls and glaciers in cold white and blue… and beyond this, in the background, rolled wave after wave of distant Zaskar snow-peaks clad in chameleon robes of crimson, mauve, and gold, as the sun poured its sheen of light upon their dazzling flanks.' Taking the memory of these warm colours to bed, she and Hunter turned in for a night at 19,900 feet, higher than they had ever camped before.

A howling wind rose during the night. Fanny and Hunter lay awake listening as icicles, torn from the ice-wall above White Needle Camp, thudded into the snow what seemed like feet away. Both knew they would be climbing that same wall in the morning.

'We attacked the wall immediately after starting,' wrote Fanny, 'making short and frequent halts for rest and breath, as we trod silently the white ladder of approach to the mysterious unknown.' White ladder indeed – Savoye and his men had cut steps up the wall the previous day, and porters had already carried forty-pound loads to the camp above. But for Fanny and Hunter, braving the 'sharp incline' for the first time, 'it was trying to the nerves'. 'During the halts we could not sit down,' wrote Fanny, 'but were obliged to stand upright in the narrow steps, which tires the legs and feet more than advancing. A misstep here might hurl us into the bergschrund,' she went on, 'or, if we passed that, down gruesome precipices to the glacial ice-fields thousands of feet below.'

Until now, all Fanny and Hunter had seen of the Nun Kun massif was seven peaks strung together in what looked like a straight line. Coming to the crest of the snow-slope, they saw not a single ridge but a 'dazzling white snow-plateau or basin, some three miles long by one and a half wide, enclosed by six great peaks and one smaller one, which encircle it in a tiara of great beauty'.

White Needle Peak had towered over them in the camp below. Now, from Camp Italia, they saw that it was a mere rampart of the massif's highest peak – the mountain called 'Nun', rising southwest of their position to a height of 23,447 feet. Nun's summit was only a mile away as the crow flies, but the sight of its seventy-degree ice-walls and jagged arêtes prompted the Workmans to give up any thought of climbing it. Instead, they would attempt a peak at the northeast end of the plateau. Comparable to Nun in height, it looked eminently more approachable. They would need another day, though – and another camp – if they were to climb it.

The Workmans would call it 'Camp America' – rather a grand name for two small tents at the northeast end of the Nun Kun plateau. Two miles from Camp Italia and a few hundred feet higher, it had been a stiff morning's work to get there, marching on thin air and little sleep. Now, under a searing midday sun, 'the heat was so sickening that we were at our wits' end to know where to sit,' wrote Fanny. 'Inside and outside tents it was unbearable.'

Tempers, too, were rising. The Workmans had been left alone at Camp America, after Savoye abruptly announced that he and the porters would pass the night back at Camp Italia. It was too late in the day to bring up their own tents, he insisted, with the mist closing in fast. Savoye and his men were 'brutes', Hunter wrote in his journal, but all he and Fanny could do was watch as the Italians left and the clouds rolled in. The departing figures, the plateau, the surrounding peaks, all faded into grey, like one of their photographs developing in reverse.

The day cooled. Fanny and Hunter retreated to their tent for a meal of soup and tinned meat then stepped outside to see the mist had lifted, all the world now bathed in silvery light. The metallic sky disappeared into the west, where the setting sun played on a canopy of cloud, colouring it crimson over dark mountaintops. 'Our small camp was but an atom in

who thinks he knows it all. He is foolhardy, indeed, who
...g these unexplored giants without availing himself of the
...essional skills obtainable.'

...hough, is a clue to why Fanny and Hunter's legacy has
been overlooked and understated. As mountaineers they relied
a little much on guides and porters, and are rarely spoken of in
the same breath as adventurous amateurs like Mummery, Eckenstein
and Longstaff. As explorers they too often followed in the footsteps of
others, passing it off as pioneering work of their own. And it was only
on their final expedition that they started to produce maps of a standard
deemed acceptable at the RGS, by which time too many mistakes had
been made, too much credibility lost.

As a result, Fanny tends to be remembered for her most obvious
point of distinction – something she addressed in her account of their
final expedition. 'The object of placing my full name in connection with
the expedition on the map,' wrote Fanny, 'is not because I wish in any
way to thrust myself forward, but solely that in the accomplishments
of women, now and in the future, it should be known to them and
stated in print that a woman was the initiator and special leader of this
expedition. When, later, woman occupies her acknowledged position
as an individual worker in all fields, as well as those of exploration, no
such emphasis on her work will be needed; but that day has not fully
arrived, and at present it behoves women, for the benefit of their sex, to
put what they do at least on record.'

'In stating this,' she went on, 'I do not wish to ignore or under-
rate the valuable cooperation on this expedition of my husband and
joint worker, Dr W. Hunter Workman.' Here was the unimaginable:
a wife munificently acknowledging the tireless efforts of her husband.
The first woman to lecture at the Sorbonne in Paris, one of the first
women granted membership of the RGS, who received medals of
honour from ten European geographical societies and was elected a
member of the American Alpine Club, Royal Asiatic Society, Club
Alpino Italiano, Deutscher und Österreichischer Alpenverein and
Club Alpin Français.

the wide arctic basin, now ashen in tone from the falling night,' wrote
Fanny. 'The air was silent with that mountain-stillness more potent than
speech. But we were human, and the cold penetrated our vicuña-coats
as, leaving the ice-wilderness to the fast-encompassing pall of darkness,
we turned shivering into our tents.'

The click-clack of ice-axes alerted them to the approach of the Italians
early the next day. Fanny had been watching the grey light creep across
the canvas overhead, but now she and Hunter wrestled on their frozen
boots while Savoye and his men did battle with a failing primus stove, a
portent of the struggles ahead. They were at an altitude where nothing,
not even the routine operation of the human brain, happened without
a fight. All were feeling the effects of three sleepless nights, but 'as *l'ap-
petit vient en mangeant*', wrote Fanny, 'so strength came with climbing'.

Leading a rope of five, Savoye cut steps up a steep slope 'broken by
dangerous ice-falls and gashed by gruesome crevasses'. The snow was
weeks old and, though it made for firmer steps, it was hard work for the
guide. After thirty minutes he carved a small shelf for them to sit on,
where they enjoyed a breakfast of tinned tongue and chocolate, washed
down with weak tea and coffee. Then it was back to work, Savoye leading
for two and a half hours before letting another man take over.

By noon they were standing on the crest of the ridge. The surrounding landscape was extraordinary, looking east over Suru, looking west
back along the plateau, but clouds were already forming around the
mountaintops and the first traces of mist were creeping over the rim of
the Nun Kun. Soon the whole ridge would be shrouded in thick cloud.
Anxious to take some photographs, Hunter decided to remain there with
one of the porters. The summit would be for Fanny alone.

For Hunter, this was no great loss. To the best of his knowledge, he
was the current holder of the world altitude record, having climbed –
he believed – to 23,394 feet on Pyramid Peak in 1903. He had gone so
far as to deliver a paper staking his claim on the record. Hunter wasn't
to know he had misidentified the mountain in question – that he had

been standing a thousand feet or more below the 23,054-foot summit of a mountain called Spantik. In reality, the crest of the Nun Kun plateau was probably the highest Hunter had ever climbed. Now Fanny was about to go higher.

The summit was five hundred feet above, up a ridge so steep snow had little chance to settle. This meant rockwork, 'requiring strength, endurance and breathing power'. For Fanny it was 'more exhausting at high altitudes than on snow' and even Savoye took frequent rests. They were climbing at a height few humans had ever visited, as Fanny closed in on yet another record. They were getting closer all the time to a summit she and Hunter reckoned at around 23,300 feet.

With a few steps left to take, Savoye and the porter stepped aside, allowing Fanny to arrive alone at what she named 'Pinnacle Peak'. There, she looked out over 'a wide galaxy of mountains running in snaky lines surmounted by winding crests, equally tortuous glaciers, and ribbon-like valleys wrapped in a vast chaos'. Fanny had claimed a record even she, with all her ambition, could not have imagined.

The height of Pinnacle Peak is given today as 22,740 feet – five hundred feet less than Fanny and Hunter believed. Higher, though, than the 22,639-foot summit of Zokputaran, which William Johnson *might* have climbed in 1861. Higher, crucially, than the height of 21,329 feet given today to Pioneer Peak, reached by Martin Conway's party in 1892. Yes, William Graham had gone higher on Dunagiri and Kabru, but by his own admission he had not reached the summit of either mountain. Likewise, Tom Longstaff had not reached the top of Gurla Mandhata. Their achievements were uncertain, their altitudes unclear, whereas a summit was then, as it is today, something absolute.

And, as of late July 1906, nobody – woman or man – had reached a higher Himalayan summit than Pinnacle Peak, first ascended by Fanny Bullock Workman.

Only a few of the names Fanny gave to mountains are still in use today. Pinnacle Peak is one of them. The name is fitting, too, the highpoint

of her mountaineering career. For a third time [...] twenty thousand feet in the Himalaya. Nobody a[...] on so much of the range from such lofty heights[...] old guard of the Survey of India, now gathering du[...] Room of the RGS.

The Workmans had traversed tens of thousands o[...] subcontinent, had traded hundreds of thousands of f[...] They would make further expeditions, to the Hispar glac[...] the Siachen glacier in 1911–12, completing a programme [...] exploration unrivalled in its day. On the final expeditio[...] accompanied by trained alpine surveyors who produced[...] such accuracy it went more or less unchallenged by the geo[...] establishment.

When she wasn't back in the Himalaya, Fanny was busy de[...] her record and her reputation. In 1908 her great rival Annie Smith[...] returned from Peru having summited Huascarán, giving its heig[...] 24,000 feet. Fanny was unconvinced. At a cost of $13,000 she engage[...] team of surveyors from the Service Géographique de l'Armée to tra[...] to Peru and measure the height of Huascarán. They concluded th[...] Peck's altimeters had been at fault and, by triangulating the mountain[...] returned a measurement of 22,205 feet – the height still given to it today. Her rival chastened, Fanny tightened her grip on a record that would stand for another twenty-five years.

Fanny also had an answer for, in her words, 'certain "guideless" climbers' who 'have characterised guides as ignorant peasants with a taste for alcoholic drinks.' She might as well have named Aleister Crowley directly. She advised against listening to those 'who themselves have attempted Asiatic peaks, but have not achieved such measure of success as to entitle their opinion to any great weight'.

And, though it was anathema for Crowley, far more people tread the highest Himalayan summits today taking the approach favoured by the Workmans, led by experienced guides. 'On the unknown glaciers and peaks of Himalaya,' wrote Fanny, 'men whose profession is mountaineering are more in their place as leaders on the rope than the fairly

Who died in Cannes, France in 1925 after an illness lasting eight years, her ashes buried first in Massachusetts and later reinterred with those of her husband under a monument in Worcester Massachusetts Rural Cemetery. The monument is still there today, inscribed with three words – 'Pioneer Himalayan Explorers'.

'Party ascending the Chang La' from *The Assault on Mount Everest* by Charles Granville Bruce, 1923.

PART 4

APPROACH TO EVEREST

Wheels began to turn.

'I had no idea,' the guide told Mumm,
'there were so many mountains in the world.'

English mountaineers Tom Longstaff (left) and Charlie Bruce (centre),
and the Swiss guide Moritz Inderbinen (right) in the Rishi valley,
16 June 1907. Photograph by Arnold Mumm (1907).

CHAPTER 20

Trident of Shiva

Half a century had passed since the founding of the English Alpine Club – the world's first society of mountaineers. Now, in 1906, on the eve of its golden jubilee, three members aimed to honour the occasion with more than just a glass of champagne. Arnold Mumm, Charlie Bruce and Tom Longstaff were finalising plans to lead an expedition onto the slopes of the world's highest mountain.

The British had long speculated about the possibility of climbing Mount Everest – ever since, in 1856, the surveyor-general of India had written to a colleague to inform him that the mountain was 'most probably... the highest in the whole world'. It was not until 1885 that the matter had been taken up by a mountaineer of any great repute. 'I do not for a moment say that it would be wise to ascend Mt Everest,' wrote Clinton Dent, 'but I believe most firmly that it is humanly possible to do so.'

In October 1892, with the Himalaya back in the headlines following Conway's expedition to the Karakoram, Dent had expounded on his ideas in an article entitled *Can Mount Everest Be Ascended?* For Dent, the central question had not changed: could the human frame withstand the rigours of life at 29,000 feet? 'The effects of respiration will impose limitations on the range of man,' Dent concluded, 'but it does not seem conceivable this limitation is below the level of the highest point on the earth's crust.' 'The attempt,' he went on, 'would be costly, laborious, long, and possibly not free from risk.'

The first challenge of any attempt to climb Everest would be to reach the foot of the mountain, through Nepal to the south or Tibet to the north. Both had long closed their borders to outsiders, but it was only a matter of time before the British found cause to intervene in the affairs of India's closest neighbours. A matter of ten years, before the British expedition to Tibet of 1903–04 seemed, for a moment, to have cleared a path to Everest.

The 'expedition' was, to all intents and purposes, an invasion. Dreamed up by the Viceroy of India, Lord Curzon, who was concerned about the extent of Russian influence in the region, it was led by the veteran soldier and explorer Colonel Sir Francis Younghusband. Commanding a force of eleven hundred soldiers, Younghusband advanced at a cost of up to three thousand Tibetan lives. The worst of the bloodshed occurred in a pitched battle at a town called Guru, where the Maxim machine guns of the British mowed down soldiers armed with spears, broadswords and, if they were lucky, matchlock rifles, which had to be reloaded after every shot. Six hundred and twenty-five Tibetans were killed within the space of less than five minutes. Not a single life was lost on the British side.

Reaching Lhasa, Younghusband found that the Dalai Lama had fled the capital, so there he 'negotiated' the hugely inequitable Treaty of Lhasa with the Tibetan officials left behind. However, as Sathnam Sanghera points out in *Empireland: How Imperialism Has Shaped Modern Britain*, 'the settlement proved ineffective: it harmed relations with Russia in ways neither Curzon nor the government wanted; its provisions were mainly superseded by a subsequent treaty; and Britain conceded that it still accepted Chinese claims of authority over Tibet. The mission created a political vacuum which China filled,' Sanghera goes on, 'the effects of which are arguably still felt today.' Yet, if this extraordinary act of military adventurism would ultimately prove counterproductive, it did bring one unforeseen benefit. The British opened a new line of communication with Lhasa and, somehow, their prospects of securing safe passage to Mount Everest improved.

Wheels began to turn. Lord Curzon was no mountaineer, but he well understood the lustre of conquest. He wrote to the English mountaineer Douglas Freshfield in 1905 pledging his support for an attempt to climb Everest. There was little appetite at the Alpine Club to fund such an expedition, but one of its members, Arnold Louis Mumm, was ready to put his hands in his own deep pockets. 'I had always looked upon those who had visited Himalaya as the most enviable of mortals,' wrote Mumm, 'but had never dreamed of such a piece of good fortune befalling myself.'

Mumm's plans gathered pace following a chance encounter with Charlie Bruce. Bruce had served under Younghusband, had stood with him on the polo ground at Chitral in 1893 discussing the logistics of an attempt on Everest. 'The sketch of the action that he suggested we should take was, to say the least of it, ambitious,' wrote Bruce. 'This, I believe, was the first concrete suggestion ever made with such an object.' Now, twelve years later, Mumm found Bruce's plans for an expedition 'fully matured'. 'He already had his eye on another fellow-member of the Alpine Club, Dr T. G. Longstaff,' wrote Mumm, 'as a likely person to make up the party.'

With Mumm's money and Bruce's ideas, for a moment it seemed as though all was set. Then, in January 1907, 'just as we felt the venture was likely to go through, the Olympian Lord Morley put down an illiberal foot.' Secretary of State for India, Morley ruled out any approach to the mountain from the Tibetan side, citing 'considerations of high Imperial policy'. Mumm, Bruce and Longstaff appealed against the decision but it was no good – a new and insurmountable obstacle had placed itself between them and Everest, in the form of a 'dry-as-dust little man, ambitious and determined to use all the powers he had now acquired'. Like that, the mountain was gone once again, swallowed up in a cloud of diplomatic duplicity and political expedience.

Mumm, Bruce and Longstaff gave up on Mount Everest, but not on the Himalaya. Lord Minto, Curzon's successor as Viceroy of India, proposed an attempt on Kangchenjunga, reasoning that the world's third-highest mountain presented none of the problems of access posed by Everest. That was precisely why Mumm, Bruce and Longstaff were not interested. 'It was accurately mapped,' noted Mumm, 'Mr Freshfield's party had been completely round it, and its attraction centred entirely in the attempt to climb it, which would probably prove both dangerous and unsuccessful.' What they wanted was the opportunity for a piece of pioneering exploration, with an itinerary to keep them occupied for several months.

Longstaff had the answer. Inspired by the example of William Graham, he had long imagined following the Rishi Gorge into the 'inner sanctuary' of Nanda Devi, a lost world enclosed within a horseshoe of high peaks. Now, with Mumm and Bruce eager for adventure, he could revisit his childhood dream.

Longstaff and Mumm left London on 4 April 1907 to be met at Marseilles by three men, all professional guides. 'The brothers Alexis and Henri Brocherel, of Courmayeur, had accompanied Longstaff on his previous journey, and shown very great ability, endurance, and resourcefulness in emergencies,' wrote Mumm. 'They were chosen naturally and inevitably.' The third man was Moritz Inderbinen of Zermatt, Mumm's go-to guide for more than twenty years. 'I hankered after the presence of someone who would be a stand-by in case I could not do as much as the others,' wrote the 48-year-old Mumm. 'I should have been very much less happy than I was if he had not come.'

From Marseilles they sailed for Bombay, en route for the hill station of Almora, where Bruce was waiting. He had selected nine Gurkhas to join the expedition, eight riflemen under the orders of an officer, Karbir Burathoki. 'A regular Indian Ulysses', Karbir had travelled 'as far afield as Wales,' wrote Mumm, 'and enjoyed an extensive and varied experience both of climbing and fighting'. He had been a member of the Conway expedition in 1892 and had joined Conway on his traverse of the Alps two years later. A case of the mumps had prevented Karbir from joining Mummery's Nanga Parbat expedition in 1895, and had probably saved his life – his good friends Raghubir Thapa and Goman

Singh were the two men lost with Mummery. 'Senior in age and rank of the Gurkhas,' noted Mumm, Karbir was 'one of the most important members of our party'.

From Almora they marched north through lush Kumaon valleys, thronged with birds, butterflies and the scent of jasmine. Longstaff, an ardent botanist, was in his element, finding the roadside jungle 'almost impenetrable from the profusion of flowering creepers and masses of wild roses more delicate than ours at home.' After three days they reached Gwaldam, greeted by 'a rare tropical sunset when day seemed to be dying for the last time... only the steadfastness of the eternal snows seemed to give any promise of a morrow in this twilight of the gods'.

Now their approach to the mountains became long and 'toilsome', as they laboured up the valleys and deep-cut gorges of Garhwal, leading a caravan of more than a hundred porters. For Longstaff, the highlight was a run-in with a dozen lungoors, big grey Himalayan monkeys chattering angrily on the branches of a silver fir. Thinking they might be 'mobbing a panther', he went charging into the jungle beneath them, not much minded by the possibility he might be right.

On 5 May they crossed the Kuari pass, their doorway to the mountains. 'A single stride,' wrote Mumm, 'and I was gazing at a panorama that made one catch one's breath. The day was clear and cloudless, and a brilliant sun illumined every detail of a bewildering multitude of mountains, of every variety of shape and outline.' The scene made an especially powerful impression on Inderbinen. 'I had no idea,' the guide told Mumm, 'there were so many mountains in the world.'

Two days later they reached a camping place called Towa. From there they hoped to follow the 'back-door' William Graham had discovered over the Lata ridge into the Rishi valley in 1883. Their prospects seemed much improved when 'in the afternoon a shikari called Bhop Chand presented himself,' wrote Mumm. 'He said he was also the man who had accompanied Graham and Emil Boss into the Rishi valley, and produced a chit, signed by them, speaking in the warmest terms of his pluck and fidelity.'

Was this the man who had transformed Graham's fortunes twenty-four years earlier? It was impossible to know. Written testimonials had been known to change hands for money, often several times, and this would have been a much-faded document by this time. But for Longstaff, whose ambition had first been fired by Graham's adventures, it was a rare thrill to think this might be the veteran of the 1883 expedition.

Within days they pitched their tents at Lata Kharak, where they could look for the first time down into the great enclave of Nanda Devi. 'The toils, the fatigues and the discomforts of the entire journey,' wrote Longstaff, 'were repaid a thousand times by the visions of the next two days.' 'We could see into the depths and up the whole length of the Rishi nullah, while above the inviolate gorge towered Nanda Devi.' But for now, all they could do was look. Bhop Chand brought word that the path leading down into the deep-cut gorge was thick with snow and would be impassable for at least three weeks. That left the party with time to kill.

It had been Bruce's idea. They might have spent three weeks bagging easy peaks, waiting for the snow to thaw. Instead, he had produced an old map, pointing to an untrodden pass at the head of the Bagini glacier. He had devised a circular route taking them over the pass into the great glacier basin beyond, then back along the sheer-sided gorge of the Rishi Ganga.

Now here they were, high on the pass in question, facing a drop so steep they could see little of what lay beyond. If they lowered themselves into the unknown, it would be with little prospect of retreat. What would they find between themselves and their return to base camp? They were travelling light, at a point of no return, about to descend a thousand feet or more to the head of a second glacier that led they-knew-not-where.

Alexis and Henri Brocherel hadn't carried six hundred feet of rope all this way for no good reason. They had been straining at the leash on Longstaff's last expedition and Henri had complained bitterly whenever their client sounded retreat. They were joined by Karbir and the three other Gurkhas – the tall and slight Kal Bahadur, the impassive Buddhi Chand and Dhan Lal, 'heavy-jowled, and rather sleepy looking,' wrote Mumm, 'discovered by degrees to be a heaven-born clown'. It was said of Bruce's men that they would follow him anywhere. Here was an opportunity to put that to the test.

Longstaff went first, anchored by Alexis as he rappelled into the unknown. One by one the others followed, working their way down the cliffs in rope-lengths, with Alexis bringing up the rear. The elder Brocherel hammered metal spikes into the rock as he went, lowering himself off these then pulling the rope through behind. The only mishap came when Dhan Lal lost his load, as 'bags of flour and tins of preserves cataracted down the cliff,' wrote Longstaff, 'exploding amid the gibes of stalwart Karbir'.

At three o'clock in the afternoon the eight men reconvened at the foot of the cliff and looked again at Bruce's map. It was the same map William Graham had dismissed as 'highly inaccurate', the same map that had betrayed Longstaff and the Brocherels two years earlier. Sure enough, the map was wrong. The branch of the basin they had expected to arrive in was 'purely imaginary', wrote Mumm, and the glacier they stood on 'had not only never been visited, but its very existence was unknown'.

The men passed a freezing cold night camped at the head of the glacier, knowing all they could do was follow it downwards. It was six hours to the snout, where the meltwater led them on, from rock to rock, over the snow-bridges that crossed its foaming waters. Ahead of them was the Rishi Ganga. 'At six o'clock we reached the level of the first birch thickets,' wrote Longstaff. 'After many days spent on glaciers the first trees are always irresistible, with their beauty, the scent of foliage and the material blessing of wood fires. So in this lovely spot we camped; surely the first humans to get there.'

Low on provisions, Longstaff took his rifle and bagged a couple of burrhal. Bruce was unconvinced by his companion's marksmanship, which 'only showed what casualties result from unaimed fire', but was happy enough falling asleep with a belly full of mutton. Waking the next morning, spirits were high and, as they carried on down the Rishi Gorge, they came to where William Graham's party had turned back, coming the other way. Longstaff, who had pored over his predecessor's itinerary, understood now where they were. Sure enough, they reached Graham's 'fairy meadow', at the place called Dibrugheta, the following day.

And still, the 'Bliss-Giving Goddess', Nanda Devi, was not quite ready to let them go. Unable to find the path Graham had taken, Bruce attacked the problem with characteristic forthrightness, marching directly uphill. Alexis Brocherel struck out in a different direction and did at least happen upon some rudimentary sheep pens, habitation enough to suggest a campsite. From there, Longstaff followed a spur running west, only to find his way smartly interrupted by a 6,000-foot drop back down to the Rishi Ganga. 'Truly the Seven Sages,' wrote Longstaff, 'had barred their gate.'

They woke the next morning of one mind to 'break out somehow'. The sheep pens ought to have suggested a shepherd's path, but the men missed it and instead climbed into thick cloud. Coming, three and a half hours later, to the ridge above, they roped up and rappelled down the other side. There was just time for lunch amid the ferns, then they raced back to their camp at Surain Thota. 'So ended my eight days' adventure with Charlie Bruce,' wrote Longstaff, 'to whom I owe it that it was the happiest, most enchanting week I have ever spent in the mountains.'

On the ocean voyage from Marseilles to Bombay, Mumm had imagined 'bringing back the top of Nanda Devi to grace the Alpine Club Jubilee'. 'One day I asked Longstaff, "How many big peaks do you think we shall manage? Four or five?" I was much disconcerted,' wrote Mumm, 'when he answered soberly "I shall be very satisfied if we get up one."'

Longstaff had known, even then, the identity of the mountain he hoped to climb. It was Trisul, taking its name from the Sanskrit word for 'Trident' – the weapon of the Hindu goddess Shiva. Longstaff hoped to summit the highest of its three peaks, measured by the Survey at 23,406 feet.

He and the Brocherels had passed within sight of Trisul in 1905, though it had offered little by way of encouragement – its face to the west was 'implacable' and to the southeast 'unpromising'. 'It was my job to persuade Bruce and Mumm that, having seen two sides of a mountain, I could tell what the invisible third side was like,' wrote Longstaff. 'They understood and believed, so our course was set.'

Longstaff believed, too, that he had discovered a path onto the slopes of the mountain. He had noticed it as they were descending the Rishi Gorge – a stream of water flowing from a smaller valley to the south. Coming from the direction of Trisul, it had the look of glacial meltwater, grey and discoloured, discharged on the mountain's northern side. Longstaff was intent on investigating further and, with the pass leading into the Rishi valley almost free of snow, the way was clear to lead loaded porters – he hoped – to the foot of the mountain.

They would be leaving Bruce at base camp. He had been suffering from acute pain in one of his legs ever since they had arrived in the mountains, the result of an abscess. Now, owing to their recent exertions, he could hardly walk. Nobody could equal Bruce for enthusiasm, but no amount of pep could replace a working knee. Longstaff and Mumm would push forward, with Bruce following behind as best he could. 'We had already decided,' wrote Longstaff, 'that not even a death in the party should prevent one of us from getting up the mountain.'

Not everybody felt quite the same way. They would need to cross the Rishi Ganga, and Longstaff's plan was to bridge it with two freshly felled pines. It would be a promenade for the climbers but, where the local men were concerned, just to venture up the Rishi Ganga was to risk the ire of the goddess Nanda. Now they were being asked to totter over its foaming waters. According to Longstaff, it would be Karbir who found the solution. The Gurkha officer placed one hand on his kukri and informed the porters that he would cut off the head of the first man who refused to cross.

Was Karbir joking? Presumably. But Gurkhas had a reputation as fierce Nepalese warriors, recruited from tribes known for decapitating their foes. And, however hollow Karbir's threats, it was a telling moment,

as he fell into step with the European members of the party. The attitude
of the climbers, it appears, was that if they were going to risk their lives
trying for the summit of Trisul, the least they could expect of the porters
was to brave a crossing of the Rishi Ganga. They were true agents of
Empire in that respect, measuring their expectations of the local men
against their own skewed worldview.

Longstaff's instincts were correct. They carried on up the valley to
find its waters flowing from the glacier northeast of Trisul. On 6 June
they established a camp to the west of the glacier at 16,500 feet, on the
last patch of moraine before the snowline. Above, Longstaff observed 'a
magnificent ice-fall and above that steep wastes of desolate snow'. After
all the preparation and planning, all the distractions and diversions, the
ascent of Trisul could begin.

They were away before dawn, steering between the icefall and a line of
dark cliffs to their right, hard work for loaded men. The slope eased,
but now the sun did its worst, tormenting them with its reflected glare.
Then it steepened again and a bitter wind rose, whipping up snow and
flinging it at them with such force that it went right through their tweeds.

A little after two, at around twenty thousand feet, 'the Brocherels
halted rather unexpectedly', wrote Mumm, 'and proceeded to unpack
the tents and pitch them in the snow'. Mumm was unconvinced by their
choice of campsite, which 'sloped considerably', but he would soon be
grateful of shelter. 'The tents were hardly up when the wind began to
blow pretty hard... There was nothing for it but... to get snug in one's
tent before sundown; so Inderbinen and I retreated to ours with a tin
of biscuits, two large bags of candied fruit and raisins, and a thermos
bottle of melted snow.'

By the time darkness fell the wind had risen into a full-blown storm,
raging around them 'as if it had never had tents to play with before'.
Mumm 'heard voices muttering through it... as though the storm
demons were debating what to do next. Then would come a short lull,
followed by a flap or two, and then a violent bang against the bottom

of the canvas, just as if a gigantic fist was punching snow underneath the tent.'

All night it went on. By daybreak Mumm could see that Inderbinen was faring badly, so he took advantage of the first lull in the storm to confer with Longstaff. The two agreed to send Inderbinen and three of the Gurkhas down to the camp below. Then, the discussion over, there was nothing for Mumm to do but return to his tent. 'At 12.30 in the afternoon,' he wrote, 'Longstaff solemnly bade me "Good-night".'

Alone, at twenty thousand feet, Mumm occupied himself experimenting with some Pneumatogen cartridges – small cylinders of inhalable oxygen. 'In the interests of science I tried whether a dose of the Pneumatogen cartridge would assist me to enjoy a pipe. I think it certainly did; and I found I could smoke with satisfaction for several minutes continuously, which I had not been able to do before inhaling the oxygen.' Whether he knew it or not, Mumm had just made history. There, in the midst of a maelstrom, he had made the first recorded use of supplementary oxygen to assist a climbing effort.

Meanwhile, a few yards away, Longstaff and Karbir were grateful of a tent with the groundsheet sewn in – it seemed at times as though their weight was the only thing stopping it from being blown away. All through the night the canvas 'flapped unceasingly, clapping and banging like rifle shots, which made sleep impossible'. Instead, the two lay awake, Karbir regaling Longstaff with tales of his soldiering life. The Gurkha had fought forty actions under Bruce, he reckoned, and passed the night recounting his many adventures along India's northern frontier.

The storm was still raging when the light came up. They had held out long enough. Accepting that their first attempt on Trisul had failed, Longstaff and Mumm signalled retreat. Pulling their tents up 'by the roots', they tore down the mountainside, 'and… were revelling in the Capuan luxuries of Juniper Camp by two-thirty.'

Capuan luxuries indeed. Just as the ancient Italian city of Capua had once been a home to the headiest excesses of the Roman Empire, Juniper

Camp was a cornucopia of pleasures for men who had spent forty-eight hours starved of heat, sleep and sustenance. 'I was so weak with hunger I could scarcely crawl', wrote Mumm, who revived himself 'by swallowing a whole tin of sardines'.

The next day they rested, but Longstaff was not getting comfortable. He was already planning their next attempt on the summit, 'grimly determined to make another start,' wrote Mumm, 'come what might'. Longstaff's plan showed 'considerable traces of that Spartan element in his mountaineering habit of mind', Mumm went on – he intended 'to put rush tactics to the test' by climbing six thousand feet to the summit, then back down, in a single day.

Mumm understood that his own best chance of climbing Trisul had come and gone. Twenty-four hours earlier he had felt the summit within reach, but since arriving back at Juniper Camp he had developed severe diarrhoea. At 6 a.m. on 11 June he wished the climbing party good luck, then started down to join Inderbinen at the camp below.

Mumm woke the next morning knowing that, somewhere above him, Longstaff, Karbir and the Brocherels were at the beginning of a very long day. Thinking much of their 'scattered band', he and Inderbinen ascended a crag opposite their camp, some of it 'a real climb', for a view all the way up the Rishi Gorge. There Mumm had time to reflect on what a successful ascent of Trisul would mean.

Nobody wanted the summit more than Longstaff – from what Mumm could tell, his friend did not set much stock by so-called 'altitude records'. Longstaff, like Mumm, understood that little could be *known* about the expeditions of the past, and what they had or had not achieved. Neither Longstaff nor Mumm would ever have questioned – openly, at least – the honesty or integrity of their predecessors or peers. Even then, so much uncertainty remained.

Half a century earlier the Schlagintweits had arrived in India with the best instruments available, but with little experience of how to use them. They claimed to have reached a record-breaking height on Ibi Gamin, but had returned describing symptoms of altitude sickness that appeared, in retrospect, quite imaginary.

Less than a decade later William Johnson, one of the Survey's best men, described going to the 23,890-foot summit of the peak designated as E61. But Johnson had orientated himself by a map shown to contain errors. He, too, had probably misidentified the mountain he had climbed.

Martin Conway had fashioned a record on 'Pioneer Peak', trumpeting it at every opportunity in the years to come, albeit his so-called summit was, to the minds of some, barely a peak at all. It had since been remeasured at an ignominious 21,329 feet.

And, while much of the criticism directed at William Graham had been unduly harsh and badly misinformed, he had made mistakes of his own. Even now, seeing the peaks Graham claimed to have ascended in the vicinity of Nanda Devi, Mumm found that some of the questions raised by his itinerary were 'outside the range of reasonable discussion'.

William Hunter Workman had misidentified 'Pyramid Peak', substantially overreporting the height he and his guides had reached on the mountain known today as Spantik. Aleister Crowley had been wildly optimistic about the 1905 expedition's highest mark on Kangchenjunga – he was not among the men who climbed, by his reckoning, to 'a height of approximately twenty-five thousand feet'. Longstaff, on Nanda Devi East, Nanda Kot and Gurla Mandhata, had returned with more modest estimates, judged in relation to their untrodden summits. 'It will start to be apparent,' concluded Mumm, 'that any one who starts to form a decided opinion as to what persons now are, and have in the past been, entitled to the honour of having reached the highest elevations, and made the highest ascents, on record, has a pretty tangle to unravel.'

Little wonder that Longstaff wanted the summit of Trisul so badly. The only two records that stood uncontested – Fanny Bullock Workman on Pinnacle Peak and Matthias Zurbriggen on Aconcagua – were summit records. A summit was something definitive, a measure of confidence and conviction, not just inches and feet. That was what they were bidding for on the highest slopes of Trisul. That was what an ascent of the mountain would mean. It would be 'the highest point on the earth's surface which had been reached by man,' wrote Mumm, 'beyond all doubt and controversy'.

So, Mumm waited. The next morning, he and Inderbinen went out again, climbing the slopes behind the camp this time. 'I only succeeded in bagging one ptarmigan,' he wrote, 'and a very poor lot of photographs... the day was cloudy and overcast, and my hopes for the Trisul party sank low.'

Then, returning to camp that afternoon, Mumm saw that additional tents had appeared. 'To my surprise and delight I found Bruce lying in one of them, weak and feverish, but overflowing with conversation and in excellent spirits.' And, even as the two exchanged news, a figure walked into camp. His face was 'skinned and swollen almost beyond recognition', wrote Mumm, but there, alive – looking like death warmed up, but alive – was Alexis Brocherel.

That evening, reunited with Bruce and Mumm, Longstaff recounted all he, Karbir and the Brocherels had done in the two and a half days since starting out from Juniper Camp. On that first day they had climbed, as planned, to 17,450 feet. Away by half five the next morning, they had moved fast over familiar ground, Karbir and the Brocherels carrying the lightest possible loads, and Longstaff nothing at all. He knew his companions were fitter than him, and stronger. He would be working hard just to keep pace.

With memories of two nights at twenty thousand feet still fresh in his mind, Longstaff didn't want to spend any more time on Trisul than necessary. He meant to climb six thousand feet, summit the peak, and be much of the way back down by nightfall. The gamble was whether there were any surprises waiting higher up the mountain, obstacles to slow them down, to bleed their time. By ten they had reached the site of their old camp, where they stopped for a short rest and a little food. Now they roped up, wary of crevasses ahead. Alexis led, Karbir coming next, then Henri – the younger Brocherel quietly hoping, perhaps, that they would spend a night on the mountain, if only so he could dig one of his beloved holes.

Last came Longstaff. The ground was steep, the air thin, but the snow was in good condition and he felt the benefit of the wind, which seemed to breathe a little life back into him. Seeing from his barometer that they had passed 21,000 feet, he noticed his mind beginning to wander. 'I seemed to be confined in an endless chicken-run, with wire-netting on either side of me. I was breathing too fast, and I doubted my capacity to hold the pace.' There was a mountain, yes, it was there in front of him, but he was also playing among the peaks and precipices of his own mind.

'All the peaks except Nanda Devi sank below us,' wrote Longstaff. Alexis had been leading for many hours, almost uninterrupted, and there was no sign of him or his brother beginning to tire. Meanwhile 'angles were narrowing; the slope was becoming a defined ridge; we were seeing round corners. We must be nearing the top. The bitter wind swooped down on us more strongly, rattling the icicles on our beards and moustaches.'

'Suddenly the slope ended and Alexis turned and shouted back to me: "The top!" At four o'clock we stood together on a dome of snow and Henri stuck in the little flag of tent-cloth he had concealed in his sack, so certain was this giant of success. But I was not quite satisfied.'

Longstaff had seen a second hump, beyond a dip in the ridge ahead, that 'seemed to me a few feet higher than the one on which we stood'. He stepped forward and took the lead, cutting steps up to the cornice of snow cutting off the view to the south. Then, with Henri anchoring the rope from a safe distance, Longstaff crawled out until the lip of snow thinned to nothing.

'I craned over on my belly to look down on the astounding southern precipice. Spread below were all the middle hills we had marched through: then the foothills: then the plains with rivers winding. To the west all was clear; the whole scarp of the Western Himalaya so vast that I expected to see the earth rotating before my eyes. The western foothills gave the impression of those little waves that on a calm day are born as the sea shallows and lap gently at the shelving shore of some great bay. I was very lucky. I had not the very least feeling of exultation on achievement: the reward was far greater.'

Longstaff could see that the first point was, after all, the higher of the two. He made his way back and took two photographs. One showed Alexis, Henri and Karbir, their silhouettes crisp against the snowy summit ridge. The second was a view north, the three men now resting on the snow-slope ahead. There would be no confusing their position, no mistaking the identity of the mountain they were on. It was Trisul, the 'Trident of Shiva' – the first 7,000-metre mountain climbed to the top.

Reunited the next day, the leaders of the expedition had every reason to celebrate. Mumm had his trophy for the golden jubilee, Bruce, yet another high adventure to add to his collection, and Longstaff, at long last, his Himalayan summit – something he owed, by his own admission, to the men climbing with him. 'I had felt the altitude more than any of my companions,' he wrote. 'Success was entirely due to them. Alexis had led for ten hours, broken by one halt of half an hour, to cover 6,000 feet of ascent.'

Success had come in a single day, but it had been a long time in the making. For Tom Longstaff it had begun in his grandfather's library all those years ago, reading about the adventures of William Graham in the latest edition of *Good Words*. Now, twenty years later, his ascent of Trisul brought some vindication for his childhood hero. Graham's 1883 ascent to the near-summit of Kabru had been disputed partly on the grounds that he, Boss and Kaufmann could not have gained so much elevation in a single day. Longstaff had climbed further, faster, in comparable conditions – and had photographs to prove it.

If it had the look of an Alpine-style ascent – a hit-and-run in an opportune weather window – that was only part of the story. Four men had raced for the top of Trisul, but their accomplishment was the result of many months of work, and not just on the part of the Europeans. The Gurkhas might have lacked the Alpine pedigree of their western counterparts but they were trained in the same techniques. They might have lacked the brute strength of the Brocherels, but they had them beaten for fitness.

Nowhere was the infighting of the Eckenstein expedition or the tyranny of Crowley's 'leadership' on Kangchenjunga. Mumm, Bruce and Longstaff were not as domineering as the Workmans, nor as hopelessly reliant on their porters and guides. 'We were that rare combination,' wrote Longstaff, 'an integrated party without a "leader". Each knew the value of the other's opinion so well that discussion easily decided every move.'

The Brocherels had brought an irrepressible can-do spirit of their own and Alexis – 'a bit of a philosopher', according to Mumm – was deeply impressed with the relationship he observed between Bruce and the Gurkhas. 'That an officer should be on such terms of good-fellowship with his men, and that the elements of respect and discipline should not be in the least degree impaired, was to him novel,' wrote Mumm, 'and, if he had not seen it, incredible.'

If it seemed too good to be true, that is because it was. Bruce was hugely charismatic, a born soldier with his own backslapping approach to command. His fellow officers considered him liberal and humane, a paternalistic figure 'who knew the name of every man in his regiment, together with the most intimate details of their private lives'. A law unto himself, he had been brought up 'under the old slack and obsolete regime', with a reputation for taking far more than his fair share of regimental leave. The Gurkhas he took with him, men like Karbir, were among his closest circle. Theirs was the devotion Alexis Brocherel had observed.

Bruce had a darker side. In *Imperial Warriors: Britain and the Gurkhas*, Tony Gould reveals a man at the mercy of his 'prodigious appetites'. He had a reputation as 'the only officer who screwed every Gurkha wife in the battalion' and could become violent when drunk, 'so powerful… it took four or five to quiet him'. When he first joined the 5th Gurkha Rifles, Bruce had dreamed up his hill race as a way of boosting regimental pride. It was now an annual tradition, but for Bruce's star athletes it could be a blight on their military careers. They lost any prospect of promotion and, when Bruce found a good runner, he ran them into the ground. Revered by many, there was a grim brutality to him, lost to history behind, in the words of Jonathan Westaway, 'the occluding meta narrative of… heroic white masculinity'.

Bruce had shown that same single-mindedness, masterminding the rise of Gurkhas as a force in Himalayan mountaineering. Now, with the ascent of Trisul, they had a hero of their own. Karbir Burathoki had climbed with a frostbitten toe – one he would lose – 'but for him,' wrote Longstaff, 'the honour of his regiment was at stake.' Karbir's participation was a highpoint for Gurkha involvement in early European mountaineering expeditions.

A highpoint, and the end of an era.

For, within a matter of weeks, an expedition would leave Darjeeling. Led by two Norwegians, Carl Rubenson and Ingvald Monrad-Aas, the majority of its members were not Europeans or Gurkhas. They were not Baltis, Lepchas or Bhotias.

They belonged to an ethnic group set to become synonymous with Himalayan mountaineering.

They were Sherpas.

The wealthy young Norwegian had arrived knowing only that he wished to climb in the Himalaya...

Norwegian mountaineer Carl Rubenson.
Photographer unknown.

CHAPTER 21

A Sporting Effort

In the late fifteenth century, war came to eastern Tibet, prosecuted by an invading Mongol army. Refugees fled first to south-central Tibet, then across a high pass east of Mount Everest into the Khumbu region of northeast Nepal. There, making homes for themselves on the mountainsides around the Everest massif, they lived off the land in villages eleven thousand feet or more above sea level. They grew buckwheat and barley, staple high-altitude crops, and reared yaks as high as pastures grew. They were the first of the Sherpas, living within sight of a mountain that would one day make them famous around the world.

More than three hundred years later, around the middle of the nineteenth century, some of the Sherpas would migrate again. This time it was seasonal, as the men left their villages for the summer and made the 150-mile journey east to Darjeeling, seeking work in British-administered India. They took on manual labour of any kind, working in construction and agriculture, building roads and railways, and offering their services to various sporting and scientific expeditions that assembled there.

There is a tantalising possibility that Sherpas were among the men recruited by William Graham in 1883. He described being accompanied by a 'splendid set of coolies' led by a sirdar named Gaga, 'a sturdy honest Tibetan', and were joined by 'a merry little Bhootea cook'. Of the porters Graham offered only that they were 'Indo-Chinese'.

There may have been Sherpas among the porters recruited by the Workmans in 1898, Douglas Freshfield in 1899 and Aleister Crowley in 1905. Yet, looking at the written accounts of those expeditions, the porters were described as either Lepcha or Bhutia people, indigenous to Sikkim. This owed itself, in part, to the colonial bias of the expedition leaders – the indigenous Sikkimese were, to British eyes at least, subjects of the Crown. Compared to other forms of labour, porterage was prestigious and potentially lucrative work. As economic migrants, the Sherpas would not have been first in line.

The first time Sherpas are known to have participated in a European-led expedition was in 1907. A wealthy young Norwegian named Carl Rubenson, independently minded and of independent means, had arrived in India a year earlier knowing only that he wished to climb in the Himalaya, 'not in the direction of scientific exploration, but merely for pleasure'. He was accompanied by his friend and compatriot Ingvald Monrad-Aas. With no itinerary to speak of, and little serious mountaineering experience between them, the pair were travelling very light indeed.

Rubenson and Monrad-Aas settled on trying the mountains of the Sikkim, arriving in Darjeeling in the autumn of 1906 intent on mounting an expedition before the end of the year. 'Everyone we met in India who had any ideas of mountaineering,' wrote Rubenson, 'warned us of the impossibility of climbing in the winter-time. However, we thought we would make a sporting effort, as we had taken the trouble of coming thus far. As could be easily foreseen,' Rubenson went on, 'the expedition proved an absolute failure. We went out with the intention of climbing Mount Kabru, but only reached the foot of it at a place called Jongri, at an altitude of about 13,000 feet.'

Marching back down into the foothills, contemplating a winter on the plains, the two were not about to give up. Both had enjoyed 'a most interesting journey in Sikkim,' wrote Rubenson, 'but what proved greater value to us was the experience gained in the way of organisation. Without having had this experience we should hardly have been able to accomplish anything later on.' All they could do for the time being, however, was kill time in warmer climes. 'We travelled about in the East,' wrote Rubenson. 'This was not the right kind of training for mountaineers, as the heat encouraged us to be lazy beyond measure.'

Late the following summer the two men arrived back in Darjeeling, ready to try again. They recruited one hundred porters, a few Lepchas, 'but most of our men were descendants of Tibetans,' noted Rubenson, 'very strong, willing and high-hearted people'. He saw to it that these men were properly equipped, believing it 'a matter for more consideration than has generally been given to it; frequently such items have been neglected'. 'It is no good fitting oneself out like a Polar bear,' Rubenson would tell the members of the Alpine Club in 1908, 'if one does not look after the men in the same way. One must always remember,' he reflected, 'that they have no personal interest in the success of the expedition.'

As a result, the party that left Darjeeling on 16 September 1907 was unlike any ever seen before. Its indigenous members were well outfitted and equipped, with a large number of Sherpas among them. Indeed, besides Rubenson and Monrad-Aas, there was only one other European in the party, a Scot named Mason. He was their transport officer and would spend the duration of the expedition stationed at the village of Yuksom. Meaning the two Norwegians had another good reason for looking after the porters – from Yuksom they would march on towards the mountains 'more or less at the mercy of our men'.

Carl Rubenson was familiar with William Graham's exploits on Kabru. The Englishman claimed to have gone within fifty feet of the 24,040-foot summit – still, a quarter of a century later, higher than anybody was known to have climbed. Only a pillar of ice had stood between Graham's party and the true summit of Kabru, too difficult a final obstacle with time slipping away. Now, as Rubenson and Monrad-Aas approached the mountain along the Rathong glacier, they hoped they could go as high as Graham, Boss and Kaufmann. Maybe fifty feet higher.

They arrived on the glacier, where firewood was hard to come by, to find that the porters had been helping themselves to the supply of methylated spirits. 'They had used it to make up fires in the forest,' wrote Rubenson, 'and, in order to hide their sins, they had filled up the bottles with water, and thus, of course, ruined the remainder.' This did nothing to sour relations between the men – on the contrary, they were getting on famously. Reaching sixteen thousand feet, close to the foot of the mountain, they came to 'a most beautiful little spot with a small tarn and grassy slopes'. They established a permanent camp there, their tent pitched 'just below a big rock'. 'We used the rock for climbing practice during the days we stayed here,' wrote Rubenson, 'and put up prizes for the best climbers among the coolies, and they took a keen interest in the competition.'

Three weeks out of Darjeeling, Rubenson, Monrad-Aas and two Sherpas reconnoitred above the camp, climbing over loose rocks to around eighteen thousand feet. There they took a first good look at the higher reaches of Kabru. For 'the first time', recalled Rubenson, 'Monrad-Aas looked into the real fairyland of the mountains. And it made a great impression on him.' Ahead was a dramatic icefall, where the lower part of the Kabru glacier presented 'a perfect chaos of broken-up ice, crevasses, and grottoes'.

'With regard to myself,' Rubenson went on, 'my delight was by no means unmixed... I could not help but feel the responsibilities of my position, as I was the only one among the party who knew anything about mountaineering.' The Norwegian could see that 'to cross the glacier here would be impossible', and his thoughts turned to something he had seen back in Darjeeling, examining Kabru 'through a strong telescope'. Above was 'the Dome', a southern buttress of the mountain, below it 'a narrow white strip'. 'Here,' wrote Rubenson, 'I thought the glacier might be possible to cross.'

The Norwegians established a camp at eighteen thousand feet, 'where we had to leave the rocks for the snow. We were not going to touch rock again for a considerable time.' The next day they pushed higher still, making the most of 'glorious weather' to pitch their four tents at 19,500 feet. There, Rubenson confessed to feeling 'somewhat down-hearted... gazing upon the labyrinth of crevasses in this broken up ice-fall'. Here was the place he had hoped to cross and, though he believed it possible for 'a light party of mountaineers', he felt less confident in the abilities of the fourteen Sherpas they had with them.

All they could do was try. Rubenson began to puzzle his way through the difficulties and dead ends, and soon found that, 'contrary to expectations, the coolies proved very eager'. Seeing that the Sherpas 'often took the initiative when they had a good idea', the Norwegians began to understand that they were more than just manual labourers, more than just porters. 'After having been trained in the use of a rope and ice axe,' wrote Rubenson, 'our men proved quite mountaineers.'

But the icefall would not go easy. Each day it drew them in with the promise of fresh progress, then crushed their hopes with some new obstacle. 'Very often when we came to a difficulty impossible to overcome we had to return and start anew,' wrote Rubenson, 'but as a rule we got on a bit further every day.' At night the wind often rose into a gale and the sound of thunderous avalanches could be heard close by, as the two Norwegians lay awake with a lamp burning, 'expecting every moment to be hurled, together with our tents, into the valley below'.

Each morning, finding they were still alive, they took up their ice-axes and marched back into the icefall. As the days went by, Rubenson saw the Sherpas improvising and adopting practices of their own. Coming to an especially difficult place, they often refused to form a rope at all, knowing a fall for one might mean death for all. 'Though it isn't the way a European mountaineer would look at things,' wrote Rubenson, 'yet there is a good deal of common sense in their reasoning.'

One incident in particular hinted at the bond forming between the men. Somewhere in the innards of the icefall, Monrad-Aas observed a hallowed mountaineering tradition – he lost his hat. It was blown from his head into a nearby crevasse and was quickly given up by the Norwegian, on the grounds that he 'had plenty more'. Putting aside the question of exactly how many hats Ingvald Monrad-Aas had with him, it must have given him some satisfaction 'when about ten minutes later one of the coolies overtook us and, wreathed in smiles, presented

Monrad-Aas with his hat. He had been let down by his comrades twenty feet or so to obtain it.'

On their fifth day in the icefall, the men established a camp at around 21,000 feet. They called it 'Halfway House'. Rubenson thought the worst behind them but, with their tents pitched at the foot of a sheer ice-wall, danger had never seemed closer. All around were huge ice boulders, 'the remains of previous avalanches', and they knew fresh debris might come thundering down at any moment. Shivering in their tents at night, the temperature below zero, they could take comfort in the knowledge that the ice-wall was frozen more rigid than they were.

Two days later they emerged onto an ice-strip at around 22,000 feet, level with the top of the Dome. They were now two thousand feet below the summit of Kabru, with a string of camps connecting them to the 'lower world', all run by Sherpas. It was a line of communication so effective the Norwegians would receive letters from Europe at their highest camp. 'Undoubtedly,' noted Rubenson, 'the highest point at which mail has ever been delivered.'

It was a fine place to smoke a pipe.

The day was beautifully clear and their eyes were drawn out across an ocean of cloud stretching away below. They had thought they might reach the summit that day but, gaining the crest of a ridge leading to the mountain's northeastern peak, they had lost something of their resolve. 'The day was very hot,' wrote Rubenson. 'We felt very lazy.' So, they sat down, lit their pipes and enjoyed the view.

Rubenson took some photographs, one of their 'great neighbour' Kangchenjunga and another of the view down onto the plateau nested on top of the Dome. At 22,700 feet, the two men had surpassed what many would have considered possible. Anxious to avoid the same fate as Graham, Rubenson was being careful to make sure he had pictorial evidence of all they had seen and done.

Short on food, they had sustained themselves for two days on a single tin of ox tongue, but both were committed smokers, finding it a welcome distraction and a useful appetite suppressant. 'One thing we found of very much use in "keeping our pecker up" was brandy,' Rubenson told the Alpine Club. 'Even in this matter the coolies were at one with us. But of course we took nothing before the evening.'

After a night in a single tent, huddled together with two Sherpas, it was now or never. 'We couldn't wait any longer, as semi-starvation is hardly the right training for strenuous work. A nasty wind was blowing and the result was that we did not get out of our warm sleeping-bags till rather late in the morning. Not until after nine did we make a start.'

On 20 October, a little over a month since leaving Darjeeling, they started up towards a summit nobody, but nobody, would have backed them to reach. One of the Sherpas went with them, but he soon turned back, leaving Rubenson and Monrad-Aas alone on the mountain.

They had given up on nailed boots – the cold wormed in through the metal nails, piercing the soles of their feet – so the steps they cut needed to be that much better. But the snow was hard, meaning 'we had to slice five or six times for making a step', and the ground was not especially steep, so they gained altitude slowly. 'Very often we were forced to stop and turn around when we were met by an extra-strong gust of wind,' wrote Rubenson. 'The rocks just under the peak did not seem to get any nearer at all.'

They had planned to climb to a saddle between Kabru's two peaks but as they worked their way upwards the wind strengthened, driving them onto the sheltered eastern side of the mountain. Their best hope now was to climb to the northeastern summit, hidden several hundred feet above. Time was against them, but Rubenson felt fit and strong and, aside from one bout of giddiness lasting just a few minutes, Monrad-Aas was there with him.

It was extraordinary, really. Monrad-Aas had never climbed a mountain before. Now here he was among the handful of people to have gone above 23,000 feet. He and Rubenson had been living above nineteen thousand feet for more than a fortnight and had not eaten properly for days, sharing every moment with the pervasive cold. And still they climbed, steeply upwards, towards a summit they could not see. 'At last at nearly five o'clock we got up to the lower rocks,' wrote Rubenson, 'and sat down to rest for a moment below a big rock. Our hands and feet were numb with cold, and we felt very hungry.'

After a short rest they resumed the climb, moving between slippery rock and steep snow. Within an hour they saw that the saddle between the two peaks was beneath them. This put them perhaps two hundred feet below the summit, but the light was fading, the sun poised on the horizon, the temperature plummeting. 'The cold had increased immensely,' wrote Rubenson, 'and our teeth were chattering violently. But a short distance above us we saw a dark-hued rock, which we thought was the actual summit, and we made our last effort to reach it.'

Another thirty minutes and they were there. But the mountain had played a last trick. The point they had seen was just an outcrop, a false summit. Beyond was the true top of Kabru, up a small snow crest that, in gathering darkness and crippling cold, was a ridge too far. 'Under ordinary conditions it would have taken us about a quarter of an hour to get there,' wrote Rubenson, 'but up here, so close underneath the ridge, the wind met us with all its force, and we did not dare continue.'

'We did not even get a view over to the other side,' he went on, 'which would indeed have been the most wonderful upon which the human eye has ever gazed.' Out of time, but not – quite – mountain, they turned back. The Norwegians, like Graham before them, had come up fifty feet short.

Two weeks later an account of the expedition appeared in *The Englishman*, an English-language newspaper published out of Calcutta. 'The altitude reached was about 23,900 feet,' wrote Rubenson. A few months later, addressing the Alpine Club, he offered that 'the height we reached, even if it was not the highest hitherto attained, still was pretty near the limit to which human beings have been able to reach'.

First to speak, once Rubenson had delivered his paper, was Tom Longstaff. 'It is, if not the highest, at least the highest unchallenged ascent that has ever been made,' noted Longstaff, 'those of Graham and Johnson having been disputed on various grounds.' 'It is a very great pleasure to me,' he went on, 'to find that Mr Rubenson has not himself in any way called in question Graham's ascent of the highest peak of Kabru in 1883.'

On the contrary, Rubenson had come down in Graham's favour. 'I must confess,' the Norwegian told the Alpine Club, 'that I found it hard to realise that Mr. Graham could have made such progress as he claims to have made in one day; but Mr. Longstaff on his last expedition proved that such rapid progress was not impossible, and I do not venture to dispute Graham's statements any longer.'

It was 2 June 1908. The Alpine Club had recently celebrated its jubilee by toasting Longstaff's ascent of Trisul and now here was Carl Rubenson describing a guideless climb to take him higher still, with a 'graphic series of photographs' to prove it. More than ever, it must have seemed as though the highest mountains of the Himalaya were coming into range.

But there was another talking point at the Alpine Club that night, another reason to be optimistic about what European mountaineers might now accomplish in the near future. As Tom Longstaff, Arnold Mumm, Cecil Slingsby and Norman Collie all congratulated Rubenson on what he and Monrad-Aas had accomplished, each acknowledged, as Mumm put it, 'his astonishing skill in managing the coolies and his enterprise and success in training them to ice-work. Indeed, the more one realises the length and the arduous character of the expedition,' offered Mumm, 'the more one is struck by the patience and the quiet, unhurried perseverance displayed by the party.'

These were some of the most distinguished alpinists in the world, noticing that something about this expedition was different. Their first instinct was to give the Norwegians credit, but Rubenson would see to it that the Sherpas had their talents recognised. He had seen how well they had performed high on the mountain. 'Very few of our men got sufficiently ill for it to be necessary to send them back again,' he noted, 'and upon some of them the altitude seemed to have no effect whatever.'

Rubenson was onto something, a physiological trait not to be properly understood until more than a century later. In 2017, scientific researchers would show that Sherpas are genetically adapted to outperform other ethnic groups at high altitude, making more efficient use of the oxygen in their bloodstream at a cellular level. This evolutionary advantage is thought to have been gained over the nine thousand years since they had first moved up onto the Tibetan Plateau, and they brought it with them when they migrated into Nepal's Khumbu valley. In their search for better stewardship through the mountains of the Himalaya, the Norwegians had discovered a rare example of natural selection in the recent evolution of human beings.

Nor was it a coincidence that the first European mountaineers to discover the traits and talents of the Sherpas came from beyond British shores. Unencumbered by imperial bias, Rubenson brought word of a mountain tribe uniquely well-adjusted for work as high-altitude porters and guides. 'Sherpa coolies, properly fitted out and well treated,' he told the Alpine Club, 'will prove more useful... than any European professional mountaineer.'

*The Duke had shown that mountaineering could be
a national project, that the hopes of a whole country
could be carried to a mountain's summit.*

Italian mountaineer and explorer Prince Luigi Amedeo, Duke of
the Abruzzi at the summit of Mount Margherita, from *La Domenica
del Corriere* (1906). Engraving by Achille Beltrame (1906).

CHAPTER 22

Rarefied Air

Early on the morning of 25 June 1909 a party of three Italians left their camp on the northeast ridge of K2 and began to climb. They had passed the night at Windy Gap, a saddle at around twenty thousand feet christened by the Eckenstein expedition of 1902. But, where Eckenstein's party had used Windy Gap as a staging point for their ill-fated attempt on K2, the Italians moved in a northeasterly direction, away from the mountain, up the slopes of what they knew as Staircase Peak.

'Staircase Peak.' Yet another of the fanciful names dreamed up by their predecessor in the Karakoram, Martin Conway. The Baltis knew it as Skyang Kangri, but Conway – rarely one to trouble himself with discovering a mountain's local name – had been inspired by the five giant steps leading to its 24,754-foot summit. It was up the first of those steps that the three Italians made their way.

Two of them, the veteran Italian guide Joseph Petigax and his son Laurent, were in the Karakoram for a second time. They, along with Cyprien Savoye, had guided the Workmans to the head of the Chogo Lungma glacier in 1903, where Fanny twice improved on her women's world altitude record. Now, six years on, they were back with a client who had royal rank to explain away his airs and graces. He was Prince Luigi Amedeo Giuseppe Maria Ferdinando Francesco di Savoia-Aosta, better known by his title – the Duke of the Abruzzi.

The elder Petigax led them across the first of the step-like plateaux, where they joined a ridge leading to the next. The guide was feeling good but, as they gained height, his son began to struggle with the thinness of the air, as did the Duke. Increasingly they found their path blocked by crevasses, each wider and more awkward than the last, until, crossing a sloping terrace, they met a gap twenty feet across, thirty in places. The men searched for a snow-bridge, or some other way over, but it was useless. With no path forward, they stopped to rest.

The Duke had more than one reason for attempting to climb Skyang Kangri. He had hoped to go as high as he could on the mountain – to its summit, if possible – but that was not his only reason for trying. Now, seeing that this was as far as they would go, he and the Petigaxes began to unpack his camera, setting it up facing away from the mountain. The day was still, the air clear. Nobody had ever commanded so fine a view of K2.

The Duke took a photograph, capturing the northeast face in crystalline clarity. It shows the mountain smouldering under spindrift and vapour, hulking shoulders beneath epaulettes of snow; the lightest shrug promises to release a tumult on anyone foolish enough to brave its slopes. Then you see it, the true face of the mountain, eyes of shadow, sunk beneath a corniced brow. K2, monarch of the Karakoram, photographed by royalty.

The Duke took another picture, and another, piecing together a panorama encompassing all he could see. For weeks he and his men had been exploring the glaciers encircling K2; in his mind he could form a complete picture of the mountain – and of all the possible routes to its summit. Now his reconnaissance was over, nothing could have been clearer – he and his companions would not be able to climb it.

The Duke had known mountains from a young age. His mother had died when he was just three and a half years old and his father, heartbroken, had left the care of his sons to others. As soon as he was old enough, Luigi was enrolled at the Royal Naval Academy at Genoa, then in the summer holidays he and his brothers were entrusted to a Barnabite monk named Francisco Denza. Denza belonged to a school of Italian educators who believed mountaineering was integral to a young man's spiritual development, so as well as tutoring the boys in geography and geology he took them hiking and climbing in the Graian Alps. Under Denza's influence, Luigi came to see mountains as a place of physical and intellectual rigour – a proving ground for body and mind.

Another formative figure for Luigi was his aunt, Queen Margherita. She had visited her sister-in-law on her deathbed, promising that she would take an active interest in the boy's upbringing. She would give Luigi the closest thing he knew to a mother's love. Margherita visited the mountains to escape her philandering husband, King Umberto, and, though there is no record of her climbing with her nephew, he learned from her example. Mountaineering and exploration became a diversion from what he would one day describe as 'the hypocrisies of men'.

Luigi thrived at naval college. His father had sent instructions that he be treated no differently to the other cadets, but the young prince understood that he *was* different. For ten years he worked harder, ran faster, aimed higher, and in 1889 he got his reward – he was promoted to midshipman, joining the crew of the *Amerigo Vespucci*. He was aboard the *Vespucci* one year later when he learned his father had died; arriving back in Italy in 1891, he was an orphan, the newly entitled Duke of the Abruzzi.

When he was not at sea, the Duke made straight for the mountains. In 1892 he completed his first significant ascent in the Alps, the 11,031-foot Punta Levanna. The following year he climbed the Gran Paradiso in the Graian Alps, made an ascent of Mont Blanc and summited the spiry Dent du Géant – proof he was becoming an adept young alpinist. Then, in 1894, he and his guides were following the trails leading up to the Matterhorn's Zmutt Ridge when they came into the rarefied sphere of true mountaineering royalty.

The Duke recognised Albert Mummery immediately. The Englishman was one of Europe's most famous mountaineers, known for daring ascents of ridges and rockfaces once considered unclimbable. The Zmutt

Ridge was a case in point – Mummery and his guides had pioneered the route in 1879 and fifteen years later it had only once been repeated. So, when Mummery advised the Duke against trying the ridge, saying it was in poor condition, the Duke took heed.

A few weeks later, arriving back in Turin, the Duke received a telegram from Mummery. Conditions on the Zmutt Ridge had improved and the Englishman planned to climb it. The Duke rushed back to Zermatt and early on the morning of 27 August he, Mummery, Norman Collie and their guide scrambled up the broken boulders skirting the Tiefenmatten glacier. Mummery had one eye on an approaching storm, but with the ridge in good condition the men found the going 'which in 1879 had been very formidable,' wrote Mummery, 'comparatively easy and simple'.

Mummery and Collie led the final pitches without incident, arriving at the summit a little before 10 a.m. The Duke was overcome with emotion. 'Enraptured by the climb and the camaraderie shared with his new companions,' wrote one biographer, 'the twenty-one-year-old Luigi di Savoia pledged then and there to devote all his spare time and energy to mountain exploration.' The Duke's love of climbing would forever be bound up in the affinity he felt with Mummery on the Matterhorn that day.

Less than a year later Mummery was dead. The Duke was aboard the *Cristoforo Columbo* – circumnavigating the world for a second time – when he heard. The Englishman had been lost with two Gurkhas on the slopes of Nanga Parbat. He had pursued his do-or-die ethos to its logical conclusion.

The Duke's first thought was to 'avenge' Mummery by leading his own attempt on Nanga Parbat. Upon arriving back into Venice harbour in 1896 he had already begun planning an expedition, only for larger forces to intervene. Famine took hold in India, followed by an outbreak of bubonic plague, leaving little prospect of safe travel to the Himalaya. This was probably for the best, where the Duke was concerned. It was folly to think vengeance could be exacted upon a mountain, least of all a behemoth like Nanga Parbat.

Intent on mounting his first major expedition, the Duke's thoughts turned to a peak named Mount Saint Elias. He had first learned about the mountain some months earlier, as the *Cristoforo Colombo* stopped over at Vancouver Island. There Charles Fay, one of the founders of the Appalachian Mountain Club, described the 18,008-foot peak overlooking the North Pacific on the border of Alaska and the Yukon. Fay explained that several attempts had been made to climb it – all had failed. At the time the Duke's mind had been set on Nanga Parbat. Now, seeking a fresh objective, he thought again.

The first obstacle was a political one. The Duke had arrived back from his latest voyage to find the Italian economy in ruins, with the government seemingly powerless to do anything about it. At home and in its colonies, Italy faced civil unrest fuelled by failing crops and widespread corruption, leaving the country shame-faced before the eyes of the world. The Duke feared mounting an expensive expedition in pursuit of a far-off mountaintop might go down badly with the beleaguered Italian public.

Queen Margherita thought otherwise. She convinced her husband that the expedition was a unique opportunity to lift the morale of the people, and to improve the image of Italy's ruling family. The King agreed to sponsor the expedition in full. Margherita had honoured her promise to the Duke's dying mother, clearing the way for her nephew to take this first step towards realising his ambitions as an explorer.

Situated deep in the snowbound wilds of Alaska, Mount Saint Elias presented a unique challenge for the Duke and his men. At 18,008 feet, it might have seemed small by Himalayan standards, but, approaching by boat and starting at sea level, they had to first transport thousands of pounds of food, fuel and climbing equipment across fifty miles of glacier, just to stand at the foot of the mountain. They did so knowing another expedition was several days ahead, a party of Americans hoping to beat them to the summit. But, with their rivals forced to turn back short of the mountain, the Italians persevered. On 31 July 1897, the Duke's guides stepped aside to form a guard of honour, as he arrived at the windswept summit. The top of Mount Saint Elias would not be trodden again for another fifty years.

Queen Margherita was right – the Duke arrived back to a hero's welcome, having championed the Italian people in the eyes of the world. His friend, Dr Filippo De Filippi, wrote an enthralling account of the expedition, brought to life by the photographs of Vittorio Sella. Suddenly the Duke was the envy of royal houses everywhere, a paragon of aristocratic exceptionalism. He had shown that mountaineering could be a national project, that the hopes of a whole country could be carried to a mountain's summit.

He did not stop there. Two years later the Duke sailed out of Oslo harbour on his new ship, the *Stella Polare*, joining the race for the greatest prize in exploration – the North Pole. The expedition lasted sixteen months and saw four of its members reach a latitude of 86°34' – the furthest north anybody had gone, by a distance of twenty-three miles. The record came, though, at a terrible price. Three sledding teams set out from their base at Teplitz Bay but only two returned. The Duke himself lost two fingers to frostbite and, though he and his men were received as heroes by the Italian people, in private the Duke doubted whether it was worth the price of three lives. He gave up the idea of any further voyages into the polar wilds, leaving it to those for whom it was a true obsession to reach the ends of the earth.

In 1905 the Duke mounted yet another expedition, this time to the Ruwenzori mountains of eastern equatorial Africa. The British explorer Henry Morton Stanley had returned from the region expressing his hope that 'some lover of Alpine climbing would take the Ruwenzori in hand'. There had been seven other expeditions within the space of five years, but when the Duke arrived in June 1906 all of the significant peaks remained unclimbed. Over a period of six weeks, he claimed sixteen first ascents, including the highest peak of all, the 16,815-foot Mount Stanley.

In between his expeditions the Duke delivered lectures on his experiences, sharing his findings and observations with distinguished audiences all over the world. In December 1907 he was speaking at the

Scottish Geographical Society when he was asked if he would take on the challenge of the Himalaya. His first thought, ten years earlier, had been to climb in India. Now he revealed his plan to revisit that ambition. His next expedition would take him to the greatest mountain range on earth. There, he would attempt to set a new world altitude record, for himself and for Italy, on the slopes of the world's second-highest mountain – K2.

On 26 March 1909, an expedition unlike any other sailed from Marseilles, bound for India. Aboard the steamer *Oceana* were eleven Italians, members of the first Himalayan mountaineering expedition organised and funded by a continental European power. It signalled the dawn of a new era in mountain exploration and the beginning of an Italian obsession with K2.

The Duke was well-versed in the Himalayan expeditions of the past. He knew that the greatest successes had been achieved by compact climbing parties, groups of two or three Europeans making opportune ascents in fleeting weather windows. The expeditions of William Graham, Tom Longstaff and Carl Rubenson had been intimate affairs, led by amiable amateurs who maintained good relations with the men around them.

The Duke knew, too, that larger expeditions had sometimes foundered. Conway had fallen out with Eckenstein in 1892, Eckenstein had struggled with dissenting voices in 1902, and Crowley had faced a full-blown 'mutiny' in 1905. As for Fanny and Hunter Workman, they had led some of the largest Himalayan expeditions to date, and the most ill-tempered. None had succeeded in climbing above 23,000 feet. Fraught with disagreements, plagued by problems, they had only been as strong as their weakest links.

The Duke envisioned something different, something new. His would be the largest European expedition yet *and* the tightest knit. His guides were led by Joseph Petigax, who had joined the Duke on all his major climbs and had been among the party of four who reached a record latitude in the Arctic in 1899. Alexis and Henri Brocherel were also on board, two years after claiming a world summit record on Trisul with Tom Longstaff. De Filippi travelled with them, as did Sella, veteran of Mount Saint Elias and the Ruwenzori. Sella had taken a little convincing before agreeing to join the party, with the Duke offering that the photographer might have had enough of his short temper, 'which is not so easy during these trips'. But the men were old friends now, with a kinship stretching back over many years, over many thousands of miles.

Reaching Srinagar in April 1909, the Italians stayed as the guests of Sir Francis Younghusband. Ten years the Duke's senior, Younghusband had been the first European to see K2 from the north, passing the mountain in 1887 at the end of an extraordinary journey across, as he called his book, *The Heart of a Continent*. 'It was one of those sights which impress a man forever,' wrote Younghusband, 'and produce a permanent effect upon the mind – a lasting sense of the greatness and grandeur of Nature's works – which he can never lose or forget.' For the Duke it was an opportunity to find out all he could from a man whose first thought, beholding the mountains of the Himalaya, had always been to see them climbed.

Younghusband saw the Italians off in style, as they took to the Jhelum river 'in two splendid state shikaras, each with a crew of fifteen rowers dressed in tunics and turbans of flaming red'. Word raced on ahead that a foreign prince was coming, and at every town and village they came to the Italians were given a lavish welcome, entreated to ceremonial polo matches and musical performances amid throngs of local officials. In truth, they would have preferred time to rest after long days keeping pace with an aggressive itinerary. Arriving at Askole in mid-May, they had covered almost three hundred miles in just three weeks, marching through the challenging terrain of the Western Himalaya.

Cold and unwelcoming as the Karakoram was, the Italians could at last leave the crowds behind, alone together in the sort of frozen wilderness they knew well. 'The impression made upon us was so strong, so moving,' wrote De Filippi, 'that no words can convey it to the reader… So inconceivably vast are the structural lines of the landscape, that the idea comes into one's mind of being in the workshop of nature, and of standing before the primeval chaos and cosmos of a world as yet unvisited by the phenomenon of life.'

On the morning of 25 May they came for the first time within sight of K2. 'For a whole hour we stood absorbed,' wrote De Filippi. 'We gazed, we minutely inspected, we examined with our glasses the incredible rock wall. All the time our minds were assailed with increasing doubt, culminating almost in certainty, that this side of the mountain was not accessible, and did not offer even a reasonable point of attack. Meantime the atmosphere grew gradually thicker, the veil of whitish vapour heavier, stretching and expanding and melting together, until even the last spectral image disappeared and a uniform grey curtain of mist filled the end of the valley. The vision was gone.'

Anxious to take advantage of the good weather, the Duke ordered an immediate attempt on K2's south ridge. The guides led the way, climbing to more than twenty thousand feet, but they were hard-fought gains with everything more difficult than they had expected; every ridge more precarious, every slab more steep. Even Joseph Petigax, who had climbed in the Karakoram with the Workmans, found he was having to recalibrate his senses for K2. Time and again a point on the mountainside that appeared minutes away would take the climbing party hours to reach.

Retreating to their camp below, they turned their attention to the glacier west of K2 – the Duke would name it the Savoia glacier – leading to the mountain's northwest ridge. Again, the going was slow, as they climbed a steep ice-wall to almost 22,000 feet. There the Duke hoped to see the north face of the mountain, thinking he might discover an easier route to the top. Instead, he and his guides found their view obscured by a broad cornice of ice and snow. 'And that was all,' wrote De Filippi, having watched all day through a telescope. 'The Duke thus saw utterly annihilated the hopes with which he had begun the ascent.'

All that remained was to reconnoitre the east face, following the Godwin-Austen glacier to Windy Gap at its head. From his vantage on

Staircase Peak he would look along the north face of the mountain to the same point they had glimpsed from the head of the Savoia glacier. He had seen enough of K2 to give up any thought of climbing it. 'He might now abandon the struggle,' wrote De Filippi, 'in the consciousness that he had left undone nothing within human power to convince himself of the impossibility of the undertaking.'

The Duke, though, was far from beaten. Indeed, as he and his companions turned their backs on K2, starting south along the Godwin-Austen glacier towards the sweeping superhighway of the Baltoro, he already knew the identity of the mountain they would attempt instead.

The Duke had come to the Karakoram hoping to claim a new world altitude record.

That meant climbing to 24,000 feet or more. Some still doubted whether William Graham had reached that height on Kabru in 1883, but few questioned the corresponding claim of Carl Rubenson and Ingvald Monrad-Aas. The two Norwegians had gone to 'about 23,900 feet' on the same peak in 1907 and returned with photographs to prove it. 'Their account,' wrote De Filippi, 'must inspire the most complete belief'.

There was no shortage of mountains well in excess of that height in the vicinity of K2. The problem was that most – Broad Peak, Masherbrum, the four peaks of Gasherbrum – would have been just as difficult to climb. What the Duke needed was a mountain rising to a record height and not too much higher. And one existed. Its name was Chogolisa. The Italians knew it as 'Bride Peak'.

It was Conway, of course, who had given the 25,157-foot mountain that name, as he and his party climbed at least some of the way up the icefall flowing from its eastern ridge. The Italians entered that same icefall on 3 July, confident they were more than equal to Conway's party. The Duke thought it 'the work of two days at most'.

Burdened with heavy loads, they worked their way up a first cascade, amid 'a chaos of blocks... piled up in confusion'. They were soon lost in a labyrinth of jagged seracs, 'cut in every direction by crevasses and covered with snow, into which one sank up to the waist'. The Italians would spend a long first day searching for a way through, only to find, as darkness fell, they had gained just thirteen hundred feet on the camp below.

The next day they tried again, determined to overcome the next wall of seracs. One of Sella's most famous photographs shows the Italians taking the fight back to the icefall; it opens a fascinating window into this vertical world. The men stand like tin soldiers, poised on the snowy ramparts, tiny dark figures frozen in time. Tongues of ice loom over them, reared up in reproach. Throats of shadow gape open, ready to swallow them whole.

Looking at Sella's picture, it is easy to understand how the icefall became their home. They succeeded in reaching a height of nineteen thousand feet but there, even as they were setting up their tents, it began to snow. They woke the next morning to find it falling heavily. 'All day the bad weather held,' wrote De Filippi. 'The air was full of white semi-opaque mist, sky and snow were indistinguishable, and they could not see 100 yards ahead.'

With Sella and his guides stranded at the high camp, the Duke and his men at the camp below, all they could do was wait in their tents as the hours passed, 'occasionally shaking the canvas to prevent their being buried'. They were 'prisoners', wrote De Filippi, 'on a narrow table of glacier surrounded by crevasses and buried in snow. This was only the beginning of a long siege.'

On 7 July the Duke sent three guides 'to liberate Sella from his blockade' and the men were reunited at the lower camp. It was now their fifth night in the icefall. For two more days they stayed hunkered down then, on the ninth, De Filippi watched from below as the weather began to clear. 'Gradually the mountains stripped off their mist, and came out one after another in purest and most dazzling white. Where the sun shone through the mists these were of a silvery brilliance, and the whiteness of the landscape enhanced the deep blue of the sky. Little spirals of snow-dust curled along the crests, lifted by the wind.'

The Duke was on the move. He and his guides climbed back up to Sella's high camp and the next day they went higher still. Only a little way up, the chaos of the icefall gave way to broader, gentler slopes and, after climbing for five hours, they at last set down their loads on the crest of the Chogolisa Saddle, three thousand feet above their camp on the Upper Baltoro. The Duke had thought they would need two days. It had taken a week.

With the air perfectly bright and clear, now was a moment of respite, a chance to savour an extraordinary view. All around were mountains, some of the highest on earth. Broad Peak with its three summits, Gasherbrum with four, K2 dominating the horizon to the north, sending a ridge west to the harrowing upper reaches of the Mustagh Tower. Looking northeast they saw Baltoro Kangri, and to the west, Chogolisa. 'The view was nothing but ice and snow and rocky wilderness spreading out to the horizon,' wrote De Filippi. 'One felt as if the inhabited earth had been left behind forever.'

Another week had passed. Seven days since they first set foot on the Chogolisa Saddle. Seven long days, and here they were, still camped where they had set down their loads, still eyeing the summit of Chogolisa from five miles away. It stood 4,500 feet above them to the west, along a ridge that had already defeated them once.

The Duke's first thought had been to establish a camp further along the ridge, but even that had been a struggle, the men weighed down as they waded through deep snow. It was 'a performance the fatigue of which cannot be measured,' wrote De Filippi, 'by those who have never tried it'.

On the second night, back at their camp on the saddle, the Duke had noticed dark clouds rolling in from the southwest. He and three guides got away at five the next morning, thinking they would try for the summit that day. It took three hours just to cross the long depression leading to the foot of Chogolisa's true east ridge. In that time a fog moved in, which thickened as they climbed.

The path up the ridge was flanked with danger. To the left a layer of fresh snow looked ready to slide, to the right great cornices rose, tempting the climbers out over the abyss below. Stray too far in one direction and an avalanche might take them, too far in the other and the ground could give way beneath their feet. Meanwhile, the fog became thicker still, limiting visibility as the wind tried to blow them off course. For two and a half hours they climbed. When they stopped to rest, on a rock projecting out of a snowy crest, it was almost midday. They could see a few feet ahead and the summit was still more than fifteen hundred feet above them. 'The danger was too imminent,' wrote De Filippi, 'and it increased at every step. They must go back.'

That evening the fog lifted to reveal a storm raging. 'Masses of threatening black cloud were constantly rolling up from the lower Baltoro,' wrote De Filippi. 'The snows reflected their tones of deep violet and ash colour. The entire party slept heavily, being greatly fatigued, while the snow fell silently and ceaselessly outside.'

The Duke held fast. Making the most of their extraordinary situation, he used small windows in the storm to study the surrounding landscape. Looking east he had a clear view of Conway's Golden Throne, and the route the 1892 expedition had taken on the way to Pioneer Peak. To the south he made out a pass first sighted by Francis Younghusband in 1884. Half a century after Haversham Godwin-Austen had stolen his first good look at K2, the mountains of the Karakoram told a human story. The Duke still hoped to add a show-stealing chapter of his own.

Then his chance came. With food and fuel running low, the Italians woke on 17 July to find the snow had stopped and the skies had cleared. Looking down, they saw an even more welcome sight – porters, Italians and Baltis, coming up the slopes below. Their arrival, coinciding with the first sustained spell of good weather, prompted a flurry of action at the camp on the saddle. 'Experience had taught that the respite would be brief,' wrote De Filippi, 'and was to be profited by to the uttermost.'

The snow lay deeper than ever. The Duke and four guides marched all day and, late that afternoon, pitched their tents at 22,500 feet, around 2,600 feet below the summit. It had begun to snow again, but in the failing light 'it did seem as though fate intended to be kind at last, for all was clear at sunset, and a magnificent starry sky gave promise of a clear morrow'. The Duke understood that this was it, 'the die was cast'. The next day would see success or failure, then only retreat.

They emerged from their tents at five in the morning, to find that 'the air was lifeless, the sun weak and pale and surrounded by a watery aureole of clouds, a sight of most unfavourable augury'. They moved quickly to reach the outcrop of rock where they had turned back at the last attempt, with the ridge ahead rising into thick mist.

Climbing higher still, they saw a crevasse to the left running parallel with the ridge, where the 'ominous creaking of the snow' warned them away. Using their ice-axes to steady themselves, they watched as snow detached itself from the slope beneath them and slid down into the waiting darkness. Bearing to the right, they moved obliquely up out over the hanging cornice, until they felt 'the breath of a cold wind' from below. 'Nothing could be seen beyond a few yards,' wrote De Filippi, 'but they realised that bottomless gulfs opened on every side.'

After four and a half hours, climbing into the unknown, they rested briefly at the foot of a promontory of stone, knowing that to go further they would have to climb it. This demanded hands as well as feet, on rock glazed with ice. Now the rarefaction of the air began to tell, as this new effort left them rasping for breath. Midday came and went and still they carried on, until finally they saw the lip of the rock above. This was it, the Duke was certain of it. All that remained above was the summit.

As they hauled themselves over the top of the rockface, their hearts sank. Ahead, the ridge continued its remorseless rise into thick mist, no summit in sight. They had seen nothing of this part of the mountain from below, they had little sense of its shape or character. Somewhere to the right would be the cornice, to the left they could just make out the tops of rugged seracs, where the slope fell sharply away. 'It would have been madness to go on blindly,' wrote De Filippi. Instead, they stopped, allowing themselves to rest.

There was still time. The day was calm and mild. So, they waited. Waited, 'in the faint hope that some fugitive wind would brush away the mists'. Sitting less than five hundred feet beneath the summit of Chogolisa, the Duke could reflect on all he had thrown at it. So much for 'siege tactics'. The mountain had not grown tired, or hungry. It had not felt the sting of wind, or the searing cold. The Italians had laid siege only to themselves, on a mountain indifferent to the outcome. And now, as one hour became two, they were defeated. Late in the afternoon, with the mist hanging heavier still, they started down.

'The giant ranges into which His Royal Highness the Duke of the Abruzzi led his expedition were not kind to him,' wrote De Filippi, 'nor was the weather favourable. Nevertheless, he succeeded in making a step forward toward the conquest of the greatest heights after such a struggle as was perhaps unexampled in the history of mountaineering.'

The Duke and his guides had turned back, according to their instruments, at 24,600 feet, surpassing the existing altitude record by around 600 feet. This was made the more remarkable, De Filippi was at pains to point out, 'under such unfavourable conditions of snow and weather. This gives it a value,' he continued, 'above any of the others in relation to the problem of the possible ascent of our greatest peaks.'

The Duke's thoughts, though, had not been on the obstacles presented by other mountains. They had been five hundred feet above him, at the summit of Chogolisa. To reach it would have been to give his public a monument to Italian mountaineering supremacy. Instead, what he and his fellow countrymen had achieved was more ambiguous, more difficult to define.

The Duke had been robbed of the ultimate apex for his climbing career, but with the thoughts of the British turning again to the ascent of Mount Everest, his influence was plain to see. He had shown that mountaineering could be a political project, the chance to light a beacon of conquest atop the world's highest peaks. And, if the ascent of such mountains was to be a flag-waving exercise, there were those at the Alpine Club already determined that, where the world's highest mountain was concerned, the flag in question must be the Union Jack.

*Unmarried, living alone, his was an unremarkable
story through to the advent of middle age.*

Scottish chemist, explorer and mountaineer
Dr Alexander 'Alec' Kellas. Photographer unknown.

CHAPTER 23

Fearlas Mòr

In 1891 the English mountaineer Norman Collie had not yet travelled to the Himalaya; a fateful attempt on Nanga Parbat was still four years into his and Albert Mummery's future. Collie had not even visited the Alps. To date, he had done all his climbing on the mountains of Scotland, which is exactly where he was on the day in question.

Collie was descending from the summit of Ben Macdui, Scotland's second-highest mountain, when he became aware of someone – or something – following close behind. 'I was returning from the cairn on the summit in a mist,' he told a meeting of the Cairngorm Club, 'when I began to think I heard something else than merely the noise of my own footsteps. For every few steps I took I heard a crunch as if someone was walking after me but taking steps three or four times the length of my own.'

'I said to myself, "This is all nonsense",' Collie went on. 'I listened and heard it again but could see nothing in the mist. As I walked on and the eerie crunch, crunch, sounded behind me I was seized with terror and took to my heels, staggering blindly among the boulders for four or five miles nearly down to Rothiemurchus Forest.'

Some poked fun at Collie when he told them about the experience, but one of his colleagues at University College London would have given the story more credence than most. Alec Kellas, a young postgraduate working alongside Collie, knew him as a scientist and mountaineer with

343

celebrated powers of observation. Moreover, Kellas knew something of what Collie was describing. Many years earlier he had experienced a supernatural encounter of his own on the slopes of Ben Macdui.

Kellas had been seventeen years old, out with his younger brother Harry in the summer of 1885. The boys had hiked thirty-five miles from the village of Ballater to the shores of Loch Avon, sustaining themselves on a loaf of bread and a bottle of lemonade. They passed a night beneath Clach Dhian, the so-called 'Shelter Stone', and were up at five the next morning, washing themselves in the freezing waters of the loch. Then, consulting their guidebook, they decided to make for Ben Macdui's summit by scrambling up the Feithe Buidhe burn, 'which was,' noted Alec in his account of the trip, 'the most difficult and by far the steepest route'.

By midday the brothers were adding stones of their own to the cairn at the top of the mountain. And, like Collie, it was as they came down from the summit that their day took a turn for the uncanny. 'Suddenly they became aware of a giant figure coming down towards them from the cairn,' wrote W. G. Robertson, a friend of Harry Kellas, in the *Aberdeen Press and Journal*. 'They saw it pass out of sight in the dip on the side of the fold remote from themselves, and awaited its reappearance. But fear possessed them ere it did reach the top, and they fled. They were aware it was following them, and tore down by Corrie Etchachan to escape it.'

Collie and the Kellas brothers had encountered Britain's only mountain ghost – *Fearlas Mòr*, in Gaelic, the 'Big Grey Man' of Ben Macdui. Described as a shadowy figure of anything from ten to twenty-five feet tall, the legend is as vague and vapourish as the lumbering grey man it describes. But for Alec, who would display a heightened sensitivity to such things, it foreshadowed the troubled future of a man who would be forever haunted in the hills.

Alec Kellas was a shy, unassuming child, growing up in a house on the busy quayside in Aberdeen. To the rear of the building was the city's great central slum, a maze of warehouses and industrial buildings; out front, famous ships came and went, unloading precious cargoes from

places with exotic-sounding names. Intelligent, with an inquisitive disposition, Alec saw from a young age that he was growing up in a world
of hard facts and infinite possibilities.

In 1878, when he was ten years old, his family moved to the city's
West End. He took up a place at Aberdeen Grammar School, but his time
there was cut short. No record remains of why Alec left the school three
years early, but he was in good company – the school's most famous
alumnus, Lord Byron, failed to complete the curriculum. Like Byron,
Alec sought sanctuary in the nearby Cairngorm mountains, where he
cultivated what became a lifelong passion for mountaineering.

Kellas did most of his early climbing in Scotland and would turn
thirty before he first travelled to the Alps. He ascended the Breithorn
in 1899 and the Finsteraarhorn the following year, but his shy manner
could not have been conducive to the showy Alpine scene. Instead, in
1901, he eschewed Zermatt and Chamonix in favour of a cycling tour
of Norway, climbing a selection of little-known peaks along the way.
Career-wise, he showed correspondingly modest ambition, taking up a
position as a lecturer at Middlesex College Hospital. Unmarried, living
alone, his was an unremarkable story through to the advent of middle age.

In 1907, all that changed. His father died and, shortly thereafter,
Kellas prepared his last will and testament. Then, with a minimum of
fuss, he sailed for Bombay.

Kellas did not consider his 1907 season in the Himalaya an 'expedition' –
it was, in his words, 'merely a tour'. Some years later he sent details of
his itinerary to the president of the Alpine Club, Captain Percy Farrar,
prefaced with an insistence 'that you will not waste a line of the *Alpine
Journal* with it at any time'.

Kellas blamed the worst of his problems on his Swiss guides. He had
hoped to climb as high as 23,000 feet on Kangchenjunga. Instead, he
struggled to persuade the two men to ford rivers that could have been
crossed by 'a well-grown schoolboy'. The season culminated with three
attempts on the 22,700-foot Simvu – all were unsuccessful. 'Our failure

made me determined to return and try climbing with Nepalese coolies,' wrote Kellas, 'who seemed to me more at home under the diminished pressure than my European companions.'

History does not record whether the Scot had been at the Alpine Club in 1908 to hear Carl Rubenson describe how Sherpas had transformed the Norwegian's fortunes on Kabru. It may be that Kellas read about it in the *Alpine Journal*, or that he formed his own determination based on his experiences in 1907. Whatever the case, he was about to share in Rubenson's success. In 1909 he went back to the mountains of the Sikkim with Sherpas as his guides.

Kellas would have one European companion, but not for long. The Scot left Darjeeling accompanied by Alcesti Rigo De Righi, the Italian manager of the Drum Druid Hotel, whose part in the 1905 Kangchenjunga expedition had not put him off Himalayan exploration altogether. Kellas found the Italian 'a pleasant companion, and a good walker', but he proved 'somewhat easily affected by altitude' and was soon on his way back to Darjeeling, leaving Kellas alone with his porters and guides.

The only record of what Kellas accomplished in the weeks to come was his itinerary, sent to the president of the Alpine Club with a few accompanying notes. 'You will see,' wrote Kellas, 'that there were many failures, but also a few successes, and I learnt a great deal regarding Himalayan snow conditions. It must be noted, however, that we were greatly handicapped, because I was carrying out scientific experiments when possible.'

'The incident which pleased me best of all,' noted Kellas, 'was my first completed Himalayan ascent.' The mountain in question was the 22,800-foot Langpo Peak, summited by Kellas and two Sherpas on 15 September 1909, after they had first been driven back by a violent snowstorm. According to Kellas, the Sherpas had 'refused to move' at 21,900 feet, but he had convinced them to go on. 'It gives me,' he wrote, 'a slight satisfaction even now. There was no real difficulty because the snow was in excellent order on the final peak, although deep and troublesome below.' Before Langpo Peak, the highest mountain Kellas had climbed was the 14,022-foot Finsteraarhorn in the Bernese Oberland. Now he and two Sherpas had gone to within a few hundred feet of the world summit record.

The account of the climb appearing in the *Alpine Journal* was thin on detail, but if Kellas was a man of few words, his photographs spoke for him. He preferred to operate his camera himself, perhaps out of concern to make sure it was used correctly. Remaining forever out of sight, the subjects of his pictures were the Sherpas who climbed with him. His photograph of Langpo Peak is a fine example, showing one of the men with the snow-covered mountain in the background. Kellas was giving the world a look at a new Himalaya – of untrodden peaks pioneered by those who had grown up in their shadow.

In 1911 Kellas took a picture of two Sherpas, identified as Sona and 'Tuny's brother', at the summit of a peak named Pauhunri. Both are well-clothed, with ice-axes and snow-goggles, and are smiling broadly. They have the bearing not of guides or porters, but mountaineers.

According to the Survey map Kellas had with him, Pauhunri was a peak of 23,180 feet – within 200 feet of the world summit record set by Longstaff's party on Trisul in 1907. Kellas had made an unsuccessful attempt on the mountain in 1909, but now, with the two Sherpas, he had finished the job. They had established their first camp at 18,000 feet then, 'on the following day,' wrote Kellas, 'an ascent to 20,700 feet was made, but we were driven back by a high wind which whirled the fine surface snow into dense clouds. The camp was next moved up to 20,000 feet, and on the following day we reached the summit, 23,180 feet.'

Sharing his photographs with the members of the Royal Geographical Society a few months later, Kellas was showing them something they had never seen before. The view from the top of Pauhunri was 'spoiled by clouds beneath us', he told them, 'but… nevertheless interesting. West and south nearly everything was obscured by a rolling sea of mist, above which some of the great peaks, Kangchenjunga, Chumiumo, and the Kangchenjhau, showed their crests like rocky islands.' But it was

not the peaks of the Sikkim the members of the RGS were seeing for
the first time. Kellas's pictures revealed a relationship with the Sherpas
anchored in compromise and co-existence. All were issued with the same
bedding, clothing and equipment as Kellas, and he brought his diet into
line with theirs, starting the day with 'a large bowl of soup, thickened
with rice and with added butter', and ending it much the same. Their
campsites were correspondingly no-nonsense affairs – pictures of the
higher camps showed a single, sagging tent in which he and the men
lived together cheek by jowl.

As it turned out, the ascent of Pauhunri was more significant than
even Kellas would ever know. The Survey map was wrong – years later,
Pauhunri would be remeasured at 23,375 feet. Meanwhile Trisul – and
the summit record of Longstaff's party – would be revised downwards,
to 23,359 feet. There, pictured on Pauhunri, the Scot and two Sherpas
had been at the summit of the highest mountain ever climbed to the top.

Kellas recounted the ascent of Pauhunri at the RGS in April 1912.
Speaking afterwards, Douglas Freshfield declared the Scot's expedition
'one of the most fruitful that has ever been accomplished by a mountaineer in the Himalaya'. Arnold Mumm, veteran of the Trisul expedition of 1907, concurred. For Mumm, the key to Kellas's success was
his accumulated experience over three visits to the Sikkim. 'If anyone
light-heartedly imagines that he can follow Dr. Kellas and go out without
any Himalayan training and accomplish anything like the same amount
that he did,' offered Mumm, 'he will be very grievously disappointed.'

Three months later, Kellas was back in Darjeeling, where he recruited
two Sherpas known to him from previous seasons. He identified them
as Nema and Anderkyow. (The first is a common Tibetan name, the
second perhaps a phonetic spelling of Ang Dorji.)

Nema was 'extraordinarily cautious', Kellas told an audience at the
Alpine Club in 1913, but not so Anderkyow. 'In 1909 he might have
been described as timid, as he refused to do anything above the snow,
but since then he has developed into the rashest coolie I have ever met

with.' Nema and Anderkyow would be the two Sherpas who accompanied Kellas on the most ambitious climb of the 1912 season – the 22,700-foot Kangchenjhau.

Revisiting the ascent at the Alpine Club some months later, Kellas described it in detail. Camping at twenty thousand feet, he, Nema and Anderkyow had gained the crest of a col at around 21,000 feet, leading to a stretch of harder ground, windswept ice that led in turn to a belt of rocks. There, one thousand feet above the col, they moved onto a steep, exposed snow-slope falling three thousand feet down to the glacier below. 'Nema... was a trifle nervous over this portion,' recalled Kellas, 'and protested several times to Anderkyow, who merely responded with a laconic "Sahib mahlum" (*i.e.*, Sahib understands).' 'We were as cautious as seemed reasonable', offered the Scot, and once they cleared the rock, he saw that they had made it over the worst of the ground. Just a steep slope of deep snow remained, bringing them, soon after 1 p.m., onto Kangchenjhau's dramatic summit plateau.

They remained at the top for an hour and a half, studying the surrounding peaks through intermittent breaks in the cloud. They stayed there, by Kellas's own admission, far too long. When they finally began to descend it felt 'leisurely' at first; they reached the col at 21,000 feet at 4.30 p.m., thinking themselves home and dry. But, looking further down the mountain, they saw 'that the condition of the ice-slope had entirely altered since morning'.

The sun, less in evidence at the mountain's windy summit, had done its worst. Gone was the layer of fresh snow, gone too were the steps they had cut. Instead, they would have to descend more than one thousand feet of steep ice-slope, bare and brutally exposed. Anderkyow began to cut what footholds he could and the men took tentative steps downwards in the failing light. They had gone around three hundred feet when, reaching an especially worrying part of the face, they came to a halt.

Looking around, Kellas could see they were in trouble. A zigzag to the left would alleviate the immediate precariousness of their position, only to bring them to the edge of a sheer ice-cliff. To the right was a ridge of rock glazed with ice, sloping deviously downwards, where a slip 'might have been serious'. Some distance below, Kellas saw a large pile of stones, the debris from some heavy rockfall they had heard during the night. The men were surrounded by objective danger. Darkness was beginning to fall.

'Mountaineering,' Kellas had told the members of the Alpine Club at the start of his talk, 'is the most philosophical sport in the world. [...] Being a philosophical pursuit, it presents innumerable fascinating problems.' Now, late in the day, high on Kangchenjhau, Kellas had plenty to think about. It would be Anderkyow, however, who stumbled upon a solution. The Sherpa slipped, and fell.

Kellas watched as Anderkyow slid away down the mountain. He watched, as the rope to Nema went taut, yanking the second Sherpa from his feet. He watched and, ever the scientist, kept careful inventory of his thoughts, understanding that within a matter of seconds he would be joining the Sherpas, 'whizzing down that ice-slope with the speed of an express train'.

'In the fraction of a second between Anderkyow's slip and my being pulled down,' Kellas told the Alpine Club, 'the following four thoughts occurred to me: Firstly, these two men on their backs look exactly like that picture of the accident on the Matterhorn in Whymper's *Scrambles Amongst the Alps*; next, "I think I could hold one man, but am doubtful about two"; thirdly, "Now you will have the novel experience you have speculated about"; and, lastly, "What should we do with our axes – should we keep them or throw them aside?" These latter two thoughts occurred at the instant I started moving.'

Lost in these and other pressing considerations, Kellas fell. It felt, he explained, like only a few seconds before he was thrust back into the moment by 'two tremendous jolts'. The first came as they made contact with the pile of rocks he had seen some two hundred feet below. 'The impact threw me on my side with my length almost at right angles to our direction of motion, and for a critical second my feet were slightly higher than my head.' Summoning all his strength, Kellas was able to rotate himself into 'the normal glissading position' only for a second jolt to turn him back around, 'so that the snow nearly enveloped me, some getting into the breast pockets of my coat, and also down the back of my neck'.

Kellas noticed, much to his surprise, that they were beginning to slow down. They would have to act quickly to avoid being buried by the great mass of snow following behind. As they came to a halt, he and the Sherpas 'simultaneously half rolled, half scrambled, out of the accompanying avalanche before it packed, and anchored ourselves as best we could'.

Kellas was 'flushed and exhilarated'. Looking around, he was astonished to see they had fallen the best part of one thousand feet and were now just a short distance above their camp. Finding they had sustained only superficial injuries, he noted down every detail of the fall, 'however trivial, from the instant the slip occurred until our wild career was checked'. These observations, he was quick to volunteer, could be of 'only very mild scientific interest'.

Perhaps, but Kellas had written a chapter of his own in the history of Himalayan misadventure. And, for anybody who has ever wondered what it would feel like to fall in the mountains, there is something oddly reassuring about the knowledge that, at a moment of such urgent danger, the Scot's first thought was to note the uncanny likeness of the situation to a picture he had seen, in a book he had once read.

A few weeks later, a group of Sherpas went missing, Anderkyow among them. There was some suggestion they had absconded into Tibet, taking the expedition's money and scientific equipment with them. Almost a week passed before they reappeared. It turned out they had lost their way and had gone many miles in the wrong direction. Kellas found Anderkyow 'greatly distressed' because he had been 'forced to use some of my private stock of provisions'.

'I was glad to remember afterwards that I never thought harshly of Anderkyow,' Kellas told the Alpine Club. Of the Sherpas in general, he offered that 'a few may pilfer a little from the provision stores, and some may shirk work, but they are almost without exception loyal to their employers as far as my experience goes. Many of these Sherpa Nepalese,' he finished, in terms any fellow Briton could understand, 'are really splendid fellows.'

Kellas had shared the most difficult and dramatic moments of his life with men like Sona, Tuny, Nema and Anderkyow, storm-wracked nights and snowbound days eking out an existence in some of the most inhospitable places on earth. Eating together, what food was available, sleeping together, what sleep would come, they had passed many long evenings around a campfire communicating in what common tongue they had.

Sometimes, though, it was not the Sherpas the Scot was talking to.

'Some people hear voices at high altitudes,' wrote the biologist J. B. S. Haldane, an acquaintance of Kellas. 'Dr Kellas also heard them at sea level. Indeed, he once told me that he wondered if a very sensitive microphone might not render them audible to others. [...] He said that in the mountains, when no other Europeans were there, he answered these voices, and his Sherpas had great confidence in a man who had long conversations with spirits at night.'

It might have given the Sherpas confidence, to hear Alec Kellas communing with the wilderness. The members of the Mount Everest Committee saw things a little differently.

Everest waited, patient as stone.

'Lower Kama-Chu' from *Mount Everest:*
The Reconnaisance by Charles Howard-Bury, 1921.

CHAPTER 24

Sleep of the Just

Seven members of the 1921 Mount Everest Reconnaissance Expedition had arrived for a dinner, held in their honour, in the banquet hall of Darjeeling's Government House. Among them was a young climber named George Leigh Mallory. He, like the other six, was immaculately turned out in full evening dress, despite having arrived in Darjeeling only a few hours earlier.

Mallory had been disappointed to learn he was to be quartered at Government House rather than with his old school pal Guy Bullock at the Mount Everest Hotel. This was according to the wishes of the leader of the expedition, Charles Howard-Bury, who, even now, was trying to ingratiate himself with their host, Lord Ronaldshay. Watching Howard-Bury, Mallory had already taken a singular dislike to the man.

Howard-Bury was, at least, the worst of them, as far as Mallory could tell. Bullock had been a good friend during their time at Winchester College, and Sandy Wollaston, the expedition's naturalist and physician, Mallory also knew and admired. This was his first encounter with Henry Morshead, but he had been at school with his brothers and instantly recognised Morshead's warm features and gentle manner. Meanwhile, seeing the geologist Charles Heron in conversation with the veteran Scottish mountaineer Harold Raeburn, Mallory understood that he was observing the dullness of one man cancelled out by the disinterest of the other.

Mallory had met Raeburn, the expedition's lead mountaineer, at a meeting in London, back in February 1921. The Scot was a certain type of cragsman, immovable as the mountains he climbed, addressing them always in the lexicon of conquest. Volatile and humourless, he wasn't the sort to let bad judgement get in the way of bludgeoning a decision through. And yet, Raeburn did at least share Mallory's disdain for the pomp and puffery filling the air. Not so Howard-Bury, the consummate High Tory, whose principal qualification for leading the expedition was that he had bankrolled it.

That left Oliver Wheeler, a second surveyor. Mallory had already taken exception to him, for no better reason than that he was Canadian. Wheeler was the last of the seven members of the expedition seated at the table.

Except that the membership of the expedition ran to nine.

Mallory gazed enviously at the empty seat.

Francis Younghusband had been the first to raise the prospect of an attempt on Everest. He and Charlie Bruce had been at Chitral in 1893 when Younghusband set out some plans that were, 'to say the least of it,' wrote Bruce, 'ambitious'.

Bruce was involved again in 1907 when Arnold Mumm turned his mind to Everest, on the eve of the fiftieth anniversary of the Alpine Club. For a time, it looked as though the expedition might go ahead, only for the British Secretary of State for India, Lord Morley, to intercede, amid concerns 'that Russian susceptibilities are easily awakened by reports of movements, however innocent, in the heart of Asia'.

One young British officer, Captain John Noel, wasn't waiting for permission. Noel had travelled extensively along India's borders with Tibet and Nepal; by 1913 he was ready to do whatever it took to get a closer look at the world's highest mountain. 'Everest!' wrote Noel. 'Hitherto unapproached by men of my race; guarded, so fantastic rumour said, by the holiest lamas dwelling in mystic contemplation of the soul of the giant peak, communing with its demons and guardian gods! It was an alluring goal.'

In 1913 Noel crossed into Tibet disguised as 'a Mohammedan from India', accompanied by a Bhutia named Adhu, a Garhwali named Badri, and Tebdoo, 'a Sherpa Nepalese, a rough but golden-hearted fellow who knew everything there is to be known about mountains and wild sheep'. Favouring the higher and more hazardous mountain passes avoided by the Tibetans, the men travelled together for six weeks, making it to within forty miles of Everest before an exchange of fire with Tibetan soldiers turned them back. Noel had been ready to force the issue 'but my men,' he wrote, 'thought the whole of Tibet would descend on us. They absolutely refused to go on.'

Within a few months Noel was contacted by Colonel C. G. Rawling, a British officer and explorer who had seen Everest from the north serving under Younghusband on the 1903–04 'expedition' to Lhasa; ten years later, inspired by his former commanding officer, Rawling was intent on making the ascent of the mountain a reality. He proposed a comprehensive reconnaissance in 1915, laying the groundwork for an attempt to climb Everest the following year. Rawling's first step was to recruit Noel, one of two men who had seen more of the approach to Everest than any other Briton alive. The other was Alec Kellas.

Since standing with Anderkyow and Nema at the summit of Kangchenjhau in 1912, Kellas had continued to broaden his knowledge of the Himalaya. Little is known about his 1913 and 1914 expeditions, but it appears he visited two entirely new regions of the Himalaya. A paper published by Kellas a few years later described Nanga Parbat seen at close quarters, and a presentation of his photography in 1920 at the Cairngorm Club featured an image of K2.

Kellas was in India in August 1914 when word reached him that war had broken out in Europe. At forty-six he was too old for active service, so he returned to London and resumed his position at Middlesex Hospital where, with the staff stretched thin, he was busier than ever. Determined to do his bit, Kellas also joined the Hampstead Volunteers, a division of the home guard offering visible reassurance that, should the enemy reach British shores, it would not sweep through that particular borough unchallenged.

Kellas was at Middlesex Hospital when he received a visit from Noel. The two started working together to devise the most viable route to Everest's summit, while Kellas also busied himself addressing some of the wider questions any expedition would face. Several of these were addressed in his paper, *A Consideration of the Possibility of Ascending the Loftier Himalaya*, published in 1916. Kellas set out his belief that 'a man in first-rate training, acclimatised to maximum possible altitude, could make the ascent of Mount Everest without adventitious aids, provided that the physical difficulties above 25,000 feet are not prohibitive'.

In another paper, *The Possibility of Aerial Reconnaissance in the Himalaya*, Kellas considered the use of aircraft to conduct remote survey work. But the field showing greatest promise was the use of supplementary oxygen to assist a climbing effort. In a letter written in 1916, Kellas explained that he had 'been considering whether a climbing suit like that of a diver... would not be a great advantage on a first ascent of Everest'. This, he believed, in conjunction with optimal acclimatisation and nutrition, held the key to climbing the world's highest peak.

Kellas had one problem. Limited by what he could achieve in a laboratory, he needed to take his research into the field. To do that, he would have to return to his beloved mountains. But, with war still raging in Europe, all he could do was wait.

The Armistice came in November 1918. Within a month of the war ending, the president of the Royal Geographical Society, Sir Thomas H. Holdich, declared the ascent of Everest 'the outstanding task which remains for geographers to accomplish'. In 1919 John Noel delivered a paper at the RGS and, out of the discussions that followed, the Mount Everest Committee was formed. One of the main functions of the committee, a joint body of the RGS and the Alpine Club, was to select the members of a prospective reconnaissance expedition.

Kellas must have thought himself a shoo-in. Few alive could match him in terms of high Himalayan mountaineering experience. He had cultivated a unique relationship with the Sherpas, upon whom any expedition would rely, and had engaged in pioneering research that could prove the difference between success and failure.

Nor was Kellas wasting his time now the war was over. In 1916 he had drawn up plans for an expedition to Kamet, a 25,446-foot peak in the Garhwal Himalaya, to research the use of supplementary oxygen. With the appetite for Himalayan exploration renewed, the expedition could now go ahead. It would be plagued by difficulties and delays – the transportation of the oxygen cylinders was delayed for a month following their classification as 'high explosives' – but Kellas and the surveyor Henry Morshead succeeded in climbing to 22,000 feet on Kamet. It was the fifth time Kellas had reached that altitude in the Himalaya. The question of his participation in an Everest expedition was, surely, a foregone conclusion.

Arthur Hinks, one of the Joint Secretaries of the Mount Everest Committee, was not so sure. Hinks knew Kellas had a troubled psychiatric history and was especially unsettled by a letter he received in October 1919, written by the Scot in anticipation of his expedition to Kamet. 'I am looking forward to the journey,' Kellas wrote, 'as a means of finally getting rid of a disturbance which medical men tell me is due to overwork, and which takes the form of malevolent aural communications, including threats of murder.'

In December 1920, only months before the Everest expedition was due to depart, Hinks wrote to Norman Collie, a fellow member of the Committee. Collie knew Kellas as well as anybody. He reminded Hinks that the Scot had surpassed expectations time and again, bringing credit to the Alpine Club and RGS in the process. If Kellas was to be excluded, Collie went on, it would be a disappointment from which he would probably never recover.

Ten minutes after those at Government House had sat down for dinner, Alec Kellas shuffled into the room. Soaked through and utterly dishevelled, he took his seat at the table, muttering his apologies in a broad

Scottish accent. He had overslept, the Scot explained, then walked four miles from his lodgings at Ghoom.

Mallory saw immediately that Kellas was gravely unwell. Could this really be the man expected to go higher on Everest than any other? On paper there seemed little reason to doubt it. But this was not Kellas on paper, it was the man in three dimensions, if not fully fleshed out. To Mallory's eye, the good doctor was pushing his 53-year-old frame harder than it was designed to go but, whatever concerns he might have felt, Mallory did not let them dampen his enthusiasm. 'Kellas,' he confided, in his next letter to his wife, Ruth, 'I love already.'

Within a few days the expedition was ready to leave Darjeeling. Besides its eight European members, it included a contingent of Sherpas, including several men Kellas had climbed with in previous years. 'Sherpa' was by now both an ethnic classification and a labour category, on its way to becoming synonymous with the indigenous guides of the Himalaya. There was still a way to go – to most of the European members of the 1921 expedition, Sherpas were little more than glorified porters. But for the Nepalese this limited perspective was an indignity worth suffering. The work was much better paid than other types of manual labour, and Kellas had shown that Europeans might one day meet them on more equal terms.

From Darjeeling they faced a 300-mile march to Everest, through the Sikkim and on into Tibet. Kellas, accustomed to the simple diet he shared with the Sherpas, was now at the mercy of Howard-Bury, who insisted they eat the tinned food they had brought with them. 'We've been living very badly,' wrote Mallory to Ruth, a little over a week out. 'The substitutes for bread are abominable and our cooks produce nasty messes which are most unappetising.'

By the time they reached Phari at the head of Tibet's Chumbi valley, Kellas had grown so weak he had to be carried into town on a litter. Unfortunately, with the other Europeans experiencing gastric problems of their own, it was too easy to overlook the deterioration in the Scot's condition, made worse by his complicity in its concealment. He was careful to start out a little later than the others each morning, fearful that if Howard-Bury saw how ill he was, he would be sent back to Darjeeling.

Kellas rallied once or twice over the days to come, but had stopped eating and was incapable of proceeding under his own steam. With Wollaston, Wheeler and Raeburn also struggling, Howard-Bury had little option but to let each expedition member go at his own pace. It was in dribs and drabs that they bore down upon the fortress town of Kampa Dzong, the culmination of a long day's march over a 17,200-foot pass. Howard-Bury and Wollaston were still being welcomed to the village when one of their men hurried in after them.

They could hardly believe what he had to tell them.

Kellas was dead.

Wollaston raced back up to the pass. There, he found the Scot's lifeless body still lying in his litter. From what he could see, Kellas had suffered a massive heart attack. More probably, the cause of death was acute gastric dysentery. Kellas had grown weaker and weaker, until he had no reserves left to draw on. The expedition had lost the first man to die in the quest for Mount Everest.

The sixth of June dawned.

'It was a perfect morning,' wrote Mallory, 'as we plodded up the barren slopes above our camp, rising behind the old, rugged fort which is itself a singularly impressive and dramatic spectacle; we had mounted perhaps a thousand feet when we stayed and turned, and saw what we came to see. There was no mistaking the two great peaks in the West: that to the left must be Makalu, grey, severe and yet distinctly graceful, and the other away to the right – who could doubt its identity? It was a prodigious white fang excrescent from the jaw of the world.'

Mallory was seeing Everest for the very first time.

There, on that stony hillside, they buried the body of Alec Kellas, then conducted a short funeral service. Among the mourners were four Sherpas, 'his own trained mountain men,' wrote Mallory, 'seated in wonder on a great stone near the grave while Bury read out the passage from I Corinthians'. Also in attendance, south to southeast of their position, were the peaks of Pauhunri, Chumiumo and Kangchenjhau, the three mountains on which Kellas had made his reputation. They would forever watch over his place of rest.

A few days after the funeral, George Mallory and Guy Bullock made their way up a steep hill to a spike of rock. They were that much closer to Everest now, but had not seen it again since Kellas's funeral. 'We were able to make out almost exactly where Everest should be; but the clouds were dark in that direction,' wrote Mallory. 'We gazed at them intently through field glasses as though by some miracle we might pierce the veil.'

'Presently,' he went on, 'the miracle happened.' 'Gradually, very gradually, we saw the great mountain sides and glaciers and arêtes, now one fragment and now another through the floating rifts, until far higher in the sky than imagination had dared to suggest the white summit of Everest appeared. And in this series of partial glimpses we had seen the whole; we were able to piece together the fragments, to interpret the dream. However much might remain to be understood, the centre had a clear meaning as one mountain shape, the shape of Everest.'

For Mallory, for whom mountains were objects of desire more than conquest, for whom climbing was an affair of the heart as well as head, this moment marked the birth of a romantic obsession. The 1921 expedition would continue as it had begun, a haphazard tramp into the heart of the Himalaya, laying the foundations for a bold and exacting attempt to reach Everest's summit the following year. For all the seasoned campaigners around him, it would be Mallory who became the mountain's intimate; it, his star-crossed love. He would return in 1924, with no good argument for doing so, except the pull, the draw, that makes of mountains haunts for restless souls.

Everest waited, patient as stone.

Bullock turned and started back down the uneven slope, leaving the lone figure of his old friend studying the mountain. Mallory read its lines and contours like musical notes, a symphony of the sublime, carried on a breeze that brushed his face, danced circles round his ears. Everest was calling to him, a sound only he could hear. Beckoning him closer, offering to share its secrets, promising to never let him go. Singing that same siren song that reached its end, for Alec Kellas, at Kampa Dzong.

*'We weren't just looking at a body, we were looking at
an era, one we'd only known through books.'*

Artist's impression of George Mallory (top) and Andrew Irvine (bottom)
climbing the 'Second Step' on Everest. Illustration by D. Macpherson (1924).

Go Ask the Past

At 10.30 a.m. on 1 May 1999, a party of five men arrived at what they knew as Camp VI, 27,230 feet above sea level, on the north ridge of Mount Everest.

Conditions were ideal. The wind had dropped, the sky was perfectly clear and brilliantly blue but, at 10.30 a.m., with the top of Everest less than thirteen hundred feet above, it was too late to go for the summit. From Camp VI the route lay up the treacherous crest of the northeast ridge, taking in the infamous 'Second Step' – a near-vertical ninety-foot escarpment – where the men would be breathing air so thin they called it the 'Death Zone'. They might make it to the summit before darkness fell; they would not have made it back to Camp VI.

Which was fine. The men were not there to summit Everest. Two had done so before, the remaining three were happy to leave it for another day. Instead, after resting for thirty minutes, they spread out west of Camp VI and started across the overlapping slabs of the mountain's north face.

They had not gone far when one of the men saw the first body. It was impossible to miss, a burst of bright colour against the mottled grey of the mountainside, crumpled and contorted where it had come to rest. They had known to expect this, but that was no preparation at all. Seeing another body, and another, they realised they had walked into 'a kind of collection zone for fallen climbers'. 'Death is like a fog that looms in the air over the North Face of Everest,' wrote Tap Richards.

'It hit me really hard. Seeing those first few bodies was eerie, grim, and humbling.'

The further they went the more bodies they found – half a dozen in all, wrapped in garish shrouds of Gore-Tex and quilted down. Each time they would radio in the details and, within seconds, the voice of Jochen Hemmleb crackled back by reply. Stationed at Base Camp seven miles away, the 28-year-old German – the expedition's 'historical advisor' – had a list of everybody lost on that side of Everest. Just from the make and colour of their clothes, boots and climbing equipment, Hemmleb quickly identified whose remains they had likely found.

Then, a little before midday, the voice of Conrad Anker crackled across the radio. Anker, the lowest of the five men, was moving along the bottom edge of the terrace, near where it fell away to the Rongbuk glacier thousands of feet below. 'Come on down,' said the American, choosing his words carefully. Anybody on the mountain might be listening. 'Let's get together for Snickers and tea.'

He waited. Three of the men had barely heard him, their radios stuffed deep inside their down-filled jackets. When only Jake Norton replied, Anker sent another message, his voice harder this time.

'I'm calling a mandatory group meeting, now.'

Following the death of Alec Kellas, the 1921 Mount Everest Reconnaissance Expedition carried on much as it had begun, its members spending the next four months engaged in the circuitous exploration of the peaks, valleys and glaciers around Everest. After a string of diversions and disappointments, they succeeded in pioneering a route onto the mountain's North Col, laying the groundwork for a first attempt on the summit the following year.

Returning in 1922, Mallory held himself responsible when seven Sherpas were killed in an avalanche, judging that he should have foreseen the danger. But, all the while, he and his companions pushed higher and higher – up the East Rongbuk glacier to the North Col, up the dangerous North Ridge to within thirteen hundred feet of the summit. Momentum, if nothing else, compelled Mallory back to the mountain for a third time in 1924. That and a sense – however misguided – that he owed it to the dead.

The third expedition had a different energy to it, with Mallory cutting an authoritative figure in the customary 'team photo', one foot planted on the shoulder of the man sitting cross-legged in front of him. To his right is Sandy Irvine, beaming from beneath the narrow brim of his sunhat. The two formed a firm friendship; Irvine had none of Mallory's mountaineering pedigree but was extremely good-natured, 'strong as an ox' and adept at making running repairs to the expedition's makeshift oxygen apparatus. After two summit bids failed, it was Mallory and Irvine who led one last attempt, leaving the highest camp and disappearing into light cloud on a still June day.

Many books have been written about the disappearance of Mallory and Irvine, working with a paucity of cold, hard facts. The men were last sighted at 12.50 p.m. on 8 June, as Noel Odell looked up to see two tiny figures two thousand feet above him, climbing one of three steps high on the Northeast Ridge; even then, Odell later confessed to being unsure which step it was. What he was certain of, climbing alone to Camp VI two days later, was that Mallory and Irvine had not made it back to their tent. Odell knew right away that both men were dead.

Percy Wyn-Harris, a member of a British Everest expedition mounted in 1933, would discover the first clue to what became of them. He was 250 yards short of the First Step when he found Sandy Irvine's ice-axe. For some, this suggested Irvine had fallen somewhere around this point, but others – Odell among them – were not so sure. The ridge was quite broad where the ice-axe had been found, not the sort of place a climber would fall. For Odell, it seemed more likely that, for whatever reason, it had been placed there.

Another British expedition was approaching the mountain three years later when one of its members, Frank Smythe, spotted 'something queer in a gully below the scree shelf'. Smythe was at the base camp of the 1936 expedition studying the North Face through a telescope when he noticed a mysterious object 'at precisely the point where Mallory and Irvine would have fallen had they rolled on over the scree slopes'. Believing he was looking at a body, Smythe wrote to Edward Norton, leader of the 1924 expedition, notifying him of what he had seen. 'It's not to be written about,' he told Norton, 'as the press would make an unpleasant sensation.' As it was, Smythe's letter remained a secret until his son discovered it in 2013.

Like Mallory before him, Smythe joined three expeditions to Everest, in 1933, 1936 and 1938. If the mountain was in danger of becoming a national obsession, the British were in good company – German climbers spent the 1930s fixating on Nanga Parbat and the Americans led two fraught attempts on the summit of K2. None of these expeditions succeeded – at the outbreak of the Second World War all the world's 'eight-thousanders' remained unclimbed. But records continued to be broken, including one terrible mark of distinction. Nine Sherpas and seven German mountaineers were asleep in their tents on Nanga Parbat in 1937 when, a little after midnight, an avalanche swept over their camp, burying the men beneath a thick blanket of snow. All sixteen were killed, in by far the worst mountaineering accident up to that point.

In the 1950s the eight-thousanders finally began to fall. A French expedition climbed Annapurna, the Italians summited K2, and a German named Herman Buhl went to the top of Nanga Parbat (now known as the 'Killer Mountain', for all the lives it had claimed). Where Everest was concerned, the British were almost beaten to it. In 1952 a Swiss expedition turned back eight hundred feet short of the summit, after two of its members had been reduced to crawling on all fours under the weight of their malfunctioning oxygen apparatus. One of the two, a Sherpa named Tenzing Norgay, was back with a British expedition the following year, as he and a beekeeper from New Zealand named Edmund Hillary became the first to go, at last, to Everest's summit. It was, they might have thought, the record to end all records. There was nowhere higher left to climb.

*

16 October 1986. A 32-year-old German named Reinhold Messner arrived at the summit of Lhotse, the fourth-highest mountain in the world. For many mountaineers, an ascent of Lhotse would be the highlight of their climbing career – for Messner, it was the last of fourteen boxes ticked. In the sixteen years since he and his brother stood at the summit of Nanga Parbat, Messner had climbed all of the world's eight-thousanders, the first person to do so. More remarkable still, he had done it without the use of supplemental oxygen. The first to climb Everest solo, pioneer of countless routes up many of the world's highest peaks, Messner was a talismanic figure for a new generation of mountaineers breaking records as quickly as they could conceive of them.

This was the 'age of extremes', as mountaineers vied for solo records, speed records, new routes and winter ascents, completed in conditions their nineteenth-century counterparts could scarcely imagine. The record books kept inventory not just of who had been to the highest Himalayan summits – their ages, genders and nationalities – but how many times and, in some cases, how they came down. Today, Everest alone accounts for more than forty different skydiving records, not to mention those who have descended the mountain by skis, snowboard and paraglider.

For some expeditions, as they grew in ambition, so they grew in size. Approaching Everest in 1976, Pete Boardman rounded a corner to see 'the British Raj in all its glory... tents erected, crowds kept at a distance'. It was 'a Bonington Everest Expedition,' noted the young Briton sardonically, 'one of the last great imperial experiences life can offer'. Chris Bonington was a British mountaineer who, a year earlier, raised what was then an eye-watering £100,000 of corporate sponsorship from Barclays Bank, allowing him to rope in fifteen British mountaineers and thirty-three climbing Sherpas. The return on their investment was to see Everest climbed 'the hard way' – in 1975 Bonington's team completed a first ascent of the mountain's harrowing southwest face, and only – *only* – at the cost of one life.

Governments, too, bankrolled major expeditions. In 1988 climbers from Nepal, China and Japan made a multinational attempt on Everest. One party climbed the mountain's north face in China; the other, the south face in Nepal. Meeting at the summit on 5 May – the first such rendezvous of its kind – they congratulated each other and spilled whisky on the ground in honour of lost climbers. This has a claim as the largest Everest expedition ever mounted, with a total membership of 252.

Then there were those who went to the other extreme. Seeing the paths into the Himalaya becoming thoroughfares, leading to base camps strewn with rubbish, two British mountaineers, Pete Boardman and Joe Tasker, tried something different. Attempting the 'ludicrously steep' West Wall of Changabang in 1976, they climbed on a budget so tight their Indian liaison officer abandoned them. For Tasker, the opportunity as a smaller party was to 'do much less damage to the personality of a people and the ecology of a region... a healthy development from the anonymous servant role, a legacy which expeditions have inherited from a colonial past'.

For the Sherpas themselves, this was not progress at all – they preferred the earlier expeditionary model, 'not,' according to Isserman and Weaver, 'because they craved servitude but because they sought employment'. 'Despite its risks, high-altitude climbing support on an expedition remained the best-paid economic opportunity available to most Sherpas, offering ten to fifteen times the annual per capita Nepalese income of $160 for two months' work.' With the ongoing commercialisation of the Himalayan experience, demand for their services would only increase.

And, out of this age of extremes came a new generation of professional mountaineers, among them a headstrong young American named Conrad Anker. Whether on the big walls of Yosemite, the soaring granite towers of Patagonia, the unclimbed peaks of the Karakoram or the hidden mountains of Antarctica, Anker gained a reputation as one of the best exploratory mountaineers in the world. In 1998 the 37-year-old was at the peak of his powers, but there remained one conspicuous gap on his alpine résumé – he had never bagged an 'eight-thousander'.

Then his chance came. Anker was contacted by Eric Simonson, one of the organisers of a forthcoming expedition to the Himalaya. Simonson assured him that, as a member of the expedition, he would have an opportunity to go for Everest's summit. There was just one caveat – first he must join a search, high on the mountain's north face, for the body of Sandy Irvine.

The skin was bleached white, the clothing blasted from it, like a statue in alabaster face down on the mountainside. 'We weren't just looking at a body,' recalled Dave Hahn, 'we were looking at an era, one we'd only known through books. The natural-fibre clothes, the fur-lined leather helmet, the kind of rope that was around him were all so eloquent.' And the hobnail boots. Only *two* men had been lost on Everest wearing hobnail boots. There, in front them, was all that remained of one.

Allowing for where Irvine's ice-axe had been found, the members of the 1999 expedition had always understood that, if they were going to find either man lost in 1924, it would be him. This had become such accepted wisdom that, when one of the men summoned the nerve to touch the body, and discovered a name tag reading 'G. Mallory', their first thought was to wonder what Irvine had been doing wearing one of his companion's shirts.

Then they found a second tag. Then a third.

Mallory.

'I just sat down,' recalled Politz. 'My knees literally got weak. My jaw dropped. Next to me Dave was saying, "Oh my God, it's George. Oh my God."'

George Mallory. His leg broken. His body tangled in rope. 'As we stood there,' Hahn went on, 'this mute but strangely peaceful body was telling us answers to questions that everyone had wondered about for three-quarters of a century.' 'It had been understood that George Mallory was infallible,' added Jake Norton, 'he didn't fall, he couldn't fall. It was a shock to discover that he was fallible, he did fall. We couldn't quite get used to the idea.'

The men chipped away at the ice cementing the body into the scree, with ice-axes at first then, as it became more intricate, with the blades of their pocketknives. Once they were able to lift his lower body, they went through his pockets, placing his various possessions in Ziploc bags. The last thing they collected was a DNA sample. 'I cut an inch-and-a-half-square patch of skin off the right forearm,' recalled Anker. 'It wasn't easy… like cutting saddle leather, cured and hard.' The American would later question 'whether this was a sacrilegious act… on the mountain, I had no time to reflect whether or not this was the right thing to do.'

It was almost 4 p.m. With what time they had left, they covered Mallory's body with rocks, then Andy Politz read Psalm 103, a prayer of committal.

'As for man, his days are as grass; as a flower of the field, so he flourisheth,' spoke Politz. 'For the wind passeth over it, and it is gone…'

22 May 2019. A Nepal-born mountaineer named Nirmal 'Nims' Purja stood at the top of Mount Everest, as the sun came up over the Himalaya. It was not his first ascent – in 2017 he had summited Everest, Lhotse and Makalu, three of the world's eight-thousanders, within the space of five days. Now, two years on, Purja hoped to climb them again in half the time. The sun, though, was holding him in its spell. For a moment he felt as though he could have stayed there all day, soaking up its warmth.

'Brother, we should go.' Purja's climbing partner, Lakpa Dendi, tugged at his summit suit. 'If you want to break that record, we need to turn around now.'

The pair had ascended the southeast ridge in darkness but, as they turned to go down, they could hardly believe what they saw. A string of climbers, 150 or more, snaked along the narrow crest of the ridge. Some had summited and were on their way down, but most were still waiting for their turn to stand, however momentarily, at the top of the world.

Purja could see the line was moving slowly, barely at all. That 'people… were angry. They had invested a lot of money, time and effort to scale Everest and their progress had been stopped dead.' The further he descended, the more concerned Purja became. 'People were arguing around me,' he wrote. 'Everything was madness.'

It may seem crazy, to see men and women queuing for a mountain's summit. But for some who climb Everest, no other mountain will do. That is the pull of the absolute.

For the rest of us, it is a world of mountains.

There is K2, approached along the Godwin-Austen glacier, climbed via the Abruzzi Spur. Kangchenjunga, where climbers pay their respects at Pache's Grave, following a route devised by Aleister Crowley. Nanga Parbat, still one of the deadliest challenges in mountaineering, climbed in winter by the Mummery Rib. Nanda Devi, 'the Bliss-Giving Goddess', seen in all her splendour from Longstaff's Col.

Conway's 'Golden Throne', Baltoro Kangri. The 'Siegfriedhorn', 'Mount Bullock Workman' and 'Pinnacle Peak'.

The Matterhorn, seen from the Whymper Suite of the Monte Rosa Hotel. Mont Blanc, and somewhere in its massif, punctuated by so many towering spitzes and needle-like aiguilles, Pointe Graham, atop the northeast pinnacle of the Dent du Géant.

Popocatepetl, Chimborazo and Lluillaillaco, the once-smoking volcanoes of Latin America. Portents of a tumultuous future. Windows into a primordial past.

There are all the rocks and blocks and boulders in the world. Oscar Eckenstein, a pioneer of 'balance climbing', turned every one into a mountain of its own.

There is Lhotse. *There, two miles south of Everest, was Lhotse.* Nims Purja and Lakpa Dendi could see it, from their vantage on the southeast ridge. The fourth-highest mountain in the world, their next objective, just across the South Col.

Purja would be two hours on Everest's southeast ridge, marshalling climbers like 'a traffic policeman', gauging from other Sherpas whether their clients were fit to go on. By the time he and Dendi moved on, most of the climbers had either summited or turned back.

Purja went on to summit Lhotse and Makulu within the next forty-eight hours, smashing his record from 2017. And that was just a record *within* the record. On 29 October he stood at the top of the 26,335-foot Shishapangma. Located in Tibet, it is the fourteenth highest mountain in the world – the last of the eight-thousanders.

Reinhold Messner had taken sixteen years to reach all fourteen summits.

Nims Purja did it in six months and six days.

For a few weeks of every summer, high on Everest, the Death Zone comes alive. Dots of colour appear, inching along its summit ridges, moving up and down. Some days, nowadays, the dots form a line.

And, every summer, a few dots are left behind. Hunched, in whatever shelter they could find. Sprawled, at the foot of wherever it was they fell. For the winter to come, they have Everest to themselves. They become part of the mountain, just as it was once part of them.

Mallory is still up there, in the shallowest of graves. Lying, good leg folded over as if to shield the break in the bad.

In his final moments, he knew what we all know. That the mountain is within. The *why* is all we have. We die on the slopes of our own ideals.

The discovery of his body sent shockwaves around the mountaineering world. For some, those who found him were heroes, honouring the legacy of Everest's true pioneer. For others, they were graverobbers, selling their pictures to the highest bidder. Either way, they had added an intriguing new chapter to the greatest mountaineering mystery of them all.

But the mystery remained unsolved.

Even as some questions were answered, others arose. Where *was* the body of Sandy Irvine? Had he fallen elsewhere on the northeast ridge, his body covered by avalanching snow, or carried beyond hope of discovery? Was there any truth to the suggestion that Irvine's corpse had already been found, by the members of a Chinese expedition, in 1975; that they had buried him on the mountainside and had taken possession of the two men's Kodak Vest Pocket camera, along with the undeveloped pictures it might contain? Had they found proof that Mallory and Irvine had indeed gone to Everest's summit?

Various personal effects were recovered from Mallory's body, clues to his final days and hours. His green-tinted snow goggles were in his pocket, suggesting that he and Irvine had been descending at night. His wristwatch had stopped between one and two, but was that in the morning or the afternoon? And where was the photograph of Ruth, the one he carried with him everywhere he went; the one he had promised to place at the summit of Everest?

There are no real endings to mountain stories. Beyond one summit stands another. And death, the epilogue of one adventure, soon becomes a prologue to the next.

Acknowledgements

Thanks to my wife Emma, a truly brilliant woman, who has guided me on this adventure for twenty-five years. To our two loving daughters, Lola and Ruby, who inspire with their kindness, industry and ambition, at home, in the classroom and on the climbing wall.

To my mother, to whom this book is dedicated, and also my father (assuming he has not skipped to the end). To my sister Charlotte, and to my brother Barney, who first took me into the mountains.

To Saffron Wilding Mackenzie, Ollie Tucker and everybody at Glass Eye for making this possible, and humouring me when it was all that seemed to matter in the world.

To Kathy Gale, who taught me to write for others, and to everybody I have worked with as a member of her Writers' Studio. To Andrew Gordon at David Higham Associates, for adding some of my favourite chapters. To Sam Carter at Oneworld, for never letting me doubt that this was a book he would pick up for fun, and Tom Mayer at W. W. Norton, for his deftness and drive. To the industrious Hannah Haseloff.

To Glyn Hughes at the Alpine Club; to Seema Desai, for *The Kangchenjunga Adventure*; to Eva Luthi, John Keay, Ian R. Mitchell, Nicholas Gledhill, Will Brook, Nokmedemla Lemtur, Joe Fratianni, Sonia Purnell, Maurice Isserman, Stewart Weaver and Emma Hargrave; to Cienna Hewitt, Oscar Banyard and the gang at Yonder.

To all the climbers, musicians and poets I have taken inspiration from along the way, with honourable mentions for Frank Smythe, Public Service Broadcasting and my friend Jo Hay.

Finally, to James Scudamore, a friend of forty years, always encouraging me to put things down on paper, so generous with the dividends of his own career. The origins of this book can still be found in dozens of postcards written to his son, my godson, Clem, long before Scudamore Jnr was able to read.

Bibliography

Sources are arranged in alphabetical order by chapter. Each source is noted once under the first chapter in which it appears.

Epigraph

Fanny Bullock Workman, *Peaks and Glaciers of Nun Kun* (London: Constable and Company, 1909), p. 34.

Prologue – Because It Is There

Wade Davis, *Into the Silence: The Great War, Mallory and the Conquest of Everest* (London: Vintage, 2012).

Peter and Leni Gillman, *The Wildest Dream: Mallory, His Life and Conflicting Passions* (London: Headline, 2000).

Tom Holzel and Audrey Salkeld, *The Mystery of Mallory and Irvine* (London: Pimlico, 2010).

Charles Howard-Bury and George Leigh Mallory, *Everest Reconnaissance* (London: Hodder & Stoughton, 1991).

R. L. G. Irving, 'George Herbert Leigh Mallory 1886–1924', *Alpine Journal*, Vol. 36 (1924), pp. 381–5.

George Mallory, *Climbing Everest: The Complete Writings of George Mallory* (London: Gibson Square, 2021).

George Mallory, 'The Second Mt. Everest Expedition', *Alpine Journal*, Vol. 34 (1922), pp. 425–39.

Sherry B. Ortner, *Life and Death on Mt. Everest: Sherpas and Himalayan Mountaineering* (Princeton: Princeton University Press, 2009).

Walter Unsworth, *Because it is There – Famous Mountaineers: 1840–1940* (London: Victor Gollancz, 1973).

Geoffrey Winthrop Young, *On High Hills* (London: Methuen, 1933).

Francis Younghusband, *The Epic of Mount Everest* (London: Edward Arnold, 1926).

'Mountain Climber Trains in Walk-Ups', *New York Times* (3 February 1923), p. 8.

Part 1 – All They Surveyed

Chapter 1 – Under a Foreign Sky

Allen H. Bent, 'Early American Mountaineers', *Appalachia*, Vol. 13, No. 1 (June 1913), pp. 45–67.

Edwin Bernbaum, *Sacred Mountains of the World* (Cambridge: Cambridge University Press, 2022).

Ronald W. Clark, *Men, Myths & Mountains: The Life and Times of Mountaineering* (London: Weidenfeld & Nicolson, 1976).

Hernán Cortés, *Letters from Mexico*, trans. Anthony Pagden (New Haven: Yale University Press, 1986).

William Dalrymple, *The Anarchy: The Relentless Rise of the East India Company* (London: Bloomsbury, 2019).

Bernal Diaz, *The Conquest of New Spain*, trans. J. M. Cohen (London: Penguin, 1963).

H. Byron Earhart, *Mount Fuji: Icon of Japan* (South Carolina: University of South Carolina Press, 2011).

Lachlan Fleetwood, *Science on the Roof of the World: Empire and the Remaking of the Himalaya* (Cambridge: Cambridge University Press, 2022).

Alexander Gerard, *An Account of Koonawur in the Himalaya* (London: James Madden, 1841).

Alexander von Humboldt, *Personal Narrative of a Journey to the Equinoctial Regions of the New Continent*, trans. Jason Wilson (London: Penguin, 1995).

Alexander von Humboldt, 'About an attempt to climb to the top of Chimborazo', trans. Vera M. Kutzinski, *Atlantic Studies*, Vol. 7, No. 2 (2010), pp. 191–211.

Buddy Levy, *Conquistador: Hernán Cortés, King Montezuma, and the Last Stand of the Aztecs* (New York: Bantam, 2009).

William Lloyd, *Narrative of a Journey From Caunpoor to the Boorendo Pass in the Himalaya Mountains, Via Gwalior, Agra, Delhi, and Sirhind* (London: James Madden, 1840).

William H. Prescott, *The History of the Conquest of Mexico* (London: Continuum, 2009).

Johan Reinhard, *The Ice Maiden: Inca Mummies, Mountain Gods, and Sacred Sites in the Andes* (Washington: National Geographical Society, 2006).

Richard Henry Stoddard, *The Life, Travels and Books of Alexander Von Humboldt* (New York: Rudd & Carleton, 1859).

E. Theophilus, 'Reo Purgyil – Beneath the Shroud', *Himalayan Journal*, Vol. 48 (1992).

Hugh Thomas, *Conquest: Montezuma, Cortés and the Fall of Old Mexico* (New York: Simon & Schuster, 2005).

Clae Waltham, *Shu Ching: Book of History* (London: George Allen & Unwin Ltd, 1972).

Gwendolyn L. Waring, *The Natural History of the San Francisco Peaks* (Gwendolyn L. Waring, 2018).

Andrew S. Wilson et al., 'Archaeological, radiological, and biological evidence offer insight into Inca child sacrifice', *PNAS* (13 August 2013).

Andrea Wulf, *The Invention of Nature: The Adventures of Alexander von Humboldt, the Lost Hero of Science* (London: John Murray, 2015).

Chapter 2 – Ahead of the Game

Helga Alcock, 'Three Pioneers: The Schlagintweit Brothers', *Himalayan Journal*, Vol. 36 (1980).

Moritz von Brescius, *German Science in the Age of Empire: Enterprise, Opportunity and the Schlagintweit Brothers* (Cambridge: Cambridge University Press, 2018).

Ed Douglas, *Himalaya: A Human History* (London: The Bodley Head, 2020).

Gabriel Finkelstein, '"Conquerors of The Künlün"? The Schlagintweit Mission to High Asia, 1854–57', *History of Science*, Vol. 38, No. 2 (June 2000), pp. 179–218.

Horst H. Geerken and Annette Bräker, *The Karakoram Highway and the Hunza Valley, 1998: History, Culture, Experiences* (Books On Demand, 2017).

Maurice Isserman and Stewart Weaver, *Fallen Giants: A History of Himalayan Mountaineering from the Age of Empire to the Age of Extremes* (New Haven: Yale University Press, 2008).

Kenneth Mason, *Abode of Snow: A History of Himalayan Exploration and Mountaineering from Earliest Times to the Ascent of Everest* (London: Diadem Books, 1987).

C. F. Meade, 'The Schlagintweits and Ibi Gamin (Kamet)', *Alpine Journal*, Vol. 33 (1921), pp. 70–5.

Hermann and Robert Schlagintweit, *Official Reports on the last Journeys and the Death of Adolphe Schlagintweit in Turkistán* (Berlin, 1859).

Hermann, Adolphe and Robert Schlagintweit, *Results of a scientific mission to India and High Asia, undertaken between the years 1854 and 1858, by order of the Court of Directors of the Honourable East India Company.*

With an atlas of panoramas, views, and maps (Leipzig and London: F. A. Brockhaus, 1861–66).

J. Stogdon, 'Schlagintweit's Himalayan Travels', *Alpine Journal*, Vol. 6 (August 1872), pp. 43–9.

H. Strachey and Herbert B. Edwardes, 'On the Death of M. Adolphe Schlagintweit', *Proceedings of the Royal Geographical Society*, Vol. 3, No. 6 (1858–9), pp. 172–4.

Chapter 3 – Fresh Blood

Mick Conefrey, *Ghosts of K2: The Race for the Summit of the World's Most Deadly Mountain* (London: Oneworld Publications, 2015).

H. H. Godwin-Austen, 'Notes on the Valley of Kashmir', *Journal of the Royal Geographical Society*, Vol. 31 (1861), pp. 30–37.

H. H. Godwin-Austen, 'On the Glaciers of the Mustakh Range', *Journal of the Royal Geographical Society*, Vol. 34 (1864), pp. 19–56.

H. H. Godwin-Austen, 'The Survey of the Mustagh Range', *Geographical Journal*, Vol. 22, No. 6 (December 1903), pp. 707–8.

Kenneth Hewitt, 'Rediscovering Colonised Landscapes: The First Europeans at the Mustagh Pass, Karakoram Himalaya, Inner Asia', *ResearchGate* (January 2009).

Charles Houston and Robert Bates, *K2: The Savage Mountain* (London: Collins, 1955).

John Keay, *When Men and Mountains Meet: The Explorers of the Western Himalayas 1820–75* (London: John Murray, 1977).

John Keay, *Himalaya: Exploring the Roof of the World* (London: Bloomsbury, 2022).

Kenneth Iain MacDonald, 'Push and Shove: Spatial History and the Construction of a Portering Economy in Northern Pakistan', *Comparative Studies in Society and History*, Vol. 40, No. 2 (April 1998), pp. 287–317.

Catherine Moorehead, *The K2 Man (and His Molluscs): The Extraordinary Life of Haversham Godwin-Austen* (Glasgow: In Pinn, 2013).

G. T. Vigne, *Travels in Kashmir, Ladakh, Iskardo* (London: Henry Colburn, 1844).

Derek Waller, *The Pundits: British Exploration of Tibet & Central Asia* (Kentucky: The University Press of Kentucky, 1990).

John Noble Wilford, *The Mapmakers: The Story of the Great Pioneers in Cartography – From Antiquity to the Space Age* (London: Pimlico, 2002).

Chapter 4 – The Khan of Khotan

Douglas Freshfield, 'Notes on the Himálaya and Himálayan Survey', *Alpine Journal*, Vol. XII (1886), pp. 58–60.

H. H. Godwin-Austen, 'Obituary: Mr. W. H. Johnson', *Proceedings of the Royal Geographical Society*, Vol. 5, No. 5 (May 1883), pp. 291–3.

W. H. Johnson, 'Report on His Journey to Ilchí, the Capital of Khotan, in Chinese Tartary', *Journal of the Royal Geographical Society of London*, Vol. 37 (1867), pp. 1–47.

T. G. Longstaff, 'Mr. Johnson's Ascent of E 61', *Geographical Journal*, Vol. 31 (March 1908), p. 345.

T. G. Longstaff, 'Journeys of the Late W. H. Johnson', *Geographical Journal*, Vol. 32, No. 1 (July 1908), pp. 94–5.

T. G. Longstaff, 'A Note on W. H. Johnson's Ascents in the Kuen Luen', *Alpine Journal*, Vol. 24 (1909), pp. 133–8.

Kenneth Mason, 'Johnson's "Suppressed Ascent" of E61', *Alpine Journal*, Vol. 34 (1922), pp. 54–68.

Mary Louise Pratt, *Imperial Eyes: Travel Writing and Transculturation* (New York: Routledge, 2008).

H. C. Rawlinson, 'On the Recent Journey of Mr. W. H. Johnson from Leh, in Ladakh, to Ilchi in Chinese Turkistan', *Proceedings of the Royal Geographical Society*, Vol. 11, No. 1 (1866–1867), pp. 6–15.

M. Aurel Stein, *Sand-buried Ruins of Khotan: Personal Narrative of a Journey of Archaeological and Geographical Exploration in Chinese Turkestan* (London: T. Fisher Unwin, 1904).

M. Aurel Stein, *Ruins of Desert Cathay: Personal Narrative of Explorations in Central Asia and Westernmost China* (New York: Dover Publications, Inc, 1987).

H. Trotter, 'On the Geographical Results of the Mission to Kashgar, under Sir T. Douglas Forsyth in 1873–74', *Journal of the Royal Geographical Society*, Vol. 48 (1866–1867), pp. 173–234.

William Hunter Workman, 'The Question of Mr. Johnson's High Camp', *Geographical Journal*, Vol. 31, No. 6 (June 1908), pp. 683–4.

'Mr Johnson's Ascents in the K'un-lun south of Khotan', *Geographical Journal*, Vol. 59, No. 4 (November 1921).

Part 2 – The Alpinists Arrive

Chapter 5 – The Golden Age

Bob Bridle, ed., *Mountaineers: Great Tales of Bravery and Conquest* (London: Penguin Random House, 2011).

D. F. O. Dangar, 'The Fuhrerbuch of "Young" Peter Taugwalder', *Alpine Journal*, Vol. 59 (1954), pp. 436–41.

D. F. O. Dangar, 'The Parkers and the Matterhorn', *Alpine Journal*, Vol. 68 (1963), pp. 285–90.

D. F. O. Dangar and T. S. Blakeney, 'The Rise of Modern Mountaineering and the Formation of the Alpine Club', *Alpine Journal*, Vol. 62 (1957), pp. 16–38.

D. F. O. Dangar and T. S. Blakeney, 'The First Ascent of the Matterhorn: The Narrative of "Young" Peter Taugwalder', *Alpine Journal*, Vol. 61 (1957), pp. 484–506.

D. F. O. Dangar and T. S. Blakeney, 'The Matterhorn: A Diary of Events after the Disaster of 1865', *Alpine Journal*, Vol. 70 (1965), pp. 199–204.

Fergus Fleming, *Killing Dragons: The Conquest of the Alps* (London: Granta, 2000).

Arnold Lunn, 'Taugwalder and the Matterhorn', *Alpine Journal*, Vol. 60 (1955), pp. 290–6.

Arnold Lunn, 'The Matterhorn Centenary', *Alpine Journal*, Vol. 70 (1965), pp. 7–47.

Arnold Lunn, 'Whymper Again', *Alpine Journal*, Vol. 53 (1966), pp. 228–35.

Alan Lyall, *The First Descent of the Matterhorn: A Bibliographical Guide to the 1865 Accident & its Aftermath* (Llandysul: Gomer Press, 1997).

Gus Morton, 'A Conversation with Whymper', *Alpine Journal* (2013), pp. 193–9.

Frank S. Smythe, *Edward Whymper* (London: Hodder & Stoughton, 1940).

Walter Unsworth, *Matterhorn Man: The Life and Adventures of Edward Whymper* (London: Victor Gollancz, 1965).

Edward Whymper, *Scrambles amongst the Alps* (London: John Murray 1871).

Chapter 6 – Mountain Sickness

Douglas William Freshfield, *The Life of Horace Benedict de Saussure* (London: Edward Arnold, 1920).

Vanessa Heggie, *Higher and Colder: A History of Extreme Physiology and Exploration* (Chicago: The University of Chicago Press, 2019).

Caroline Schaumann, *Peak Pursuits: The Emergence of Mountaineering in the Nineteenth Century* (New Haven: Yale University Press, 2020).

John Sutton, 'Medical problems of high altitude', *Alpine Journal* (1973), pp. 153–60.

Edward Whymper, *Travel Amongst the Great Andes of the Equator* (London: Thomas Nelson, 1891).

Chapter 7 – No Higher Purpose

Willy Blaser and Glyn Hughes, 'Kabru 1883 – A Reassessment', *Alpine Journal*, Vol. 114 (2009), pp. 217–28.

Mor. Déchy, 'Mountain Travel in the Sikkim Himalaya', *Alpine Journal*, Vol. IX (August 1880), pp. 1–11.

D. W. Freshfield, 'In Memoriam – Emil Boss', *Alpine Journal*, Vol. XIV (August 1888), pp. 67–9.

W. W. Graham, 'The Dent du Géant (II.)', *Alpine Journal*, Vol. XI (November 1882), pp. 73–8.

W. W. Graham, 'Mountaineering in Sikhim', *Alpine Journal*, Vol. XI (February 1884), pp. 402–7.

W. W. Graham, 'Travel and Ascents in the Himálaya', *Alpine Journal*, Vol. XII (August 1884), pp. 25–60.

W. W. Graham, 'Travel and Ascents in the Himálaya', *Proceedings of the Royal Geographical Society*, Vol. 8 (August 1884), pp. 429–47.

W. W. Graham, 'Up the Himalayas – Mountaineering on the Indian Alps', *Good Words 1885* ed. Donald Macleod, (1885), pp. 18–23, 97–105, 172–8.

J. W. A. Michell, 'Twenty Years' Climbing and Hunting in the Himalayas', *Alpine Journal*, Vol. 11 (May 1883), pp. 203–15.

Alessandro Sella, 'The Dent du Géant (I.)', *Alpine Journal*, Vol. 11 (November 1882), pp. 72–3.

Clement M. Smith, 'A Walking Tour through the Himalayas, from Hindostan to Tibet', *Alpine Journal*, Vol. 3 (1867), pp. 52–68.

Walt Unsworth, *Hold the Heights: The Foundations of Mountaineering* (London: Hodder & Stoughton, 1994).

Walt Unsworth, ed. *Peaks, Passes and Glaciers: Selections from the Alpine Journal* (London: Penguin, 1981).

Chapter 8 – The Climber's Flower

Edwin Swift Balch, 'The Highest Mountain Ascent', *Bulletin of the American Geographical Society*, Vol. 36, No. 2 (1904), pp. 107–9.

J. Norman Collie, 'The Highest Climbs on Record', *Alpine Journal*, Vol. 22 (1905), pp. 626–7.

Douglas Freshfield, 'Himálayan and Alpine Mountaineering', *Alpine Journal*, Vol. 12 (1886), pp. 99–108.

Douglas Freshfield, 'The Highest Climbs on Record', *Alpine Journal*, Vol. 19 (1899), pp. 48–54.

William Hunter Workman, 'The Highest Climbs on Record', *Alpine Journal*, Vol. 23 (1907), pp. 82–3.

'Mountaineering in the Himalayas', *Pioneer Mail* (24 July 1884), p. 82.

Chapter 9 – Friction

C. G. Bruce, *Twenty Years in the Himalaya* (London: Edward Arnold, 1910).

C. G. Bruce, *Himalayan Wanderer* (London: Alexander Maclehose & Co., 1934).

W. M. Conway, 'Centrists and Excentrists', *Alpine Journal*, Vol. 15 (1891), pp. 397–403.

W. M. Conway, 'Mr. Conway's Karakoram Expedition', *Proceedings of the Royal Geographical Society*, Vol. 14, No. 11 (November 1892), pp. 753–70.

W. M. Conway, 'Climbing in the Karakorams', *Alpine Journal*, Vol. 16 (1893), pp. 413–22.

W. M. Conway, 'Exploration in the Mustagh Mountains', *Geographical Journal*, Vol. 2, No. 4 (October 1893), pp. 289–99.

William Martin Conway, *Climbing and Exploration in the Karakoram-Himalayas* (London: T. Fisher Unwin, 1894).

William Martin Conway, *Mountain Memories: A Pilgrimage of Romance* (London: Cassell and Company, 1920).

Oscar Eckenstein, *The Karakorams and Kashmir: An Account of a Journey* (London: T. Fisher Unwin, 1896).

B. E. M. Gurdon, 'Obituary: Brigadier-General the Hon. Charles Granville Bruce, M. V. O., C. B.', *Geographical Journal*, Vol. 96, No. 4 (October 1940).

T. G. Longstaff, 'Obituary: Lord Conway of Allington 1856–1937', *Geographical Journal*, Vol. 90, No. 1 (July 1937), pp. 93–4.

Kenneth Mason, 'Bruce, Charles Granville', *Oxford Dictionary of National Biography* (6 January 2011).

Charles Roy, 'Mountain Sickness', *Science Progress (1894–1898)*, Vol. 3, No. 14 (April 1895), pp. 85–98.

Chris Williams, 'Eckenstein, Oscar Johannes Ludwig', *Oxford Dictionary of National Biography* (25 September 2014).

Matthias Zurbriggen, *From the Alps to the Andes; Being the Autobiography of a Mountain Guide* (London: T. Fisher Unwin, 1899).

Chapter 10 – Pioneer Pique

W. M. Conway, 'Mr. Conway's Karakoram Expedition', *Proceedings of the Royal Geographical Society*, Vol. 14, No. 11 (November 1892), pp. 753–70.

William Martin Conway, 'Some Reminiscences and Reflections of an Old-stager', *Alpine Journal*, Vol. 31 (1918), pp. 146–157.

Joan Evans, *The Conways: A History of Three Generations* (London: Museum Press, 1966).

Peter H. Hansen, 'Conway, (William) Martin, Baron Conway of Allington', *Oxford Dictionary of National Biography* (23 September 2004).

A. D. McCormick, *An Artist in the Himalayas* (London: Macmillan, 1895).

Framley Steelcroft, 'Illustrated Interviews: No. LIV. – Sir W. Martin Conway', *Strand Magazine*, Vol. 13 (1897), pp. 665–77.

Chapter 11 – World of Giants

Edward Charles Cyril Baly, 'John Norman Collie 1859–1942', *Biographical Memoirs of Fellows of the Royal Society* (1 November 1943).

C. G. Bruce, 'The Passing of Mummery', *Himalayan Journal*, Vol. 3 (1931), pp. 1–12.

J. Norman Collie, 'Climbing on the Nanga Parbat Range, Kashmir', *Alpine Journal*, Vol. 18 (1897), pp. 17–32.

Norman Collie, *Climbing on the Himalaya and Other Mountain Ranges* (Edinburgh: David Douglas, 1902).

F. G. Donnan, 'Collie, John Norman', *Oxford Dictionary of National Biography* (23 September 2004).

Peter H. Hansen, 'Mummery, Albert Frederick', *Oxford Dictionary of National Biography* (23 September 2004).

A. F. Mummery, *My Climbs in the Alps and Caucasus* (London: T. Fisher Unwin, 1895).

Walter Unsworth, *Tiger in the Snow: The Life and Adventures of A. F. Mummery* (London: Victor Gollancz, 1967).

Part 3 – Amateur Hour

Chapter 12 – Lord of the East Face

E. A. Fitzgerald, *Climbs in the New Zealand Alps; Being an Account of Travel and Discovery* (London: T. Fisher Unwin, 1896).

E. A. Fitzgerald, 'Exploration on and around Aconcagua', *Geographical Journal*, Vol. 12, No. 5 (November 1898), pp. 469–86.

E. A. Fitzgerald, *The Highest Andes* (London: Methuen & Co., 1899).

Peter H. Hansen, 'FitzGerald, Edward Arthur', *Oxford Dictionary of National Biography* (27 May 2010).

Horace-Bénédict de Saussure, *Voyages dans les Alpes*, (Neuchâtel: 1803).

Stuart Vines, 'The Ascent of Aconcagua and Tupungato', *Alpine Journal*, Vol. 19 (1899), pp. 565–78.

Chapter 13 – Nature at Her Wildest

Dorothy Middleton, 'Some Victorian Lady Travellers', *Geographical Journal*, Vol. 139, No. 1 (February 1973), pp. 65–75.

Michael Plint, 'The Workmans: Travellers Extraordinary', *Alpine Journal* (1992/3), pp. 231–7.

Cathryn J. Prince, *Queen of the Mountaineers: The Trailblazing Life of Fanny Bullock Workman* (Chicago: Chicago Review Press, 2019).

Fanny Bullock Workman, *In the Ice World of the Himalaya: Among the Peaks and Passes of Ladakh, Nubra, Suru and Baltistan* (London: T. Fisher Unwin, 1900).

Fanny Bullock Workman, 'Amid the Snows of Baltistan', *Scottish Geographical Magazine*, Vol. 17, No. 2 (1901), pp. 74–86.

Fanny Bullock Workman, 'Expedition Journal, India 1898–9', National Library of Scotland.

Fanny Bullock Workman, 'Drafts for literary works including "A Vacation Episode" and "Adele, the Pride of the Donnerkoning"', National Library of Scotland.

William Hunter Workman, 'Expedition Journal, India 1898–9', National Library of Scotland.

Chapter 14 – Rough Diamonds

T. S. Blakeney and D. F. O. Dangar, 'Oscar Eckenstein, 1859–1921', *Alpine Journal*, Vol. 65 (1960), pp. 62–79.

Martin Booth, *A Magick Life: A Biography of Aleister Crowley* (London: Hodder & Stoughton, 2000).

Charlie Buffet, *Jules Jacot-Guillarmod: Pioneer am K2* (Zurich: AS Verlag, 2012).

Aleister Crowley (John Symonds and Kenneth Grant, ed.), *The Confessions of Aleister Crowley: An Autohagiography* (London: Jonathan Cape, 1969).

Jim Curran, *K2, Triumph and Tragedy* (London: Hodder & Stoughton, 1987).

H. C. A. Gaunt, 'Guy John Fenton Knowles 1879–1959', *Alpine Journal*, Vol. 64 (1959), pp. 288–9.

Dr Jules Jacot-Guillarmod, *Six Mois dans l'Himalaya: Le Karakorum at l'Hindu-Kush* (Auvernier: Chaman, 2019).

Richard Kaczynski, *Perdurabo: The Life of Aleister Crowley* (Berkeley: North Atlantic Books, 2010).

Guy Knowles, 'Expedition Journal', *The Alpine Club* (1902).

Galen Rowell, *In the Throne Room of the Mountain Gods* (San Francisco: Sierra Club Books, 1986).

Lawrence Sutin, *Do What Thou Wilt: A Life of Aleister Crowley* (New York: St. Martin's Griffin, 2000).

Simon Thompson, *Unjustifiable Risk? The Story of British Climbing* (Cumbria: Cicerone, 2010).

Chapter 15 – Monarchs of a Void

Wilhelm Kick, 'Chogo Lungma Glacier, Karakoram', *Geographical Journal*, Vol. 122, No. 1 (March 1956), pp. 93–6.

Fanny Bullock Workman, 'Expedition Journal, India 1902–3', National Library of Scotland.

Fanny Bullock Workman, 'First Exploration of the Hoh Lumba and Sosbon Glaciers: Two Pioneer Ascents in the Himalaya', *Geographical Journal*, Vol. 27, No. 2 (February 1906), pp. 129–41.

Fanny Bullock Workman, *Ice-Bound Heights of the Mustagh: An Account of Two Seasons of Pioneer Exploration in the Baltistan Himalaya* (New York: Charles Scribner's Sons, 1908).

William Hunter Workman, 'Expedition Journal, Himalayas 1902–3', National Library of Scotland.

William Hunter Workman, 'From Srinagar to the Sources of the Chogo Lungma Glacier', *Geographical Journal*, Vol. 25 (March 1905), pp. 245–65.

William Hunter Workman, 'Ascent of the Bhayakara La, Baltistan', *Alpine Journal*, Vol. 22 (1905), pp. 16–20.

William Hunter Workman, 'Some Obstacles to Himalayan Mountaineering and the History of a Record Ascent', *Alpine Journal*, Vol. 22 (1905), pp. 489–506.

William Hunter Workman, 'Dr. and Mrs. Workman in the Himalayas', *Geographical Journal*, Vol. 22, No. 5 (November 1903), pp. 541–4.

Chapter 16 – Baptism of Ice

Fergus Fleming, *Barrow's Boys* (London: Granta, 1998).

Tom Longstaff, *This My Voyage* (London: John Murray, 1950).

T. G. Longstaff, 'Notes on a Journey Through the Western Himalaya', *Geographical Journal*, Vol. 29, No. 2 (February 1907), pp. 201–11.

Chapter 17 – Because I Must

A. Henry Savage Landor, *Tibet and Nepal* (London: A. & C. Black, 1905).

Charles Sherring, *Western Tibet and the British Borderland* (London: Edward Arnold, 1906).

Chapter 18 – Five Brothers

Mick Conefrey, *The Last Great Mountain: The First Ascent of Kangchenjunga* (Mick Conefrey, 2020).

Aleister Crowley, 'On the Kinchin Lay: Prospect and Retrospect', *Pioneer Mail* (10 August 1905).

Aleister Crowley, 'On the Kinchin Lay: Bandobast', *Pioneer Mail* (17 August 1905).

Aleister Crowley, 'On the Kinchin Lay: The March', *Pioneer Mail* (20 September 1905).

Aleister Crowley, 'On the Kinchin Lay: The Glacier', *Pioneer Mail* (September 1905).

Aleister Crowley, 'On the Kinchin Lay: Mountains or Metaphysics?', *Pioneer Mail* (26 September 1905).

Charles Evans, *Kangchenjunga: The Untrodden Peak* (London: Hodder & Stoughton, 1956).

Douglas Freshfield, *Round Kangchenjunga: A Narrative of Mountain Travel and Exploration* (London: Edward Arnold, 1903).

Dr J. Jacot-Guillarmod, 'Vers le Kangchinjunga', *Jahrbuch des Schweizer Alpenclub 1905*, (1905), pp. 190–205.

Dr J. Jacot-Guillarmod, 'Dans l'Himalaya: La Catastrophe du Kangchenjunga', *Gazette de Lausanne*, (11 November 1905).

Dr J. Jacot-Guillarmod, 'Dans l'Himalaya: Du Glacier de Yalung a Jongri', *Gazette de Lausanne,* (17 November 1905).

Dr J. Jacot-Guillarmod, 'Dans l'Himalaya: De Jongri a Darjeeling', *Gazette de Lausanne* (1 December 1905).

Charles Reymond, 'L'Expedition de l'Himalaya', *Journal de Genève* (5 February 1906).

A. C. Rigo De Righi, 'To the Editor', *The Pioneer* (29 September 1905).

Chapter 19 – Camp America

Kenneth Mason, 'A Note on the Topography of the Nun Kun Massif in Ladakh', *Geographical Journal,* Vol. 56, No. 2 (August 1920), pp. 124–8.

Fanny Bullock Workman, 'Expedition Journal, India 1906', National Library of Scotland.

Fanny Bullock Workman, *Peaks and Glaciers of Nun Kun* (London: Constable and Company, 1909).

William Hunter Workman, 'Expedition Journal, Himalayas 1906', National Library of Scotland.

William Hunter Workman, 'An Exploration of the Nun Kun Mountain Group and Its Glaciers', *Geographical Journal,* Vol. 31, No. 1 (January 1908), pp. 12–39.

Part 4 – Approach to Everest

Chapter 20 – Trident of Shiva

Clinton T. Dent, 'Can Mount Everest be Ascended', *Nineteenth Century,* Vol. 32 (1892), pp. 604–13.

Patrick French, *Younghusband: The Last Great Imperial Adventurer* (London: Harper Collins, 1994).

Tony Gould, *Imperial Warriors: Britain and the Gurkhas* (London: Granta, 1999).

George Taubman Goldie and John Morley, 'A Himalayan Barrier', *Alpine Journal,* Vol. 23 (1907).

T. G. Longstaff, 'A Mountaineering Expedition to the Himalaya of Garhwal', *Geographical Journal,* Vol. 31, No. 4 (April 1908), pp. 361–88.

A. L. Mumm, *Five Months in the Himalaya: A Record of Mountain Travel in Garhwal and Kashmir* (London: Edward Arnold, 1909).

J. B. Noel, 'A Journey to Tashirak in Southern Tibet, and the Eastern Approaches to Mount Everest', *Geographical Journal*, Vol. 53, No. 5 (May 1919), pp. 289–308.

Captain J. B. L. Noel, *Through Tibet to Everest* (London: Edward Arnold, 1927).

Sathnam Sanghera, *Empireland: How Imperialism Has Shaped Modern Britain* (London: Penguin, 2021).

Craig Storti, *The Hunt for Mount Everest* (London: John Murray, 2021).

Jonathan Westaway, 'Encountering the indigenous body in the Himalayan Borderlands', Lecture, Royal Geographical Society (16 October 2023).

Chapter 21 – A Sporting Effort

James A. Horscroft et al., 'Metabolic basis to Sherpa altitude adaptation', *PNAS* (22 May 2017).

Carl Rubenson, 'An Ascent of Kabru', *Alpine Journal*, Vol. 24 (1908), pp. 63–7.

C. W. Rubenson, 'Kabru in 1907', *Alpine Journal*, Vol. 24 (1908), pp. 310–21.

Eva Selin, 'Carl Rubenson, Kabru and the birth of the Norwegian AC', *Alpine Journal*, Vol. 113 (2008), pp. 257–63.

Chapter 22 – Rarefied Air

Filippo De Filippi, 'The expedition of H.R.H. the Prince Louis of Savoy, Duke of the Abruzzi, to Mount St. Elias (Alaska)', *Alpine Journal*, Vol. 19 (1899).

Filippo De Filippi, 'The expedition of H.R.H. the Duke of the Abruzzi to the Karakoram Himalayas', *Geographical Journal*, Vol. 37, No. 1 (January 1911), pp. 19–30.

Filippo De Filippi, *Karakoram and Western Himalaya 1909: An Account of the Expedition of H.R.H. Prince Luigi Amedeo of Savoy Duke of the Abruzzi* (London: Constable and Company, 1912).

Mark Haworth-Booth et al., *Frozen in Time: The Mountain Photography of Vittorio Sella* (Rome: Gangemi Editore, 2008).

Mirella Tenderini and Michael Shandrick, *The Duke of the Abruzzi: An Explorer's Life* (London: Bâton Wicks, 1997).

C. W. Thornton, 'The Ascent of Mount St. Elias', *Overland Monthly*, Vol. 31, No. 184 (April 1898).

Chapter 23 – Fearlas Mòr

Affleck Grey, *The Big Grey Man of Ben Macdhui* (Aberdeen: Impulse Books, 1970).

Alec Kellas, 'Our Tour to Cairngorm Mountains' (1885).

A. M. Kellas, 'The Mountains of Northern Sikkim and Garhwal', *Geographical Journal*, Vol. 40, No. 3 (September 1912), pp. 241–60.

A. M. Kellas, 'Mountaineering in Sikkim and Garhwal', *Alpine Journal*, Vol. 26 (1912), pp. 52–4.

A. M. Kellas, 'A Fourth Visit to the Sikkim Himalaya, with Ascent of the Kangchenjhau', *Alpine Journal*, Vol. 27 (1913), pp. 125–53.

Ian R. Mitchell and George W. Rodway, *Prelude to Everest: Alexander Kellas, Himalayan Mountaineer* (Edinburgh: Luath Press, 2011).

'Obituary: Alexander Mitchell Kellas', *Geographical Journal*, Vol. 58, No. 1 (1921), pp. 73–5.

'The Late Dr. Kellas' Early Expeditions to the Himalaya', *Alpine Journal*, Vol. 34 (1922), pp. 408–14.

Chapter 24 – Sleep of the Just

C. K. Howard-Bury, 'The 1921 Mount Everest Expedition', *Alpine Journal*, Vol. 34 (1922), pp. 195–214.

A. M. Kellas, 'A Consideration of the Possibility of Ascending the Loftier Himalaya', *Geographical Journal*, Vol. 49, No. 1 (January 1917), pp. 26–46.

Francis Younghusband, 'The Mount Everest Expedition: Organisation and Equipment', *Geographical Journal*, Vol. 57, No. 4 (April 1921), pp. 271–82.

'Dr. Kellas' Expedition to Kamet in 1920', *Alpine Journal*, Vol. 33 (1921), pp. 312–9.

Epilogue – Go Ask the Past

Conrad Anker and David Roberts, *The Lost Explorer: Finding Mallory on Mount Everest* (New York: Simon & Schuster, 1999).

Peter Firstbrook, *Lost on Everest: The Search for Mallory & Irvine* (London: BBC Worldwide, 1999).

Jochen Hemmleb, Larry A. Johnson and Eric R. Simonson, *Ghosts of Everest: The Authorised Story of the Search for Mallory & Irvine* (London: Macmillan, 1999).

Nimsdai Purja, *Beyond Possible* (London: Hodder & Stoughton, 2022).

Tony Smythe, *My Father, Frank* (London: Bâton Wicks, 2013).

Mark Synott, 'Climbing Everest – to try to solve its greatest mystery', *National Geographic* (8 July 2020).

List of Illustrations

1. A traveller following a trail up the Sutlej valley in Himachel Pradesh, India. Photograph by Samuel Bourne (c. 1865). V&A.
2. Two illustrations of the first attempt on Popocatépetl (top) from the title page to Herrera's *Historia*, 1601 and (bottom) from an engraving in Ogilvy's *America*, 1671. Collection of The Library of Congress.
3. German naturalist and explorer Adolph Schlagintweit. Portrait by A. Graefle. Alamy.
4. English naturalist, soldier and surveyor Henry 'Haversham' Godwin-Austen at Cherraponjee, India. Photographer unknown (1869).
5. 'Crossing the Burzil Pass', from *Climbing and Exploration in the Karakoram-Himalayas* by William Martin Conway (1894). Illustrator unknown.
6. 'The Ascent of the Matterhorn, on July 14th 1865: Arrival at the Summit'. Illustration by Gustave Doré (1865). Wikimedia.
7. 'Whymper's Fall on the Matterhorn', from *Edward Whymper* by F. S. Smythe (1940). Illustration by Edward Whymper.
8. 'Chimborazo from 17,450 feet', from *Edward Whymper* by F. S. Smythe (1940). Illustration by Edward Whymper.
9. English barrister and mountaineer William Woodman Graham. Illustrated by Ruby Light from photograph.
10. Illustration from 'Up in the Himalayas', an article by W. W. Graham in *Good Words* (1885). Illustrator unknown.
11. 'Climbing Party of Goorkhas', from *Twenty Years in the Himalaya* by C. G. Bruce (1910). Photographer unknown.
12. 'On the Top of Pioneer Peak', from *Climbing and Exploration in the Karakoram-Himalayas* by William Martin Conway (1894). Illustration by A. D. McCormick (1892).

13. English mountaineer Albert 'Fred' Mummery, from *My Climbs in the Alps and the Caucasus* by A. F. Mummery (1895). Photographer unknown.

14. 'In a Crevasse at Snow Lake', from *Ice World of the Himalaya* by Fanny Bullock Workman (1900). Illustration by Arthur Cooke (1900).

15. 'The Accident on Sefton', from *Climbs in the New Zealand Alps* by Edward Fitzgerald (1896). Illustration by H. G. Willink.

16. Cover of *Journal des Voyages* No. 686, 23 January 1910. Illustration by F. Conrad.

17. English mountaineer Oscar Eckenstein. Illustrator unknown. Collection of The Royal Asiatic Society of Great Britain and Ireland.

18. 'Two Record Climbers', from *Ice World of the Himalaya* by Fanny Bullock Workman (1900), showing Swiss guide Matthias Zurbriggen and American mountaineer Fanny Bullock Workman. Illustrator unknown.

19. Italian guides Alexis and Henri Brocherel on Nanda Devi Saddle, 8 June 1905. Photograph by Dr Tom Longstaff (1905). Collection of The Alpine Club.

20. 'A Perilous Crossing', from *Tibet and Nepal* by A. Henry Savage Landor (1905), showing English writer and explorer A. Henry Savage Landor and his Tibetan guides. Illustration by A. Henry Savage Landor.

21. Camp IV on Kangchenjunga, August 1905. Photograph by Dr Jules Jacot-Guillarmod (1905).

22. American mountaineer Fanny Bullock Workman at the summit of Pinnacle Peak, from *Le Petit Journal* (1906). Illustrator unknown. Alamy.

23. 'Party ascending the Chang La' from *The Assault on Mount Everest* by Charles Granville Bruce, 1923.

24. English mountaineers Tom Longstaff (left) and Charlie Bruce (centre), and the Swiss guide Moritz Inderbinen (right) in the Rishi valley, 16 June 1907. Photograph by Arnold Mumm (1907).

25. Norwegian mountaineer Carl Rubenson. Photographer unknown. Collection of The Alpine Club.

26. Italian mountaineer and explorer Prince Luigi Amedeo, Duke of the Abruzzi at the summit of Mount Margherita, from *La Domenica del Corriere* (1906). Engraving by Achille Beltrame (1906). Collection of Museo Nazionale della Montagna.
27. Scottish chemist, explorer and mountaineer Dr Alexander 'Alec' Kellas. Photographer unknown. Collection of The Alpine Club.
28. 'Lower Kama-Chu' from *Mount Everest: The Reconnaisance* by Charles Howard-Bury, 1921. Collection of the Library of Congress.
29. Artist's impression of George Mallory (top) and Andrew Irvine (bottom) climbing the 'Second Step' on Everest. Illustration by D. Macpherson (1924). Alamy.

Plate Section

1. 'The Chain of the Kuenlúen, from Súmgal, in Turkistán' by Hermann Schlagintweit (August 1856). Wikimedia.
2. 'The Himalaya Mountain Scenery of Baltistan, or Little Thibet' by H. H. Godwin-Austen (August 1861). Bridgeman Images.
3. English mountaineer Edward Whymper, aged twenty-five. Photographer unknown (1865). Alamy.
4. 'The Ascent of the Matterhorn, on July 14th 1865: The Fall' by Gustave Doré (1865). Wikimedia.
5. English art critic, mountaineer and explorer Sir William 'Martin' Conway. Photograph by John Thomson (1894).
6. 'A Group of Climbers outside Pen-y-Gwryd, North Wales, 1898', from *The Victorian Mountaineers* by Ronald Clark (1953). Photograph by the Abraham Brothers.
7. Conway's 1892 expedition to the Karakoram included four Gurkha soldiers: Karbir Burathoki, Harkabir Thapa, Amar Sing Thapa and Parbir Thapa. Illustrations by A. D. McCormick (1892).
8. Albert 'Fred' Mummery and Charles 'Charlie' Bruce on the Nanga Parbat expedition of 1895. Photographer unknown (1895). Collection of The Alpine Club.

9. Matthias Zurbriggen and Edward Fitzgerald in New Zealand's Southern Alps in 1895. Photograph by Sir Joseph James Kinsey (1895). Alexander Turnball Library, National Library of New Zealand (Ref: 1/1-003232-G).
10. American alpinist Fanny Bullock Workman. Photograph by Maull & Fox. Collection of The Library of Congress.
11. Poet and occultist Edward Alexander 'Aleister' Crowley. Photographer unknown (1902). Bridgeman Images.
12. The European members of the K2 expedition of 1902. Photograph by Dr Jules Jacot-Guillarmod (1902). Alamy.
13. 'Al fresco lunch, Riffel Camp', from *Ice-bound Heights of the Mustagh* by Fanny Bullock Workman (1908). Photographer unknown (1903).
14. The 1907 Trisul expedition. Photograph by A. L. Mumm (1907). From *Five Months in the Himalaya* by A. L. Mumm.
15. Italian mountain guides Henri and Alexis Brocherel, and Gurkha mountaineer Karbir Burathoki, on the summit ridge of Trisul. Photograph by Dr Tom Longstaff (1907). Collection of The Alpine Club.
16. Prince Luigi Amedeo Giuseppe Maria Ferdinando Francesco di Savoia-Aosta, Duke of the Abruzzi. Photographer unknown (c. 1913).
17. The northeast face of K2. Photograph by Prince Luigi Amedeo, Duke of the Abruzzi (1909). Wikimedia.
18. The Duke of the Abruzzi and two guides in the icefall at the head of the Upper Baltoro glacier. Photograph by Vittorio Sella (1909). Wikimedia.
19. 'Memorial Cairn Everest' from *The Fight for Everest* by Lieutenant-Colonel E. F. Norton, 1925.

Index

References to images are in *italics*.

Abbottabad (Pakistan) 119–20, 121
Abdullah 23
acclimatisation 205, 211
Aconcagua (Argentina) 172–83, 227
Adirondack Mountains (NY) 186
Africa 231, 232, 332, 334
Ali, Nazar 126
Alpine Club 56–7, 64, 66, 72, 295
  and Conway 121, 132
  and Eckenstein 124, 201
  and Everest 297, 358, 359
  and Graham 96–7
  and Kellas 345, 346, 348, 350
  and Rubenson 322–3
Alpine Journal 79, 97, 112, 115–16
  and Eckenstein 213
  and Kellas 347
  and Workman 227
alpinism 58, 63, 72, 123–4
Alps 11, 47, 77–9, 265
  and Conway 134–5
  and Crowley 263
  and Eckenstein 123–4, 200
  and Kellas 345
  and Longstaff 232–4
  see also Matterhorn; Mont Blanc; Monte Rosa

altitude 13, 16–17, 50, 104–5; *see also* mountain sickness; world altitude record
Amar Sing Thapa 121, 126, 127, 137, 141–2, 143
Amazonian rainforest 11–12
Amin, Mohammed 24
Anderkyow 348–9, 350–1
Andes 11, 19, 25, 172–3
  and Whymper 79, 80
Anker, Conrad 366, 370–1, 372
Annapurna (Nepal) 368
Antarctica 231
anti-Semitism 124
archaeology 18–20
Arctic 231, 232
Argentina, *see* Aconcagua
Askole (Karakoram) 41–2, 128, 129, 204, 205
Atlantic Ocean 231
Avalanche Camp (Karakoram) 191–2, 193, 194
avalanches 2, 162, 217, 250–1, 366

balance climbing 123
Balmat, Jacques 78
Baltoro glacier (Karakoram) 44–6, 133–4, 135–46, 206